# Africa Betrayed

Also by George B. N. Ayittey

*Africa's Economic Crisis: The Indigenous Solution*
(forthcoming)

*Developing Southern Africa After Apartheid*
(forthcoming, International Freedom Foundation, Washington, DC)

*Indigenous African Institutions,*
1991. New York: Transnational Publishers, Inc.

# Africa Betrayed

George B. N. Ayittey

St. Martin's Press
New York

A Cato Institute Book

First published in the United States of America in 1992

Printed in the United States of America

ISBN 0-312-08058-1

Library of Congress Cataloging-in-Publication Data

Ayittey, George B. N., 1945-
   Africa betrayed / George B. N. Ayittey.
          p.   cm.
   Includes bibliographical references and index.
   ISBN 0-312-08058-1
   1. Africa—Politics and government—1960- 2. Political
corruption—Africa. 3. Military government—Africa.
   4. Apartheid—Africa. I. Title.
JQ1875.A55C63   1992
320.96—dc20                                        92-16026
                                                        CIP

# THE BOOK IS DEDICATED TO:

The traditional rulers of Africa (chiefs and kings) who never copied foreign systems to impose on their people. The hundreds of thousands of peasants killed by Africa's "educated" leaders and to the following, who were punished, jailed, killed, or exiled for expressing their viewpoints:

**Algeria:** Abdennour Ali-Yahia, president of the Algerian Human Rights League.

**Angola:** Jonas Savimbi.

**Benin:** Leon Yelone and Moussa Mama Yori.

**Burundi:** Leon Bantigira, Aloys Habonimana, Deo Hakizimana, Terence Ndayakire, Leonce Ndikumana, Augustin Nasnse, and Salvator Sunzu.

**Cameroon:** Ambroise Kom, Bassek Ba Khobio, Martin Soua Ntyam, Ebona Myetam, David Ndachi, Jean-Marie Nzekoue, Jean Mboudou, Jean Luc Kuomo, and Yondo Black, former president of the Cameroonian Bar.

**Chad:** Saleh Gaba, a journalist.

**Ethiopia:** Said Osman Hamid, Mohamed Ker Geblan and the peasants in the village of Milhab.

**Gabon:** Joseph Rendjambe, the late leader of Gabon's Progress Party, Georges Koupangoye and Louis de Dravo.

**The Gambia:** Baboucar Langley.

**Ghana:** Fred Poku Sarkodee, Mrs. Justice Cecilia Koranteng-Addow, Mr. Justice Kwadwo Agyei Agyepong, Evangelist Akwasi Amoako and Dr. Edmund N. Delle.

**Ivory Coast:** Professor Laurent Gbagbo and Bamba Morifere.

**Kenya:** Achiya Echakapa, the late Dr. Robert Ouko, former Minister of Foreign Affairs and International Cooperation, Professor Wangari Maathai, Kitobu Imanyara, editor and publisher of *The Nairobi Law Monthly* (NLM), Bishop Alexander Kipsang Muge, and Bishop John Okullu.

**Lesotho:** Joel Moitse.

| | |
|---|---|
| Liberia: | Mr. Robert Phillips and Emmanuel Weh. |
| Libya: | Yousef Khreybish and Muhammad Feheima—assassinated in Rome and Athens, respectively. |
| Malawi: | The late Osborne Mkandawire, former Malawian journalist, and Mkwapatira Mhango, an exiled Malawian journalist assassinated in Zambia on October 13, 1989. |
| Mali: | Adama Coulibaly, Souleymane Dembele, Ibrahima Tangara, and Boulkassoum Kire. |
| Mauritania: | The late Tene Youssouf, who died in detention in September 1988. Hamady Djouma Ba (a peasant fisherman), Abdoul Bouka N'Diaye, and Mamadou Gninguel N'Diaye of the village of Djeol, who were shot in January 1990 by the Mauritanian National Guard. |
| Morocco: | To the political prisoners serving sentences ranging from 15 years to life in Kenitra Central Prison. |
| Nigeria: | Dele Giwa, former editor of *Newswatch*, killed in October 1986 by a letter-bomb sent by Nigeria Security men. |
| Rwanda: | Augustin Murayi Nduhira and Rachel Ndayishimiye. |
| Sierra Leone: | Yakuba Bah and Franklyn Bunting-Davies, editor of *New Shaft*. |
| Somalia: | Safia Hashi Madar, and the late Mahamoud Mohamed Mohamoud. |
| South Africa: | Steve Biko, Chief Mangosutho Buthelezi, Nelson Mandela, Bishop Desmond Tutu, Alan Boesak, Helen Suzman, and other foes of apartheid. |
| Sudan: | Dr. Ali Fadul, Magdi Magoub, George Yustus, and Arkango Agadad. |
| Tanzania: | James Mapalala, Mwinyijuma Othman Upindo and the Reverend Christopher Mtikila, Secretary of the Full Salvation Church. |
| Togoland: | Yema Gu-Konu and Ati Randolph. |
| Tunisia: | Khemais Chamari. |
| Uganda: | Lance Sera-Muwanga. |
| Zaire: | Etienne Tshisekedi. |
| Zambia: | Tabeth Mwanza, Yotamu Chimwanga, Alfred M. Chambeshi, Joseph Chitalu, Chisala Mukunto, Alex S. Chambala, Pascal Ng'Andu, Matthew N. Kasonde, Peter C. Bwaiya, Mario Mayio, John C. Sakulanda, Fred Bwalya, Fred P. Mulenga, John S. Chupa, and Henry Kalenga. |
| Zimbabwe: | Edgar Tekere and Ndabaningi Sithole. |

# CONTENTS

## ACKNOWLEDGMENTS

I am immensely indebted to many individuals, both African and non-African, in the execution of this project. My debt of gratitude is also owed to several foundations, institutes, and agencies that actively or indirectly supported me in my research.

As most Africanists would testify, research on African subjects is often rendered especially difficult by the absence of reliable data, the uncooperative attitude of suspicious African government officials, and even concerns about personal safety in gathering data on human rights violations. In addition, field work in Africa can be daunting in the face of transportation and communication difficulties. Consequently, support for research endeavors such as this was greatly appreciated.

Deserving of foremost mention is the Earhart Foundation in Ann Arbor, Michigan, which provided me with funding for two summers (1987 and 1988) to support field trips to Africa and further research. The Hoover Institution, Stanford University, where I spent a year (1988-1989) as a National Fellow, equally deserves my gratitude. Hoover provided me with such facilities—archives, office space, outstanding computer capabilities, and excellent secretarial support—that I was able to complete three book manuscripts: *Indigenous African Institutions*, *Africa Betrayed*, and *The African Economic Crisis: The Indigenous Solution*. *Indigenous African Institutions* has been published by Transnational Publishers, Inc., New York. My special thanks go to Professors Thomas H. Henriksen, Larry Diamond, Lewis Gann, Thomas Sowell, Wendy Minkin, Silvia Sandoval, and many more of the fine staff at Hoover.

From the Hoover Institution, I went to the Heritage Foundation in Washington, D.C., to which I also owe a deep debt of gratitude. It provided me with office space, an outstanding support staff, and valuable critical reviews to make this work possible. Charles Heatherly, Teri Ruddy, Michael Johns, Ed Hudgins, and many others at the Heritage Foundation were very helpful with comments.

Other institutions also assisted. Bloomsburg University must be mentioned, as this was where my work originally started. Professors John Baird, Peter Bohling, Robert MacMurray, Robert Obutelewicz, Elis Majd, Mehdi

Haririyan, W. B. Lee, Oliver and Ann Larmie, and many others must be thanked for their support and encouragement. From the University of Manitoba must be mentioned Professors Henry Rempel, John Rogge, John Loxley, Randolph Gorvie, Percy Christian Quao, and Sandy Matheson.

I also drew particular inspiration from Professor James Buchanan, a Nobel laureate, when I was a visiting scholar at the Center for the Study of Public Choice in 1988. Thanks also to Tom Palmer and the staff at the Institute of Humane Studies, and to David Boaz, Ted Carpenter, and Ed Crane at the Cato Institute.

During my tenure at American University, I have been fortunate to receive critical reviews and encouragement from Professors Robert Lerman, Alan Isaac, Barbara Bergmann, Jim Weaver, and Jon Wisman and excellent secretarial support from Jane Dolingo, Peggy Blank, Sheila Budnyj, Sharon Childs-Patrick and many others in the Economics Department.

There are many others to whom I still owe a debt of gratitude: Professor Walter Williams, John Fund, Grace Ortiz, Lynne Criner, Melanie Tammen, Dianne Hicks, Roberto Santiago, Gregory Simpsons, Margaret Calhoun, and others.

Gratitude must also be expressed to *Index on Censorship* for permission to use extracts from their excellent magazine.

Last but not least have been the numerous Africans who have shown unflinching support for my work and writings. Among them are Dr. Isaac Amuah, Rev. G. B. K. Owusu, Silva Upusunju, Kobina Annan, Stanley Ansong, Joseph Clegg, Lily Danso, Marjorie Winfred, Dr. Emmanuel Ablo, Kwasi Agyeman-Prempeh, Dr. Kofi Apraku, Kwaku Danso, Augustine Edusei, Kwadwo Boahene, Dr. Derek Gondwe, Anis Haffar, Charles Mensah, Okezie Patrick Okezie, Dr. Victor Teye, the Rev. Ndabiningi Sithole, Peter Abbam, Sekoe Sengare, Moses Tesi, Dominic Ntube, Manfred Tumban, John Okoh, Michael Atadika, Edward Nyarko, Walusako Mwalilino, Professor Edem Kodjo (former secretary-general of the Organization of African Unity), Paati Ofosu-Armah, Fabian Makani, Maina Kaia, Nii Akuetteh, Dr. Kojo Yelpaala, Banda Ngenge, Emeka Chukunjindo, Charles Ayensu, Ablorh Odjijah, Professor Willie Lamouse-Smith, Jeddy Namfua, Kwasi Baidoo, Fatou Danielle Diagne, Verna Warren, and many, many others.

The views expressed in this book are my own, however, and any errors or misstatements are my sole responsibility.

*George B. N. Ayittey, Ph.D.*
Washington, D.C.—June 14, 1992.

# FOREWORD

Once in a while, out of the blue, comes an extraordinary book—provocative, shockingly gripping in its exposition of the truth, and yet saddening in the message it conveys. *Africa Betrayed* is one such book.

With elegant brevity, George B. N. Ayittey captures the essence of his story in the book's title: that after independence, most Africans were denied the very freedoms they struggled so hard for from colonial rule. Tyranny is rampant in Africa, according to Ayittey. Violations of human rights are committed with impunity on the continent, with the worst offenses occurring under military dictatorships. But most of Africa's "liberators" did more than oppress their people. They mismanaged their national economies and looted national treasuries for deposit in overseas bank accounts. Although external factors beyond the control of Africans played a role, Ayittey asserts that the policies of African leaders contributed in no small measure to the grinding poverty, appalling human misery, and deterioration in social conditions that are evident across much of Africa.

It is a very sad story indeed, coming at a time when the African continent is beset with political turmoil, instability, and economic disaster. It takes an extraordinary African to provide this "inside view." It is a story many would prefer not to hear. Certainly, this book is not for those who believe that African heads of state are "saints" and should not be criticized. Nor is this book for those Africans who feel that we should not "wash our dirty linen in public." But only the truth shall set us free. However ugly, it must be spoken, exposed, and cleaned. And Ayittey takes great pains to present the facts and the documentation.

As a black South African woman who has experienced the evil system of apartheid, I believe oppression must be exposed wherever it may occur, even in our own backyard. Freedom is not defined only in terms of color. If it is wrong for whites to oppress blacks, then it is even more immoral and shameful for black African leaders to oppress their own people. These leaders should know better.

Blacks in independent Africa deserve not only liberation from the naked oppression of colonial and imperial powers, but from the brutal and harsh domination and control of their own black leaders. Black people deserve to be granted equal rights and freedom of expression and to be regarded as responsible, thinking individuals, irrespective of their tribal, political, or class affiliations.

This book is a godsend for most Africans, especially black South Africans, who are still fighting for their liberation. It provides us with valuable lessons in our struggle in South Africa. The pitfalls and mistakes made in independent Africa were understandable. But we must learn from them and avoid repeating them in our own campaign for freedom in South Africa.

The tone adopted in this book may not be everyone's cup of tea. At times, it is quite strident and the exposition shocking. I do understand the rage seething in Ayittey. But he is not alone. Many other Africans are irate at their leaders for having betrayed them. Some of Ayittey's proposals are quite ingenious and insightful. He believes that Africa's salvation lies neither in the West nor the East but in returning to Africa's own *indigenous* roots and building upon them. Who will disagree with him on this? But there are other proposals that are quite controversial and, in fact, I do disagree with a few of them. Disagreements, however, are of little moment. They are natural.

In our own traditional African society, disagreements and debates were common features of our political system. The chief and his elders often differed in their positions. And when he took an unpopular position, the chief himself was rebuked and criticized. More important, however, we were able, in most cases, to resolve our differences of opinion and reach a consensus under the shade of a big tree. That was the purpose of the debates and discussions: to reach agreement on the best course of action or policy. Differences of opinion, per se, were unimportant. The *freedom* to express them and the *ability* to settle them peacefully were more important.

Freedom of expression and of political association, unfortunately, are not well understood or respected by many African leaders, both white and black. The Organization of African Unity's Charter on Human and Peoples' Rights, which was promulgated in 1986, was explicit on these freedoms. Specifically, Article 9 of the charter expressly guarantees the right of free expression.

Significantly, in our own traditional African society, these freedoms were guaranteed. Further, there were various associations in traditional Africa: *stokfel*, guilds, secret societies, *asafo* companies, religious organizations, and age-grades that Africans could join if they so wished. The chief did not ban these associations nor did he deny people the right to free expression.

I believe that black Africa will progress and move toward full democracy when our leaders begin to favor *openness* (democratic pluralism in multiparty systems and freedom of expression) and eschew everything that operates as a constraint on the free exercise of one's views or speech. It is only when they stifle freedom of speech that a debilitating "culture of silence" is produced that then leads to economic, social, and political stagnation.

We may not like what Ayittey has to say, how he says it, or what he proposes. But we must at least respect and fight for his right, as well as that of *any* other African, to express his thoughts and views freely as we do in our own traditional societies.

*Makaziwe Mandela*
February 1992

# PROLOGUE

If you look at the period after independence, the people who had fought for our independence were betrayed, not by Jomo Kenyatta, but by the entire KANU regime. The people who now run the government were actually on the other side, or at best did not take part at all. So they have been doing their best to cover up this chapter of our history. Of course, they argue that they themselves fought for independence, but those are lies.

—Maina wa Kinyatti, former senior lecturer in history at Kenyatta University, jailed for six years for alleged possession of a "seditious" document
(*Africa Report*, Jul-Aug 1989; p. 58).

The greatest malady of African politics is the unwillingness of the rulers to relinquish power. Entrenched in power by constitutions that have virtually made them kings, opposition to them is treason. Now it seems the only way a change of government can be effected in Africa is by beheading the heads of state. It is a crude option which regrettably seems to be the only workable one for Africa.

—Thulo Hoeane of Maseru, Lesotho writing in *New African* (Apr 1991; p. 4).

A nation with revolutionary youth is like a woman married to a man with undeveloped testes. No offspring means no progress, no sense of innovation. This is the reality in Africa today regarding leadership.

For President Kaunda, after 26 years in office, to talk not about Zambia's state of emergency in place for over a quarter of a century, but to claim that only he and UNIP are qualified to rule Zambia, disqualifies him as a democrat. The political and economic problems in Africa today are due to the fact that non-democrats have ruled our nations for far too long.

—P.U. Nnganyadi in *New African* (Mar 1991; p. 32).

AFRICANS ARE ANGRY—at their leaders. "One can simply see from the faces of the people the rage about to explode," wrote Adam Egeh of Somalia (*African Letter*, April 16-30, 1990; p. 3).

On February 18, 1986, President Alhaji Sir Dawda Kairaba Jawara of The Gambia, who has been in power since 1965, arrived at MacCarthy Square to deliver a speech celebrating The Gambia's 21 years of independence. A young Gambian, Baboucar Langley, evaded security measures and made his way to the front of the president's dais. As he was being dragged away, he managed to deliver this protest: "People are tired. People are hungry. We must change the system!" (*West Africa*, Feb 24, 1986; p. 436.) He was hastily convicted and sentenced to 18 months' imprisonment. Ironically, The Gambia is one of the pitifully few African states where opposition parties and dissent are somewhat allowed.

In March 1990, following the brutal murder of Dr. Robert Ouko, Kenya's former foreign minister, Waruru Kanja (the Minister for Information and Broadcasting) astonished members of parliament when he asked, "Is this the freedom we fought for? Did we fight for freedom to eliminate one another?" On April 2, 1990, President Moi of Kenya dismissed Kanja without any public explanation (*Africa Report*, May-Jun 1990; p. 20).

Though these individuals personally suffered imprisonment and career termination, they courageously spoke out for the majority of irate Africans, fed up with their leaders and yearning for "*sopi*" (change).

This book is a continuation of their struggle—for the second and true liberation of Africa from both white oppression and black tyranny. Many Africans have gripping tales of life-long crusades against the forces of tyranny and its machinations in Africa. Mine began back in 1974, when I was a professor of economics at the University of Ghana, during the tenure of the late Col. I. K. Acheampong's military government (1971-1978).

What set the wheels of my crusade in motion was the prevailing elite mentality that attributed most of Africa's economic woes to such external factors as lingering effects of Western slavery, colonialism, American imperialism, and an exploitative international economic system. There was little analysis of the contributory role played by such *internal* factors as defective and incompetent political leadership, economic mismanagement, corruption, and political repression. A scientific analysis of any crisis requires an unerring scrutiny of all possible causes—internal as well as external. But only the examination of the external factors received official sanction in most places in Africa.

About this time the world was still reeling from the effects of the 1973 Arab oil embargo. The subsequent oil squeeze forced African governments, including the Acheampong regime, to adopt extraordinary economic measures. An economic crisis had not yet fully blossomed in 1974, but the signs of an impending crisis of major proportions were ubiquitous. In a response typical of most African governments, the Acheampong government blamed "a neocolonial conspiracy" and other hostile external factors.

To be sure, external factors had been important in supplying the initial shocks to fragile African economies. But as was often the case, these shocks were magnified by defective domestic economic management and poor leadership. The Acheampong administration, in particular, was riddled with appalling corruption, administrative ineptitude, and economic mismanagement. In addition, the prevailing environment of intellectual repression provided little opportunity for sensible debate of the crisis and effectively precluded alternative analysis of the role played by internal factors.

The state owned and controlled the media. Criticisms of government management of the economy were prohibited and brutally suppressed. Even a balanced and constructive criticism of government policies was interpreted as "seditious." Nor could one dare criticize Acheampong—his leadership was above reproach.

I used to make commentaries about economic policies on Radio Ghana until I was hauled in "for questioning" at the military barracks. Subsequently, copies of commentaries I had kept for my records mysteriously vanished from my home. I was lucky. In many other African countries critics of government policies were rewarded with detention. Some did not live to regret their indiscretion. They disappeared under mysterious circumstances and were never seen again.

I left Ghana for the West in 1975, hoping for a more tolerant intellectual environment. But I discovered much to my astonishment a perverse climate that was equally debilitating. My criticisms of African governments were greeted with suspicion in North America and Western Europe. I quickly learned that in the United States, African leaders, especially those from black Africa, were viewed almost as saints. Blacks, having been colonized and enslaved in the past, could do no wrong. Criticizing African leaders, especially in the North American media, is often regarded as "blaming the victim." To do so is not "politically correct."

Since the 1960s, public discussion of African issues in the West has been restricted to impassioned expressions of pieties and even muffled apologies for despicable atrocities and political regimes in Africa. Perhaps subdued by collective guilt over past colonial wrongdoing, whites in the West have all too often been mute or ever ready to overlook the failings of the rulers of former colonies. When black African leaders oppressed and slaughtered their own people, a multitude of rationalizations and alibis, usually citing past colonial iniquities, were readily offered to explain their failings. In Europe, in particular, it was generally believed that the problems of Africa, devastated by centuries of colonialism, were exacerbated by American interference and imperialism.

For example, in response to my article, "Guns, Idiots, and Screams" (*New Internationalist,* June 1990), Sally Feather of Guilford, the United Kingdom, wrote: "In his article, George Ayittey condemns African elites for destroying Africa. But the faults he accuses them of are just as prevalent in the West. . .

Who is to blame for the deaths of 800,000 people in Uganda—Idi Amin or the Western arms producers who made their fortunes selling him guns? The guilt is ours. For the Idi Amins of Africa were trained in our Western military academies. And our entire lives are founded on the immense benefits which the West has accrued from unfair trading with Africa over the years" (*New Internationalist*, September 1990; p. 2).

When will African dictators be held accountable for their misdeeds? Holding these dictators to account is understandably difficult and dangerous in Africa. But "well-meaning" Westerners compound the problem by offering nonsensical excuses for the egregious actions of these tyrants. Past colonial iniquities or "an unfair trading" system gives no African leader the license to terrorize his people.

It may be cogently argued that it is not the responsibility of the West to guide Africa's destiny or police its affairs. Nor does the West have any moral right to meddle in the internal affairs of sovereign African nations. But the West cannot seek to defend human rights in some parts of the world and neglect them in Africa.

Exceedingly tolerant and apologetic Western attitudes that shielded African despots from public scrutiny and criticism have helped perpetuate tyranny in Africa. These attitudes are more crystallized in the African-American community, where there is an additional racial propensity to express solidarity with "the brothers and sisters" in Africa. Unfortunately this solidarity is blind and fails to distinguish between the tyrants and the victims. In Africa there are two classes of people: the real people (the peasants) and the parasitic elites. Which "victims" do African-Americans or the West seek to help?

But Westerners alone are not to blame for the repression in Africa. African elites and highly "educated" diplomats, who ought to know better, have been the most treacherous supporters of African dictatorships by supplying spurious intellectual arguments for despotism. For example, my advocacy of freedom of expression in the *African Letter* drew this attack from Okey Chigbo and Grace-Edward Galabuzi:

> The eminent columnist, George Ayittey, has stated that "Freedom of expression is more than a human right. It is one of the most critical ingredients vital for long term development." Can our good professor be serious? . . .
>
> To prate about freedom of speech as he does, or to claim like some of his less eminent followers, that there are no good arguments against liberalization is to fundamentally misunderstand the nature of economic development. It is time to state categorically that there is no correlation between freedom of speech or

political plurality and economic development. Absolutely none. Neither freedom of speech nor the multi-party system can guarantee the expanded industrial and agricultural production that propels industrial take-off and economic development. In fact, going by the evidence of the successful industrial societies, the reverse appears to be the case . . .

Ayitteyism thus represents an unbelievable callowness that expects to solve major problems of emerging modern industrial states without the full range of necessary instruments. It is known by everyone but the Ayitteyists that *coercion is one of the more important of these instruments* . . . Keen observers of Third World affairs understand that forces opposed to progress in the Third World often mask their aims by calling for freedom of speech (*African Letter*, Feb 1-15, 1990; p. 13; emphasis added).

Living in Canada, Chigbo and Galabuzi at least had the *freedom* to express their views without being arrested or detained. It was quite clear on whose side these intellectuals stood—with the tyrants and not the African people. Furthermore, there are profound difficulties with their arguments. First, the advocacy of coercion is frightening. Coercion implies the denial of volition or freedom of choice. Second and more distressing, the military dictators of Africa still subscribe to this viewpoint, believing that a prosperous economy would emerge after issuing orders and decrees and using coercion and threats of death by firing squad.

But the worst defenders of African tyrants have often been diplomats; some with high credentials and university educations who *should* know better, but are all too willing to sell off their consciences for a comfortable living. Here, for example, are statements by African diplomats. First, Zaire's ambassador to the United States, Tatanene Manata:

With regard to Zaire's protection of human rights, the Department of Citizens' Rights and Liberties was created in 1986 and was the first ministry in Africa dedicated to the protection of human rights. This department has begun to fulfil its mandate to inform the citizenry of their rights and to investigate and prosecute violations of those rights in Zaire.

In the U.S. State Department's most recent human rights report, Zaire was praised for implementing several measures that have improved its judicial system (*The Washington Post*, Oct 4, 1990; p. A26).

Second, Malawi's ambassador to the United States, R. B. Mbaya:

For the benefit of your readers, I would want them to know that Malawi believes in the freedom of the press . . . With regard to the allegation that the government of Malawi specialises in getting rid of opponents I would say this is totally untrue.

What your readers should know is that the government of Malawi rules by popular consent. The people of Malawi are staunchly behind the leadership of the country and the government. The truth of the matter therefore is that it is the people of Malawi who reject ambitious and self-appointed would be leaders and when this happens these persons indulge in misinformation and unqualified propaganda against the government of Malawi (*West Africa*, Dec 24-Jan 6, 1991; p. 3082)

Really? Even so, it is disgusting that Zaire, of all places, established "the first ministry in Africa dedicated to the protection of human rights" 26 years after independence. What happened, then, to the human rights of Africans in the *first* 26 years of independence?

Even more amazing is the alacrity with which such chameleon diplomats change their tune as soon as their governments back home are overthrown. Suddenly and quietly, they begin seeking political asylum in Western countries, the very countries they denounced when they were diplomats.

Africa needs an unwavering scrutiny of its elites and leaders. Concealing or making excuses for their shortcomings aggravates the plight of the victims of tyranny. Furthermore, atonement for past iniquities of colonialism and slavery does not require blind Western acquiescence to the hideous slaughter and other mistreatment of Africans by their leaders. One can help by shipping tents and bandages to hapless African peasants, but such aid serves little purpose when inhumane governments daily deny basic human rights and undermine economic security.

This book does not assess the leadership qualities, aims, or achievements of individual African heads of state or attempt to evaluate their objectives and policies for development. Nor is this book written to titillate the Western cultural palate. Rather, it offers an African perspective on the crisis plaguing the continent—a perspective which is often lacking in news coverage of African events.

No apologies are offered, as the pertinent theme of this book is straightforward—*freedom*. It is an issue to which Africans react passionately because they arduously fought for freedom from the colonialists in the 1950s and 1960s: freedom to express themselves, to write and publish, to move about without harassment from uniformed bandits at border crossings, to produce and trade, and to choose who should rule them. But where is this freedom today in Africa?

Instead, tyranny and intellectual repression reign over much of Africa today. Even in South Africa, blacks now have greater freedom of expression than we do in our own supposedly "free and independent" African countries. Brutally terrorized by their governments and crocodile liberators, most

Africans now live in a cocoon of fear—afraid even to whisper innocuous political comments. Ghanaians aptly have named this a "culture of silence."

Naturally, a book about freedom and its betrayal will not meet with the approval of African tyrants or the many blacks in North America who feel that "washing our dirty linen in public" only provides ammunition to racists. But the forces of freedom will not be deterred. They are continually inspired by the words and deeds of Nelson Mandela and Dr. Martin Luther King, Jr. Mandela was incarcerated for 27 years and his writings banned. But his will was not broken. After his release he stared at the repressive apartheid behemoth and declared defiantly: "I am prepared to die for my beliefs!" His words echoed those of Dr. King: "A man who won't die for a cause is not fit to live" (King, 1987; p. 23).

Freedom fighters elsewhere in Africa are not deterred by brutal repression. On the contrary, they have been emboldened by the historic events in Eastern Europe, the Soviet Union, and even apartheid South Africa. As the Nigerian journalist Pini Jason has predicted, "[t]he same tide sweeping away repression in Europe and Asia is bound to sweep away repressive and totally idiotic regimes in Africa." AFRICANS ARE ANGRY!

# Chapter 1

## Introduction:
## Black Neocolonialism

Three decades of dictatorships, phoney and misunderstood political ideologies have left a legacy of fear, poverty, refugees, outright political thuggery and theft.

The systems which have been in place for the last three decades in Africa have produced the likes of Amin, Bokassa, Nguema and the remaining political sphinx which strangle the African continent and its people.

Since assuming political power in their countries, these leaders have held their citizens hostage, have run national economies like private chicken-runs and created a national mentality of siege and a state of hopelessness.

— George Sono in *New African* (Jan 1991; p. 41).

What we need, and what enlightened Africans should be advocating, is for the masses to throw off the chains of fear which our dictators have manacled them with, and sweep the oppressive regimes that ensure the perpetuation of our enslavement out of existence.

— E. O. Gallo of Harare in *New African* (Feb 1991; p. 4).

Africa is still a foreboding enigma—a land of mystery, full of melancholy contrasts and paradoxes. For centuries it was a baffling entity that held an irresistible appeal to the valiant hearts of the adventurous and stoked their desires to look beneath its shroud of mystery.

Africa today consists of 52 countries and can be classified into four regions: the Maghreb in North Africa, which comprises the six Arab states of Algeria, Egypt, Libya, Mauritania, Morocco, and Tunisia; Francophone Africa, made up of the former French colonies; Anglophone Africa, comprising the former British colonies; and Lusophone Africa, which consists of the former Portuguese colonies.

The second largest continent after Asia, Africa occupies 20 percent of the earth's land surface. Five thousand miles long and 4,600 miles wide, Africa's total geographical size is 11,596,000 square miles—about three times the size of the United States. Africa spans four hemispheres, since the prime meridian and the equator pass over the continent and intersect in the Gulf of Guinea. Thus, Africa is squarely in the center of the world's geographical map. Africa is also symmetrically located. It stretches 37 degrees north and 35 degrees south of the equator. As such, it is the most tropical of all the continents.

Africa is also the oldest continent and bears topographical imprints peculiar to that status. It is a very rigid piece of the earth's crust on which geologic forces have made few changes. Physically, Africa is a hard land that does not admit of easy access or conquest. Littoral plains abut plateaus, and its rivers, interspersed with rapids, are seldom navigable. Africa's rain forest, which extends across an irregular and asymmetrical belt, varying in width from about 4 to 10 degrees of latitude, is dense and impenetrable. In this belt trees stand tall, reaching up in a fierce competition for the sun. Most trees do not branch out until 90 or 100 feet above the brushes and undergrowth.

The combination of high humidity and temperatures for centuries re-pulsed large-scale European settlement in Africa. West Africa, for example, was known as "the white man's grave." The principal grave-digger, it may be deduced, was none other than the tiny mosquito, which thrives in such climatic conditions. The equatorial climate terminates abruptly, however, and gives way to savanna vegetation on the wide plains of eastern and southern Africa. In West Africa the savanna recedes rather quickly before the Sahara desert, the world's greatest. Tucked in the southwestern corner is another desert, the Kalahari. These deserts, which have posted some of the hottest temperatures in the world, are generally inhospitable. But the plains and climate of eastern and southern Africa are congenial and thus were the scene of intense European settlement. It was also these same areas that saw the most protracted struggle for independence and liberation from European colonial rule. Persuading Europeans to relinquish colonial rule over hot and humid regions was relatively easy.

Africa's natural resources and mineral wealth are widely acclaimed as vast and diversified. It has 40 percent of the world's potential hydroelectric power supply, the bulk of the world's diamonds and chromium, 30 percent of the uranium in the noncommunist world, 50 percent of the world's gold, 90 percent of its phosphates, 40 percent of its platinum, 7.5 percent of its coal, 8 percent of its known petroleum reserves, 12 percent of its natural gas, 3 percent of its iron ore, and millions upon millions of acres of untilled agricultural land. In addition, Africa has 64 percent of the world's manganese, 13 percent of its copper, and vast bauxite, nickel, and lead resources. It also has such strategic minerals as cobalt, critical in the manufacture of jet engines, rhodium, palladium, vanadium, and titanium. Without these essential minerals many industrial plants in the West would grind to a standstill. As Lamb (1984) put it, "[t]here is not another continent blessed with such abundance and diversity" (p. 20).

Africa also accounts for a large share of world production in other sectors: 70 percent of cocoa, 60 percent of coffee, 50 percent of palm oil, and 20 percent of the total petroleum traded in the world market, excluding the United States and the former Soviet Union.

Equally diverse are the physical types of man, languages, and cultures. This diversity has challenged the taxonomic abilities of scholars in physical anthropology, linguistics, culture, history, and evolution. Anthropologists have classified Africans into three main groups: Bushmanoids, Caucasoids, and Negroids. Some classify Pygmies as a separate race: Negrillo. There are further subdivisions. For example, Caucasoids are subdivided into Semites and Hamites. The classifications and subdivisions often tend to be confusing. North African Arabs and Berbers, for example, are classified as Hamites. But similarly categorized are the Tuaregs, the Tebu of East Sahara, and the Fulani of Nigeria—all dark-skinned.

Of its indigenous stock, Africa has about 2,000 tribes or ethnic societies, each of which has its own language or dialect, culture, and traditions. Some, such as the Xhosa and Zulu of South Africa, occupy thousands of square miles, while other tribes are small in numerical strength and territory. The total population of Africa, in mid-1987, stood at about 559 million. (The U.S. population in mid-1987 was 244 million.) Demogr-phically, Africa is a young continent, with over 50 percent of its population 15 years old or less. The majority of Africa's population are peasants, while a small but growing educated class, or elite, constitutes the remainder.

The people of Africa have been brutally traumatized. European colonizers denigrated them for centuries as "subhumans" and denied them recognition of any meaningful intellectual, cultural, and historical accomplishments or experience. Called "savages," millions of Africans were carted off in bondage as slaves to the Americas. Even when Charles Darwin speculated that it was Africa, not a Garden of Eden in the Near or Far East, whence the evolution of the human race should be traced, intellectual prejudices of the time precipitated a spirited rejection of the notion that something good or new could originate from Africa. Allegedly, its people had no history, no culture, no civilization, and nothing of value to contribute to the creation of the human being.

It is now firmly established, however, that the earliest evidence of culture in the world is found in Africa. In 1931 Louis Leakey of Kenya discovered the fossilized remains of the creature *Proconsul*, identified by scientists as one of the primates in man's evolutionary scale, which lived 25 million years ago. Subsequent paleontological research and findings discovered the fossils of *Homo habilis* ("skillful man") and *Homo erectus* in the Olduvai Gorge, situated in northern Tanzania in the Eastern Rift.

It was also in Africa that toolmaking first appeared in the geological record. The first tools, mostly made from stone, are known as Oldowan-type tools after the Olduvai Gorge. They were used as early as 2 million years ago and have been discovered at various sites throughout Africa.

The evidence is indisputable. Yet these remarkable discoveries were generally dismissed as irrelevant and accorded little acceptance by European scholars, up until the 1920s. Studies of prehistory had nothing to offer the student of present-day cultures, it was argued. Most Africans recoil at these denials, which make a mockery of painstaking scientific inquiry. Other Africans consider them as classically monumental acts of ingratitude by man to his birthplace—the Motherland. The human race and its culture evolved in Africa. Yet after migrating to other continents and perfecting their skills, humanoids returned with a vengeance—to denigrate, enslave, conquer, and colonize.

The first to attack were the Arabs. After wresting Egypt from Byzantium in A.D. 639 to 642, they quickly advanced west to the Maghreb, where they effectively established their rule by the second half of the seventh century and imposed Islam on the Berbers.

Next to come were the European explorers, Christian missionaries, and slave traders in the fifteenth century. Jomo Kenyatta, the late president of Kenya, cynically declared: "When the missionaries arrived, Africans had the land and the missionaries had the Bible. They taught us to pray with our eyes closed. When we opened them, they had the land and we had the Bible" (cited by Lamb, 1984; p. 58). Africans were told the Bible would deliver them into Heaven. But they were not "saved" from slavery. Since the Bible spoke of slavery without condemning it, Christian missionaries argued sternly that Africans would in fact be better off as slaves than as African savages (Harris, 1987; p. 17).

Accordingly, over 15 million Africans were shipped across the Atlantic to the Americas in unmitigated misery and appalling conditions. That figure does not include the hundreds of thousands who perished during slave raids and the march to the coast. In Angola, for example, Portuguese colonizers demanded an annual quota of slaves from African chiefs. Those who failed to secure the required number were themselves enslaved or killed. "Over a hundred chiefs and other notables were sold in a single year (1609) and an equal number murdered" (Williams, 1987; p. 261).

An especially pernicious aspect of the slave trade was the fact that the victims were the strong, active members of the population—young, healthy, and able-bodied men and women. The vitality of Africa's labor force was effectively sapped, placing severe constraints on its agricultural and commercial development. It would be impossible to calculate the economic damage of the slave trade to the indigenous economies of West Africa, aside from the human loss.

Equally devastating, however, was the slave trade on Africa's east coast which, for some inexplicable reason, has received little scholarly attention. Arabs largely organized and controlled this trade. Africa also lost large, if not equal, numbers from the East African slave trade. Estimates of Africans exported range from a low of 3 million to a high of 20 million. The Zanzibar slave trade, for example, reached its zenith during the reign of Sayyid Said (1804-1856), the Sultan of Muscat and Oman. In the mid-nineteenth century between 40,000 and 45,000 African slaves were exported from Zanzibar alone.

According to Wickins (1981), "Enslaving and slave trading in East Africa were peculiarly savage in a traffic notable for its barbarity. Villages were burned, the unfit villagers massacred. The enslaved were yoked together, several hundreds in a caravan (for) a journey to the coast which could be as long as 1280 kilometres . . . It is estimated that only one in five of those captured in the interior reached Zanzibar. The slave trade seems to have been more catastrophic in East Africa than in West Africa" (p. 184).

By the 1840s the slave trade had been abolished, but it left blacks persistently stigmatized as "inferior." It was probably this, rather than the physical and economic damage of the slave trade, that wrenched the heart from the inner psyche of blacks and assailed the very cultural soul of their existence. This helps to explain why the slave trade, which occurred centuries ago, continues to draw emotive reactions from blacks in general. But while this reaction is understandable, it tends to produce a mentality among black leaders that impedes further black progress and intellectual development.

Naturally, stigmatization educes a strong and overarching inclination to confront and challenge negative imputations against blacks. Unfortunately, the all-consuming passion to change the label of "inferiority" blinds many black leaders and incapacitates them in the search for solutions to mundane black problems.

Everyone recognizes the repugnance of the slave trade, colonialism, and racism. But the obsession of many black leaders and intellectuals, as well as whites in the West, with these past travesties invariably distorts their perceptions of current black problems so that they are incapable of making a dispassionate, objective analysis.

Almost every black problem is placed or explained in terms of a racialist paradigm, giving the false impression that black problems cannot be solved until racism is totally eradicated. This is painfully unrealistic. Regrettably, there will *always* be racism in the West and elsewhere. Must we blacks wait for its end before we take the initiative ourselves to solve our own problems?

In fact, many of us are so obsessed with the racial prejudices of Westerners that we fail to see those of Easterners or of other non-Westerners. For example, the harassment and arrest of African students in China in the summer of 1989 revealed a deep-seated racial hatred against blacks. Yet those incidents elicited little protest and condemnation. More shocking is the continued enslavement of black Africans in this day and age, not by Westerners but by Arabs in Sudan and Mauritania. The slavery of blacks was abolished in Mauritania only in 1980. In Sudan it was officially abolished in 1987, but was still continuing in 1990. Arab militias, formed and armed by the Islamic government of Lt. Gen. Omar Bashir, were trafficking in slaves from the southern Dinka tribe (*The Economist*, Jan 6, 1990; p. 42). Many black leaders, both in Africa and the West, choose to ignore these moral depravities, however, and prefer to focus on past slavery by Westerners.

Africa barely recovered from the trauma of slavery before it was hit by another type of cultural adversity. The European scramble for Africa began in earnest in the 1880s, propelled by three forces that drew their impetus from Europe's Industrial Revolution. The first was the need for new markets for surplus manufactured goods. As industrial activity expanded beyond England to France, Russia, Germany, and Italy during the second half of the nineteenth century, far more goods were produced than could be absorbed locally, and new colonial markets were needed. Second, increasing industrial competition for such raw materials as cotton, rubber, and minerals added further impetus to the desire to control or own the sources of the supply. The third factor in the race for colonies was the investment of surplus capital. As more and more profit accumulated in the European countries, an outlet was needed for their investment. It was this that led Lenin, the Russian leader, to describe imperialism as the "highest stage of capitalism."

By July 1884, France, Britain, Germany, and Portugal were all actively staking out colonial claims on Africa. To lay down rules to govern this race and to avoid the possibility of open conflicts, an international conference was held in Berlin from Nov 15, 1884 to Jan 30, 1885, under the chairmanship of Otto von Bismarck. On Feb 26, 1885, the Berlin Act, which promulgated the "rules" for partition, was signed. One rule was that any power that wanted to claim any African territory should notify the other signatory powers. Another was that to be valid, any such annexations should be followed by effective occupation.

In this way Africa was carved up into colonies and transformed into economic appendages of European colonial powers. Boundaries were artificially drawn up with little regard to demographic configurations. The Ghana-Togo border, for example, ran right through the Ewe community, placing nearly half under French colonial jurisdiction and the rest under the British. The Somali people fared the worst. They were split into a British Somaliland, a French Somaliland, and an Italian Somaliland. A fourth component was absorbed into Kenya, and the fifth became the Ogaden in Ethiopia.

Colonial subjugation was a cultural and emotional humiliation suffered on top of the pervasive denigration of Africans as inferior. In many places the African people put up a gallant and fierce resistance to colonial rule. Their resistance was crushed with a merciless abandon that resulted in thousands of African casualties. But undeterred by these setbacks and their inferior weapons, Africans persisted with their struggle for freedom and independence. By 1990 most of Africa had been "liberated" from colonial rule except for Namibia and South Africa. But in most parts of Africa independence from oppressive colonial rule was in name only. All that changed was the color of the guards and the masters.

A third and far more insidious invasion began under black neocolonialism. Educated abroad and having assumed the trappings of foreign cultures and ideologies, a new wave of invaders struck Africa. They were actually returnees, sons of Africa who briefly left to pursue studies overseas or to go into exile. But they came back with a vengeance to denigrate, to enslave, to destroy, and to colonize by imposing alien ideological systems upon the African people.

The economic exploitation and political repression of the African people continued unabated. More treacherous perhaps was the continued denigration and, in some cases, the destruction of indigenous African institutions and culture—by the very African nationalists and heads of state who claimed to have liberated Africa. From what? Economically, politically, *and* culturally,

Africans today are worse off than they were at the time of independence in the 1960s.

Three decades of independence from colonial rule have produced nothing but economic misery and disintegration, political chaos, and institutional and social decay. The decline in per capita income has been calamitous for many African countries.[1] Agricultural growth has been dismal, producing chronic food shortages and an ever-present threat of famine. *The Economist* wrote that between 1986 and 1991, "real GDP grew by 2.3 percent in Africa (including Arab North Africa, but not South Africa). The population grew faster, so real GDP per head fell by 0.7% a year. The proportion of state spending devoted to health and education fell. In 1985, a quarter of Africa's pre-school children suffered from acute protein deficiency; in 1989 two-fifths did" (Aug 31, 1991; p. 33).

In sub-Saharan or black Africa, the crisis has been particularly severe. Black Africa, with a population of 450 million, has a GDP of $135 billion, which is about the same as that of Belgium, with a population of only 10 million. Between 1980 and 1989, black Africa's real GDP per capita contracted by an average 1.2 percent (World Bank, 1991; p. 3). So severe has the economic deterioration in black Africa been that, by 1990, this region had the dubious distinction of being home to 24 of the world's 36 poorest nations. Nigeria, the most populous African country, was transformed from the "Great Black Hope" into the "Great Black Disappointment."

The exceptions to the general economic atrophy in black Africa have been few. Botswana continues to serve as a shining black success story, followed by Mauritius and Cameroon, while Senegal struggles to keep its head above water. In the early 1980s the Ivory Coast and Kenya used to be members of this select club, but they now suffer from serious economic crises. The worst performers have been Ethiopia, Ghana, Liberia, Mozambique, Niger, Nigeria, Sao Tome and Principe, Sudan, Uganda, Zaire, and Zambia—all of which are characterized by civilian/military dictatorships.

The case of Zaire was most pathetic. Potentially one of the richest countries in Africa—a country with enough arable land and hydroelectric potential to feed and power the entire continent—Zaire had been looted so completely that in 1992 its economy was a hollow shell and nothing was working:

> The capital's [Kinshasa's] state-run hospitals are closed, and the patients have been sent home . . . The public sector, by and large, has ceased to function. There is a government, there are ministers and there is even an official budget, but there is an air of fantasy about it all, since the tax collection system has broken down

and virtually no custom revenues are coming in. For the most part, the government has taken to paying its bills by printing fresh batches of currency . . .

The country's official banking system has all but collapsed . . . [and] Kinshasa's telephone system has nearly shut down (*The Washington Post*, Mar 31, 1992; p. A13).

For most Africans, independence did not bring a better life or even greater political and civil liberties. Many are troubled by this comparative statement because they misinterpret it as a veiled justification of colonialism. Nothing could be further from the truth. Africans overwhelmingly rejected colonial rule. Colonialism was invidious, and Africans expected the quality of their lives to improve markedly after independence. They were sorely disappointed.

Colonial governments in Africa were generally authoritarian and paternalistic. Even the more liberal systems, such as those established in British West Africa, permitted only scant popular participation in government, and this itself was confined to a small elite. Nevertheless, colonial administrations allowed some measures of freedom of movement and civil liberties. Though a few radicals, such as Kwame Nkrumah of Ghana, Jomo Kenyatta of Kenya, and Robert Mugabe of Zimbabwe, were incarcerated for advocating armed and violent overthrow of the colonial system, the majority of African nationalists were able to work, albeit with difficulty, within the system to effect change and to win independence. Many African nationalists also traveled to Europe and within Africa with relative ease and personal safety. As oppressive as colonial rule was, almost all the nationalists who struggled against it for independence emerged *alive* to lead their countries after independence. But few Africans would be lucky to survive even two years in the jails of independent Africa.

Since independence in the 1960s there has been a systematic curtailment and virtual banishment across Africa of freedom and civil liberties. Africans asked for *more*, not less, freedom after colonial rule. But today, this freedom remains a fantasy. One word of criticism of an African government may earn a death sentence. As Makau Wa Mutua, a Kenyan lawyer and project director of Harvard University Law School's Human Rights Program, lamented:

Since independence in Africa, government has been seen as the personal fiefdom a leader uses to accumulate wealth for himself, his family, his clan. He cannot be subjected to criticism by anyone, and everything he says is final. The apex of this notion of owning government is the idea of a life president like Hastings Banda of Malawi.

Once they replaced the colonial rulers, they wanted to become just like them. They wanted to be all-powerful and omnipresent. We just replaced white faces with black faces (*The Washington Post*, Sep 9, 1991; p. A20).

Africa has been betrayed. Freedom from colonial rule has evolved into ghastly tyranny, arbitrary rule, denial of civil liberties, brutal suppression of dissent, and the wanton slaughter of peasants. This malicious betrayal drives the deep sense of disillusionment, despair, and anger pervasive among Africans. It is difficult to convey to Westerners a sense of the depth and breadth of this betrayal. But the most painful was the cultural insult.

It may be recalled that European colonialists generally held indigenous African institutions and culture in contempt. But the African elites who replaced them were no better. They deprecated the indigenous as "backward" and "primitive." In many places the elites sought the destruction of the indigenous by imposing alien systems on Africa. In some cases the destruction was premeditated, as with the dynamiting and burning of indigenous markets in Ghana during 1982 and 1983. But in most other cases functional illiteracy and acceptance of false syllogism were the motivating force: colonialism was judged to be synonymous with Western civilization and capitalism. Therefore, if colonialism was evil, so too must be capitalism. Consequently, the rejection of colonialism simultaneously meant the renunciation of Western institutions as well, even those erroneously perceived as such.

To replace Western institutions many African leaders marched off to the East and adopted socialist and communist systems for transplantation into Africa. In so doing African leaders consciously embroiled themselves in the East-West conflict and cold war, despite their protestations to the contrary. Common sense should have dictated absolute neutrality and noncommitment. African leaders should have taken heed from an ancient African proverb: "When elephants fight, it is the grass that suffers."

More insulting, however, was the African leaders' forcing culturally alien ideologies and revolutionaries down the throats of their people. In this respect the nationalists were no different from the colonialists. The African leaders' rejection of colonialism and Western institutions was an understandable reaction. But in their overzealousness to eradicate all the vestiges of Western colonialism, virtually all sense of purpose and cultural direction was lost. After independence, many African leaders, proclaiming themselves "free and independent under black rule," hauled down the statues of European monarchs and erected, not those of Martin Luther King, Jr. or Kankan Musa, but of another set of white aliens—Marx and Lenin. Even the peasants could see clearly that Marx and Lenin were not black Africans and had no cultural affinity with Africa. Yet for decades portraits and statues of Marx and Lenin graced the capitals of Angola, Benin, Ethiopia, Mozambique, and other African nations.

The waning years of the 1980s witnessed the wholesale rejection of Marxist-Leninism in Eastern Europe. Even in the Soviet Union, the communists voted to relinquish their monopoly on political power. But not so in Africa, where many leaders and intellectuals adamantly uphold the virtues of one-party rule, state ownership of the means of production, state control of the media, and other trappings of Marxist-Leninism. If you thought colonialism was dead in Africa, think again.

## PLAN OF THE BOOK

This book was not written to please anybody—white, black, or brown. It seeks to speak the truth about Africa and the betrayal of the freedom for which the people of Africa struggled. The issues raised in this book are not those that most Africans, even those living abroad, discuss with detached emotions. The task is formidably dangerous since ordinarily those Africans who embark on such a crusade do not live long enough to see its successful completion. They have been "liquidated," jailed, or exiled. The task is further confounded by the absence of statistics. Researchers of African issues have perennially bemoaned the lack of reliable data, even for economic phenomena. Statistics on political crimes and atrocities are even harder to obtain—they are simply not reported in the state-owned media. And even when reported, they are often slanted. Nevertheless, I have made every effort in this book to provide documentation and, where possible, to supply the names of those killed. From the perspective of the victims of tyranny it is essential to expose the atrocities perpetrated by "educated" African leaders. These victims would like the world to know their plight, which all too often is censored by the state-owned media in Africa.

In addition, I have made every effort to draw upon statements and quotations by Africans themselves as they assessed their own experience, political well-being, and environment. Even if a Ghanaian and an Ethiopian express the same indignation, both are quoted. This is important since in Africa their voices are not heard. In addition, this will help demonstrate that it is not only Ethiopians, Liberians, or Ugandans who yearn for *sopi* (change). The cry for freedom is widespread across Africa.

Material for this book was drawn from a wide variety of sources: books, monographs, government reports, magazines, and newspapers—both Western and African. To address the perennial complaint of African governments that Western news coverage of African events is biased, however, I placed greater reliance on African sources that are, in my view, *objective* and *constructively critical.* Unfortunately these African sources are, needless to say, few. This narrow material support base includes *West Africa* magazine, *New African* magazine, the *African Letter* newspaper, the *Continent* newspaper, and a few others. Africans produce these publications outside Africa. Wherever possible I have attempted to supplement these with sources within Africa itself. (More information about these sources appears in the bibliography.)

Every effort has been made to cite sources of quotes, facts and figures. These sources have been placed in the text, together with page numbers wherever practical. For example, an idea originally espoused by author David Lamb is cited as: Lamb, 1984; p. 123. A quick reference to the bibliography at the end of the book and a look under Lamb (1984) will indicate the title of the book, the name of the publisher and the city/country where it was first published. On certain occasions, it was necessary to expatiate on some points without breaking the flow of thought or argument in the text. Such elaborations have been placed in the notes section.

Chapter 2 discusses the myths and misconceptions about the natives of Africa and their contribution to Western civilization. Chapter 3 briefly describes how the African people traditionally ruled themselves. Their indigenous systems of government were hardly ever studied or understood. Ignorance and mythology about these institutions are still pervasive. As will become clear, the people of Africa have for centuries had a political tradition of participatory democracy that allowed them to engage freely in the political decisionmaking process *without* harassment or exclusion. There was much freedom in traditional African societies. Somehow these freedoms steadily vanished from much of Africa after independence from colonial rule.

Chapter 4 examines Africa's experience under colonialism. I analyze various colonial policies and their impact on Africa's indigenous institutions. Most analysts now agree that although colonialism was evil, it offered comparatively more freedom than did many independent African countries in the 1980s.

Chapter 5 details the relentless march toward oppression by the African nationalists who won independence for their countries. The story is one of betrayal of the African struggle for freedom. More painful, however, was the cultural betrayal.

By 1990 the political regimes instituted in most African countries were indistinguishable from the abominable system of apartheid or institutionalized racism in South Africa. In fact, the oppression of blacks in some independent African countries was even worse. Chapter 6 focuses on the other de facto apartheid regimes in Africa, not so much to justify the repugnant system in South Africa but to call for a clean-up of all of Africa's racist and tyrannical regimes.

Chapter 7 discusses military regimes. They are not only the most prevalent but the most alien of all Africa's regimes. In addition, they are characterized by carnage, savage brutality, barbarism, and even cannibalism.

Chapter 8 attempts to explain how the erosion of these civil and political liberties occurred. It begins with Ghana, which, being the first black African nation to gain its independence, provides the obvious starting point for a discussion of autocracy. Subsequent sections trace the political histories of selected African countries, both pro- and anti-West, to describe the spread of tyranny to the rest of Africa.

Chapter 9 generally surveys the prevailing atmosphere of intellectual repression in Africa. It offers a descriptive account of the arrests, detention, and massacre of dissidents or anyone with a viewpoint that deviates from the party's or the government's line.

For decades African radicals have carped incessantly about the colonial exploitation and plunder of Africa. Unfortunately they have failed to see the devastation wreaked by elite *bazongas* (raiders of the public treasury). Chapter 10 deals with the growing scourge of venality and embezzlement. The evidence shows that the problem is far more widespread than has hitherto been acknowledged. After presenting the general nature of the problem, I provide more in-depth case studies of corruption in selected African countries.

Tyranny has persisted in Africa because of various props, both external and internal. Chapter 11 discusses how foreign blocs and powers (American, French, Soviet, and Chinese), through various aid mechanisms, diplomatic contrivances, and other devices, unwittingly supported the proliferation of dictatorships in Africa and contributed to its ruin, not so much by design but by default and munificence. The focus is skewed slightly toward discussion of U.S. policy toward Africa.

Chapter 12 examines the *internal* props of tyranny, which are by far the more formidable. Among them are the military, the civil service, journalists, intellectuals and the opposition itself.

Chapter 13 examines the types of reform Africa needs to survive. It also discusses Africa's experience with economic adjustment programs sponsored by the International Monetary Fund (IMF) and offers a prognosis for Africa's development. Drawing lessons from Eastern Europe, this chapter notes that economic reform alone is insufficient; political and *intellectual* reforms are also essential. Of much greater importance, however, is the *sequence* of reform. Economic reform *without* political restructuring is meaningless. But political reform is not possible unless Africans have *freedom of expression*. Ultimately, it is the African people themselves who must determine which political and economic systems are best suited for them. But they cannot make this determination in a "culture of silence" or an atmosphere of intellectual repression. The final chapter provides some concluding remarks and looks at the way ahead.

---

## NOTES

1. Between 1965 and 1987, the average annual growth rate of GNP per capita was 1.1 for all of Africa, 0.4 for Sub-Saharan Africa, and -0.1 if Nigeria is excluded (UNDP, 1989; p. 3).

# Chapter 2

## Solving Black Africa's Problems

Maybe we can reach the "promised land" that the Rev. Dr. Martin Luther King Jr. preached about. So far, we're still wandering in the wilderness.

— Clarence Page, black American columnist (*Washington Times*, Feb 28, 1992).

I am human . . . I am a self-defining value. I can make of myself whatever I choose.

— Zulu concept of "humanness" or *buntu*.

Every political system or society has its own unique set of economic, political, and social problems. Germany, Eastern Europe, Russia, and even Japan are all grappling with their own problems. The United States is not immune. It has a chronic budget deficit problem, electoral disenchantment with the political system, and racism, to name only a few. Even freedom of expression is rapidly vanishing on American campuses.

American society generally seems to be on the decline. Art critic and *New Criterion* editor Hilton Kramer, a neoconservative, offered this view: "We are told that we won the Cold War and that Eastern Europe is looking to us for models in economics and culture. But we find in the West decadence and intellectual civil wars" (*The Washington Times*, Apr 30, 1990; p. A10).

Black Africa also has its share of problems. Famine, economic crisis, political instability, tyranny, agricultural decline, deteriorating living standards, capital flight, corruption, AIDS, and inflation are all examples of the problems Africa is wrestling with. But while other societies certainly have problems, dealing with those of black Africa is particularly challenging and exasperating—not because black African problems are unsolvable but because all sorts of myths, misconceptions, innuendoes, and extraneous and dissonant factors are allowed to intrude, scuttling reasoned analysis. This especial difficulty in solving black African problems is misused to grease the racist perception that black Africans are intellectually inferior and therefore cannot solve their own problems. This, of course, is nonsense. Problems persist in black Africa not so much because of intellectual inferiority but because of the application of the wrong remedies or policies by black African leaders.

To remedy a problem, it should first be exposed. Then one must carefully diagnose its causes, prescribe a solution, and monitor the efficacy of the prescription. In Africa, the proliferation of tyrannies—one-party state systems, government monopoly of the media, intolerance of alternative viewpoints, and the general brutalization of dissidents—precludes exposure of any problem, let alone an intelligent analysis of it. Exposing problem can be embarrassing to an incompetent African government, which naturally attempts to cover it up. In 1984, for example, the Mengistu regime in Ethiopia strenuously denied reports of an impending famine.

Even when a black African problem is exposed, an attempt to solve it seldom proceeds beyond the first stage: diagnosis of its causes. This first stage often evokes emotionally charged arguments about the causes and degenerates into heated debates, name-calling and eventual paralysis. African exiles may bear witness to numerous unproductive "meetings" that have produced more heat than light.

There are several reasons for this paralysis. The first is the difficulty of penetrating the abstruse mythology that envelopes Africa and its people. The denigration of Africans as subhuman creatures with no history, culture, or civilization is still pervasive. It is a myth that Africans were not capable of developing any viable institutions or civilization. This mythology has been a constant source of distorted, faulty analyses and has given rise to useless prescriptions that often exacerbated Africa's ills.

The East-West ideological conflict posed a second difficulty in analyzing African issues. For decades, Marxist-Leninists attributed Africa's economic decline to the lingering effects of Western colonialism, American imperialism, an unjust international economic system, inadequate foreign aid, and many other extraneous causes. Never was the decline attributed to defective domestic policies. By the early 1980s, even illiterate peasants were fed up with this "colonialism-imperialism" claptrap.

One would have thought that the demise of Marxist-Leninism in Eastern Europe and Russia would ensure clearer thinking and a more objective analysis. Unfortunately there still prevails among African leaders and intellectuals a tendency to ascribe the causes of Africa's problems to exogenous or Western factors. This predisposes African intellectuals and leaders to seek solutions to Africa's ills from abroad, reinforcing the myth that no good solutions can come out of Africa. In fact, the suggestion of *internal* solutions is likely to be met with great resistance and suspicion both by Westerners who believe that Africans are intellectually incapable of solving their problems and by African elites who spurn the efficacy of internal solutions because the problems are assumed to be of external origin.

The result of these attitudes and beliefs has been a scholarly minefield, laden with myths, prejudices, exaggerated claims, suspicions, and misconceptions about Africans, whom so many seek to help and yet are so little understood. The problems facing Africa are really not of such esoteric complexity as to defeat the human mind but are made so because too many irrelevant factors are allowed to intrude. To analyze the issues, scholars must examine all possible causes, both external *and* internal, make objective assessments, and propose viable solutions. In many cases, we never get beyond analysis of causes of a problem, let alone prescribe a solution.

## MYTHS, MISCONCEPTIONS, AND IGNORANCE ABOUT AFRICA

Western ethnocentrism prevented a recognition of the capabilities of the African people. The European colonialists generally held African culture in contempt, contending that the savages of Africa had no viable institutions and were incapable of developing them. Allegedly, indigenous African society was chaotic and barbaric, and Africans had no value systems. Occasionally, the racist assertion was made, based on the frequent tribal rivalries in Africa's history, that the black man could not rule himself. Much of this mythology was of deliberate manufacture to justify colonial rule: colonial rule was "good" for the savages of Africa. But of far more immediate consequence is the question: How can the African people lift themselves out of poverty? And with what institutions? Even these innocent questions cannot be answered without provoking intense debate.

Quite often, one also encounters the absurd claim that everything good on this earth was invented in the West and, therefore, Africa can only solve its problems by adopting *Western* institutions.

For the record, the institutions of democracy, money, and free markets were *not* uniquely Western inventions. They existed in various rudimentary forms in Africa. For example, there is a sharp contrast between a supermarket or a mall in the West and a village market under a tree in Africa. But both are different forms of the *same* institution of bringing buyers and sellers together, which is the function of a market.

Before the arrival of the Europeans, Africa had *participatory* and *direct* democracy, free village markets, and free trade. Freedom of expression also existed in traditional African societies. At village meetings, the natives of Africa freely expressed their ideas and exchanged viewpoints. Africans had a value system; they knew of the work ethic, justice, order, and fairness. "Primitive" Africa had forms of *family, social,* and *political* control. There were kingdoms, empires, and civilizations in Africa. Some were "primitive," but others were highly organized and sophisticated. Gold was being used as money by coastal peoples of West Africa before the Europeans arrived there. The initial discovery and use of this precious metal as money were distinctly due to black Africans. Gold provided the basis for a stable and robust Western monetary system. By the end of the nineteenth century, almost all Western currencies were backed by gold (or "on the gold standard"). Although the knowledge and use of gold in Africa predated the arrival of Europeans and Arabs, subsequent refinements of its use in international monetary systems were, however, made by the Europeans.

From this perspective it can be said that the Europeans never really introduced new institutions into Africa; they introduced only the advanced and more efficient forms of *already existing* institutions.[1] Over the centuries there has been a cross-cultural fertilization and borrowing of ideas and institutions between the West and Africa that makes claims of "invention" absurd. Much of this borrowing is still evident. For example, there has been a great deal of Western borrowing from African music and art. Many Western countries and organizations also use lions and elephants—animals indigenous to Africa—in their emblems. The lion, in particular, has appeared in the coat of arms of many Western institutions, and the elephant is the symbol of the American Republican Party.

A more poignant example comes from France. In 1989, Kofi Yamgnane, a black African from Togoland, was elected mayor of the village of Saint Coulitz. "He became famous throughout France not only for being a black Breton mayor but also for instituting an elected 'elders council.' This practice has been imitated by more than 400 towns around France" (*The Atlantic,* Apr 1992; p. 36). As we shall see in the next chapter, an "elders council" is an indigenous African concept.

The West can lay claims to having improved upon the institutions borrowed from various peoples, but not to inventing them. This is a unique characteristic of Western society: the capacity to take an idea or item and to accentuate its attributes to the superlative. For example, the West refined and advanced the use of gold and iron and further developed the institution of money by introducing new forms, such as paper currency, checks, and credit cards. Gold provided the foundation upon which a sound monetary system was built. Without a stable monetary system, the advance of Western civilization would have been greatly impeded. But then the West also has the capacity to develop a bad idea to the nadir of its ugliness. There is a conspicuous absence of Western claims to the invention of bad ideas.

Some of these bad ideas evolved autonomously in various societies. One is imperialism, which was not invented by the West but highly developed by Westerners to subjugate other peoples. There was also imperialism in Africa, evidenced by ancient empires, before the arrival of the Europeans. But imperial rule in Africa was not characterized by strong centralized rule. Indigenous African kings generally lacked the coercive means to centralize power. Furthermore, land was abundant in Africa, and tribes that found themselves subjugated could always move elsewhere, as we shall see in the next chapter.

Another bad Western development was slavery, which also existed in Africa before the advent of Europeans. Slavery in indigenous Africa was not completely iniquitous, however, and the term "limbry" has been suggested by Vaughan (1986). Slaves could own property and had full political rights and social mobility. In many West African societies slaves elected and sent their own representatives to the king's court and could request a hearing with the king. Slaves could even become kings. One was Jubo Jubogha (called Jaja by the Europeans), king of one of the Niger states (Nigeria): "He was born in 1821, sold as a slave to a Bonny trader in 1833 and elected head of the Anna Pepple House to succeed Alali in 1863" (Boahen, 1986; p. 92).

Narcotics are another modern day example. Tobacco, marijuana, opium, and coca were not discovered by Westerners. These substances have been used by various natives of the Third World for centuries without any noticeable harm to their societies.

The West did not invent any of these institutions, but it developed them to their ugly extremes. Slavery was pushed to its horrifying limits in the trans-Atlantic slave trade. The political art of conquering and subjugating neighboring nations was polished first by the West and subsequently by the Soviet Union into Yankee and Communist imperialism. Similarly with narcotics—it is in the West where the consumption of these substances has expanded to such horrifying proportions that it seems to threaten the very fabric and foundations of Western civilization.

Even the institution of democracy itself seems to have decayed in the United States. Many Americans would affirm that political action committees have effectively debauched the democratic process by turning legislators into political prostitutes. Less than half of Americans now bother to vote in national elections. Americans are angry with their political representatives. Governor L. Douglas Wilder, the first black governor of Virginia, said, "[i]n 1990 more and more Americans want government that is once again of, by and for the people rather than a burden to the people (*Washington Times*, Oct 4, 1990; p. G2). But the anger of Americans with their elected representatives is no different from that of Africans who are fed up with military dictators and presidents-for-life. Nor is their ire any different from that of the Eastern Europeans.

If the above statements sound vehement, it is because Western claims and assertions cause a great deal of difficulty. It is dangerous enough for a black African to speak the truth about his country's conditions, but the danger is exacerbated by Western misconceptions about Africa. Many African intellectuals now believe some of them, compounding the existing mythology. For example, Charles Mungoshi, a well-known Zimbabwean author, wrote, "Education is a Western thing and we throw away brother and sister for it but when it fails we are lost" (*The Economist*, Apr 28, 1990; p. 97). So, Africans should abjure "education" because it is a Western thing? This is ridiculous. Although "primitive" Africans had no written scripture, they educated their children.

Westerners' claims to have invented everything good on the face of the planet provokes equally absurd counterclaims. These claims and counterclaims only serve to crank up the decibel level of noisy debates and to politicize scholarly work on Africa. This distracts African scholars from the search for pragmatic solutions to Africa's woes. Whether Africa contributed more to the industrial civilization of the West than the West did to Africa's modernization is not only difficult to establish but also irrelevant when Africans are starving.

The glorification of Western values and Westerners' staking proprietary claims to such concepts as liberty, democracy, free markets, or free speech have probably done more damage to the world in the past 50 years than the two world wars combined. These claims induced hordes of scholars and national leaders to search for and produce specious confuting evidence by focusing on "the problems of Western capitalist societies."

Placing a "Western" label on various institutions made them targets for destruction by radicals. Markets are one perfect example in Africa. Somehow, they were perceived by African intellectual radicals as "a capitalist, Western institution." Accordingly, market activities were suppressed forcibly in many African countries in the postcolonial era.

The desire to reject these Western claims, by *both* Westerners and non-Westerners, was so intense and consuming that it also led to deliberate, unnatural attempts to create alternative non-Western systems (socialism and communism). The failures of these attempts at social engineering are now only too apparent in Eastern Europe, the Soviet Union, China, Latin America, and Africa.

In summary, claims of superiority of Western culture and civilization drew a backlash that has only served to complicate issues, poison the academic environment, and impede scholarly work. This backlash emanated from two sources: from the West itself ("Third Worldism") and from black intellectuals.

## "THIRD WORLDISM"

Over the past 25 years, a set of attitudes toward Third World countries has flourished among many intellectuals and journalists in the West. It is based upon a conviction that Third World countries have long been *victims* of the West—that their resources were stolen by imperialist colonialists or multinational corporations, that their cultures were destroyed by commercialism and exploitation, and that their pastoral sensitivity toward nature was corrupted by industry and pollution.

Such French writers as Fanon and Sartre were perhaps best known for arousing and legitimizing the "collective guilt" of Westerners for crimes committed in the past in their name. In his foreword to *The Wretched of the Earth*, Sartre exhorted Westerners to have courage to abase themselves and feel shame. And shame, as Marx said, is a revolutionary emotion.

Western guilt, as Bruckner (1987) explains, originates from three sources:

*Guilt by history:* You [Westerners] are responsible for the frightful genocide of colonialism that was carried on against Indians and blacks from the Renaissance to the twentieth century by your ancestors.

*Guilt by contagion:* You are guilty of being the happy descendants of these unscrupulous freebooters, and you must not forget that your prosperity is built upon the corpses of millions of natives.

*Guilt by confirmation:* You demonstrate that you are no better than your conquering forefathers because you do not react when hunger kills children and new nations are pushed into underdevelopment by your selfishness (p. 18).

Because of this guilt, many Westerners were willing to reject their own civilization and to immolate themselves to redeem the debts incurred by their fathers. Being Western or being supported by a Western power was enough to make one suspect. Being non-European was enough to put one on the side of right.

But Third Worldism soon degenerated into fanaticism. After the former colonial victim was freed from his chains, he was deemed to have a wisdom that approached the mystical. A whole generation of European and American intellectuals, fortified by Sartre's authority, subscribed to Fanon's prophecy that Europe would view the Third World as a colossus.

America was the ideal scapegoat, according to Bruckner (1987): "Four hundred years of conquest, pillage, and massacre achieved their supreme expression and converged under the roof of the White House. All the loathing for a particular culture could be concentrated in a single place, in a single people, in a single system" (p. 17). This was so because "America the Evil was showing all the symptoms by which the guilt of the West was known—she was rich to the point of satiety; imperialistic, domineering, insolent, and polluting; alienating her youth; exploiting her minorities; glorifying her foundation on genocide; and prospering only because of massacre and murder" (p. 16).

At the same time, Third Worldists were excessively glorifying the Southern Hemisphere:

> Puny insurrections and the slightest of uprisings are given enormous attention, far out of proportion to their real importance. The ignorance and sectarianism of tropical gangsters are treated with reverence. Glory is given to the parade of splendid Asians who have been called upon to destroy European civilization. The most outrageous lunacies are praised to the skies by enlightened intellectuals, who are only too happy to submit to a primitive authority to abase themselves before the splendor of a healthy barbarism. By this axiom, anyone who uplifts, praises, or celebrates the West is suspected of the worst sort of evil. Modesty, humility, self-destructiveness, and whatever else might lead Europeans to efface themselves and give up leadership are honored and saluted as wonderfully progressive. The golden rule of this masochism is simple: Whatever comes from us [Westerners] is bad; whatever comes from them is perfect. Formerly colonized peoples are prized as perfect through and through (Bruckner, 1987; p. 22).

Soon shrewd Third World dictators began exploiting Western guilt to the fullest. The West pumped much aid into Africa perhaps to soothe its guilty conscience. Did this aid help save Africa from economic ruin? The *New York Times* reported: "It is hard for the villagers of Chamkombe in Zambia to see how foreign aid from well-meaning Western sources has made much difference. At the main provincial hospital in Kasama, there has been no water for three years. Patients usually sleep two to a bed, with others on the floor. They must arrange with relatives or friends to have water brought to them" (Jun 5, 1990; p. A13).

By the early 1980s the Third Worldists themselves had become fed up with Third World dictators. After discovering a distressing capacity among these leaders to inflict cruelty on their own countrymen, "depressed intellectuals now swear that they will never again be deceived into supporting 'crazy niggers,' 'yellow devils,' cigar-smoking dictators, or emperors in Mao jackets" (Bruckner, 1987; p. 40).

## DISILLUSIONMENT WITH AFRICAN LEADERSHIP

The disenchantment of the African people with their leaders began much earlier—in the 1960s. There was no question that colonial injustices were perpetrated against the African people. But the leadership which assumed power after independence continued with the *same* denigration and oppression of the African people. It was all the more painful when the atrocities were being committed by the very leaders who claimed to have brought freedom to Africa. Some freedom.

Those who won their countries' first elections subsequently transformed themselves into "life presidents." "Power to the People!" these leaders chanted. But they declared themselves "presidents-for-life," refusing to give their people the *real* power to remove them. "Colonialism was oppressive and raped Africa of its resources!" Of course, these leaders never saw the oppression they were meting out against their own people. In addition, they looted Africa's wealth for deposit in Swiss bank accounts while their own people starved. How were these leaders different from the colonialists? Name one indigenous African chief who had such an account. "Apartheid is evil!" African leaders rightly asserted. But they never looked to see where they were standing—on the necks of their own people. These leaders turned the office of the presidency into their own personal property. Any attempt to remove them from power for incompetence was derided as "an imperialist/neocolonial plot."

Ask these leaders about the causes of Africa's problems and they will wax eloquent on colonialism, American imperialism, the pernicious effects of slavery, the unjust international economic system, and exploitation by multinational corporations. Of course, they will never mention their own incompetence and pursuance of wrong-headed policies. Obviously, without a proper diagnosis black African problems cannot be solved.

Black African leaders constantly complain about these problems but disgracefully cannot take the initiative on their own, expecting somebody else—either the government or some foreign charitable organization—to come and solve them. Aiya-Obs, an African living in Los Angeles, admonished, "We as black people have to accept our challenges and abandon excuses and white scapegoating for our lack of guts to venture into the unknown" (*West Africa*, May 14-20, 1990; p. 816). Ariz L. Issarrah of Accra added his voice: "It seems to me as though we the black society have the tendency to complain more than to act" (*West Africa*, May 20-26, 1991; p. 788).

Writing in *New African* (June 1990), Jesse Ssegayi was quite eloquent:

> Should we blame all of Africa's woes on the IMF, the colonialists, the imperialists or the population growth? NO!!!
> African governments are to blame for the poor development planning. Governments just neglect the economy and put all their efforts on ideology and politics . . . And this is all due to the fact that some governments on the continent come to power by undemocratic means. Africa needs democracy. Excuses cannot solve our problems. We have to clean our house first. Eastern Europe has just woken up, and Africa as usual is still sleeping (p. 56).

But after ruining their countries' economies, some of Africa's leaders still insist on putting the blame elsewhere. Nigeria's Ambassador to the United States, Zubair M. Kazaure, wrote: "Certainly, Nigeria is not free from worldwide economic and social malaise, largely caused by external factors, like unfavorable trade terms and fluctuating commodity prices" (*Washington Post*, Jan 15, 1992; p. A22).

In an editorial, *Ghana Drum* (March 1992) wrote:

> Some people will blame our colonial oppressors (and external factors). Well in some cases part of it is true BUT a whole lot of the blame should be put squarely on our own shoulders.
> Not many people thought that we will be fighting for the same basic rights that we fought for. We kicked the British out and replaced them with our brothers and sisters who turned out to be more brutal than the British. Because these people were our own, we woefully failed to remind them of what our elders fought for. So, as long as we enjoyed the little perks, we shut up only to see the majority of the people maimed and thrown in jail and sometimes killed. Do we then blame the West for doing this when most of us have forgotten what independence stands for?

Independence was thought to be the beginning of the golden era where political freedom and expression, freedom of association, free enterprise, economic prosperity, less ethnocentricism, responsibility and accountability of each and every one prevailed. These lofty ideals never happened because we replaced white imperialism with the black one. People who were voted into office to help build the country turned it into their own personal property . . .

It is now time to speak out. People in authority can go wrong. If they do, let's tell them (p. 3).

At the June summit of the Organization of African Unity (OAU) at Abuja, Nigeria, African leaders resolved to demand reparations from the West for the colonial exploitation and the ravages of the slave trade inflicted upon Africa. The figure mentioned was $130 trillion. Rather strangely, the OAU did not demand reparations from Arabs for the conduct of the East African slave trade, which was viciously savage even by slave-trade standards.

Said Nobel laureate Wole Soyinka: "If we are talking about the slave trade then reparations must touch all those who despoiled African humanity, often in the most barbarous manner. I don't care whether they are Europeans or they are Arabs or Eskimos or whatever. I do not want double standards. Otherwise we would look ridiculous and un-serious" (*West Africa*, Jul 15-21, 1991; p. 1155). But one African started getting serious. Dennis Akumu, a former Kenyan labor leader, demanded that African leaders should declare their assets annually: "We have a situation where leaders have salted away billions of dollars in bank accounts abroad while the continent is facing its greatest crises. These leaders should be made to bring the money back to the country where it belongs" (*New African*, Jul 1991; p. 12).

Perceptions have changed dramatically in Africa. Africans now see their leaders as *the problem*. As Claude Ake, a Nigerian scholar, put it: "The democracy movement in Africa is opposed to the authoritarianism of Africa's leaders and wants to change a leadership whose failure and exploitative practices have banished all hope of material improvement and become life-threatening" (*Africa Forum*, Vol. 1, No. 2, 1991; p. 14).

Black African leaders incessantly carped about how whites denigrated African culture and heritage. But how many African leaders built upon the indigenous African systems and tapped their great stores of knowledge?

The next time an African head of state rails against the injustices of the colonialists and other Westerners, he should be told to apply the *same* standards to himself and to rectify his own appalling injustices against Africans. African leaders must be held accountable for their actions. If they cannot be evaluated by Western or Eastern standards, then Africa's own indigenous standards must be used. By these standards, the modern leadership in much of Africa is a disgraceful failure. Said Malawi's Life President Hastings Kamuzu Banda: "I want to be blunt. As long as I am here and you say I must be your president, you have to do what I want, what I like, and not what you like and what you want. Kamuzu is in charge . . . That is my way" (*The Washington Post*, Sept 9, 1991; p. A20). Traditional African chiefs do not talk like this.

In the next chapter I spell out these standards by examining the indigenous African concept of participatory democracy and the way in which the natives of Africa ruled themselves. Then we can compare the indigenous political system with the modern systems established by African leaders and elites after independence. The defects and failures of the modern systems will then become glaring.

Only a scandalous few of the modern leaders know much about their own indigenous African heritage and standards. It is this ignorance that partly explains why Africa is currently in a deep crisis and today imports nearly 40 percent of its food needs. (Africa used to be able to feed itself and indeed exported food during the colonial era.) It is ignorance on the part of African leaders, *not* Westerners, that confounds efforts to find lasting solutions to Africa's problems.

## SOLVING BLACK AMERICAN PROBLEMS—A DIGRESSION

Although this chapter began with a discussion about solving black Africa's problems, the astute reader in North America would have noticed some uncanny similarities with difficulties in solving problems in the black American community. Rather than leave these to readers' imagination, perhaps it would be useful to discuss these parallels in some detail.

Black America, like black Africa, is also afflicted with a host of problems: drugs, violence, teen pregnancy, unemployment, destitution, despair, homelessness, and many more. "The current state of black America is gloomy and depressing," said the Urban League's 1991 "The State of Black America" report. What are the causes of black American problems?

Once again, a reasonable diagnosis of black American problems is virtually impossible without degenerating into heated debates and name-calling. Pragmatism, which ought to be the guiding principle in analysis of black American problems, is often usurped by emotionalism. Like black African leaders, there is also a tendency among black American leaders and scholars to attribute *every* black or African problem to the legacies of slavery, colonialism, racism, or "white" conspiracy—external factors. Nobody disputes the fact that slavery was at once dehumanizing and wrong. Nor would anybody deny that racism still exists in the United States, despite affirmative action and anti-discrimination laws. But to say that *all* black problems have been caused by racism is, to say the least, ridiculous.

The black American community, like any other society in this world, will have its own unique problems, whether the white race exists or not. That is a fact. Furthermore, certain problems are not race-specific. For example, poverty, unemployment, and social crimes as larceny, assault, and rape have plagued *all* societies since time immemorial. It is indeed a tall order to suggest such problems in the black American community are all due to white racism.

Certainly the causes of some black American problems have *external* origins. But not all of them do. There are many which are *self-inflicted* or *internally* caused. Pragmatism, or common sense, dictates a rigorous examination of *both* external and internal causes. As black American columnist, William Raspberry, observed eloquently: "Defeating the external enemy—racism—won't suffice unless we also defeat the internal enemies of apathy and violence and failure to be all we can be" (*Washington Post*, Jun 24, 1992; p. A19). The same dictum, as we noted earlier, applies pari passu to black Africa, whose leaders placed a great of blame on such external factors as Western colonialism, American imperialism, and exploitation by multinational corporations as causes of Africa's economic woes. These leaders neglected completely the crucial role played by such internal factors as incompetent leadership, corruption, intolerance, and civil wars. In fact, a month before Raspberry made that observation, Dr. Emmanuel Evans-Anfom had said almost exactly as much, 8,000 miles away in Ghana: "We came together and fought for our freedom from the external enemy [colonialism]. Let us now come together and unite to fight the enemy within: ignorance, hunger, poverty, disease, oppression, denial of fundamental human rights" (*Christian Messenger*, May 1992; p. 5).

The attribution of every black American problem to racism leads to a neglect of the internal causes ("the enemy within"). More perniciously, its placement in a "racism" paradigm paralyses the search for an effective solution. It suggests to blacks that they are not to be blamed for, nor should they take the initiative to tackle the problem, since somebody else caused it. Unfortunately, many blacks do subscribe to this "blame racism" banality. The result is apathy and an endless wait for "a white knight in shining armor" to come and solve black problems.

Blaming all black American problems on white people also carries the scrofulous notion that these problems will automatically disappear once the white race has been wiped off the face of this earth. Obviously, this is neither a feasible—nor morally just—solution.

But day in and day out, the monotonous drumbeat is "racism!" "racism." Fighting racism is a worthy social goal but its complete eradication is impossible. There was racism in the 8th century and there will be racism in the 53rd century. This is not to justify racism, but must black Americans wait until racism is completely annihilated *before* dealing with their problems?

## BLACK AMERICAN REACTIONS TO RACISM

Although Westerners always recognized the mathematical skills of the ancient Egyptians and their contributions to Western civilization, they extended little or no recognition to blacks, whose alleged intellectual inferiority rendered them incapable of any such contributions. Black reactions to white imputations of inferiority have been tripolar: separatism, militancy, and imitation—both on the scholarly and personal levels. All are equally self-destructive. Because each is obsessed with race, its dictates sap the creative energies of blacks and diverts their attention away from the resolution of their problems.

### *Afrocentricism*

The drift toward separatism and militancy at the scholarly level is exemplified by "Afrocentricism," which is based on the belief that Africa was the cradle of civilization and ancient Egypt was a black African society. Africa's glorious past, according to Afrocentrists, was "stolen" or denigrated by racist white historians. A group of militant black scholars are therefore determined to "reclaim" Africa's true contributions to the world and "correct" school curriculums accordingly.

An interview that the *Washington Times* conducted with Molefi Asante, the widely-acknowledged leader of the Afrocentricism movement, summed up its views:

"You can't go to school in America, K to 12, whether you are white, black or whatever and come out on the other side of the experience without having a negative attitude about Africans and African-American people,". . .

Mr. Asante said he tells black children to take two set of notes in class: "a set to pass the examination and another set to keep your sanity."

"You've got to write in the margins," he said. "When they say Shakespeare was the greatest writer who ever lived, you write it down so you can pass the test. But you write in the margins, 'This is nonsense'" (Nov 13, 1990; p. A10).

In 1982 Portland, Oregon, made an effort to restructure its inner-city public school curricula to accommodate Afrocentricism. The resource document used, known as "African-American Baseline Essays" was developed by Asa G. Hilliard, an educational psychologist from Georgia State University. These Essays maintained that:

- Africa was "the world center of culture and learning in antiquity." Ancient Greece largely derived its culture from blacks.
- Ramses and King Tut were black. Aesop was probably black. Cleopatra was partly black, partly Greek.
- Ancient Egypt was a black nation. The Greek gods, the Ten Commandments and the Olmec civilization in Mexico are all derived from black culture as well. Moses was an Egyptian and early images of Jesus and Buddha were black.

Therefore, argued Ali Mazrui (a political science professor at State University of New York, Binghampton, self-congratulatory assertions that the West contributed to the modernization of Africa are shallow, "The West has contributed far less to the industrialization of Africa than Africa has contributed to the industrial civilization of the West" (Mazrui, 1986; p. 164). Moreover, contended Mazrui, Western civilization is doomed to failure in Africa: "The materialism of Western civilization, the superiority of Western science and technology at their home base in the West, and the glitter and temptations of Western life-styles, have all combined to pose a significant threat especially to the younger generations of the Muslim world. As these Western institutions grind to a standstill in Africa, causing new areas of poverty and deprivation, the glitter of Western civilization begins to dim (p. 19). As a matter of fact, "the decline of Western civilization might well be at hand," said Professor Mazrui. "It is in the interest of humanity that such a decline should take place" (*The Washington Times*, Nov 13, 1990; p. G4).

Professor Leonard Jeffries, Jr., chairman of the Black Studies Department at the City University of New York, added a new dimension to Afrocentricism with claims of genetic superiority. He dismissed "whites as 'ice people' whose endless savagery is due to a lack of melanin, the all-important chemical that turns blacks into benign 'sun-people' and gives them intellectual advantages over whites as well" (*The Washington Times*, Nov 13, 1990; p. G4).

Ridley (1982), an African-American consultant in Philadelphia, added these thoughts:

We should understand clearly the position of white people, or so-called Cauca-sians. Their position has been outlined succinctly by Frances Cress Welsing, in that white people are indeed genetic mutations from albinism, and they did indeed spring from African people. . . .

White people have a definite fear of genetic annihilation. This means that if white people do not discover a way to survive in a world where they are a real minority, they realize they face the real possibility of genetic annihilation. If we understand that, and realize the psychological and psychiatric dynamics behind that white fear, then we will not feel intimidated by white distortions of our historical process. In other words, we cannot allow white historical distortions and false superiority claims to destroy our ability, and courage, to look at our culture critically and honestly, as we struggle to make sense out of the real dilemma of continual Black enslavement the world over. A failure to do this will mean the complete genocide of African people (p. 9).

Obviously, the notion that Africa was the source of everything good and Europe (or whites) the source of everything evil is as repugnant and prepos-terous as the assertion that everything good on this earth was "invented" by the West. In fact, many "correctionists," in their zeal to dispel myths about Africa and black people, make matters worse by overstating their claims. These claims are made either out of a vainglorious attempt to reclaim some lost pride or out of a misunderstanding of indigenous Africa. Regardless, the result is intellectual malfeasance and distortion.

Assume, for the sake of argument, that black civilization is superior to all others, as claimed by Afrocentrists. They argue that Africa has a rich history of mathematical, scientific, and literary accomplishment, mostly suppressed or stolen by whites. Study at great African universities was "fairly common" among the ancestors of slaves who were brought to America. They also claim that,

"The greatness of African science can be realized by deduction: 'Since Africa is widely believed to be the birthplace of the human race, it follows that Africa was the birthplace of mathematics and science.' Or it can be demonstrated by historical observation: The blowgun made possible the pistol and the machine gun, and the African study of electric eels may have led to the invention of the battery" (The Washington Times, Nov 13, 1990; p. G4).

Assume all this to be true. But how many Afrocentrists take interest in their own children's education in math and science? Africans educated their children through oral tradition. How many Afrocentrist parents read to their children after school? How many black American leaders have instituted any effective programs to disarm black youths and schoolchildren? How many black Americans, wearing dashikis and chanting "AFRICA, AFRICA, AF-RICA!" went to the aid of black Africans being slaughtered by their own leaders? As we shall see in Chapter 11, black Americans offered little effective aid to black Africans fighting for democracy in black Africa.

Claims of Western superiority and black counterclaims are *both* unhelpful for the development of African scholarship. But it is probably the reactions of blacks, rather than the denigration or lack of recognition, that have impeded black scholarship and the search for effective solutions to black problems. As Bishop Desmond Tutu once reminded, "It is not what is done to us that matters, but *how* we take what is done to us." On the individual or personal level, this can have disastrous consequences.

Some black Americans have been sold on a defeatist philosophy that says they cannot get anything done unless they break away to live in splendid isolation. But an isolationist policy is not possible in today's "global village," as China learned. Black militants, on the other hand, believe that progress will be elusive unless they demolish the whole racist establishment. Unfortunately such endeavors are likely to be quixotic. Other blacks, more disturbingly, accept their "inferior status" and strive to shed that label by adopting lifestyles or behavioral characteristics designed to win white "acceptance" by, for example, straightening or bleaching their hair.

Most of these activities compound rather than resolve the problem of the sense of black inferiority. How can a black be "accepted" or "respected" by whites when he has rejected himself? The fact of the matter is that no one can call blacks "inferior" *without* their consent. Blacks do not *have* to prove to anybody that they are capable—only to themselves. The problem here is that in consciously setting out to prove that one is not "inferior," one may well end up proving precisely the opposite or reinforcing existing myths.

Tragically, much of the creative energy of blacks has been misdirected or channeled into unproductive ventures to prove or disprove some specious claims. All these imitations and the frenetic obsession with white racism deflect attention from devising real solutions to blacks' problems. So the problems fester for lack of attention. According to Courtland Milloy, a black *Washington Post* columnist, "More than 3,000 people, the vast majority of them black, have died violently in the Washington area since 1987. That compared with just over 5,000 in the entire country of South Africa during the same period" (Mar 22, 1992; p. B3).

An angry Cheryl D. DeLaotch wrote:

All the pain our ancestors endured for us, all the torment they accepted, all the work they did, the calluses on overworked hands, the blisters on uncared-for feet, all that was done for us. The speeches, marches, boycotts, rallies and sacrifices. And look! Just look! Look at what we are doing to ourselves. And the majority of us don't even care.

We go yelling "Black Power!" - "Power to the People!" and other such slogans. We run around wearing clothes of African design made of a cloth we have named Kente! We walk around with likenesses of the African Continent around our necks and on our jewelry. Some of us even run around with these likenesses on our clothes! We run around wearing black, red, green and gold; colors of Africa. We run around chanting - "AFRICA, AFRICA, AFRICA!"

We do this because it looks good and we need a cause, not because we care.

If we cared, would we go around in our African images, disgracing Africa by selling drugs to our younger brothers and sisters? If we cared, would we send them to school for the sole purpose of selling drugs to their peers? If we cared, would we tell them that an education isn't necessary because crime pays better? Would we ask our little sisters to sell their bodies, if we cared? Would we tear our families apart? Would we abuse our loved ones? Would we abuse ourselves? Would we kill one another and rob each other of the life and rich heritage that we are entitled to? (*Washington Times*, Jan 11, 1991; p. F4).

The fault lies not with black American people but with their leaders who give them poor guidance. Here too, there are similarities between black African and black American leadership. Recall that those African leaders who won independence for their countries subsequently declared themselves to be "life-presidents" and the state their personal property. Any attempt to remove these failed leaders was stubbornly resisted as an imperialist plot, plunging various African countries into civil wars.

Similarly, when some black Americans are elected into office, they subsequently turn that office into a lifetime personal property. Any attempt to oust them from office is invariably dismissed as "racially motivated" or met with allegations of a racist conspiracy or plot. When black Congressman Gus Savage was defeated in the Illinois Democratic primary, he claimed, "We have lost to the white racist press and to the racist reactionary Jewish misleaders" (*Newsweek*, Mar 30, 1992; p. 32). When the Board of Trustees of City College of New York refused to reappoint Leonard Jeffries, Jr. as chairman of the Black Studies Department—a post he had held for 19 years—the controversial professor called it: "an academic lynching and media lynching" (*The New York Times*, Mar 24, 1992; p. B4). Robert L. Woodson, a black American and president of the National Center for Neighborhood Enterprise in Washington, wrote:

A black congressman is arrested for driving drunk the wrong way on a main thoroughfare. He charges racism. A black federal judge is found guilty of accepting bribes to lower the sentence of a convicted drug dealer. He charges racism. Two black deputy mayors go to jail for stealing money intended for the poor. Again, the charge is racism. A state senator was caught setting up a scheme to defraud the food stamp program intended for his low-income constituents. He too cries racism and upon release from jail attempts to run again to represent his district. And now Mike Tyson's rape case is just one more unhappy episode in the erosion of the moral legacy of the civil rights movement . . .

It is becoming increasingly clear that corruption, greed and personal indiscretion have become "entitlements" for black celebrities and elected officials. The message being sent to young blacks is also clear—"Rape your sisters; it's the racist society's fault. Rob and plunder your brothers; you have an exemption. . .

Immunity from justice by virtue of race, when expanded, can result in tragedies as horrendous as those perpetrated by Idi Amin, who terrorized and murdered millions of his people in Uganda, only to be defended by black activists who labeled the reaction of the world community against him as "racist" (*The Wall Street Journal*, Mar 20, 1992; p. A12).

Blacks will make little progress in solving their problems until there is a renewal of political leadership to bring in new blood and fresh new ideas. Once elected into office, many black leaders monopolize power, grow old and lose touch with the people. Worse, they insist on applying obsolete strategies to the resolution of black problems. For example, some civil rights activists still call for 1960s-style marches and confrontational tactics while crime, drugs, and violence rage in the black community. Clarence Page wrote: "NAACP leaders should consider how much the issues their organization confronted at its birth in 1909 have changed and that maybe now it's time to move on to new strategies to revive inner-city economies, educate our young, fight street crime and empower embattled parents in low-income households" (*The Washington Times*, Feb 28, 1992; p. F4). Self-criticism is vital if we are to make any progress. And criticism of black leadership is good because it will instigate change. For far too long we have shielded our leaders under the mantra "united we stand, divided we fall." Must we stand united behind our leaders even if they are leading us into the gutter?

Even if it were true that all black American problems are caused by white racism, does one really expect "racists" to come and solve black problems? Where is the black pride and dignity? Quite frankly, some blacks are angry and fed up with this constant portrayal of black people by their leaders as helpless and incapable of solving their own problems unless some "white knight" comes to the rescue. Problems persist in the black community, not so much because of the inferiority of blacks as a race but because of poor leadership. Too many black American leaders are full of rhetoric and little action while endlessly engaged in an unproductive "blame game." Others perform faulty analysis of the causes of black problems and thereby prescribe faulty solutions. In fact, it is the *leadership* which is the problem, not black people.

Benjamin Hooks, former head of the National Association for the Advancement of Colored People (NAACP), said as much: "It's time today—July 8, 1990—to bring it out of the closet: No longer can we proffer polite, explicable reasons why black America cannot do more for itself. I'm calling for a moratorium on excuses. I challenge black America today—all of us—to set aside our alibis (*Washington Post*, Jul 9, 1990; p. A8).

What blacks need most are *functional*, not symbolic, leaders as it does not take much to be the latter. Anybody with enough charisma and a big enough mouth can stand on a street corner and hurl charges of racism and discrimination. But this kind of leadership does not put food on the table, improve educational performance, or reduce crime. As Rosa Beavers, a drug counselor, complained: "I see the pain. I see the need. I don't see the NAACP" (*Washington Times*, Feb 28, 1992; p. F4).

The role of the Western media in helping to create *symbolic* black leaders should not be discounted. It seems that those blacks who make the loudest noise, are strident in their demands and virulently anti-white are the very ones that the white media is frightened into putting on television and radio. A perfect example were the incendiary remarks by black rap singer Sister Souljah after the Los Angeles riots. In an interview, she said:

> I mean, if black people kill black people every day, why not have a week and kill white people? You understand what I am saying? In other words, white people, this government and that mayor were well aware of the fact that black people were dying every day in Los Angeles under gang violence. So if you're a gang member and you would normally be killing somebody, why not kill a white person? (*Washington Post*, May 13, 1992; p. B1).

Few black American leaders were willing to rebuke her publicly. But when Democratic presidential candidate Bill Clinton—a white—did so, the Rev. Jesse Jackson rose to the defense of Souljah. The ensuing controversy brought the singer much fame. She appeared on numerous network programs and even graced the cover of *Newsweek* (Jun 29, 1992). The implicit message from all this cannot have been lost to blacks. Any black who spits deadly racist venom can achieve their 15 minutes of fame. Besides the impracticality of killing all whites, how does that even help solve black American problems? Are all black Americans of the same opinion?

There is little or no effort on the part of the white media to balance coverage of black opinion. On most non-racial issues, such as abortion, budget deficits, and tax cuts, the Western media go to extraordinary lengths to seek speakers on *both* sides of the issue. But on black problems, it is always one person, usually the Rev. Jesse Jackson, who is rolled out. Jackson is a respectable black leader but does not speak for all blacks. He acts and speaks for himself.

Blacks must demand choice and an end to this kind of "plantation mentality." Blacks are not one monolithic group and there is as much diversity of opinion in the black community as in the white. We would like to see other black leaders, with alternative viewpoints, discussed on television and radio. We would like to see more *functional* black leaders—the doers who can get problems in the black community solved.

In 1991, the Chicago Housing Authority (CHA) applied these tough rules to Lake Parc Place public housing project. Critics charged that the refurbishment of gang-infested housing projects was doomed to failure. They were wrong. A year later, Lake Parc Place was a success. As *Newsweek* reported:

> Much of [its] success stems from careful screening and security procedures that the CHA and many other public housing agencies abandoned decades ago. Rescorp Realty, a private company hired by CHA to manage Lake Parc, visits each applicant's current home and also checks credit, criminal and rental histories. (Conviction for a serious offense makes it almost impossible to get in.) New residents meet with managers and current residents to discuss what behavior is acceptable and what—such as loud stereos—is not. Lake Parc security "doormen," wary of dope dealers and unauthorized tenants, log guests in and out. Individuals who aren't named on a lease can't visit for more than 14 days. Rescorp president Larry McCarthy admits that the precautions can appear Orwellian: so many tenants arrive from unsanitary housing that even before families pack to move, Rescorp send exterminators to spray their belongings for roaches. But many residents say living in such clean, safe surroundings justifies the rules. And Chicago police confirm that crime in the 15-story buildings has all but vanished (Jun 22, 1992; p. 43).

The challenge is for black American leaders to come up with similar solutions to deal with other problems blacks face, instead of carping incessantly about racism. It is a shame that a white private company, Rescorp—and not the NAACP, the Rev. Jesse Jackson nor Sister Souljah—went to the rescue of Lake Parc residents.

## NOTES

1. For more on these assertions, see Ayittey (1991) (*Indigenous African Institutions*).

# Chapter 3

## Indigenous African Political Institutions

Then our people lived peacefully, under the democratic rule of their kings . . .
Then the country was ours, in our name and right . . . All men were free and equal
and this was the foundation of government. The council [of elders] was so
completely democratic that all members of the tribe could participate in its
deliberations. Chief and subject, warrior and medicine man, all took part and
endeavoured to influence its decisions.

—Nelson Mandela, 1984.

As noted in the previous chapter, mythology and ignorance about Africa are
quite pervasive. This ignorance has allowed many to acquiesce in the
imposition of tyrannical political regimes by modern African leaders. In the
postcolonial era, one-man dictatorships became rife in modern Africa. By
1990 Africa had more dictators per capita than any other region in the world!
These despotic regimes, however, cannot be justified on the basis of African
custom. For centuries most African societies have enjoyed a tradition of
participatory democracy. To evaluate modern political regimes in Africa, we
should first examine indigenous African political institutions.[1]

The organizational structure of indigenous political systems was generally
based on kinship and ancestry. Survival of the tribe was the primary objective.[2] Each ethnic group had its own system of government. There were no
written constitutions. Custom and tradition established the procedures for
government.

There were two main distinct types of indigenous political organization
and further differentiation within each. In the first type, tribal groupings
existed as separate political entities and governed themselves independently.
Of these tribes, some were led by chiefs and others were not. Tribes with
chiefs and their attendant administrative and judicial institutions were

referred to as chiefdoms or states. Tribes that dispensed with chiefs but governed themselves peacefully were called stateless societies.

In the second type, some conquered tribes came under the hegemony of others, as in kingdoms and empires. There were also two discernible political subcultures. The first was an imperial rule that afforded the vassal states extensive local independence or autonomy, as in the Asante and Zande empires of the nineteenth century. This type of indirect rule was the most common. The second type of imperial rule required the vassal states to assimilate an allegedly superior foreign culture. Notable examples included the Mandinka, Fulani, Hausa, or, in general, the Islamic empires in the eighteenth and nineteenth centuries in West Africa. This was rule by assimilation.

In virtually all the African tribes, political organization of both types began at the lineage or the village level. The lineage was the most powerful and effective force for unity and stability in early Africa (Williams, 1987; p. 165). Each lineage had its head, chosen according to its own rules. The Fanti of Ghana seldom used wealth as a criterion (Oguah, 1984). Most other lineages chose their heads on the basis of age, maturity, and relation to ancestors. The old, deferentially referred to as elders, were often chosen as lineage heads because there was a tendency to associate old age with wisdom.

## GOVERNMENT IN STATELESS SOCIETIES AND STATES

In general there were as many as four basic units of government in African societies that governed themselves. The first was the chief, the central authority. The second was the inner or privy council, which advised the chief. The third was the council of elders. If there were 10 lineages in the village, for example, their heads would form a 10-member council of elders. The fourth institution was the village assembly of commoners or the meeting.

### Stateless Societies

Stateless societies had only two of the four units of government: the council of elders and the village assembly. Although there were often leaders or headmen, around whom opinion coalesced, central authority was absent. In addition, there were no officeholders, only representatives of groups. Tribesmen could shift their allegiance or support from one leader or decisionmaker to another. To resolve conflicts, such societies reached compromises instead of making judgments or applying sanctions. Kinship governed their system of law and order. These societies included the Igbo of Nigeria, the Kru of

Liberia, the Tallensi of Ghana, the Konkomba of Togoland, the Fulani of Nigeria, the Somali, the Jie of Uganda, and the Mbeere of Kenya. These people, as well as many other African tribes, valued their freedom very highly and guarded it zealously. Because autocracy was always a theoretical possibility in government, many tribes completely dispensed with chiefs or centralized authority. Their resulting "stateless society" would seem almost a contradiction in terms to those Westerners who see the state as an institution necessary to avoid chaos and tyranny. Africans who lived in stateless societies, on the other hand, tended to view the state as unavoidable tyranny. According to Bohannan (1964, p. 195), they found order in other institutions.

There were two such alternative institutions. The first involved maintaining justice as well as cultural and territorial integrity through extended family organizations and invoking kinship behavior in both domestic and wider spheres. The hunting and pastoral peoples, such as the Bushmen, the Pygmies, and the Fulani, adopted this institution. The second institution was a system of checks and balances in which two or more power centers (judicial, legislative, and military) were balanced against each other. This system was applied in all levels of the community so that no single center predominated. This system was widely adopted across Africa by such ethnic societies as the Tiv and Igbo of Nigeria, the Nuer of Sudan, and the Bedouin Arabs throughout North Africa.

## African States

Other African societies that ruled themselves had all four units of government: a chief, an inner council, a council of elders, and a village assembly. Tribes that had chiefs included the Fanti of Ghana, the Yoruba of Nigeria, the Mossi of Burkina Faso, the Swazi, and the Zulu of South Africa. The chief, in most cases, was a male. He was the political, social, judicial, and religious head of the tribe. As such, he had wide-ranging powers.

The term "chief" is often used indiscriminately to represent a king, a chief, or even a headman. But in the traditional African hierarchical system of authority, the chief is the person immediately subordinate to the king. When there are several chiefs subordinate to the king, the principal chief is the paramount or head chief. The others are just chiefs, and those under them are subchiefs. Strictly speaking, the leader of the village is a headman.

The chief was usually assisted in governance by a small group of confidential advisers called the inner or privy council. Membership was not limited, but was drawn mainly from the inner circle of the chief's relatives and personal friends, who may have included influential members of the community. The inner council served as the first test for legislation. The chief would privately and informally discuss with the inner council all matters relating to the administration of the tribe. He might consult his advisers severally or jointly to form an opinion before bringing an issue to the people. The meetings might be held in the privacy of the chief's home or in some secluded spot after dusk, when there was little chance of interruption.

The chief was not bound to follow the inner council's advice, but he would not deliberately ignore it lest the inner council withdraw its support and call for his divestiture. Thus, the inner council was the first line of defense against despotism. The duty of the inner council was not only to keep the chief in touch with happenings in the tribe but to keep a check on the chief's behavior. If the chief ruled incompetently, the tribe would reproach the inner council for failing to act responsibly (Olivier, 1969).

After the chief had raised an issue with his inner council, he might take it to the council of elders. This was a much wider and more formal body comprising all the hereditary headmen of the wards or lineages; in essence, the council of elders represented the commoners. According to Mensah Sarbah, "[t]he village council [represented] the fountainhead of the common life, and its determination [found] expression in the popular voice" (1897; cited by Langley, 1979; p. 20). With the concurrence of the other councilors, the chief could appoint to the council of elders a few young, competent, and intelligent men.

In matters of serious consequence, the chief had to summon all the members of the council of elders. Such matters included additional tributes, market tolls, proposed new laws, the declaration of war, and serious quarrels. The chief presided over this council and sought its opinion. Essentially, the council of elders had two functions: to advise and assist the chief in the administration of the tribe and to prevent the chief from abusing his power. Olivier (1969) noted that the council of elders voiced its dissatisfactions, criticized the chief, and kept him "under the necessary control." It is important to keep in mind how the chief was checked and criticized because modern African leaders do not tolerate criticism or rebuke.

Under normal governance, the chief would inform the council of elders of the subject to be dealt with, and those wishing to do so would then debate it. Routine matters were resolved by acclamation. Complex matters would be debated until the council reached unanimity. Decisions so reached were sure of acceptance by the rest of the tribe since the councilors were influential members of the community.

Generally, the chief would remain silent and watch the councilors debate. His role was to weigh all viewpoints and assess the majority opinion or consensus. It was not his function to impose his decision on the council, as that would defeat the purpose of the council's debates. The chief did not rule; he only led and assessed the council of elders' opinions. Occasionally, however, in the course of debate, the chief would attempt to persuade the councilors to accept the opinion previously reached by him and his inner council. If the majority of the headmen opposed that position, however, the chief had to abide by their decision, "unless he [was] looking for trouble" (Schapera, 1955; p. 78). This relationship between the chief and the council of elders was prevalent from West Africa to southern Africa.

The key feature of the indigenous African political system was unanimity. Majority opinion did not count in the council of elders. This explains the African penchant for debating, sometimes for days, to reach unanimity. The primary reason for unanimity was survival. If a head of a lineage was irreconcilably opposed to a measure, he could leave the village with his lineage to settle elsewhere. This, of course, was a frequent occurrence in African political history, as evidenced by migrations of families and even whole tribes. To prevent such break-ups of the tribe, unity of purpose was always advanced.

The chief, however, did not generally use coercive powers to achieve unity. Instead, he and the councilors used persuasion and appeals to win over recalcitrant members. Quite often, such lobbying included visits to dissident councilors' homes to influence their opinion in privacy. If the council could still not reach unanimity on a contested issue, the chief would call a village assembly to put the issue before the people for debate. Thus, the people served as the ultimate judge or final authority on disputed issues. In many tribal organizations the village assembly served other important functions. The Bantu assembly had to ratify all new laws before they came into force (Olivier, 1969). Although the laws were not recorded, they were often very well known to the people.

At village meetings the chief began by explaining the purpose of the meeting. He would not announce any decision reached in council meetings; he would merely state the facts involved and order discussions to begin. His advisers would open the debate and would be followed by headmen or elders. Then anybody else wishing to speak or ask questions might do so. If two men stood up together, precedence was given to the more elderly. Speakers stood bareheaded or bowed as a sign of respect and faced the chief. According to Olivier (1969), they were "usually allowed to speak fully and freely but [might] occasionally be interrupted by a comment or question. The senior advisers and headmen finally [would] sum up and express their opinion after which the chief [would] announce his decision" (p. 135). At village meetings, the majority opinion ruled if a consensus could not be reached. Unanimity was not the objective. Unanimity could not be insisted upon since meetings were often called because the council of elders themselves could not reach a unanimous verdict. Flight Lt. Jerry Rawlings of Ghana observed that traditional decisionmaking in Africa involves the chief and council of elders' creating a forum "at which every member of the community can make his or her voice heard." Rawlings noted that "as the discussion goes on and new points are made, a majority position emerges" (*New African*, Dec 1988, p. 11). Other African leaders agreed. Julius Nyerere, for example, once said: "The very origins of African democracy lay in ordinary oral discussion. The elders sat under a tree and talked until they agreed" (cited in Mazrui, 1986; p. 75).

At the village assembly, if the chief saw that he had sufficient support after lengthy debates, he would regard the decision as favorable and would proceed with his policy. According to Olivier (1969), however, if the chief's supporters were in the minority, he had to accept defeat as graciously as he could. Although the chief was "in strict theory able to override the wishes of his people . . . in practice he rarely venture[d] to do so. Their cooperation [was] essential for the successful government of the tribe; and should any Chief act contrary to the public opinion the result would be disaster" (p. 143).

Freedom of expression was an important element of village assemblies. Anyone—even those who were not members of the tribe—could express his views freely. Sensible proposals or ideas were often applauded, and inappropriate ones were vocally opposed. Dissent was open and free, with due respect to the chief, of course. Dissidents were not harassed, arrested, or jailed. If a dissident made an intelligent argument, he was praised for having offered an idea that could help the community. If he made a silly remark, he set himself up for ridicule. The choice was his.

In the indigenous African tribal political system consensus was possible because ordinary tribesmen were free to express themselves at both the council of elders and the village assembly levels of the decisionmaking process. Many African tribes—especially the Igbo, the Yoruba, the Ga, the Asante, and the Abesheini—fiercely defended the right to free speech. Chiefs did not incarcerate those who held different opinions because the collective survival of the tribe, not the chief's individual survival, was at stake. As we shall see, if the chief refused to tolerate dissent or pay heed to criticism, he was removed, abandoned, or killed.

## The Traditional Role of the Chief

"A nation without a culture has no soul. We are the custodians of our culture."

—Nana Kwame Nyi XII, paramount chief of the Assin Apimanim tribe of central
Ghana and president of the central region's House of Chiefs, 1990

In the chiefdoms, or states, rules for selecting chiefs varied from one ethnic group to another. In most tribal systems chieftaincy was hereditary and reserved for certain lineages by right of genealogical link to the founding ancestors. Generally, the man who first settled on a piece of unoccupied land with his followers was regarded as the owner of the land and the ancestor. His offspring and their descendants constituted the royal or ancestral lineage.

This ancestral lineage chose the chief, who was often the eldest son of the deceased chief. But succession was not always automatic. The choice of the heir was subject to approval by the "royal" lineage members. The chief's eldest son could be blocked from succession if he was found to be unfit or mentally incompetent to govern. Other considerations included his past conduct, his mannerisms, his capacity to lead, his valor, and his popularity. In general, the chief was never elected by balloting. He was appointed, but he could not appoint himself.

The traditional African chief performed many functions. First, as the political (administrative) head of the tribe, he was responsible for maintaining good order, handling public affairs, and acting as the ultimate authority in all matters affecting the welfare of the state. Second, he presided over the Chief's Court, which was the final court of appeal unless there was a king, in which case his court was the final. Third, he was the religious head of the tribe, the presumed direct living representative of the ancestral spirits that guarded the tribe and whose goodwill and cooperation were considered essential to the everyday existence of the tribe.

As a central figure in the village, the chief played many other roles. The survival of the tribe was his imperative, and reason as well as custom compelled him to consult with his tribesmen. He listened to a variety of viewpoints and proposals and seldom dismissed any out of hand. He was required to explore every possible way of preserving the integrity of his tribe—its numerical strength, culture, history and religion—as well as ensuring its survival.

The chief received tributes, court fines, and market tolls. As the main repository of wealth, he had to assist members of the tribe who were in need, to treat visitors to his residence in a chiefly fashion, and to supply food and drink to all those who were at his residence on official business—for example, members of his council or regiments of his army that had been called up.

It is crucial to note, however, that such wealth did not belong to the chief as a person but to the "stool" or the office of chieftaincy. The chief merely held the wealth in trust for the tribe as a whole. He could not loot the tribal treasury or dispose of tribal wealth at will. When the chief died, this wealth was not divided among his children. Instead, it passed on to the next chief. For example, among the Bantu, the chief's most important source of wealth was cattle. As a rule, he possessed by far the largest herds in the tribe, but they were tribal cattle; the chief held them in trust for the tribe and could not "use them recklessly for his own ends" (Olivier, 1969). This was indeed the general rule in many other African ethnic societies, including the Asante, Fante, and Ga.

Many analysts and historians have failed to make the distinction that the wealth given to the chief was *stool* property to be held in trust.[3] They misinterpreted the wealth of the chief as evidence of the unequal distribution of income. Indeed, the chiefs lived well and were better off than commoners, but they did this to maintain the custom that required them to live in a manner appropriate for a chief and to entertain guests in a manner that enhanced the stature of the tribe.

The traditional practice of offering gifts or "dash" to chiefs has often been misinterpreted by scholars to provide a cultural explanation for the pervasive incidence of bribery and corruption in modern Africa. In most West African countries, a bribe is often called a "dash." But this characterization reflects a confusion or misunderstanding of the traditional practice. In the traditional legal system of the Vais of Sierra Leone, the plaintiff called upon the chief and presented him with a "dash"—cold water or a drink. Among the Shona of Zimbabwe, each party to a dispute offered a token (usually a court fee of $1.50 from the plaintiff and $.50 from the defendant). After the case was decided, the tokens were divided among the chief, his messengers, and the appointed advisers. In addition, the guilty party paid the full costs of the case by refunding to his adversary the court fees paid at the beginning. The party who won the case gave the chief a portion of the compensation he received as a token of his gratitude for a fair hearing. This practice was observable among the Asante of Ghana as well, where payment by the winner (*aseda*) was similarly shared by the chief and his advisers. (See Ayittey [1991] for a more extensive discussion).

In these contexts the dash or token payment hardly constituted a bribe or corruption. The Shona court tokens were offered for all to see. The Asante *aseda* was openly shared by the chief and his advisers. The dash of the Vais was a payment for a service to be performed by the chief, who was not otherwise paid for his judicial services. By contrast, today's bribe is demanded or extorted clandestinely by civil servants before they perform a service they are paid to render. More important, historical evidence suggests that the natives of Africa themselves did not tolerate corruption. Diop (1987) cited a popular revolt against corrupt leaders in Ghana between the sixth and eighth centuries A.D.: "Ghana probably experienced the reign of a corrupt dynasty between the sixth and eighth centuries. Kati tells of an extremely violent revolt of the masses against it. The members of that dynasty were systematically massacred. In order to wipe it out completely, the rebels went so far as to extract fetuses from the wombs of the royal family" (p. 65).

Corruption, then, cannot be excused by references to indigenous African tradition.

## Checks against the Powers of the Chief

In theory, the African chief wielded vast powers that led many observers to characterize him as autocratic. But in day-to-day administration and legislation, the chief rarely made policy. If the village had a social problem—for example, rebellious youth—the chief would raise the issue with his inner council and then with his council of elders for proposals and debate. As we observed earlier, he would normally remain silent during the course of the debates and would assess the various positions. If there was no unanimity, the issue would be discussed before the village assembly for a majority opinion before he took further action. In this sense, the chief did not rule or dictate. He only led—an important distinction. In fact, Olivier (1969) observed that the Bantu chief was surrounded by various bodies and institutions that prevented him from becoming an abusive ruler. Thus, the Bantu government was "a peculiar type of democracy, although it [was] not based on the principle of free elections and on individual or communal voting" (p. 145).

The chief's governing role was not autocratic but consultative, since his foremost concern was the preservation of his tribe and the protection of the interests of all his tribesmen as individuals. He acted as an umpire to ensure fair play and equal justice for all. In mediating disputes, he was expected to weigh all sides impartially. Native courts existed to assist the chief in dispensing justice fairly. As a judge, he was not infallible; his decisions at court could be reversed or invalidated.

It is useful to keep in mind that the institution of chieftaincy still exists in many parts of Africa today, but chiefs' roles and functions have been changing. Thus, chieftaincy is a dynamic and adaptive institution. Neil

Henry of the *Washington Post* studied Chief Amakuade Wyete Ajeman Labie II of Awutu Breku of Ghana in 1990. He wrote:

> In modern Africa, the life of a village chieftain—or the king, as he is also known here—is not an easy or simple one.
>
> Once upon a time, a Ghanaian king needed to know only a few things well—how to lead his warriors in battle, punish miscreants, settle disputes between villagers and apportion the richest farmland fairly enough to keep most of the peasants happy. A wise chief also made sure there was enough liquor or fruit juice on hand to pour regular libations to the revered ancestors.
>
> But nowadays, a chief must know how to lobby the state for public works, how to get emergency assistance in times of epidemics or other hardships and how to interpret and explain the government's policies to the people (*Washington Post*, Jul 27, 1990; p. A34).

Despite the demands of his position, the chief traditionally solicited and encouraged dissenting or alternative viewpoints. He never considered such solicitations demeaning. In fact, he served his traditional political role by seeking these views. He frequently asked his people to "bring their minds"—the vernacular invitation to express an opinion. And those who brought their minds expressed their opinions willingly and freely, without fear of arrest.

Under this traditional system of government there were two main factors that generally made it unthinkable and unfeasible for the chief to impose his will on his people or to act despotically. First, the chieftaincy, as the repository of ancestral spirits, was sacred. The chief could not oppress his people and then expect the blessing or cooperation of his ancestral spirits. He was supposed to be the guardian of his people, not their oppressor. The African chief was also expected to be humble among his people but belligerent with rival tribes. It was very rare to see an African chief shout at his people. That would violate his code of conduct. Second, such dictatorial tendencies would bring shame to his lineage. A member of the founding lineage might be provoked to replace a chief who acted dictatorially. Busia (1967) observed, "Those who elected [appointed] the chief also had the power to depose him if he did not perform the duties of his office satisfactorily" (p. 23).

If these two checks failed, there was the inner or privy council of advisers, who monitored public opinion and passed the information on to the chief. If the chief persisted in his despotic ways, the advisers could abandon him. If this check also failed, there was a fourth, and the most important, line of defense—the council of elders.

As noted, the council of elders was the representative body of the commoners. Without this council the chief was powerless and could not make laws. Council approval or unanimity was needed on all matters affecting the community. The chief could not dismiss the council of elders since their offices were hereditary and were restricted to nonroyal lineages. Therefore, he could not use family ties to suborn them.

If the chief overran the council of elders, the people themselves could still rebel against his despotism by calling a village strike or ceasing to pay tributes to the chief. If these measures still did not remedy the situation, the people would leave the village. The chief lacked the means to stop them from abandoning him.

## The Removal of African Chiefs

Although it took time for each line of defense against despotism to be tested, the despotic chief would usually be removed long before the people needed to consider a rebellion. Thus, although in theory the chief ruled for life, in practice and under normal circumstances he ruled only as long as his people allowed it—a distinction many observers failed to note. He could be destooled (removed) at any time if he failed to perform his traditional duties or if his people so wished, irrespective of how long he had been in office. Oguah (1984) observed with respect to the Fanti of Ghana: "Though the chief [was] not elected by popular vote, he [had] to govern in accordance with the popular will. For the people retain[ed] the right to destool their chief at any time . . . [T]he Fanti chief's rule [was] not autocracy but a consultative system of government" (p. 54).

The African chief was held accountable for his actions at all times. Errant chiefs were punished, as Olivier (1969) pointed out: "[W]hen it became evident that the tribe was discontented and not likely to tolerate . . . oppression much longer, the fathers of the tribe would hold a great *pitso,* and in the presence of the tribe denounce the chief for his wrong-doings, and intimate that some other member of the royal household had been elected to act in his stead. A chief so deposed would be murdered if he remained to contest the position" (p. 163).

Since independence in the 1960s there have been some improvements in the native system of government. A chief can be removed in several ways: by the people according to traditional procedures, by kingmakers and traditional councils, or by a House of Chiefs—a body composed solely of chiefs. (The House of Chiefs was created by the British colonialists in an attempt to formalize the native system of government.)

The first step in removing a chief involved bringing up "destoolment charges" against him. He was then given ample opportunity to answer the charges. He was destooled if he could not respond satisfactorily. To guard against capricious vendettas, the chief was also given a chance to appeal a destoolment verdict.

## GOVERNMENT IN NATIVE AFRICAN EMPIRES AND KINGDOMS

While tribes that were independent or autonomous governed themselves with or without chiefs, other tribes were subject to imperial rule by their conquerors. Differences in imperial rule generally lay in the degree of independence or autonomy conquerors granted to the subjugated tribes. At one end of the spectrum were the Islamic empires such as the Mandinka, which made conscious efforts to supplant existing cultures by forcing the subjugated tribes to assimilate an allegedly superior culture. At the other end were the Asante and the Zande, who adopted a policy of indirect rule by according the traditional rulers of the subjugated tribes extensive autonomy.

### The Mandinka Empire, 1870-1898 (Imperial Rule by Assimilation)

At its zenith the Mandinka Empire occupied much of what is today Mali and the northern part of the Ivory Coast. The basic Mandinka stock was the Diula, who were Muslims. According to Boahen and Webster (1970), they moved freely throughout the Mandinka country and beyond because of the foreign goods they sold and their skill as craftsmen, weavers, and blacksmiths (p. 42).

The Mandinka Empire was divided into 162 cantons, each of which consisted of 20 or more villages. The cantons were grouped together to form 10 large provinces. The empire was governed by three parallel levels of authority: the traditional, the military, and the religious. Supreme to all three were the *almani* and his state council.

The village chiefs were chosen by traditional methods of lineage, but their power was limited by the *almani's* appointee. Canton chiefs were also chosen by traditional methods but held mostly honorary positions. The provinces were headed by relatives or close friends of the *almani*, who was the supreme political, judicial, and religious head of the empire as well as its military commander. He ruled through a state council comprising the provincial heads of the three lines of authority. His rule was based upon the assimilation of local cultures: "The major aim of Samori's [the almani's] administration was to destroy tribalism and promote national loyalty among the Mandinka. He did this by placing less emphasis on the village groups and more on the canton which brought villages together irrespective of their past relations... Images, ancestral houses and sacred groves were replaced with mosques and schools, the major agents in creating new values and goals of the younger generation" (Boahen and Webster, 1970; p. 46).

## The Nineteenth-Century Asante Empire (Indirect Rule)

This empire, which stretched over much of what is now Ghana, consisted of two parts: metropolitan Asante and provincial Asante. Metropolitan Asante comprised Kumasi, the capital state, and all the states within a 30- to 40-mile radius from Kumasi. The inhabitants of metropolitan Asante considered themselves to be of the Asante tribe, that is, owing allegiance to a golden stool, believed to have descended from heaven. Provincial Asante consisted of vassal tribes.

Each part of the empire had its own system of administration. The central government of metropolitan Asante consisted of the Confederacy Council, made up of all the kings, or *Omanhene* (properly designated as paramount chiefs) of the various states, over whom the *Asantehene* (king) presided. It also had an executive council (inner council) or cabinet, which comprised a few of the principal chiefs of the Kumasi division and was the home of the divisional chiefs.

In Kumasi the Asantehene sat on the golden stool. In addition, there were 77 stools, representing 77 public functionaries such as the Bantuma chief, the Ateni chief, the chief of the Royal Burial Grove, and the chief of the Lamplighters. Many were chiefs of the states within metropolitan Asante, each of which had its own state council. The local government of Kumasi was in the hands of the *Kwintsira*, a body of men who were the keepers of the golden stool. They also formed the Department of War. According to Boahen and Webster (1970), neither the king nor any paramount chief "enjoyed uninhibited dictatorial powers," and "each of them would be destooled whenever he was considered to have abused his power" (p. 118). In fact, in provincial Asante the states continued to govern themselves as they had before they had been conquered and annexed.

This kind of rule was rather benign imperialism, and conquered tribes could make a bid for independence if they so wished. Many did so throughout the eighteenth century, but "it was the superior military techniques and the bravery of their army that enabled the Asante to crush all these rebellions and to preserve the empire intact" (Boahen and Webster, 1970; p. 118).

The internal structure of the Asante governmental organization was one of confederacy, however. A confederation is a rather loose form of political association in which the constituent states retain more autonomy and powers than the center in a federation. In a unitary state, virtually all powers are concentrated in the center.

As Busia (1967) asserted, "The first feature to note about the Asante system is that it was based on decentralization which gave a large measure of local autonomy to the smaller units" (p. 29). It is important to note that confederation was apparently quite widespread on the former Gold Coast in the nineteenth century. According to Hayford (1911), "In the Gold Coast proper we have, for example, the native states of Asante, Fanti, Ahanta, Insima, Ga, Wassa, and others, having more or less the same laws and customs, and speaking generally the same language, or dialects of the same language. Each federal State takes rank in the order of its importance in the native State union, and its composition and constitution is the same as that of the principal or premier State, which is usually the State of the paramount King" (cited in Langley, 1979; p. 59).

Beyond the Gold Coast, there were other kingdoms and empires. Indeed, their political structures were remarkably similar. Wickins (1981) emphasized: "Strong centralised rule was exceptional in sub-Saharan (black) Africa. Poverty of communications made it difficult to prevent states from breaking up, and it is no accident that some of the most stable and enduring ones had navigable rivers, notably the kingdoms of the western Sudan, served by the middle Niger . . . [E]ven relatively wealthy rulers, like the Mwene Mutapa, could not maintain a professional army of any size to enforce commands" (p. 228).

These factors necessitated delegating administrative powers to appointed officials or to subordinate rulers. But appointed positions in African states tended to become hereditary, and hereditary subordinate rulers to become less zealous in carrying out the directives of the paramount ruler. Control became more nominal than real, the more remote the center was.

It was perhaps to avoid the danger of uncontrollable officials that members of the royal family were given some administrative and tax-collecting duties, as in the Ovimbundu states of the Benguela highlands in the nineteenth century, the Hausa state of Nupe, the empire of the Mwene Mutapa, and the sultanate of Fez in Morocco. Still, delegation of authority was the imperial norm across much of Africa. As Wickins (1981) asserted:

Some of the large territorial states—Funj is an example, the kingdom of the Mwene Mutapa another—were virtually confederations of autonomous areas. Poor communications, together with local particularism and dynastic intrigue, made it frequently difficult for a central government to assert its will. This was to be seen even in Ethiopia, a region subject to the unifying force of religion and faced with threats from both Muslim pastoralists, chiefly Galla and Somali, and Muslim sheikdoms, which, however, were themselves constantly at odds with one another despite the bond of Islam (p. 229).

Only a few African kingdoms and empires, such as sixteenth-century Benin and nineteenth-century Zulu, were able to impose a strong centralized rule. In the Hausa states, however, there was a trend, often promoted by the influence of Islam, toward greater power at the center with closer control over official positions and the extended use of forced and slave labor, as well as the establishment of servile standing armies (Wickins, 1981; p. 229).

But where centralization was attempted with military force, such empires crumbled as rapidly as they were built. For example, the Oyo empire collapsed in the first half of the nineteenth century, the Akwamu in the Gold Coast in the eighteenth century, and the Zulu empire in the latter part of the nineteenth century. It is instructive to note that the factors that militated against strong centralized rule are still valid today—a poignant lesson to modern-day African leaders. These factors included the absence of an efficiently developed administrative and communications system as well as the cultural desire for independence. Government administration in most modern African countries is run by a small cadre of bureaucrats and communication with the rural areas is generally poor. It takes ages, if ever, for bureaucrats in the capital city to attend to problems in the rural areas. Devolution of authority, under these circumstances, would make much sense. These and other issues are discussed in greater detail in Ayittey (1991).

## The Traditional Role of African Kings

To understand the role of kings, we should first briefly consider the African concept of the universe. Africans believed that their universe comprised three levels: the sky, the world, and the earth. The sky was the domain of spirits of both the living and the yet to be born as well as of powerful forces such as lightning, thunder, rain, and drought. The earth was the domain of dead ancestors, other dead tribesmen, and the activities of the living, such as agriculture, fishing, and hunting. The world, occupied by the people and other tribesmen, was therefore the domain of war, peace, trade, and relations with other tribes.

A god usually represented each of the three orders. For example, among the Yoruba, the sky god was the *Olorun Oldumare*, the supreme god, and the earth goddess was the *Onile*. The earth god was the *Ogboni*, and the principal organ of the Ogboni was the *Oyo Mesi* or council of state.

It was imperative to maintain proper harmony among the three components of the universe at all times. Otherwise, there would be war, floods, famine, and disease. African societies adopted various methods to preserve order. Some societies invoked the gods' intervention; others reserved that function for the king. Thus, in the ethnic societies that had a king, his function was precisely defined: to "maintain harmony between society and its natural environment by means of ritual action" (Davidson, 1970; p. 192). For example, the duties of the Nigerian Junkun king in this sphere were threefold: to perform the daily rites for which he was uniquely qualified by office; to provide for and direct the activities of other cults; and to sustain and control his own spiritual potency.[4] To accomplish this, he had to possess the greatest vital force in the kingdom. Only in this way could he serve as mediator with the superior universe, without creating any break within the ontological forces (Diop, 1987). The king's powers were thought to be enhanced by those of his dead ancestors as well as of his people because he sat on a sacred stool, the repository of the powers of the kingdom.

Thus, the vital force of the king should never decline; nor should he die, since he embodied the spiritual and therefore the material well-being of his people. The consequences would be devastating: Droughts would occur, women would become barren, and epidemics would strike the people. Great care, therefore, had to be taken to prevent a break in the line of transmitted power.

It was not possible, however, to set aside the qualifications a king needed to provide the vital link with the universe. When an electoral council met to assess the legitimacy of claimants to the throne, it generally did not select the wealthiest but, in accordance with tradition, the one who had the requisite qualities necessary to provide the vital link. Ideally, the king had to be strong, generous of mind, humble, bold in warfare, and devout in everyday life. Descent from the founding ancestors was desirable. He had to epitomize a people at one with its moral order, at peace with itself, and at every point in harmony with its ancestors.

The king had two roles to play: political, as head of the kingdom, and spiritual, as the link to the universe. Kings had certain fundamental duties, such as serving as ultimate judicial appeal. In practice, however, the provincial heads made the laws and even waged wars. According to Hayford (1911), "The Asante king never directly interfere[d] in the internal government of a province, but he [could] bring external pressure to bear in suitable cases" (in Langley, 1979; p. 60). The kings, like most chiefs, were not rulers; they were leaders. The spiritual function of the king was always paramount and eternal. As Davidson pointed out:

> [W]hat the kings did was to subsume in their persons the many ancestral powers formerly invested in a more or less large number of lineage leaders, and so enable a people's unity to survive. They were, in other words, the guardians of a social charter which contained a network of otherwise separate charters. Willingly accepted only when legitimate, they could not become kings except when recognized as standing at the ritual apex of their people's socio-moral order. Hence the accent on "divinity." For the king's existence as a political or military person was a secondary thing (1970; p. 191).

Vansina (1975), who extensively studied the kingdoms of Central Africa, also found that "the king's role is small: he is the representative or symbol of the chiefdom and may have some religious duties, but his participation in the political decision-making process is insignificant" (p. 29). In fact, the king rarely made policy or spoke. He had a spokesperson, called a linguist, through whom he communicated, and his advisers and chiefs would determine policies and present them to him for royal sanction. His role in legislation and execution of policy was minimal and severely limited.

African kings were divine. The emphasis on the spiritual meant a separation of kingship and political leadership. Kingship as an office was regarded as the spiritual repository of the collective soul of the people as well as of the powers of ancestors. Thus, the office was sacred, protected by many taboos and rules. The king and kingship would be identical only if the king obeyed these rules. As the Ga said: "If the big man does not respect, the small man will not respect."

Once the king deviated from the rules, he corrupted or endangered the kingship and therefore the state or the soul of the people. By transgressing the boundaries of the right and natural, he allowed evil to intrude. For example, the Barotse emphasized that the king was bound by the law, and that if a king ruled cruelly, "his council and people were entitled to rebel against him and to try to dispose of him" (Gluckman, 1965).

To stay on as legitimate kings, they had to provide the vital link and also obey the taboos and the rules. "And the rules—the constitutional rules—were repeatedly developed in the direction of 'checks and balances' to control the growth of centralizing power. There is perhaps no more fascinating subject in the history of African institutions" (Davidson, 1970; p. 198).

The king's life was strictly regulated by custom to fit his role. Among the Mossi, the monarch's schedule was planned down to the slightest detail. At one time he did not have the right to leave the capital. In many tribal societies, the less public exposure of the king, the better. His primary function was to deal with the universe and ancestors. He was not expected to perform terrestrial functions, except the ceremonial. The king (Oni) of Ife (Yorubaland, Nigeria) "could return home to visit his relatives only incognito and under cover of darkness. He appeared in public only once a year" (Bascom, 1984; p. 31). Similarly, the king in Diara in the Termes region (Upper Senegal) was obliged to remain in his palace and never leave it; the people paid little attention to him (Diop, 1987; p. 64).

In African kingdoms chiefs held whatever authority the kings delegated to them. One of the functions expected of chiefs in the kingdoms was raising tribute for the king. All the kingdoms Vansina (1987) investigated exacted some "taxation" in the form of tribute and labor. Tribute was collected at one level of the system and handed up to the next higher level so that ultimately the king received some from each level. The lines of communication between chiefs and kings varied. The most common, however, was for the chiefs to form councils, or to send representatives as intermediaries to the councils of the king. Membership on the councils varied from one kingdom to another, but the councils were the primary deterrent to royal despotism (Bohannan, 1964; Vansina, 1987).

## The Selection of African Kings

Like chieftaincy, kingship was also restricted to certain lineages in most tribal systems. Such lineages were often those that traced their descent from the original settlers of the land.

### The Ga Mantse.

With the Ga stool in Accra (Ghana), succession was automatic. "No one, however normal or probable his election would be, has any inherent right to succeed," according to Field (1940, p. 51). The appointment of the Ga mantse (king) involved two steps. The first was the selection of a nominee by the members of the stool house (known as dzase), akin to a royal lineage and with its head known as dzasetse. Although some Ga towns selected the nominee on a rotational basis from the constituent clans, the town of Accra restricted the choice to the Abola clan. The second step was the election proper of the nominee by the representatives of the people called manbii. Field (1940) described the procedure thus: "The manbii first send to the dzase asking for a candidate. The *dzase* meet under the presidency of the *dzasetse* and elect a nominee. The *manbii* meet again and consider the nomination. If they reject the candidate, they demand another. They go on demanding and rejecting till they get an offer they can accept. Differences of opinion in any of these meetings are put to the vote. The elected candidate is privately enstooled by a small group of officials and is afterwards publicly exhibited to the town in his new capacity of *mantse* (p. 51).

When the Europeans arrived in Africa, they patronized the Ga *mantse*: "From those early days Europeans had it in their heads that an African tribe must necessarily be under a single ruler, monarch, or "chief," and that this ruler must be the most suitable agent to go between themselves and the tribe, whether they are giving orders to the tribe, trading, or otherwise negotiating" (Field, 1940; p. 75).

The Europeans conferred upon the Ga *mantse* the political authority that he lacked. Before that the *mantse* was only useful in times of warfare. He was not an integral part of the native government. Feeling that they had the support of the Europeans, however, a few Ga *mantses* began to act autocratically. The Ga people tried to persuade the Europeans to cease dealing with such despots. When that failed, the Ga people destooled the despots.

### The Asante King.

The Asante of Ghana had an elaborate system of king selection and succession. The king, the *Ohene*, was selected from the Akwuamus, who were considered to have "the best blood in the land." This made the Akwuamus the aristocrats of Kumasi and conferred upon their lineage the right to be consulted in all internal matters (Hayford, 1911).

When a king died the council of elders began the process of selecting a successor by asking the *Gyasehene*, the head of the household functionaries, to communicate to the queen mother (*Ohemma*) its desire to have a successor named. The *Ohemma* would then convene a meeting of the heads of the houses, *afiepanyin*, within the royal family group (the Akwuamus) and ask for suggestions on a successor. He might be the cousin or nephew of the deceased king. With matrilineal descent, such a cousin or a nephew would be the son of the sister of the deceased king. The choice of the nominee "was probably determined by the personal valor, intelligence, and capability of the individual to lead the forces of the community in time of war" (Hayford, 1911).

When there was agreement within the royal family group, the *Gyasehene* would be asked to communicate to the council the name of the person nominated. In nominating a person, the *Ohemma* and the elders of the royal family had to follow three principles. First, eligible candidates of the generation of the deceased ruler should succeed before members of the next younger generation. Second, where the family group was divided on the basis of descent from several women, the succession should rotate among the descendents of those women. The third rule served to ensure that the second was observed: that the male and female stool-holders should belong to different sections of the family group.

The person nominated would be presented to the council of elders, and upon being approved, would be placed by the councilors on the stool (enthroned). The process, however, might not always be smooth. During the reign of the old king there might be several heirs apparent, each favored by different groups: the royal family, the king himself, and the councilors. But the councilors retained the final right of veto.[5]

The council of elders could reject the nomination if the *Ohemma* ignored these three principles or if the nominee was unacceptable to the political community. If a candidate was rejected, then the consultation process had to start all over again. The *Ohemma* had three chances to produce an acceptable candidate. If she failed on the third attempt, the representatives of the political community made the selection.

The queen mother could not impose her choice on the Asante people. Although the royal family had its own army, the political community also had an army made up of all adults armed with their own purchased muskets, powder, and shot. This "people's army" could resist such impositions. Indeed, such was the case in the latter part of the nineteenth century when the queen mother, Yaa Akyiaa, insisted on having her own son, Kwaku Duah, as the Asante king in contravention of all three principles governing succession. Some Asante chiefs objected, saying that a man called Atwareboanah, not Kwaku Duah, should be king. The dispute escalated into a civil war that lasted for three years (1885 to 1888). Although war ended with the defeat of Atwareboanah's forces and Kwaku Duah became the king (Prempeh I), it became firmly established in the Asante mind that the imposition of a candidate could lead to a civil war, a destructive event regardless of the outcome.

If the choice of successor met the approval of the Council and the people, the new ruler was enstooled by following certain procedures and observing numerous rituals and ceremonies. The candidate would take a stool name, usually that of a renowned deceased ruler or occupant of the stool—say "Prempeh." He would be raised and lowered three times over the "blackened" stool of his ancestors.[6] In this way, the idea of continuity of the office and the political community was conveyed to him. Thereafter, he became the rightful occupant of the stool and assumed the name of, say, "Prempeh III." He and his office became sacred.

In lightly touching the stool with his buttocks, the candidate was also subtly informed that he was distinct from the stool or the nation for which it stood. The nation was immortal but he was not. In being lowered onto the Prempeh stool, his person became sanctified. He acquired physical immunity while he occupied the stool. But the sanctity flowed from the stool and the office. For failing to meet his responsibilities, he could be desanctified and therefore destooled.[7]

At the enstoolment ceremony, the candidate was given instructions and advice on how to rule. The typical advice, recited by the linguist, or *okyeame*, would run as follows:[8]

We do not wish that
    he should disclose the origin [ethnicity] of any person.

We do not wish that
    he should curse us.

We do not wish him to be greedy.

We do not wish that
    he should refuse to listen to advice.

We do not wish that
    he should call people "fools."

We do not wish that
    he should act without advice.

We wish that
    he would always have time for his advisers.

We do not want personal violence—(In Arhin, 1985; p. 38).

Upon being enstooled, the king would be allowed to govern as long as he was a man of character and capacity and could lead the people. But, as Hayford (1911) indicated, the community still retained an important power:

The community would still continue to possess the power of veto in case a given member of the royal family was found incapable of performing the kingly functions. They would say, in effect, to the incompetent aspirant, "We appointed your ancestor to the kingly office as a reward for uncommon abilities, and we are prepared to honor his family by seeking election to the kingly office from and by it; but we must object to being ruled by any unfit person. We will, through the [royal] family council, decide which member of the family shall govern us, if we are dissatisfied with the family's own selection (in Langley, 1979; p. 61).

Hayford (1911) asserted that "no Asante king was born a king." There were a number of circumstances that prevented an heir or the person nearest to the stool from ever occupying it: "A junior heir may be selected to sit upon the stool if a senior heir is a profligate, or otherwise incapable of maintaining the kingly dignity. Nor does a king acquire an indefensible title to the stool when once he has sat upon it. It is the right of those who placed him thereon to put him off the stool for any just cause" (in Langley, 1979; p. 61).

The Asante king was the one in whom the various lineages that comprised the tribe found unity. He symbolized their identity and continuity as a tribe and embodied their ancestral values. His golden stool, the symbol of his power, was also the "soul of the nation," the sacred emblem of the tribe's permanence and continuity. Since the Asante placed supremacy in the spiritual world, the king was the link—the intermediary between the living, the dead, and the yet to be born.

### The Yoruba King.

The Yoruba kings of Nigeria were distinguished by the right to wear beaded crowns, the symbols of their authority. In many respects they were divine. The *Oni* was chosen from the royal patrilineal clan; the largest clan in Ife. The position was hereditary but did not pass from father to son. Males of four lineages or branches of the royal clan were eligible to become king in rotation, but lineages were skipped if they had no suitable candidates, and the same lineage could even provide two *Oni* in succession. Each of the eligible clans might campaign for its own candidate by spending money to entertain the town and palace chiefs who selected the king and by acting deferentially toward all who could influence the final choice.

Wealth was important in these campaigns, but it was not an essential qualification for a king or a chief; nor was a candidate selected simply on the basis of how much he and his family spent, although this was a measure of his generosity and of how well he was liked by those who knew him best. The main objective was to select the best candidate; and the qualities that were most important were good character, unselfishness, and the willingness to listen to advice. Seniority was not a factor, although it might have been in earlier times. The candidate had to be at least 30 years of age and married, and his father had to be dead, for no chief should have a father to whom he must bow.

## Checks against Royal Despotism

Monarchical divinity is often confused with either absolutism or tyranny. In the African scheme of kingship, despotism could not be reconciled with the traditional role of the king. Philosophically, the one who was supposed to provide a vital link to the universe for his people could not at the same time sever this link by taking repressive measures or distancing himself from his people.

A big gap between real and apparent despotism was observed in the nineteenth century. The Asante king appeared absolute, yet according to Carlston (1968), he had to procure the consent of the chiefs to bring about group action" (p. 127). The Zulu king could make no decisions of national importance without the *ibandla*, the highest council of state (Olivier, 1969). Similarly, in the kingdom of Swaziland the authority of the Swazi king, *Ngwenyama*—chosen by the *Ndovukazi* (queen mother)—was checked by the *Liqoqo* (inner council) and the *Libandla* (general council).

The tendency of many tribes to decentralize government by delegating authority and responsibilities to local entities and by instituting a complex system of checks and balances to curb autocracy evidenced the tribes' fear of tyranny. In central Africa, delegation of the king's authority usually amounted to delegation of almost all authority save religious—and on a few occasions, even religious authority was delegated (Bohannan, 1964; p. 192).

The Oyo Empire of the Niger delta (Nigeria) developed an elaborate system of checks and balances to guard against despotism. The political system centered around four powerful figures: the *Alafin*, the *Basborun*, the *Oluwo*, and the *Kankafo*. Theoretically, all power came from the *Alafin*, who was considered semidivine. Next to the *Alafin* was the *Basborun*, the leader of the *Oyo Mesi* or Council of Notables, made up of seven prominent lineage chiefs of the capital. The councilors held judicial power with the *Alafin* in the capital. But the *Alafin* had no control over the appointment of the councilors since, as chiefs, they were lineage-appointed. Thus, the *Basborun*, who dominated the Council of Notables, had an ultimate check upon the *Alafin*. The third power in the empire was the *Ogboni*, headed by the *Oluwo*. The *Ogboni* chiefs, like the Council of Notables, were lineage-appointed. They also had judicial functions, but their primary function was to preserve the Ife oracle, which could accept or reject the *Basborun's* decision to command the *Alafin's* suicide. (Ife was the founding lineage or ancestors). But the *Alafin's* representative sat on the *Ogboni* council, and his opinion carried considerable weight. Thus, he could use this position to check an ambitious *Basborun*. The *Kakanfo* was the field marshal with his 70 war chiefs, the *Eso*, who were expected to be loyal to the *Alafin*. The army was responsible to the Council of Notables, who appointed and promoted its officers. But would the *Kakanfo* not overthrow the Council of Notables and seize power? That was not possible, according to Boahen and Webster (1970), because the political system placed a check on his power: "Civil authority feared the potential power of the *Kakanfo* and in order to isolate him from politics he was usually of humble [slave] origin and was forbidden to enter the capital city. The political system was thus a complex and delicate balance with checks and counterchecks against concentration of power in one man's hands" (p. 90).

In most cases these checks and balances were sufficient to prevent the king from abusing his power. If for some reason, however, an African king failed to rule according to the will of the people or pursued policies inimical to the interests of the state, he was removed after all counsel had failed.

## Destoolment (Removal) of African Kings

To lead his people well, the African king had to obey the rules and save his people from calamities such as droughts and famine. When such evil occurred, according to the beliefs of the Junkun (northeastern Nigeria), the king had not ruled well and was to be deposed or killed. "Kings were supposed to be killed if they broke any of the royal taboos on personal behavior, fell seriously ill, or ruled in time of famine or severe drought: whenever they could no longer be regarded as fit guardians of the 'right and natural' " (Davidson, 1970; p. 201).

The king was put to death when the level of his vital force was perceived to have declined. For example, among the Serer, "[a] *Bur* who reached old age was subject to ritual murder because it was believed he could no longer guarantee that cattle and women would remain fertile" (Klein, 1968; p. 13). This practice, known as regicide, has been abolished, however.

In the kingdom of Cayor the king could not rule when he was wounded. In other societies a king was revitalized when he grew old. It was believed that he would symbolically die, be born again, regain the vigor of his youth, and be fit once again to rule. This ritual was found among the Yoruba, Dagomba, Tchamba, Djukon, Igara, Songhai, Wuadai, Haussa of the Gobi, Katsena, and Daoura, the Shillucks, among the Mbum, in Uganda-Rwanda, and in what was ancient Meroe (Diop, 1987; p. 61).

In most indigenous systems the people brought sanctions against a ruler who did not heed advice or govern according to their will. The Dagomba *Na* or Asante *Ohene* could find himself isolated by his subjects as a consequence of misrule. They would shun him, withdraw their services, or rebel.

The Akan people of Ghana called this rebellion *adom ye.* But before that stage was reached, there were various institutionalized sanctions that could be taken during the ruler's reign. He could be admonished privately and publicly on ceremonial occasions and festivals. His subjects could also file grievances of misconduct (Arhin, 1985; p. 81).

If a ruler committed a very grave offense and his removal was necessary, two rules had to be observed in his destoolment. First, only those who enstooled him could destool him. Thus, only members of the ruler's council could make formal statements of grievances and start the procedures for destoolment. Council members normally acted in response to public opinion and pressures from the villages, districts, or the state as a whole. If the council failed to act, the people would either move elsewhere (vote with their feet) or rise up in open rebellion. Second, potential successors to the stool were not allowed to lead destoolment proceedings. Among the Akan states of Ghana, members of the royal family were debarred from these procedures. Enstoolment and destoolment were the right of the people.

After the satisfaction of these two rules, destoolment had to follow certain prescribed procedures. First, in accordance with customary law, the authority that called the king to the stool was the only authority that could call for his destoolment. Second, only a properly enstooled king can be destooled and before he could be properly destooled, he must be given an opportunity to defend himself. Third, not every petty act of misconduct justified calling for a king's destoolment. He must have been convicted of acts seriously detrimental to the state or otherwise gravely unbecoming the kingly dignity. Fourth, in accordance with customary law, the proper tribunal had to try the king, and the law had to dictate the procedure on such occasions.

If the ruler was found at fault during these proceedings, he would be asked to "beg" the council's apology. But if the spokesperson of the aggrieved party refused to accept this apology, the judge presiding over the case would pronounce the ruler destooled. Thereupon, functionaries present at the hearing would remove his sandals, so that his bare feet touched the ground, and would lower his buttocks to the ground. He would thus be desanctified and would lose immunity derived from the stool. After this, sheep would be slaughtered to pacify the spirits of the Earth and dead ancestors who, many believed, had been defiled.

A destooled ruler was normally asked to leave the town. His people would make a village for him. He was allowed to take a wife and a boy to settle in the new village. He had no access to the village treasury. Nor could he dip his hands into the treasury to take whatever loot he could for his exile. He would remain in this new village until the elders of the town decided that his presence would no longer pose a threat to their peace and tranquillity.

In the case of the headships of the large Akan political communities, formal charges were often not made for destoolment purposes. If the council agreed to destool the head of state, they informed the Gyase division, which handled royal matters. Then at a major festival, after the ruler had been carried in a palanquin through the town, he was not conveyed back to the palace but to a place already agreed to and prepared as his new home. This was done to avoid protracted political strife and acrimony, as it was believed that the ruler's supporters would accept his removal but would fight vigorously against any destoolment proceedings.[9]

The Asante people in this way destooled three kings: Osei Kwame in 1799 for, among other reasons, absenting himself from Kumasi and failing to perform his religious duties during the Adae festivals; Karikari in 1874 for extravagance, among other failings; and Mensa Bonsu in 1883 for excessively taxing the Asante people.

Many other destoolments occurred among the Akan and Ga peoples as well as other tribes. Each tribe had its own procedures for divestiture. While the Serer tribe of Senegal adopted a distinctive drumbeat to signal the end of a king's reign, the Yoruba of Nigeria demanded the king's suicide by a symbolic gift of parrot's eggs (Isichei, 1977; p. 71). In the kingdom of Cayor "the prime minister was the one who could initiate the procedure which would lead to the deposing of the king, if the latter disagreed with him, that is, with the people; if, in fact, he ceased to rule wisely" (Diop, 1987; p. 76).

## MYTHS AND DISTORTIONS BY AFRICAN LEADERS

Many foreign observers misunderstood the native system of government. When the Europeans arrived in Africa they did not find a written constitution, a parliament, or a ballot box. In addition, the African king ruled for life and could theoretically wield absolute powers. Other foreign observers were more obsessed with the external manifestations of the indigenous institutions. Primitive tom-toms called the assembly, not public announcements broadcast on the radio or published in a newspaper. There were no administrative clerks to record the proceedings meticulously. The venue was under a tree or at an open market square, not in an enclosed roofed structure. The Europeans, as a result, hastily dismissed the indigenous system of government as undemocratic, authoritarian, and primitive.

Granted, the facilities were primitive. But there was a tradition of reaching a consensus. There existed both a forum (the village assembly) and the freedom of expression needed to reach consensus. There was a place (the village market square) to meet and the means (talking drums)—however primitive—to call such a meeting. Viable political institutions with checks and balances to prevent the abuse of power existed in Africa before the colonialists set foot on the continent.

The key was the existence of the institutions, not their outward manifestations. Although elections were not held in precolonial Africa, the councilors and the chiefs were chosen. More important was the political tradition of consensus. Oguah (1984) argued, "If a democratic government is defined, not as one elected by the people, but as one which does the will of the people, then the Fanti system of government is democratic." The Kenya government concurred. A sessional paper (No. 10 of 1963/65) asserted:

> In [traditional] African society a person was born politically free and equal and his voice and counsel were heard and respected regardless of the economic wealth he possessed. Even where traditional leaders appeared to have greater wealth and hold disproportionate political influence over their tribal or clan community, there were traditional checks and balances including sanctions against any possible abuse of power. In fact, traditional leaders were regarded as trustees whose influence was circumscribed both in customary law and religion. In the traditional African society, an individual needed only to be a mature member of it to participate fully and equally in political affairs (paragraph 9).

Other myths originated from careless generalizations, for example, that all African chiefs were as brutally despotic as Shaka the Zulu. Still other myths were invented out of calculated attempts to portray Africans as savages and thereby provide European governments and missionaries with the colonial justification to civilize them and convert them to Christianity.

As we observed in Chapter 2, it is *not* solely Westerners who need to be educated about indigenous African political culture. Rather, it is the *African leaders (and elites)* who so loudly berate Westerners for their ignorance but are themselves shamefully ignorant of their own political heritage. Although Julius Nyerere, former president of Tanzania, noted that "[t]he very origins of African democracy lay in ordinary oral discussion—the Elders sat under a tree and talked until they agreed" (cited by Mazrui, 1986; p. 75), he did not lay the foundations of an African democracy. Rather, as we shall see in a later chapter, he imposed a Marxist one-party state system on Tanzania and arrested anyone who opposed it.

The real tragedy of the African story is the persistent misconception that Africa's educated leaders hold about Africa's political heritage. In their indigenous political systems, the natives gathered under a tree or at the village market square and talked. The colonialists put up a building and called it parliament, which means a place to talk. What is the difference?

But African leaders saw a big difference. After independence, many of them saw parliament as a colonial institution and destroyed it. But did they establish a national tree, under which their people could sit and discuss national affairs? To blow up the parliament just because it was a "colonial institution" without providing a "national tree" betrayed a shameful lack of understanding of the *purpose* of parliament. I shall later detail how this destruction of colonial institutions was extended to other areas, such as markets, roads, and schools, which are now in various stages of disrepair and disintegration in much of postcolonial Africa.

The most treacherous development after independence, however, was the African leaders' characterization of democracy as a colonialist invention and imperialist dogma. One would have expected them to show a much deeper operational understanding of their own indigenous political heritage. But after independence, African leaders abused the indigenous African political heritage to justify the institution of cruel dictatorships, authoritarianism, one-party state systems, life-presidents, censorship, and flagrant violations of human rights. For example, President Mugabe took the name of his country from the Great Zimbabwe, the city-state and capital of the Mwene Mutapa empire that flourished for 300 years beginning in the twelfth century. That empire was *not* a one-party state, as is the new Zimbabwe, but a confederation of many states, of which Great Zimbabwe was one. These states were scattered across the region, including modern Mozambique.

The rulers of the empire bore the title *Mwene Mutapa* and appointed their male brothers as provincial governors. But the governors or rulers of the city-states took no direct orders from the king. They had extensive local autonomy, and by the end of the fifteenth century, some of them had asserted their independence.

President Felix Houphouet-Boigny, who has ruled the Ivory Coast since independence in 1960, spoke on behalf of all African dictators when he remarked, "There is no number two, three or four . . . in Côte d'Ivoire there is only a number one: that's me and I don't share my decisions" (*West Africa*, Aug 8, 1988; p. 1428).

As we have seen, in the indigenous political system it was not the chief or king who acted as "number one" and dictated policy. Consensus was the rule, and all participated in the decisionmaking process. Because the African chief ruled for life, many other African heads of state conveniently declared themselves "presidents-for-life" and their countries one-party states. Few recognized that the chief was appointed; he did not appoint himself. Military dictators pointed to the warrior tradition in tribal societies to justify their rule, while other African dictators claimed that the people of Africa did not care who ruled them. Most of these claims, of course, betrayed a rather shameful ignorance of indigenous African heritage. It is necessary to dispel some of these myths now propagated by African leaders.

## Myth 1: "Democracy Is Alien to Africa"

After independence, the view that democracy was a Western invention and therefore alien to Africa somehow gained rapid acceptance. Ghana's first head of state, the late Dr. Kwame Nkrumah, was probably also the first to expound this view. He further castigated democratic institutions as imperialist propaganda ploys. He wrote:

> To achieve this objective [of weakening liberation movements], the colonial power uses its arsenal of alliances, its network of military bases, economic devices such as corruption, sabotage and blackmail, and equally insidious, the psychological weapon of propaganda with a view of impressing on the masses a number of imperialist dogmas:
>
> 1. That Western democracy and the parliamentary system are the only valid ways of governing.
> 2. That capitalism, free enterprise and free competition, etc., are the only economic systems capable of promoting development (Nkrumah, 1968; p. 8).

President Mobutu Sese Seko of Zaire echoed these criticisms of democracy: "Democracy is not for Africa. There was only one African chief and here in Zaire we must make unity" (*Wall Street Journal*, Oct 14, 1985; p. 1). Many other modern African leaders used this same "African tradition" to justify their autocratic rule. No such justification is defensible. Professor Eme Awa, a former chairman of Nigeria's National Electoral Commission, said in a recent interview: "I do not agree that the idea of democracy is alien in Africa because we had democracy of the total type—the type we had in the city-states where everybody came out in the market square and expressed their views, either by raising their hands or something like that (*West Africa*, Feb 22, 1988; p. 310).

Ellen Johnson-Sirleaf, the finance minister of Liberia from 1985 through 1986, also defended democracy:

> They tell us that democracy is a luxury in Africa; that a multiparty political system is inappropriate to our traditions; that the electoral process is foreign to our heritage and that participatory politics is potentially exploitative of our masses. Such rubbish is repeated in one form or fashion by even some of our renowned continental leaders. But we know and can see clearly through their attempts to halt the development of political institutions merely to perpetuate themselves in power. This social African legacy has led to succession only through the barrel of a gun—a legacy which now threatens us with two political forces—the military and the civilian, the latter with no means to ensure full political choice or expression. Add to this a growing disguised military as a political force in the form of civilianized soldiers and we will realize how much behind Africans are falling in this important aspect of national development. (*Index on Censorship*, May 1987; p. 14).

It is true that the natives did not care who ruled them. In fact, some tribes in Ghana just went out in the streets and picked anyone to be their chief when the ruling one died. A few whites, mostly British, became chiefs in this way. If the natives did not care who ruled them, it stemmed from the fact that in their system of government, their "rulers" exercised little effective power. Real power lay with the people, not the chief. Furthermore, they had complete freedom to go about their activities without harassment. The tribal government did not intrude into every minute aspect of their lives. Besides, they could remove the chief, in sharp contrast to modern African dictators who cannot be removed without destroying the entire economy (as happened in Cameroon, Ethiopia, Liberia, Somalia and Zaire in the 1990s).

## Myth 2:
### "Socialism and One-Party Rule Are Indigenous African Ideology"

One frequently hears the argument that there was no organized opposition in indigenous African political affairs because the emphasis was always on unanimity and unity. Therefore, one-party state socialism must be the most suitable system of government for a modern African nation.

The late Kwame Nkrumah of Ghana first espoused this idea: "The choice of [socialism] is based on the belief that only a socialist state can assure Ghana a rapid rate of economic progress without destroying that social justice, that freedom and equality, which are a central feature of our traditional way of life" (*Seven-Year Development Plan*, 1963; p. 1). It was Julius Nyerere of Tanzania, however, who articulated more cogently the link between socialism and African culture:

Nyerere claimed that the traditional African economy and social organization were based on socialist principles of communal ownership of the means of production in which kinship and family groups participated in economic activity and were jointly responsible for welfare and security. The socialist system of cooperative production appeared to be more compatible with African culture than the individualism of capitalism and on the basis of these cultural roots Nyerere sought to emphasize the distinctive characteristics of African socialism (cited by Bell, 1987; p. 117).

In 1962 Nyerere asserted that the extended family system was the basis for socialism in Africa:

The foundation and objective of African socialism is the extended family system. The true African Socialist does not look on one class of men as his brethren and another as his natural enemies ... He regards *all* men as his brethren—as members of his ever extending family. That is why the first article of Tanzania African National Union (TANU) is:*"Binadamu wote ni ndugu zangu, na Afrika ni moja"* ["I believe in Human Brotherhood and the Unity of Africa"]. *"Ujaama,"* then, or "Familyhood" describes our Socialism. It is opposed to Capitalism, which seeks to build a happy society on the basis of exploitation of man by man; and it is equally opposed to doctrinaire socialism which seeks to build a happy society on a philosophy of inevitable conflict between man and man (cited by Bell, 1986; p. 117).

Such a rationale for socialism stemmed from a complete misunderstanding of indigenous economic institutions and the native system of government. Socialism, as an economic ideology, cannot be based on African tradition. Nyerere was wrong—dead wrong. The indigenous African economic system was never fundamentally socialist. The means of production in traditional Africa were emphatically *privately-owned* and never owned by the chief or king. Even land was not owned by the chief. He was a mere *custodian*—the land actually belonged to the ancestors (or first settlers). Further, the indigenous economic system was not characterized by pervasive controls. Village markets were free and chiefs did not fix prices. These issues are explored in greater detail in Ayittey (1991).

There was no organized opposition in the indigenous African political system simply because there was no need for opposition. The traditions of free expression and consensus ensured that in the process of governance each person's viewpoint was heard, regardless of his wealth, status, or membership in an organization.[10] There were no winners or losers.

Under the one-party socialist systems instituted in many African countries, those who did not belong to the official party had no right to participate in government. Only party members became ministers and enjoyed access to government programs. Nonparty members were completely shut out. In some African countries, membership in the official party was required to secure employment. Clearly, such a system was a far cry from the indigenous system. The one-party system operating in many African countries is more of a degenerate Western system where the winner takes all forever. Although elections are held under the one-party state system, they are of the type in which only one candidate runs and always wins.

While it is true that Africans have a strong sense of community awareness, many African leaders misunderstood this feature of the indigenous system of government or used it to justify the imposition of alien political regimes on Africa. Julius Nyerere, for example, mistook the peasant's emphasis on kinship and communication as readiness for socialism—Ujaama (Nyerere, 1962). But being communalistic or social does not necessarily mean that the African peasant is communistic or socialist and therefore willing to share his wealth equally with all members of the extended family or everyone across a huge nation. The confusion originated from the failure to distinguish between communalism and communism or to differentiate between man as a social animal and socialism as an ideology.

It is true that in traditional African society contributions to the family pot were expected, but they were based on ability, discretion, and in some cases volition. It is also true that the lineage land was apportioned among the members. But the farmer was free to decide what type of crops to cultivate and in what amount—an exercise of freedom of choice. The farmer's decision was based not only on subsistence but on market conditions. If he chose to pursue an occupation other than farming, he did so on his own initiative, not at the behest of his chief. Profits made were his to keep, with a contribution, of course, to the family pot.

The head of the extended family was held accountable for the money in the pot. Rare were cases of embezzlement. In fact, within that traditional system of values and beliefs, embezzlement would be a sacrilegious act that would assail not only the ingrained sense of kinship but also the ancestral will. It would be un-African.

It is true that there was only one chief and that he ruled for life. But he was appointed. The chief did not appoint and impose himself on his people. More important, he could be removed. It is also true that unity was the guiding principle among the tribesmen, but only when they were in imminent external danger. In other cases, unity was achieved through the process of consensus-building as independence was the cultural trait. In any case, unity was not enforced by declaring the village to be a "one-party state." Certainly, the councilors did not all come from one lineage. One-party states cannot be justified on the basis of African political culture.

Granted, the tribal governments were gerontocracies. But the elders were not considered infallible. Nor was respect for the elders a form of servility. They could be criticized and challenged. Young adult members of the community could attend council meetings or the village assembly and voice their opinions openly and freely. The chief or councilors did not jail dissidents. Nor did the chief loot the tribal treasury and deposit the booty in Swiss or other foreign banks.

Moreover, African nationalists themselves affirmed the right of the people to participate in government. In 1919, the maiden Pan-African Congress, convened in Paris, issued a series of resolutions. One of them was the following:

> The natives of Africa must have the right to participate in the Government as fast as their development permits, in conformity with the principle that the Government exists for the natives, and not the natives for the Government. They shall at once be allowed to participate in local and tribal government, according to ancient usage, and this participation shall gradually extend, as education and experience proceed, to the higher offices of states; to the end that, in time, Africa is ruled by consent of the Africans . . . Whenever it is proven that African natives are not receiving just treatment at the hands of any state or that any State deliberately excludes its civilized citizens or subjects of Negro descent from its body politic and culture, it shall be the duty of the League of Nations to bring the matter to the notice of the civilized world (cited in Langley, 1979; p. 740).

But as we shall see in a later chapter, African rulers of self-proclaimed "free and independent" countries continue to this day to deny Africans the right to participate in their government.

## Myth 3: "Military Rule Is Uniquely African"

Many scholars, including Africans, have acquiesced to brutal military regimes in Africa by citing Africa's warrior tradition. But an exhaustive study of indigenous African political systems does not reveal soldiers or men in uniform serving as chiefs or heads of village governments. The heads of these governments were always civilian.

The traditional function of warriors or soldiers was to defend the village and the tribe against rival tribes or slave raiders. It was in such defensive encounters that the soldiers proved their valor and earned the respect of their people. Indeed, there were warrior tribes, and a warrior could become chief, but if he did, the government could hardly be characterized as a military government in the sense that soldiers occupied all positions of power.

Many tribes did not have standing armies. As Boahen and Webster (1970) noted, "professional military classes were small and standing armies rare" (p. 228). In the face of an imminent external threat, the chief would summon young men of a certain age and present them to the king for war. According to Bates (1987), "[i]n most states, the people were the army and the monarchs had no independent full-time forces of their own" (p. 41). After a war, the army was disbanded.

The proper function of the military in indigenous Africa was well understood. Only in a few African empires and kingdoms, such as Dahomey and Zulu, did the military play an active role in government. But three or four of over 2,000 chiefdoms, kingdoms, and empires in Africa's history hardly constituted a traditional pattern. Even then, the allegedly backward and primitive Dahomean and Zulu warriors did not turn their spears and guns against their own people, the very ones they were supposed to defend against marauding neighboring tribes. By contrast, most of the modern soldiers who make up the national armies in much of Africa today cannot distinguish between their real enemies and the citizens they are supposed to defend.

The historical and cultural evidence does not lend support to military rule as uniquely African. In fact, "historical accounts revealed tension between the military and trading interests in the precolonial societies of Africa" (Bates, 1987; p. 36). According to Wilks (1975), the Asante formed a political party that advocated "peace, trade, and open roads" and opposed the continuation of warfare by the Asante military elite that threatened commercial interests and development. Elsewhere in Africa, where military forces threatened the commercial activities of subjects within the state, "these interests withdrew their support from that element of centralized polity [the army]" (Bates, 1987; p. 32). Thus, military rule was not a feature of indigenous African political systems. Such rule was as alien to Africa as was colonial rule.

## LESSONS FOR A MODERN-DAY AFRICAN GOVERNMENT

In discussing indigenous African political institutions, it is important to note that many of these structures still exist in Africa today, although they are tattered and battered. There are still chiefs and kings operating in Africa as well as tribal councils. For example, "[a]mong Ghana's 32,000 chiefs, there are 200 paramount chiefs, 2,000 divisional chiefs and about 30,000 'Odikros' [village chiefs] and headmen" (*West Africa*, Feb 8, 1988; p. 232). Furthermore, today's traditional African rulers are not illiterate and politically primitive. The *West Africa* detailed the impressive academic and professional credentials of 20 of the region's leaders, including those from the northern states, where the article asserted that the "myth of undereducated feudalism needs even greater demystification." The group included attorneys, accountants, engineers, educators, writers, and prominent businessmen. For example, the article reported: "In Bendel State, the Cambridge-educated Oba of Benin, Omo N. Edo, Uku Akpokpolo Erediawa, was B.A. (Hons) and a federal permanent secretary before his resignation and coronation in March 1979. The Olu of Warri, Godwin Toritseju Emiko, ran a highly successful legal practice in Warri between 1982-1987, and Charles Abangwu held an LL.B. and had been commissioner of agriculture in the East-Central State before his appointment as Igwe of Isienu" (Mar 20-26, 1989; p. 432).

Whether indigenous African political institutions are primitive or advanced is not the pertinent issue here. They are an integral part of indigenous African culture. This is not to suggest that the indigenous system was free of defects. Far from it.

## STRENGTHS AND WEAKNESSES
## OF THE NATIVE SYSTEM OF GOVERNMENT

Like other systems, the indigenous African political system had its weaknesses and strengths. One of its weaknesses was the fact that chieftaincy and kingship were restricted to certain lineages; one could become a king or a chief only if he had *bulopwe* (royal blood). In that sense, the native system could be faulted, although it might be argued that this criterion was not overriding. The Igbo, for example, considered other qualities, such as leadership abilities, good character, and oratorical skills.

The second weakness pertained to the fact that the native system was based upon kinship, a rather poor cohesive force beyond the village or the town boundaries. The Oyo and the Zande kingdoms were unified on this basis. The kings of the subsidiary Oyo kingdoms traced their descent from their ancestral home of Ife. It is doubtful, however, whether the average citizen in the outlying kingdoms could make such a connection.[11]

The Asante, on the other hand, strengthened their kingdom by declaring allegiance to the golden stool, which was said to embody the collective soul of their people. Tradition held that *Okomfo Anokye*, a fetish priest, caused this stool to descend from the sky and provided the Asante with a powerful means of cohesion. But the frailty of this cohesion was demonstrated in the latter part of the nineteenth century when British forces launched successive raids on the golden stool and threw the kingdom into disarray.

By contrast, Islam provided a more cohesive force and a stronger basis for empire-building. It was no accident that the Islamic empires, such as Ghana and Kanuri, lasted the longest in Africa's history. The Luba Empire must also be mentioned as having successfully found a satisfactory solution to the cohesion problem. These empires perpetually combined positional succession with kinship: certain offices were perpetually assigned to certain lineages.

The general lack of cohesion in African communities reflected the cultural passion for independence. Although many African tribes converted to Islam, they still retained their indigenous cultural identities. The endless process of segmentation and splintering off to form little independent states attests to the characteristically African desire for independence. By nature, Africans are rebellious of authority and fundamentally anti-imperialistic. Witness the fact that over 2,000 tribes managed to preserve their independence and identities even during and after the process of colonization.

Africa's traditional institutions were of course not perfect. However, there was much merit in its system of government. Busia (1967) emphasized the success of the Asante decentralized government in serving the needs of the community: "The tribe was administered on a policy of 'decentralization.' The chief communicated directly with the elders, they in turn with the headmen of the villages under them, and they with their subjects. When the system functioned well, it was democratic. It could check those in power and protect those who were ruled, and regulate behavior for the peace and well-being of the community" (p. 22). The political structures were not rigid and were adaptable to economic and environmental exigencies. They were reformed when social conditions required it. Furthermore, they were stable and fairly democratic in the sense that the people could participate in the decisionmaking process.

The process of consensus-building ensured that minority positions were not only heard but also taken into account in negotiations. Majority vote, on the other hand, ignored minority positions. Moreover, it could lead to a tyranny of the majority. Some political scientists believe that consensus-building through dialogue is superior as it is existential, distinct from the dialectics of adversarial democracy based on majority vote and "the winner takes all" principle. But of course consensus-building has its drawbacks. It was far more difficult to reach on important issues, which explains the lengthy deliberations that characterize decisionmaking by African elders. Nevertheless, there was unity of purpose once a consensus had been reached since *all* participated in the decisionmaking process. This unity, it must be stressed, was not achieved by the chief or king's demanding blind allegiance to his leadership and directives. In fact, contrary to popular misconception, few indigenous African chiefs and kings displayed such despotic tendencies.

It is the responsibility of *every* African head of state to preserve and build upon this culture, not only for cultural but for political and economic reasons. American journalist Neil Henry noted:

> While the power of Ghana's governing political authorities has proved ephemeral during the nation's first three decades of independence, the popular influence of village chiefs has never waned. They remain virtually indispensable to the fabric of Ghanaian culture and society . . .
>
> "The people know their chief better than any government official," said T.K. Boahene, clerk of the Central House of Chiefs. "That is why the government cannot do away with the system. The chief is everything in the community. He is judge, economist, planner; he is the link between the ancestors and the future."
>
> The power and respect they command from their followers seem to derive from their intelligence and wisdom and the model of behavior they set for the community (*Washington Post*, Jul 27, 1990; p. A34).

It is obvious to most, except educated African heads of state, that the chief ought to play the pivotal role in economic development—especially agricultural development. For example, a "chief's farm" would make more sense than a "state or government farm" since "the people know their chief better than any government official" and could possibly work for free on a "chief's farm."

Another important issue is what type of government might be most suitable for a present-day African nation. Should an African country be considered as one huge tribe or a federation of several tribes under one rule?

At one level, an African country may be considered an amalgam of diverse lineages, as in a typical village. If the chiefs were able to keep the different lineages together in a village, surely an educated African head of state ought to be able to keep his country unified. The chiefs succeeded by instituting a type of government that permitted a high degree of autonomy and independence. Council meetings over which the chiefs presided were open and free. Any adult could participate in the decisionmaking process. Thus, the people were not alienated from the village government; they felt that they were part of it.

At the other level of generality, an African country may be considered a federation, comprising several different tribes under one rule. In that case, the constitution of a modern African nation can profit from some historical lessons. The empires that lasted in Africa were the Islamic ones. The Ghana Empire lasted the longest, over 900 years, from A.D. 300 to 1276. Next were the Mali and Songhai empires: from 1238 to 1488 and from 1488 to 1591, respectively (de Graft-Johnson, 1986; p. 109). The strictly African Lunda Empire which expanded considerably during its three centuries of existence, may be mentioned.

Two reasons explain the longevity of these empires. One was religion. The other was confederation or indirect rule. At the tribal level, kinship ties and genealogical links with ancestry were sufficient to provide a cohesive force and serve as the basis for government. But more was needed to build an empire comprising several different tribes with different ancestral allegiances. For the Islamic empires, religion supplied this unifying force. The Lunda achieved unity by investing the office, rather than the individual, with the privileges of kingship. In addition, by adopting a confederacy type of government, the Islamic and Lunda empires allowed their constituent tribes to enjoy a considerable degree of autonomy. For example, seven dynasties of the kingdom of Cayor, a province in the Ghana Empire, never accepted Islam. Yet they were tolerated and allowed to remain in the empire until it was sacked by the Almarovids in the thirteenth century. These dynasties included the Akans of modern-day Ghana (the Asante, the Akim, the Akwapim, and the Fanti). The Wolof, the Tulucor, and the Serer of Senegal also refused to embrace Islam in the beginning but still remained part of the Ghana Empire.

The high degree of tolerance shown toward non-Muslims was demonstrated by the fact that, in the Ghana Empire, imperial succession was matrilineal—an old African tradition. That is, in the event of the death of the emperor, only his sister's son would succeed him. It may be noted that matrilineage was the custom of the Akans, but a practice that was diametrically opposed to the Islamic code under which women have little power.

Furthermore, Islam was not forcibly imposed on the subjects. Conversion was gradual and generally peaceful. According to Diop (1987), "[w]hile the Arabs did conquer North Africa by force of arms, they quite peacefully entered Black Africa . . . [and] owe their influence and later acceptance to spiritual and religious virtues" (p. 102). Attempts by a few Islamic rulers to impose their religion by force merely accelerated the destruction of their empires. Examples include the Oyo and Bornu empires in the nineteenth century.

In sharp contrast to Islam, military force proved to be an ineffective tool of empire-building. The Asante Empire, which used military force, would have lasted much less than a century were it not for the autonomy granted the vassal states. In the Zulu Empire the centralization of power and militarization of the society under Shaka proved unworkable. Several vassal tribes broke away from Zulu domination, and Shaka's reign lasted only 10 years.

Above all, the basic lesson from African empire-building is that tolerance, accommodation, peaceful coexistence, and autonomy worked best with a collection of different ethnic societies. Davidson (1970) observed: "What [conquerors] actually imposed was not their rule, but a rule modified by accommodation with the customs of the peoples among whom they settled . . . Superior military power at a crucial point had always to be reinforced by ritual acts of compromise. Out of these accommodations came systems differing from the Luba kingdom . . . but the differences . . . remained of form, not of content" (p. 194).

When the Europeans employed this accommodative approach to government, they enjoyed fruitful relationships with Africans for over 400 years (from 1456 to 1880). But when they carved up Africa into pieces at the infamous Berlin Conference and imposed their rule on Africa, they were expelled in less than a century.

If an African nation today is considered a conglomeration of diverse tribes, what type of government would be most suitable for such a nation? A black African drew up a constitution for such a system:

There should be elected a king-president, two ministers—viz., one superintends internal and external affairs, and the other industry and education—and a chief justice. For the purpose of deliberating on the mutual affairs of the Confederate states, a Confederate Diet should be established at Mankessim, having two divisions—the Royal, in which all the kings, with the principal chiefs or grandees, should have seats; the other, the Representative Assembly, to which each province should send a certain number of representatives (one chief and one educated person), obtained by the votes of all citizens. The fundamental law of the country should guarantee to every citizen equal rights and protection, and direct and indirect participation in the Government. The King-President is to be elected from the body of kings. He should be made an ex officio member of the Legislative Council, where his presence should be only required when subjects affecting or relating to the interests of the Confederation are about to be discussed; and should he hold that appointment as a Government nominee prior to his election, he should be called upon to resign it as such, but assume the position of membership as President of the Confederation.

That was written back in 1868 by Dr. James Africanus Horton, in his book *West African Countries and People* (London: W. J. Johnson). The book was a plan for self-government for West Africa that included the Fanti Confederation and a Republic for Accra—both in Ghana. I echoed these themes in a guest column in the *New African*: "Confederation is the type rooted in indigenous African culture. It guarantees the greatest amount of autonomy than under federation and even unitary-type. It was this local autonomy that generated Africa's immense cultural diversity by allowing the various tribes to cultivate and maintain their own distinctive identities. The confederate type of government should, therefore, be adopted for every African nation" (Jan 1992; p. 27).

After decades of independence and vast sums of money spent on education, how many African leaders and elites can boast of having drawn up a constitution that even comes close to the one drawn up by Horton in 1868? They were too busy copying Marxist and other foreign systems.

---

## NOTES

1. What follows is a necessarily brief account of the general features of the native political systems. A more detailed and extensive discussion of Africa's native institutions (economic, legal, political, and social) can be found in my book, *Indigenous African Institutions*.

2. Although the past tense is used, it needs to be kept in mind that most of the tribes in Africa still exist today, together with their institutions.

3. The term "stool" depicts a backless and armless chair. In the olden days, the chief sat on such a chair draped in royal regalia. This seat or "throne" symbolized the collective soul of the tribe and the repository of ancestral powers. Although modern chiefs no longer sit on such stools, the use of the term "stool" has remained. Thus "stool property" means that belonging to the office of chieftaincy or, in the final analysis, to the people.

4. The kings of medieval Western Europe also had three fundamental duties: to ensure the spiritual welfare of their people by acts of piety and the protection given by the true faith; to defend their people against outside enemies; and at home, to safeguard justice and peace. "The forms of kingship might be different: the content in Africa and Europe was essentially the same" (Davidson, 1970; p. 193).

5. Hayford (1911) cited a 1900 court case, *Enima v. Pai*, in which the plaintiff (Enima) sought to be declared the rightful successor to the Kwimbontu's stool in the Wassaw district to which the Werempims or

councilors had elected Pai and upon which they had actually placed him. The plaintiff and defendant were cousins and as such both were qualified. The court upheld the councilors' choice and recognized Pai as the legal king.

6. The stool of a dead chief was charred or immersed in a black substance and preserved. It symbolized the "presence" of the departed as well as his "powers."

7. One may note the clear separation between the sanctity of the office and the fallibility of the occupant. Kingship was divine in many indigenous African systems. But it did not mean that the king as a person was infallible. He could be removed, and the sanctity of the office would be preserved.

8. The advice to the *Na* of Dagomba (northern Ghana) ends with the following: "If anyone is oppressed, and he comes to you, save him. Do not look behind you when you walk; do not be afraid. Do not beat people. Do not go after men's wives. If we advise you, hear our advice. If you advise us, we will listen."

9. Modern scholars may object to this procedure of "quiet removal" as undemocratic. But it should be pointed out that the council was a representative body of the people, and decisions such as the removal of a ruler that affected the entire community had to be unanimous. The council could not act in this way if people opposed the removal. Often, those opposed, the ruler's supporters, tended to be small but vocal factions.

10. In nineteenth-century Angola, the African king, Alfonso, allowed the Portuguese merchants to send their own representative to his court. In nineteenth-century Senegal, slaves elected their own representatives to the king's court.

11. It may, however, be argued that a government based upon kinship in fact served a very useful purpose. It checked despotism. Authority was derived from kinship relationships. As such, an outsider who did not possess such a relationship could not arbitrarily impose his rule on strangers unless such rule was accepted. If imposed by force, such rule would be illegitimate, without authority or consent, and would only be transitory.

# Chapter 4

## Africa under Colonial Rule

> One white man come and make book [treaty] and another white man come tomorrow and break it; white man be fool, because treaty is in my head.
>
> —Dappa Pepple, chief of Bonny (Niger Delta); quoted in Wickins, 1981; p. 274.

To the defenders of colonialism, Africa had no history, culture, or institutions. Therefore, they believed colonialism was good for Africans because it liberated them from their despotic chiefs. As we saw in the previous chapter, this was a gross distortion of reality to justify the imposition of foreign rule on Africans.

There were other distortions, however, that were introduced by African scholars and leaders as well as American experts. They asserted that the imperialistic colonialists completely destroyed Africa's native political structures and replaced them with colonial institutions. Therefore, they argued, at independence Africa had to uproot these colonial institutions and restructure its society from scratch. General Moussa Traore, who ruled Mali for 22 years, asserted, "Many African problems stem from the newness of the national institutions we are trying to create in the post-colonial period" (*Washington Times*, Oct 8, 1990; p. A8).

Traore's statement betrayed a fundamental misunderstanding of the nature of African institutions and the colonial experience. As we noted in Chapter 3, the colonialists never really introduced new institutions into Africa. They merely brought advanced forms of institutions *already existing* in Africa. Unfortunately, many African leaders did not make this distinction. In their zeal to replace what they perceived as colonial institutions with new ones, several African leaders destroyed a large part of their own indigenous institutions.

Mercifully, other African leaders and elites recognized that Africa indeed had its own native institutions. But they held these institutions in contempt as too backward and primitive to use in their countries' development. Kwame Nkrumah of Ghana best exemplified this attitude. He decided that he would not rely on peasant farmers and their primitive technology to achieve the rapid social transformation of Ghana. Instead, he sought modern, scientific methods. This belief resulted in the adoption of inappropriate foreign technology and institutions across Africa.

Can the indigenous institutions be used to develop Africa? Before answering this question, we must address a more pertinent question. Did colonialism completely obliterate these institutions? Exactly how did they fare under colonialism? We address this question next.

## THE ADVENT OF COLONIALISM

The abolition of the slave trade in the late 1840s allowed commerce and trade to prosper along the West African coast. Intertribal rivalries flared up occasionally, however. For example, a few tribes raided each other's cattle and battled among themselves for control of lucrative markets and trade routes. Tribes under siege from warring neighbors found it convenient to seek protection from them with European traders. These alliances, however, soon drew the natives into much broader European commercial hostilities.

In the eighteenth and nineteenth centuries, for example, the Fanti and the Asante on the Gold Coast were frequently at war. When the Asante allied themselves with the Dutch, the Fanti thought it wise to seek British protection. But in March 1867 the Dutch and the British signed an agreement to end their commercial rivalries that included the transfer of territory. News of the agreement infuriated the Fanti because they had not been consulted. On January 16, 1873, rioting broke out in Sekondi to protest the transfer of the British protectorship. The suppression of the riots and the settlement of the issue of transferability intensified the level of colonial involvement in tribal affairs.

Until the 1860s the Europeans were generally unwilling to extend protectorates over Africans, as that would have required additional expenditures. In fact, in 1843 the African Committee of the British House of Commons passed a resolution expressing Britain's reluctance to further engage in colonial affairs. According to Boahen and Webster (1970), the British resolved that their future policy in Africa "should be to encourage in the natives the exercise of those qualities which may render it possible for us more and more to transfer to the natives the administration of all Governments, with a view to our ultimate withdrawal from all, except probably Sierra Leone" (p. 210).

Growing commercial competition, however, forced the British to reconsider their position or face being squeezed out of Africa. Throughout the second half of the nineteenth century the British, French, Dutch, Portuguese, and other Europeans brutishly jostled one another for influence and control over the trade of certain valued commodities. They built forts and castles, especially along the West African coast, not only to defend commercial interests against foreign interlopers, but to expand trade. To secure commercial advantages, they signed friendship treaties with African chiefs and kings. There is evidence to suggest that African chiefs, although illiterate, knew how to deal with treaties.

So intense was the competition for commercial hegemony that in 1884 Chancellor Bismarck of Germany convened a conference of European nations with the avowed purpose of reducing tensions among them. The effect of the conference was to establish rules for recognizing spheres of commercial suzerainty. A frenetic scramble ensued to establish such spheres of dominance where none existed before.

Tendentious treaties were extorted from African rulers, in some cases by sheer military force. De facto protectorates became colonies. Various rationales were proffered to justify colonialism. One claim was that African savages needed to be civilized to be freed from the oppressive regimes of their traditional rulers. Missionaries soon entered the rush, independently at first but subsequently in collusion with colonial authorities, to convert the African pagans. The betterment of the natives, each party asserted, was the objective of the intrusion. Others had a different view of colonial interests. Said Herbert Macaulay in 1905, "The dimensions of 'the true interests of the natives at heart' are algebraically equal to the length, breadth and depth of the white man's pocket" (cited by Boahen and Webster, 1970; p. 225). Similarly, the Christian mission in Africa provoked the following parody in a Gold Coast newspaper:

Onward Christian Soldiers unto heathen lands,
Prayer books in your pockets, rifles in your hands,
Take the happy tidings where trade can be done
Spread the peaceful gospel with the Gatling gun (cited by Boahen and Webster, 1970; p. 225).

Colonial rule was never accepted by Africans. In many parts of Africa resistance was ferocious. In North Africa the Arabs of Mauritania revolted in 1905 and killed the French governor Coppolani. In 1896 the Ethiopians routed the Italians at Adowa with furious vindictiveness. In West Africa historians have documented the resistance of the Sarakolle kingdom of Mamadou Lamine from 1885 to 1887, the *jibad* of Ma Ba Tall from 1861 to 1867 in Senegambia, revolts by the Abe people of eastern Ivory Coast from 1891 to 1918, the Asante of Ghana in 1891, and many other states. Colonial rule was not accepted on the East African coast either. The Maji-Maji revolt in 1890 was a mass movement that encompassed many ethnic groups—the Shambaa, Zaramo, Zigula, Yao, Ngoni, Ngulu, Kwere, Hehe, Kami, Sagara, Makonde, Mbugu, Arab, and Swahili. In addition, a relatively large number of powerful and wealthy merchants vigorously opposed the colonial powers. Among them were Mirambo (from 1871 to 1884) on the great ivory route of Tabora (Tanzania), Msiri in Katanga (from 1860 to 1891), and, until he allied with the Belgians in the Upper Congo, Tippu-Tib in Maniema. In southern Africa, the Sotho and the Zulu (under Shaka) rebelled against colonial domination in the 1880s, and the Shona and the Ndebele did so during the following decade.

Elsewhere in Africa there were sporadic revolts. But African resistance to colonial rule was in general weak because of the vast military superiority of European weapons. In particular, the Maxim gun (a machine gun) proved decisive. Frequently, African armies of 20,000 or more were routed by European-led armies of 2,000 or less.[1] Such victories bred overconfidence and caused the Europeans to surmise erroneously that the weak resistance was due to the oppression of Africans by their rulers. The Europeans thus overestimated their welcome and acceptance.

In all, the early colonial years brought political subjugation and humiliation to Africans. Scores of African rulers died on the battlefield; many more were executed or exiled after defeat. Those who signed treaties and remained as protected rulers soon found themselves demoted from king to chief and required to collect taxes or recruit laborers for their French or German overlords. At a later stage, most were dismissed altogether (Manning, 1988; p. 57).

Though Africa was conquered with relative ease militarily, the cultural battle proved far more formidable and costly than the Europeans had anticipated. It was one thing to subjugate a people and demand obedience and taxes by military force. But it was quite another to force them to shed centuries-old traditions, to adopt alien ways of doing things, and to respond willingly to the dictates of a foreign culture.

## COLONIAL PLUNDER AND ATROCITIES

Although there were some rudimentary checks against colonial plunder, abuses, and misrule, the potential for the mistreatment of African natives was enormous. A Frenchman in his 20s, who had just finished school, would suddenly find himself posted to a colony as *commandant de cercle* with complete authority over 200,000 African natives. He could literally do as he pleased since his personal powers were guaranteed by the *Statut de l'indigenat*, the most hated feature of the colonial system in French West Africa. The *indigenat* consisted of regulations that allowed colonial administrators to inflict punishment on African subjects without obtaining a court judgment or approval from the metropolis. It allowed the colonial officers to jail any African for up to two years without trial, to impose heavy taxes and punitive fines, or to burn the villages of those who refused to pay.

Colonialism was an extractive, generally profitable operation, the objective of which was to maximize revenue at the lowest cost. To do this colonialists used cheap sources of raw materials and, where possible, forced the natives to work without pay. There were no considerations of equity or ethics. Reluctant to make new expenditures unless they were absolutely necessary or could yield greater returns to recoup their initial investment, the colonialists were intolerant of native activities that threatened their profit objective. Thus, they relentlessly crushed native rebellions or civil disobedience.

The profitability of colonialism is now subject to much dispute, however. Revenues rarely matched the costs of colonial rule very closely; sometimes they were much higher, other times much lower. According to Curtin et al. (1988), the "Belgian Congo was the only colony that paid off directly to a European government" (p. 477). Even then, profit was realized only by resorting to terroristic and brutal methods. To recoup his investment in the Congo Independent State, King Leopold turned half of the colony over to concessionary companies, which, with a small amount of capital, undertook to guarantee the commercial profitability and the mineral exploitation of these areas. These companies brutally forced inhabitants to collect rubber. In 1884 an Englishman observed: "Everywhere rubber and murder, slavery in its worst form. The missionaries are so completely at the mercy of the state that they dare not report these barbarous doings" (cited by Bauer, 1934; p. 187).[2]

## INDIGENOUS AFRICAN INSTITUTIONS UNDER COLONIALISM

The main object of our inquiry in this chapter is to determine how the native institutions fared under colonialism. This question is of crucial importance since many African scholars and leaders, as well as American experts, have claimed that the native system of government was completely destroyed under colonialism.

We have seen that kinship was the basis of political organization in indigenous Africa—leaders derived authority from kinship. Political structures could be weakened or destroyed, but authority was both inviolable and nonsubstitutable. In the indigenous system leaders appointed by the colonialists were not accepted because they lacked kinship.

Of the two general types of political organizations in Africa, the colonialists had more difficulty in dealing with stateless societies, in which they had to appoint leaders who lacked the traditional legitimacy and authority to govern their people. Many of the appointees, feeling that they had the full force of the colonial military to back them, became autocratic and corrupt. A case in point was the Ga *mantse*, and it is worth discussing this in detail since the colonial government's attempt to restructure this native institution not only proved to be a fiasco but also created immense difficulties for both subjects and masters. In addition, this restructuring exposed the colonial government to ridicule and exploitation.

As we noted in Chapter 3, the Ga kingdom of the nineteenth century was a confederation of six independent republics with no paramount chief. Each city-state conducted its affairs independently of the rest and had a *mantse*. But the *mantse* was not a chief in the sense that was usually reserved for the title.

The Ga *mantse* was considered magically useful in war. But he had no political authority and was not part of the government of the Ga people. Even in war, the *mantse* was not a military leader. He carried his stool—supposedly endowed with magical powers—to war, but he never directly engaged in combat. In fact, he and his stool stood aside, protected by a special bodyguard.

When the Danes came to Osu in the nineteenth century, they insisted on dealing with a chief. There was none among the Ga people. But to the Danes, the Ga *mantse* was good enough; they began dealing with him as the chief. The Ga people refused to accept the elevation of their *mantse* to a political position that he traditionally did not hold. In response to this Danish intrusion, the people of Osu created a *mankralo*, transferred allegiance to him, and deserted the *mantse*. The Danes, adamantly refusing to recognize the *mankralo*, continued to deal with the *mantse* as chief. The British colonialists also conferred new importance and authority upon the Ga *mantse*. As a result, whenever the post became vacant, those seeking a lucrative appointment scrambled for it. Although the responsible elders of the town would elect the new *mantse* constitutionally, invariably another group, relying on the colonial government's ignorance of the native constitution, would produce a rival candidate—often a passive puppet—and declare him to be the rightful *mantse*. Field (1940) contended: "A 'government's *mantse*' is, as often as not, merely the puppet of a small gang who have financed him from the first, and are running him as a speculation. Apart from Government, the only recognition he gets in his own town is from the disreputable band of hangers-on who invested in him and hope for an income from the investment" (p. 80).

Meanwhile, the elders would refuse to enstool the colonial government's *mantse* and would never go near him. Responsible members of the tribe would also ignore him and take all their affairs to the elders. This state of affairs could exist because in the Ga system of government, the *mantse* was politically inessential. Trouble erupted, however, when the government-appointed *mantse* tried to extend his authority or attempted to intervene in native affairs by, for example, selling town land. Such actions prompted immediate destoolment proceedings by the people.

A broader discussion of the fate of African chiefdoms and kingdoms under colonialism requires us to examine specific colonial policies and the strategies African rulers adopted to preserve their political integrity.

## Various Styles of Colonialism

Because colonial policies differed among the Europeans, some African chiefdoms had better chances of surviving under one colonial policy than under another. The British and the Germans, on the whole, regarded their colonies as complete entities and therefore treated each one separately. The French and the Portuguese, on the other hand, saw their colonies as integral parts of the metropolitan countries and therefore as overseas provinces. Thus, while the British did envisage a day when each of its colonies would become an independent state in its own right, the French did not recognize this as a possibility until the late 1950s. The Portuguese never changed their unbending attitude. Furthermore, although all the colonial powers regarded the black race as inferior to the white race, "the British did show a great deal of respect for the Africans and for many aspects of their culture and institutions, while the French and the Portuguese condemned practically everything African as primitive and barbaric" (Boahen and Webster, 1970; p. 123).

## British Colonialism

The British adopted a colonial policy of indirect rule by which they generally made little conscious effort to supplant the indigenous rulers. They left in place, especially in West Africa, the administrative machinery that the natives had created. Two factors influenced this colonial policy. In the 1860s Britain was generally reluctant to extend direct rule over territories thousands of miles away, as this would entail considerable expense. Furthermore, Britain was more preoccupied with its Asian empire, particularly India, than with its African possessions, which were to be prepared for eventual self-rule.

Under the British colonial system each colony was divided into regions under regional or chief administrators, each region into provinces under provincial commissioners, and each province into districts under district commissioners. Each district consisted of one or more of the traditional states, and the day-to-day affairs and local ordinances were left in the hands of the traditional rulers and their council of elders.

The African chief was the instrument of local government. He appointed all officials who were responsible to him. He or his officials presided over the law courts, which, as far as possible, applied African law. His agents levied taxes for the local treasury. Part of the revenue was sent to the central government and the remainder kept for local improvements such as roads, sanitation, markets, and schools, and to pay the salaries of local officials (Boahen and Webster, 1970; p. 242).

The use of the existing native administrative machinery allowed the British to govern lightly and inexpensively. More important, the use of traditional chiefs as intermediaries ensured that potential conflicts between the two cultures were identified and resolved. Thus, compared to other colonial systems, indigenous institutions faced the least danger of annihilation under the British system. Their chances of survival were somewhat more assured.

## French Colonialism

The colonial policies of other Europeans, such as the French, posed the gravest danger to indigenous African institutions. These policies were highly centralized and authoritarian. The French adopted a policy of deliberate destruction of the great paramount chieftaincies. By 1937 only 50 of them remained, most of which had been deprived of their prestige (Boahen, 1986; p. 127).

French colonial policy had two strands. One was *assimilation*, the approach taken by Louis Faidherbe in Senegal under which the colony became an integral part of the mother country rather than a separate but protected state. Further, the colonized were expected to assimilate French culture. The rationale for assimilation was based on the belief of French cultural superiority. In fact, French colonialists felt they had a *"mission civilisatrice."*

The other strand in French colonial policy was *association*. This concept was developed and applied by Savorgnan de Brazza in Central Africa. Those advocating association believed that, though assimilation was desirable, it was impracticable because non-Western people were racially inferior and would never be accepted, even if fully assimilated. Association, on the other hand, would permit the subject people to develop within their own cultures.

Association was akin to the British policy of indirect rule. The French version differed in some fundamental respects, however. The French colony was part of France rather than a separate political entity. The French also had no intention of using the traditional rulers as intermediaries. They allied themselves with African rulers in order to neutralize them until they could be eliminated or deposed at convenience. Those who remained were put in the position of serving as agents of the colonial state rather than rulers in their own right. For example, when the French conquered Dahomey in 1894, General Dodds dismembered the kingdom. Only the central province, the area around the capital of Abomey, remained; the rest of the provinces were placed under direct French rule or made into new kingdoms. Where there were no central authorities, as in stateless African societies such as the Fulani and Somali, the French created new chiefs.

### Belgian Colonialism

Other European governments sometimes ruled indirectly by subcontracting colonial government to private companies—rule by corporation. Belgian King Leopold's private Congo Independent State was a form of company government with three sources of authority: the crown, the church (Roman Catholic), and large companies in which the crown held substantial stock.[3] While British colonial officials would use persuasion to get something done, Belgian officials would issue commands: "Plant 40 rubber trees here next month or else!" The brutality, exploitation, and forced labor that marked rule by the companies ultimately forced the Belgian parliament to annex the Congo Independent State and bring it under Belgian state control.

After 1908, Belgian colonial policy was one of paternalism or tutelage. This involved a much tighter political and economic control over the colonies than under the French policy of assimilation. Further, under Belgian paternalism Africans were considered to be incapable of guiding their own destinies. Therefore, the colonialists controlled every aspect of the Africans' welfare.

The Belgian Congo was administered directly from Brussels. The governor-general was the representative of the crown, all edicts and directives came from Brussels, and the Congolese were not consulted in the administration of their own affairs. Belgian overlords felt free to interfere in the selection of African leaders in their protected states. There were no local legislative assemblies to guide or check the governor-general.

Although the French and Belgian colonial policies of assimilation and tutelage posed the greatest threat of obliterating indigenous African culture, in many places the culture survived. Assimilation turned out to be a failure. For one thing, effective implementation required extraordinary expenditures on education and cultural indoctrination that the French colonial government was unwilling to make. For another, there was African disenchantment with French citizenship and Belgian tutelage.

In the latter half of the nineteenth century, absolutism had noticeably retreated from the political arenas of France, Belgium, and Germany. Politics were becoming increasingly dominated by republican ideals of legal equality of all citizens. As these nations sought to expand their colonies, a dilemma emerged as to the political status of the new territories and their inhabitants. If the colonies were part of the mother country, would their African subjects be regarded as citizens as well?

Because of the perceived inferiority of African culture, most European governments were reluctant to grant citizenship to their colonial subjects. Citizenship, if necessary at all, was to be granted under special circumstances. Only when Africans had become sufficiently well educated and acculturated could they become French citizens with full political and other rights. Such Africans were to become known as *évolués*.

Of all the Europeans the Belgians were probably the most contemptuous of their colonial subjects and imposed the most stringent conditions on them. The African could not travel in the Congo without a permit, possess firearms, or drink anything stronger than beer. He could become a carpenter or a mechanic, but not an engineer. He could be a bishop, a journalist, an accountant, a medical assistant, a teacher, a civil servant, or a druggist, but not an architect or an attorney. By the 1930s there were several lawyers in British and French West Africa, but not a single one in the Congo. To the Belgians, lawyers meant politics, and politics would instigate demands for political rights outlawed for the Africans.

One vital point of difference between the Belgian system and that of the British and French was that the Belgians did their utmost to keep their African subjects out of Europe, particularly out of Belgium itself. Africans in other colonies could attend universities in Europe but not the Congolese. Belgians did not normally countenance citizenship for Africans. But if unavoidable, citizenship was to be granted under very strict conditions. Africans had to be fully educated and acculturated before they could become Belgian citizens. In addition, Africans had to have permanent employment with Europeans before they could become *immatricules* (registered) and live under Belgian law. These requirements were so rigid that only a few Africans became *immatricules*.

Although more liberal than the Belgians, the true colors of the French began to show through their much vaunted policy of assimilation. In West Africa, French opposition to citizenship quickly emerged. In 1908 French administrators and French settlers in Senegal began calling for systematic restrictions of the citizenship rights of the *originaires* (the inhabitants of the four communes of St. Louis, Goree, Rufisque, and Dakar) on account of their alleged illiteracy in French. Bowing to this pressure, the government of French West Africa promulgated a naturalization decree that tightened the qualifications for citizenship. Until 1946 an African desiring French citizenship had to fulfill one of the following requirements: to have been born in any of the four communes; to have held with merit a position in the French service for 10 years; to provide evidence of good character and possess a means of existence; or to have been decorated with the Legion of Honor or the Military Award. By 1922 less than 100 persons in all of French West Africa had qualified for citizenship (Manning, 1988; p. 79). In 1936 there were 78,000 French citizens in Senegal and only 2,400 in the remaining French West African colonies out of a total population of 15 million (Bell, 1986).

To secure citizenship in the Portuguese colonies the African had to be well educated, Christian, and monogamous. Once his application was accepted and he became a Portuguese citizen, he was saved from the indignity of having to carry a passbook and exempted from compulsory labor. Few Africans became citizens. In the Portuguese colony of Guinea, for example, only 1,418 out of a total African population of 550,457 had become *assimilados* by 1950.

European administrators frequently adopted others nations' colonial policies. The failure of assimilation prompted the French to replace it with association. British colonial policy, on the other hand, increasingly took on a French character. The traditional paramount ruler or sultan was no longer the head of the social and political order but was rather a subordinate of the British overlord, who used him to implement such unpopular measures as compulsory labor, taxation, and military enlistment for two world wars. Those traditional rulers who had armies lost control over them and had no say in the conduct of foreign affairs and legislation. Furthermore, the British could depose traditional rulers and replace them with their own nominees. Finally, the British often interfered with existing paramountcies by breaking some of them up and raising subordinate chiefs to the status of paramount chiefs, as they did in Sierra Leone.

European colonial policies also underwent various reforms, in phases. The first phase occurred in the period preceding the outbreak of the First World War. The exposure of colonial scandals by European anti-imperialists forced the phaseout of private companies as direct colonial administrators in the Belgian and Portuguese possessions. The next phase of colonial reform occurred after the Second World War with the introduction of constitutions, which allowed Africans greater participation in the colonial government.

Thus, over time, colonial government policies became remarkably uniform, regardless of the European power in charge (Curtin, et al. 1988; p. 482). Berman (1984) noted: "[W]hen we probe beneath the surface of formal structure and rhetoric, we find that the experience and internal processes of French and British colonial administration were not only similar, but also in many instances practically identical" (p. 176).

General administrative officers were amazingly few for the extent of territory governed. The whole of French Equatorial Africa in the mid-1930s was run by only 206 administrative officers, with 400 specialists and technical officers to assist. The whole of British tropical Africa at the same period (leaving aside Egypt, the Sudan, and southern Africa) was governed by about 1,000 general administrative officers, plus another 4,000 or 5,000 European specialists, while the Belgians ruled the Congo in 1936 with 728 officers in charge of the 104 territories. In Rwanda and Burundi, however, they ruled with an administrative staff of less than 50 Europeans, because African kingship had been preserved there.

### Indigenous Rulers' Strategies to Preserve Institutions

African rulers were not without options in dealing with colonialism, however. They could collaborate and try to seek the favor of the new masters, resist to the end, surrender when defeat was imminent, or attempt to bargain for advantage. They also had a range of similar but independent choices to make in response to Western culture. Africans could choose Western weapons and reject Christianity, or the other way around. Africans could accept Christianity and yet fight to the end against Western rule, or they could accept

Western rule as inevitable, collaborate with colonial governments, and yet remain all the more faithful to Islam. In other words, political subjugation of Africans did not necessarily yield spiritual, religious, and cultural control over them. To assure the survivability of their political entities, indigenous African rulers took various measures. Some recognized their military weakness and surrendered or cooperated with the colonialists to prevent being annihilated by either the colonialists or by a stronger neighboring tribe. The Fanti states of Ghana, Rwanda, and Burundi as well as the Ganda kingdom of Uganda acted in this way. The rulers of these states realized that surrender or cooperation, far from being an act of cowardice, was the best way to preserve their kingdoms under the prevailing circumstances and constraints. For example, at the time of the French annexation of Porto Novo in 1883, the Toffa chief was facing three enemies: the Yoruba to the northeast, the Fon kings of Dahomey to the north, and the British on the coast. He saw an alliance with the French as a tactical survival maneuver.

The Buganda preserved their indigenous systems by actually placing themselves under British protection through surrender treaties and agreements. In not opposing British annexation, the Buganda won many concessions for themselves and enhanced their bargaining position since they possessed the power to make British rule either inexpensive and comparatively easy or extremely difficult. Their greatest success was in translating their bargaining position into a written agreement, the Uganda Agreement of 1900. The political effect was to keep the title and office of *kabaka* (the king) intact but to assign real power to the *Lukiiko*, a representative body.

Many other African rulers managed to hold on to their power by timely surrender and collaboration. For example, the Muslim theocratic state in Futa Jallon and many Fulbe emirs of northern Nigeria retained a great deal of power by cooperating at the appropriate time with the first British officials to appear. Similarly, the Mossi kingdom of Burkina Faso retained its existence. Zanzibar and the Muslim states of North Africa survived after colonialism for a rather special reason: most of them had been recognized for centuries as political entities in European international law because of early trade contacts in the Mediterranean and the Indian Ocean. In southern Africa, Lesotho and Swaziland kept their identities through skill and luck in manipulating the rivalry between Britain and the Boer republics. King Moshweshwe of Lesotho requested and received British annexation to fend off the Boers in the Orange Free State in the 1880s. Prior to the Anglo-Boer War of 1899, Swaziland was under the control of the Boer republic of the

Transvaal. Following the defeat of the Boers, the British rewarded the Swazi king for his help with the grant of considerable autonomy under British rule. Other African rulers fought against colonial rule to the bitter end and saw their kingdoms destroyed. For example, Ba Bemba of Sikasso steadfastly opposed the French until 1894 when he killed himself rather than surrender his sovereignty to the French. The Ndebele, Shona and Dahomey Kingdoms were decimated when their rulers refused to give up. Chiefs who disobeyed the Portuguese in Angola paid with their lives. According to Williams (1987): "Chiefs failing to secure the required number of slaves were themselves enslaved. Over a hundred chiefs and notables were sold into slavery in a single year and another hundred murdered by the Portuguese. We may safely assume that the actual number of chiefs enslaved or murdered was greater than that stated above since the Portuguese, like other nations, generally cut casualty figures for the record" (p. 261).

The destruction of political structures, however, did not mean the complete obliteration of their immanent political cultures. For example, after a brief respite, the Ndebele and Shona rallied around the religious spirit of *Mlimo* and rose in rebellion. Similarly, when the British captured the Asante king and exiled him to Sierra Leone in January 1897, they discovered that the soul of the Asante nation was not so easily captured. It was the golden stool, not the king, that was the symbol and soul of the Asante nation. When the British made a vain attempt to capture the stool in April 1900, they met a stiff and humiliating defeat. Although this rebellion was finally crushed, the British never gained possession of the golden stool.

In eastern and southern Africa, there were cases of forced labor and expulsions of the natives from their land. But even so, the native structures were erected elsewhere. Chiefs and headmen still retained their traditional authority and administered the affairs of their people. Thus, despite the colonialists' meddling in political affairs by appointing government chiefs and deposing traditional rulers, the indigenous political cultures survived. There was no doubt that the indigenous political structures had been severely weakened and the authority of traditional rulers drastically reduced. But the claim that the indigenous system of government was completely wiped out is fallacious. As most Africans in the former British colonies would affirm, at the dawn of independence in the 1950s, the native institutions, as exemplified by chiefs, kings, and councils of elders, were still very much in existence.

This was also generally the case in French West Africa. In 1888 Gabon, the Congo, and the interior areas were merged into one large colony, known as the French Congo. But French presence in this great territory was so modest that local communities were little disturbed, except along major waterways and along the 400-kilometer porterage route from Loango on the coast to Brazzaville. Manning (1988) observed, "[E]ven where the old states lost their formal political power, they continued to exist, and the kings and chiefs could act as representatives of their constituents, not simply as tools of the administration" (p. 74).

There was one indigenous institution, in particular, that the colonialists actually sought to strengthen: the native system of courts and law. In the fields of property rights and civil and criminal matters, the Europeans drew a very sharp line. Europeans were to be governed by European law and Africans by African law.[4] This necessitated formalizing African customary law and providing law courts and legal services to administer justice for the natives. The British commissioned reports on the code of native customs and law. The jurisdiction of the native courts was recognized. In southern Africa, some attempts were made to provide the native courts with court registers and roofed buildings. According to Manning (1988):

> In both French West Africa and the Belgian Congo (but not in French Equatorial Africa), the colonial regimes sought to strengthen their legal foundations by drawing up formal codes of African law. For various ethnic groups or for whole colonies, government officials drew up written codes based on traditional law, on decisions made in the Native Courts, and on the needs of the colonial state. Their idea was to strengthen the Native Courts, to base decisions on a formal code and no longer on common law and judicial precedent, and to reduce the number of cases going before the courts of French or Belgian law. For Dahomey, the political activist, Louis Hunkarin, did much of the work of drawing up the manual of customary law (p. 84).

In sum, the indigenous system of government survived under colonialism and operated alongside the new colonial system. As Austen (1987) put it:

> Through almost all of tropical Africa, the diplomats' "paper partitions" of the 1880s and early 1890s were followed by years and sometimes decades of relative inactivity. Only the most rudimentary, if any, administration was established outside the capitals, few roads and hardly any railways were built, and *for most Africans life had hardly changed.* The reasons for these hesitations were financial: private European investors were uninterested in Africa, metropolitan legislatures opposed major public expenditures on colonies, and even the Western commercial firms already established at coastal entrepots refused to move inland ahead of piecemeal government "pacification" (p. 124, emphasis added).

Africans saw little social development of their indigenous systems under colonialism. The colonialists built a few thousand miles of road and dreadfully inadequate schools. At independence in 1961, Tanzania had only 120 university graduates. But Guinea-Bissau was not so lucky. According to Lamb (1984): "What the Portuguese left as a legacy of three hundred years of colonial rule was pitifully little: 14 university graduates, an illiteracy rate of 97 percent and only 265 miles of paved roads in an area twice the size of New Jersey. There was only one modern plant in Guinea-Bissau in 1974—it produced beer for the Portuguese troops—and as a final gesture before leaving, the Portuguese destroyed the national archives" (p. 5).

Elsewhere in Africa, the object of infrastructure, even where built, was to serve the needs of the resident expatriate community and to help evacuate minerals and cash crops from the interior. The large rural sector and the interior of Africa were largely left untouched. As Nkrumah (1973) put it:

> Under colonial rule, foreign monopoly interests had tied up our whole economy to suit themselves. We had not one single industry. Our economy depended on one cash crop, cocoa. Although our output of cocoa is the largest in the world, there was not a single cocoa processing factory. There was no direct rail link between Accra and Takoradi. There were few hospitals, schools and clinics. Most of the villages lacked a piped water supply. In fact, the nakedness of the land when my government began in 1951 has to have been experienced to be believed (p. 395).

If the colonialists never developed or poorly developed rural Africa, why then the allegation that the colonialists completely destroyed Africa's indigenous institutions?

It is true that colonial rule was marked by atrocities, plunder, and neglect. But Africa's indigenous institutions were largely left intact by colonial rule. From this perspective, the task facing African leaders after independence was clear: to develop the traditional sector that the colonialists had neglected, to restore the traditional authority that the chiefs and kings had lost under colonialism, and to rebuild the native political structures that the colonialists had tried to destroy. How did African leaders and elites attended to these tasks? We examine this question in the following chapters, which discuss the period from 1960 to 1990.

---

## NOTES

1. The unfavorable military imbalance that operated against Africans proved difficult to rectify because of controls on gun imports. By 1885 the Europeans had gained enough control over the import-export trade

along the West African coast to bar the importation of guns and ammunition. Some guns and ammunition were smuggled into the region, and Africans devised new tactics that occasionally proved effective, even with their technologically inferior weapons. But in the final analysis, better European military organization and the Maxim gun triumphed, compelling respect and obedience.

2. The literature on the barbarities of colonial overlords and the exploitation of African natives is vast. It is not the intention here to contribute to it.

3. Corporate rule was also used in the Portuguese colonies of Angola, Mozambique, and French Central Africa.

4. The dichotomy, however, left much room for conflict and contradictions that prevented the development of a coherent set of judicial institutions after colonialism.

# Chapter 5

## Indigenous Africa after Independence

It is true God's children in Africa suffer because there is *less* freedom in their countries than during the colonial times. African leaders need to be reminded that there is totalitarianism and despotism nearly everywhere in Africa. When your people are free, you can also walk freely and you will not need huge security to protect you.

— Bishop Desmond Tutu, 1990[1]

### THE BETRAYAL OF THE BLACK CAUSE FOR FREEDOM

After protracted negotiations, often punctuated by threats and acrimony, the colonial powers finally granted Africans independence. In eastern Africa, notably Kenya, and southern Africa (Angola, Mozambique, and Zimbabwe), independence was secured after sustained guerrilla warfare. Although Ghana has often claimed to be the first black African country to gain its independence—in 1957—Sudan secured independence on January 1, 1956, and Ethiopia and Liberia had been regarded as autonomous since 1847. By 1960 almost all of the French colonies had attained their sovereignty. Gambia, a British colony, was late in gaining her freedom in 1965. Later still were the Portuguese colonies of Angola, Guinea-Bissau, and Mozambique, which won their independence by 1975.

Although West African colonies generally won their freedom by nonviolent political agitation, there were a few rancorous episodes, particularly in French Guinea and the Belgian Congo (Zaire).

When Guinea voted "No" to association with France and proclaimed its independence on October 2, 1958, Charles de Gaulle ordered the withdrawal of all French functionaries from Guinea. Two weeks later, only 15 of the 4,000 French officials remained. The French emptied their cash registers and shipped the weapons of the police, the library of the Ministry of Justice, and the furniture of the governor's palace back to France. In a burst of vindictiveness, some Frenchmen went so far as to rip out telephone wires and electrical fixtures, cut fruit trees, uproot gardens, tear down walls, scrawl obscene curses on buildings, and reroute a ship carrying 5,000 tons of rice.

Zaire also obtained its independence in an acrimonious atmosphere, on June 30, 1960. King Baudouin of Belgium, who took part in the ceremonies, exhorted his former subjects to unity: "The principal dangers for you are the inexperience of your people in government affairs, tribal fights which have done so much harm and must at all costs be stopped, and the attraction which certain of your regions can have for foreign powers which are ready to profit from the least sign of weakness" (cited in Italiaander, 1961; p. 158).

In response, Joseph Kasavubu, the president of the new nation, praised the Belgian administrators of the Congo, promised future cooperation, and added that Belgium had given "an example unprecedented in the history of peaceful decolonization—leading our people directly, without transition, from foreign rule to independence under full national sovereignty." Premier Patrice Lumumba, however, resented this flattery. In a speech marked with extraordinary ferocity, he declared:

> We are no longer your monkeys! . . . No Congolese worthy of the name will ever be able to forget that this independence has been won through a struggle . . . in which we did not spare our energy and our blood . . .
>
> We have known ironies, insults and blows which we had to undergo morning, noon, and night because we were Negroes. We have seen our lands spoiled in the name of laws which differed according to whether they dealt with a black man or a white. We have known the atrocious sufferings of those who were imprisoned for their political opinions or religious beliefs, and of those exiled in their own country. Their fate was truly worse than death itself. Who will forget the rifle fire from which so many of our brothers perished, or the jails into which were brutally thrown those who did not wish to submit to a regime of injustice, oppression, and exploitation, which were the means the colonialists employed to dominate us? . . .
>
> The Republic of the Congo has been proclaimed, and our country is now in the hands of its own children . . . We are going to put an end to suppression of free thought and see to it that all our citizens enjoy to the full the fundamental liberties in the Declaration of the Rights of Man. . . We are going to rule not by the peace of guns and bayonets but by a peace of the heart and will (quoted in Italiaander, 1961; p. 159).

The last two paragraphs of Lumumba's speech are noteworthy since African nationalists never ended the "atrocious sufferings" of their people, nor fulfilled the promises they made.

In 1945 pan-Africanists such as Nkrumah, Padmore, and Nyerere were demanding and pledging equal justice, freedom of the press, freedom of expression, and parliamentary democracy for every part of the continent. The declarations of the Pan-African Congress in Manchester in 1945 were particularly telling: "We are determined to be free. We want education. We want the right to earn a decent living; the right to express our thoughts and emotions, to adopt and create forms of beauty. We will fight in every way we can for freedom, democracy, and social betterment" (cited by Langley, 1979; p. 121).

In the 1950s and 1960s African nationalists also unleashed a barrage of fiery speeches and homilies. In 1960 Dr. Nnamdi Azikiwe, the governor-general of Nigeria, asserted: "Let bygones be bygones. I mean it with all my heart. Let us go forward together towards the great day of our independence with no bitterness and no looking back to the wounds of the past. I have fought as a nationalist for nearly 25 years, and I tell you honestly that if we spoil this magnificent opportunity that lies ahead of us by quarrels amongst ourselves, by intrigues and slanders and dirty politics, it will be the biggest disappointment of my life (Langley, 1979; p.45)."

In 1958 Sir Abubakar Tafawa Balewa, the first premier of Nigeria, proclaimed: "Differences of opinion there are bound to be in any country, and in a free country they will be expressed openly, and, I hope fearlessly, but let them also be expressed honestly and unselfishly. The fear of God, honesty and tolerance are the foundations on which a nation can build peace and prosperity . . . And not only among the leaders but especially between the members of different religious and political parties let there be tolerance (Langley, 1979; p.49)."

Dr. Kwame Nkrumah, the late president of Ghana, contended: "I described Positive Action as the adoption of all legitimate and constitutional means by which we could attack the forces of imperialism in this country. The weapons were legitimate political agitation, newspaper and educational campaigns and, as a last resort, the constitutional application of strikes, boycotts, and noncooperation based on the principle of absolute nonviolence, as used by Gandhi in India (Langley, 1979; p.78)."

Julius Nyerere, the former president of Tanzania, said: "Democratic reforms are naturally well-suited to African conditions. For me the characteristics of democracy are: the freedom of the individual, including freedom to criticize the government, and the opportunity to change it without worrying about being murdered (Langley, 1979; p.134)."

And Sekou Toure, the late president of Guinea, averred: "We prefer to live in poverty in liberty to riches in slavery . . . Guinea is a small country, but we have raised high the banner of freedom and know no fear. . .No one can claim for himself the right to speak for all of Africa. But each man has the right, and the pride, to be able to attempt to express the hope and the aspirations of the peoples of Africa (Langley, 1979; p.231)."

On the eve of independence, nationalists such as Kwame Nkrumah of Ghana and Jomo Kenyatta of Kenya, jailed by the colonialists for their liberation activities, were released from jail to stand for elections. Given constitutions that the colonialists had modeled after the European parliamentary system, these nationalists won elections with strong support from the peasants. The colonialists asked the victors to form the first African governments and to have them in place on the day of the declaration of independence. In the European political tradition, the losers were to form the opposition.

Each African country celebrated its day of independence with unbounded euphoria. Freedom at last! Africans unfurled flags, broadcast national anthems on the radio, and paraded in the streets. The nationalists and other speakers displayed their oratorical skills. But not for long. That fresh breath of freedom from colonial rule was to prove ephemeral. "One man, one vote" came to Africa only one time. By the time Gambia gained its freedom in 1965, the Ghanaians, Nigerians, and Togolese were asking what had happened to theirs.

True freedom never came to much of Africa after independence. Despite the rhetoric and vituperations against colonialism, very little changed in the years immediately following independence. For many countries independence meant only a change in the color of the administrators from white to black. The new leaders began to act in the same manner as the colonialists. In fact in many places they were worse than the colonialists.

Inchoate democratic structures, hastily erected by the departing colonialists were perceived by the new leaders as "Western." They were quickly uprooted and replaced with systems that were, in many cases, far more repressive than the hated colonial system. The constitutional democracies installed in Ghana, Uganda, Tanzania, and Zambia soon degenerated into one-man dictatorships built on personality cults. Winners of the elections held on the dawn of independence subsequently used their parliamentary majorities to subvert the constitution and declare themselves presidents-for-life. Elsewhere, the rulers built a political system of patronage that served their predatory instincts. In the Ivory Coast, Malawi, and Zaire, state power was effectively and personally monopolized.

In many places in Africa the leadership that emerged after independence was characterized by pretentious, megalomaniacal venality. In other places the leadership dogmatically embraced alien revolutionary ideals, assumed the trappings of foreign cultures, and misperceived the process of development. The irony was that many African leaders came to assume some of the very same characteristics they so loudly denounced in the colonialists, imperialists, and racists.

The political patronage system these new leaders adopted rewarded idleness and sycophancy. Those who protested most loudly against Western colonialism and imperialism and praised the new tyrannical governments received ministerial appointments, sinecures, rapid promotions, and emoluments. In many countries the patronage system instigated fierce competition for political favors that pitted even relatives against one another. For ambassadorial posts, and in some cases for a mere pittance, even educated African intellectuals willingly sacrificed their moral scruples and the principles of freedom for which they had fought.

By the late 1970s tyranny had become so firmly entrenched that it could deal with the few brave intellectual critics. The intellectual community had been transformed into such a servile tool of tyranny that despite years of political and general education, few of the ruling elites understood the meaning of such simple concepts as freedom and democracy. One irate Nigerian, Peter Senam Anyomi of Lagos, wrote:

> In almost three decades of independence, Africa can hardly boast of an instance where the incumbent government or leader has been removed peacefully via the ballot box. Hence the "bullet" rather than the "ballot" has become the only effective means of removing many an inept and undesirable ruler. But as we march towards the 21st century, Africa's youths are saying enough is enough. The old rulers should give way to the more dynamic and progressive younger men. After all the throne is not the personal property of any ruler (*New African*, Aug 1989; p. 40).

Examples of despotism were rampant. Soon after independence, Nigeria suffered from bitter regional factionalism that culminated in the Biafran war from 1967 to 1970. In addition, Nkrumah of Ghana, while espousing the virtues of constitutional means to attack the forces of imperialism, denied his own people the same means to attack the forces of despotism. He declared the opposition's newspaper campaigns as well as its strikes and boycotts, which were constitutionally guaranteed rights, illegal. He incarcerated members of the opposition. Similarly, Julius Nyerere, soon after becoming Tanzania's president, asserted that "the characteristics of democracy—the freedom of the individual, including freedom to criticize the government, and the opportunity to change it without worrying about being murdered"—were emphatically *not* "naturally well-suited to African conditions." He declared Tanzania a one-party state and when Chief Abdallah Said Fundikira and James Mapalala, founders of Civic Movement, campaigned for greater political pluralism, they were immediately arrested (*Financial Times*, Nov 23/24, 1991; p. 2).

In Sekou Toure's Guinea, the people soon found themselves not living in poverty in liberty but rather in poverty in slavery and tyranny. They also found that they did not have "the right, and the pride, to be able to attempt to express the hope and the aspirations of the peoples of Africa." Thousands of Guineans fled Toure's tyrannical rule in the 1980s.

The new African leaders dismantled little of the oppressive colonial administrative machinery. In fact, they strengthened and greatly centralized much of it. They also retained and fortified—to the later chagrin of many Africans—the same instruments of coercion and tyranny the colonialists had widely used to suppress the aspirations of black nationalism. In 1990, 26 years after independence, a state of emergency was still in effect in Zambia— the very measure the colonialists had used to quell the nationalists in Northern Rhodesia. African leaders also imposed controls on the press, on freedom of movement and expression, and on foreign exchange. Even the colonialists had not prevented Louis Hunkanrin of Dahomey and Kwame Nkrumah of Ghana from publishing independent newspapers that criticized colonialist policies. But after independence in Cameroon and Malawi, for example, newspaper editors had to clear stories with the censorship board before publication.

Much of postcolonial Africa came to be ruled by "educated barbarians." The elites and nationalists proved themselves to be no "noble savages." Recall that the illiterate peasants of Africa—the so-called savages—developed political institutions of participatory democracy based upon consensus. They also recognized the fact that consensus was impossible to reach without a guarantee of *freedom of expression*. At village meetings, even nontribesmen could express their opinion freely without harassment or arrest. After independence, however, the majority of African nationalists and the educated elites denied the people these rights. In fact, in most African countries criticisms of the government became illegal. The opposition was gagged and its members, some of whom were the same nationalists who had fought for freedom alongside the new leaders, were thrown into jail or killed.

Various arguments were advanced to justify the new leaders' repressive measures against Africans. One was that the new governments needed emergency powers to check the machinations of neocolonial forces that were bent on destabilizing the continent. The Ugandan ambassador to the United States, Stephen Kampimpina Katenta-Apuli, was quite forthright: "Third World countries foolishly confused independence with surliness in those days. They thought the world owed them everything for its earlier misdeeds; and they see each business overture as a warning of neocolonialism" (*Wall Street Journal*, Apr 25, 1990; p. A14).

Another rationale for the repression was the need to spur socialist development. A wave of socialism swept across the continent as almost all the new African leaders succumbed to the contagious ideology. The dalliance and fascination with socialism seemed to have emerged during the struggle for political independence and freedom from colonial rule in the 1950s. Many African nationalists harbored a deep distrust and distaste for capitalism, which, with Lenin, they identified as an extension of colonialism and imperialism. Consequently, they interpreted freedom from colonial rule as freedom from capitalism as well.

Having rejected both colonialism and capitalism, the new leaders needed an alternative ideology. Although some elements of communism seemed appealing, its adoption would have entailed their nations' becoming satellites of the Soviet Union. European socialism, on the other hand, was a poor substitute. Its acceptance would have been interpreted as continued reliance on the European colonialists. Requiring a different ideology, the nationalists settled on "African socialism"—a nebulous concept that borrowed heavily from European socialism but with liberal usage of such terms as "communalism," thus enabling it to be portrayed as based upon African traditions. Further, the definition could be made flexible enough to permit different interpretations and applications to suit the social conditions prevailing in each African country.

As a result, a proliferation of socialist ideologies emerged in Africa, including some that were quite bizarre. They included: Julius Nyerere's *Ujaama* (familyhood or socialism in Swahili) in Tanzania; Leopold Senghor's vague amalgam of Marxism, Christian socialism, humanitarianism, and "Negritude" in Senegal; Kenneth Kaunda's humanism in Zambia; Marien N'Gouabi's scientific socialism in the Congo (Brazzaville); Muammar Gaddafi's Arab-Islamic socialism in Libya; Kwame Nkrumah's Nkrumaism ("consciencism") in Ghana; Mobutu Sese Seko's Mobutuism in Zaire; and Habib Bourguiba's *Bourguibisme* in Tunisia. Only a few African countries, such as the Ivory

Coast, Nigeria, and Kenya were pragmatic enough to eschew doctrinaire socialism.

Although African leaders were generally disposed to erasing the allegedly exploitative, capitalistic tendencies of colonial structures, they held different views on the need for the socialist ideology. Nkrumah of Ghana, widely regarded as the "father of African socialism," was convinced that "only a socialist form of society can assure Ghana of a rapid rate of economic progress without destroying that social justice, that freedom and equality, which are a central feature of our traditional life" (*Seven-Year Development Plan*, Accra: Government of Ghana, 1963; p. 1). Nyerere of Tanzania, on the other hand, misread the communalism of African traditional life as readiness for socialism, to which he was first exposed during his schooling in Scotland. He castigated capitalism and a money economy, saying it "encourages individual acquisitiveness and economic competition." He contended that the money economy was foreign to Africa and it could be "catastrophic as regards the African family social unit." As an alternative to "the relentless pursuit of individual advancement," Nyerere insisted that Tanzania be transformed into a nation of small-scale communalists (*Ujaama*) (Nyerere, 1966). In Tunisia the doctrine was Bourguibisme. The official definition was:

> To deal with the enemy of today without ever forgetting that he could become the friend of tomorrow; if relations are broken off to make untiring attempts to establish them again; to turn to force only as a last resort, and then in full public view with flags flying; to build up the nation, but to rise above narrow nationalism and carry on the fight for freedom from a moral and ideological point of view; never to allow oneself to be diverted from the principle of independence, while taking note of its various stages of development and making the compromises that may become necessary (*Insight*, Sep 15, 1986; p. 34).

However, Bourguiba himself refused to make compromises and threw many dissidents into jail. In November 1987 he was thrown out of office after a 31-year rule.

Since socialism implied one-party rule, leaders amended their constitutions to create one-party states. The chairman of the party was automatically the head of state and could not be removed by elections. To ensure continued tenure, he was unopposed in any election. The socialists justified this by arguing that allowing other candidates would be an admission of dissension in the party. Unity was the avowed imperative. Thus, once one became a party chairman, he held the post for life. Socialism proved to be a very convenient ideology for egotistical tyrants to realize their ambitions of self-aggrandizement. Political power thus became dangerously concentrated in the hands of one person. The head of state became the chairman of the only legal party, the supreme commander of the armed forces, the chancellor of all the universities, the chief judge, and so on. To emphasize their omnipotence and omniscience, heads of state took new names for themselves. For example, President Joseph Désiré Mobutu changed his name to Mobutu Sese Seko Kuku Ngbendu Wa Za Banga, which translates to "the earthy, the peppery, all-powerful warrior who, by his endurance and will to win, goes from contest to contest leaving fire in his wake."

In practice, the various socialist ideologies turned out to be convenient justifications for personal rule or one-man dictatorship, the repression of alternative viewpoints, the intolerance of criticism, and the brutal suppression of civil liberties. Samora Machel, the late president of Mozambique, said: "When a class imposes its will, those who refuse to accept this imposition must be forced to conform. Those who oppose this will be repressed" (cited in Caldwell, 1989; p. 12).

Very quickly, African independence and socialism turned into one-man dictatorships, characterized by conspicuous consumption by the elites and a "Swiss-bank socialism" that allowed the head of state and his cohort of vampire elites to loot their countries' treasuries for deposit in Swiss and other foreign banks. Billions of dollars were deposited abroad by the Babangidas, the Bandas, the Barres, the Does, the Kerekous, the Houphouet-Boignies, the Mois, the Mobutus, the Mengistus and many others. Even Nkrumah was found by the Azu Crabbe Commission of Enquiry, set up by the government of Ghana in 1966 to probe his assets, to have deposited over $5 million in foreign banks.

Mobutu's conspicuous consumption was typical of that of the new leaders. He built 11 palaces and linked some of them with four-lane highways. At his palace on the northern border, in his ancestral village of Gbadolite, called the "Versailles in the Jungle," waiters served pickled quail tongues and chilled French wines. The palaces were not enough. He acquired grand estates and chateaus in Belgium, France, the Ivory Coast, and Spain, as well as vineyards in Portugal. Almost every bridge or monument of significance in Zaire has been named after him. Only Julius Nyerere, the former president of Tanzania, proved to be a true practicing socialist by refraining from using his office for self-aggrandizement.

Throughout Africa the socialist transformation was characterized by heavy state intervention in all aspects of daily life; the government regulation of economic activity was known as *dirigisme*. Governments appropriated all unoccupied land and set up roadblocks and passbook systems to control the movement of their people. Marketing board and export regulations were tightened to exploit the cash crop producers; governments imposed price controls on peasant farmers and traders that made food for the urban elites cheap. For example, in Guinea Sekou Toure established a Marxist regime: "Unauthorized trading became a crime. Police roadblocks were set up around the country to control internal trade. The state set up a monopoly on foreign trade and smuggling became punishable by death. Currency trafficking was punishable by 15 to 20 years in prison. Many farms were collectivized. Food prices were fixed at low levels. Private farmers were forced to deliver annual harvest quotas to "Local Revolutionary Powers." State companies monopolized industrial production" (*New York Times*, Dec 28, 1987; p. 28).

Sekou Toure was the same man who had declared: "We prefer to live in poverty in liberty to riches in slavery." Private farms and traders saw no liberty under his rule. When confronted about his drift toward dictatorship, he responded:

> Before independence, there were 12 political parties in Guinea. Now there is only one: Le Parti Democratique de Guinea (PDG). Anyone who says I am a dictator because we have only one party and no opposition doesn't understand what we are trying to accomplish. The party is not a goal, but a method to achieve the goal of human freedom. Our constitution permits complete freedom for the existence of Opposition parties. However, in the last election, 91 percent of the people voted for the PDG. The Opposition received only five or six percent of the votes, and decided to join our party. This meant reconciliation, and two of their leaders received responsible posts. Actually, the Opposition's point of view can be expressed much better within the party than from outside it (Italiaander, 1961; p. 146)

His illiterate peasants understood perfectly well the "human freedom" he was trying to achieve. By the time of his death in March 1984, more than one-fifth of the country's population—some 1.5 million people—had fled the country.

In 1973 Tanzania undertook massive resettlement programs under "Operation Dodoma," "Operation Sogeza," "Operation Kigoma," and many others to create "communal villages." Peasants were loaded into trucks, often forcibly, and moved to new locations. Many lost their lives in the process. To prevent them from returning to their old habitats, the government bulldozed the abandoned buildings. By 1976 some 13 million peasants had been forced into 8,000 cooperative villages, and by the end of the 1970s, about 91 percent of the entire rural population had been moved into government villages. Regulations required that all crops were to be bought and distributed by the government. It was illegal for the peasants to sell their own produce. Recall Nyerere's principles of democracy: freedom of the individual, including freedom to criticize the government and to change it. Recall also his vaunted rhetoric about African familyhood. In reality, he meant only the family of his own creation, with him as the head. He was perfectly willing to destroy the indigenous African family by forcibly resettling peasants against their will.

In Ethiopia, Mengistu Haile Mariam overthrew Emperor Haile Selassie in 1974 and assumed power. The ailing emperor was suffocated with a wet pillow, and his body was buried in an unmarked grave. Scores of his relatives were murdered or chained to walls in the cellars of the imperial palace. Thousands of suspected counterrevolutionaries were gunned down in the streets. More than 30,000 people were jailed. When a member of his own junta questioned the wisdom of such terror tactics, Mengistu shot him in the head. In March 1975 Mengistu nationalized all land under the Land Reform Act. He instituted a villagization program in which he proposed moving 34 million people (roughly 75 percent of the total population of Ethiopia) into state-controlled communes, guarded by the army—300,000 strong and the largest in Africa. Since 1977 the Soviet Union has poured over $11 billion worth of arms into Ethiopia, largely on credit. Much of the Soviet military hardware was used to carry out indiscriminate bombings, shellings, and slaughter of civilians. Even famine relief centers in the north and along the Sudan border were bombed and burned.

Villagization was touted as necessary "to move the population away from areas where the soil was degraded to combat the erosion of agricultural land. In addition, resettlement was to provide new opportunities to people in areas affected by drought and to those in highly crowded areas where landholdings were shrinking." An Ethiopian government official asserted: "It is our duty to move the peasants if they are too stupid to move by themselves" (quoted in *Time,* Aug 4, 1986; p. 32). True, soil erosion and land degradation were problems. But the measures the Mengistu government took to solve those problems were more damaging than the peasants' "stupidity." Dr. Aradom Tedla, former director general of the Ministry of Law and Justice, pointed out: "The Mengistu Government is one that is systematically oppressing religion, denying starving Ethiopians food, brutally relocating and 'villagizing' millions of people, and persecuting political suspects through false trials—which mete out death sentences and long prison terms indiscriminately."[2]

Even if relocation was necessary, conditions in the government camps were poor and unsanitary and resulted in the deaths of more than 150,000 Ethiopians. Once in the cooperatives, peasants were forced to walk as far as five miles to and from the fields every day at gunpoint. They were ordered to turn over all their produce to the state and to attend indoctrination seminars that praised the Mengistu government. In February 1988, when drought victims refused to participate in the government resettlement program in the northern town of Korem, Ethiopian troops opened fire on thousands, killing at least 20 (*Wall Street Journal,* Feb 12, 1988, p. 1). More insidious was the fact that the real goal of the resettlement program was to eradicate the indigenous power bases of the chiefs or traditional rulers that Mengistu perceived as a threat to his power. Those who opposed Mengistu were either shot or starved into submission. Food became a weapon. Villages that opposed Mengistu were either starved or destroyed. In 1984, while thousands of Ethiopians were starving to death, Mengistu spent $200 million to celebrate the tenth anniversary of Soviet imperialism. As children died, Mengistu and his army were consuming Scotch whisky, crates of caviar, salmon, lobster, and French champagne. Ten million dollars were spent to redecorate the statues of Marx, Engels, and Lenin in Addis Ababa, the capital.

In 1986 Mengistu declared: "We are now on the threshold of the formation of the People's Democratic Republic of Ethiopia. The constitution was drafted by representatives of the people themselves. It has been submitted to all Ethiopian citizens including those living abroad, and it will be promulgated after it is put to a referendum. Such democratic participation is unparalleled in the history of Ethiopia. Once the constitution assumes its final shape, Ethiopia will never again be ruled by the personal absolutism of any one individual or a handful of individuals" (*Time,* Aug 4, 1986; p. 34).

Mengistu, of course, never saw the "personal absolutism" of his own rule. In Addis Ababa an arch that led to Revolution Square proclaimed: "The victory of socialism is inevitable!" If this was what African leaders such as Mengistu meant by socialism, it provided a disgraceful commentary on the calibre of their leadership.

The failure of Marxist-Leninism was inevitable in Ethiopia since the ideology is alien to Africa. Under siege from a coalition of rag-tag rebels, Comrade Mengistu fled Ethiopia on May 22, 1991 to Zimbabwe. Irate citizens chanting "Mengistu Thief, Lenin Thief" stomped on a smashed statue of Lenin that once graced the capital, Addis Ababa.

In many countries the political regimes established by the new leaders of Africa proved to be far more tyrannical and brutal than their colonial counterparts—a fact that did not escape the attention of Bishop Desmond Tutu, a Nobel laureate. Speaking at Nairobi's All Saints Cathedral in March 1990, he lamented that there was even more freedom during the much-maligned colonial period than in many independent African nations (*Daily Nation,* Nairobi, Mar 26, 1990).

As Bishop Tutu spoke, the Rev. Lawford Ngege Imunde of the All Africa Conference of Churches was in detention on a sedition charge. According to *New African*: "On March 28, 1990, Rev. Imunde was brought before the Chief Magistrate court and charged with printing and being in possession of a seditious publication. This 'publication' later turned out to be a personal 1990 diary which contained words offensive to President Moi and his government. He was jailed for six years" (Jun 1990; p. 21).

Another group the new leaders attacked were the market traders. Although market traders had financially supported the nationalist cause and many of the nationalists' mothers had been market traders, the word "market" had become anathema to the nationalists, who considered the market a colonialist institution. That belief demonstrated not only the nationalists' lack of understanding of the purpose and forms of economic institutions but also their ignorance of their own indigenous African heritage. There were markets in Africa before the Europeans arrived. Indeed, the marketplace was the nerve center of traditional precolonial Africa and still is today. Nevertheless, the nationalists, in complete ignorance of their culture, set out to destroy these markets. They imposed price controls, seized the goods of those who violated the controls, and imprisoned traders in the same jails in which the nationalists had been detained during colonial rule. African neocolonialism was rearing its ugly head.

"Peoples' Power!" "Peoples' Revolution!" many African leaders chanted. But in most cases, it was a nonsensical "revolution" that deprived the people of their power to remove incompetent governments they did not want.

In Zaire, for example, Mobutu's *Mouvement Populaire de la Revolution* (MPR) was the sole legal party until April 1990. Every citizen became a member of the MPR at birth. The revolution, however, was fatuous. Having accumulated his fortune, Mobutu once asserted, "It is better to die of hunger than to be rich and slave to colonialism." Indeed, some 50 prisoners starved to death in his jails in 1983, according to Amnesty International. In response to that accusation, Mobutu asked: "Why should I feed my prisoners when I don't have enough to feed my peasants?" (*Wall Street Journal*, Oct 23, 1984; p. 16). Mobutu's revolution had no sense of direction or any knowledge of its enemies. Zairian exile Lucien Naki said: "The gun, which was meant to protect the Zairian as a citizen and his property, is increasingly being used against the Zairian to take away his life and his property. People are often forced to flee so that their houses can be seized and looted. The disappearances are so numerous now that women fear for their husbands' safety if they are late in coming home from work. Many have vanished never to be seen again" (*New African*, May 1989; p. 41).

A similar situation existed in Ghana between 1981 and 1983. Those participating in the Rawlings revolution did not know who their real enemies were. The revolutionary cadres denounced as an enemy any Ghanaian who drove a nice car, regardless of the legitimacy of his acquisition of wealth. Worse, they misinterpreted the Rawlings revolution as a license to commit brutal acts against innocent people. Few Ghanaians wanted to be associated with such a revolution. The chiefs also distanced themselves from the brutal acts of the People's Defence Committee. *Daily Graphic* reported: "Most of the chiefs from the Central Region House of Chiefs at Cape Coast complained bitterly about the negative activities of the PDCs in their areas and called upon the government to take immediate action to stop acts of the PDCs which discredited the institution" (Dec 21, 1982; p. 8).

At the All-Africa Congress called by Kwame Nkrumah of Ghana in 1958, a young radical, Tom Mboya of Kenya, made an impassioned speech: "Europe is yesterday, Africa is tomorrow! . . . Hands off Africa!. . .Europeans get out of Africa! . . . Africans have had a belly full of Europeans!" By the middle of the 1980s, Africans had had a belly full of black neocolonialists, infantile revolutionaries and military buzzards who had ruined the continent.

The political regimes established by the elites were a far cry from what existed in traditional Africa. Even in that allegedly primitive and backward society there was much freedom, as we saw in Chapter 3. African chiefs did not perpetrate tyrannical acts against their own people. After independence, these chiefs watched in horror and dismay as their own traditional authority was abrogated and their powers severely curtailed by the nationalists.

## THE CULTURAL BETRAYAL

Despite their rhetoric, most African leaders did not value their own heritage and the significance of their indigenous systems. Instead, they copied alien systems to develop their countries. The new leaders stripped the traditional chiefs of their authority and actually set out to destroy indigenous systems through various government policies and civil wars.[3] Rejecting Western capitalism because of colonialism, they looked to the Eastern bloc for an alternative system. In addition, they recruited foreign ideologues and revolutionaries.

These new leaders acted as if Africa had no history, no culture, no native institutions, and no indigenous revolutionaries for its people to salute. We should recall that the Europeans used the same arguments to justify colonialism. Now the African leaders were using these arguments to support the imposition of Marxism and other alien "isms" on Africa.[4] These black neocolonialists were no different from the white colonialists.

The same African leaders who railed against Western denial of the intellectual capabilities of Africans placed more faith in expatriates and foreign systems than in their own African peoples. For years the Kamuzu Academy and Kamuzu Hospital, built and named after Malawi's Life-President Hastings Kamuzu Banda, did not employ black teachers and doctors. Blacks, according to this black African president, were not talented enough to fill these posts. Nor were they good enough to wear three-piece business suits. "Only to Banda belongs the right to wear a three-piece suit, top hat, carry a fly-whisk and ceremonial cane. Woe betide him that may exhibit the temerity to question or trample on this executive prerogative," Mabvuto Kapalepale (a Malawian) wrote (*New African*, Jul 1990; p. 36).

The *New York Times* corroborated the visible employment of expatriates: "Government bureaus are headed largely by expatriate professionals. For example, the head of the central bank is a German, and the man who runs the public works department is a Scot" (Apr 3, 1990; p. A6). The West German was Hans Joachim Lesshaft, appointed in July 1988. Before then, John Tembo, Banda's heir apparent, used to run the Central Bank but rather poorly. The IMF and the World Bank recommended the appointment of R. Mandinga, a highly experienced economist with respectable skills in the banking system. "However, Banda and his protégé John Tembo were not pleased with the recommendation. Mandinga died in a mysterious car accident between Blantyre and Zomba in July 1985" (*New African*, Jun 1990; p. 50). Decades of all-round repression drove many Malawian dissidents into exile. Banda "told dissidents in exile that they would become 'meat for crocodiles' if they came home" (*The Economist*, Mar 21, 1992; p. 46).

African leaders also proudly pointed to Timbuktu as a world-renowned ancient seat of learning and boasted of their world-class universities, comparable to those in the West. They seldom used them, however. They allowed the universities to decay, arbitrarily closed them at the slightest sign of student unrest, and jailed professors. Intellectual freedom, which was the hallmark of the ancient University of Sankore, was nowhere to be found in modern African universities.

Although African leaders declared that Africa had bright, highly qualified, locally trained experts, they never used them. When the military government of Ghana embarked upon a program of participatory democracy in 1987, it sought the services of a Bulgarian expert. Between 1986 and 1988 the government of Ghana recruited 265 foreign consultants whose fees and expenses amounted to 34 percent of the total compensation paid by the government to 200,000 of its employees. As the *West Africa* reported: "While consultancy fees paid to expatriate personnel range between $3,000 and $5,000 per month, that paid to public and civil servants with equivalent or sometimes higher qualifications and experience is $80-$200 per month . . . In addition to the huge salaries, the foreign experts receive fantastic conditions of service—furnished residential accommodation, office accommodation, logistics support, a vehicle, and the best hotel accommodation while travelling" (Dec 11-17, 1989; p. 2053).

Other examples of African leaders' failure to acknowledge African talent abound. Although they demanded respect, recognition, and various rights from the West, they rarely extended the same rights to their own people. They condemned the West; yet they secretly admired it. In fact, they went to extraordinary lengths to imitate the trappings of Western culture.

African leaders have spent billions of dollars on grandiose projects just to gain Western acceptance. For example, President Felix Houphouet-Boigny of the Ivory Coast built a $360 million basilica at Yamassoukrou. In 1977 President Jean-Bedel Bokassa of the Central African Republic spent $20 million to crown himself emperor because France once had one. In December 1989 President arap Moi announced that Kenya would build a $200 million 60-story building that would serve as the headquarters of the ruling Kenya African National Union (KANU) and would feature a four-story, larger-than-life statue of himself. "It will be the tallest office building in Africa," he boasted. When construction of the building was opposed for environmental reasons by Professor Wangari Maathai, President Moi attacked her. He claimed that because she was a woman, she had no right to criticize. The African tradition, President Moi said, was for women to respect men.[5] *The Economist* reported: "President Moi declared that she and other opponents should shut up, adding that they have 'insects in their heads.' When a lawyer wrote that such debates should be free, Mr. Moi told lawyers to be quiet" (Jan 13, 1990; p. 41).

Soon after, the Nairobi police evicted Professor Maathai's organization from the premises it had occupied for 10 years (*New York Times*, Dec 29, 1989; p. A5). On March 4, 1992, she and a group of women staged a hunger strike in a park to demand the release of political prisoners. In response, "heavily armed police officers swept through the tents in the downtown park and beat four women unconscious. Among those admitted to the hospital was Wangari Maathai" (*The New York Times*, Mar 5, 1992; p. A5).

The megalomaniacal obsession of African leaders with grandeur was driven by an inferiority complex and the need to prove something. On a personal level, this obsession was marked by punctilious attention to dress, the acquisition of grand palaces, monuments, basilicas, and other symbols of prestige. On the national level, the obsession manifested itself in the adoption of ruinous development models and projects, to the detriment of indigenous institutions.

African leaders imported or copied much from abroad in an attempt to prove that Africa was not backward but developed or developing. Tons of expensive agricultural machinery—even combine harvesters—were imported and many industries were haphazardly set up. After a very few years or even months of operation, most of these industries collapsed for lack of economic viability.

The case of food products in Ghana provides the most perverse example of imitation. The British colonialists were not used to African food and therefore imported tinned food. But Ghanaian elites never saw it that way. If the British administrators consumed it, so too should they. Accordingly, after independence, particularly from 1963 to 1985, the elite government declared 15 items that the colonialists had previously imported—including sardines, corned beef, and tinned milk—to be essential commodities and imported them. Absolutely no cognizance was taken of the fact that most Ghanaians, and indeed black Africans, do not produce the enzyme lactase, which is necessary for the digestion of milk. For these black Africans, the consumption of milk precipitates digestive disorders. But the government declared milk to be an essential commodity just because the white colonialists had consumed it. Naturally, the elites, imbued with an avid preference for imported food items, were not inclined to develop native dietary sources and spurned traditional foods. As a result, agriculture declined and the incidence of malnutrition soared.

With so much of their energy diverted toward acquiring symbols of modernity to prove their capabilities and to achieve acceptance, many African leaders and elites had little energy left to tackle the real problems facing the continent. Naturally, conditions worsened.

Black African leaders devoted much of their time to condemning the slave trade, racial injustices, colonialism, and American imperialism instead of taking steps to develop the economy of their resource-rich continent. Obsession with white injustices distracted black African leaders, like their counterparts in America, from utilizing the talents of their people.

The peasants of Africa, despite their alleged backwardness and lack of education, were capable of great achievements and economic miracles. They used their imagination and native intelligence to devise their own practical solutions to their problems. They did not copy or transplant alien solutions to Africa to prove anything. It is not Westerners but rather African leaders and elites who must accept or must be convinced of the capabilities of African natives.

And it is not the backwardness of the African people but the intellectual backwardness of African leaders and elites that keeps Africa in the economic doldrums. To turn President Moi's phrase around, it is the *leaders* who have "insects in their heads."

---

## NOTES

1. See the *Daily Nation*, Nairobi, March 26, 1990.
2. Dr. Tedla was arrested on December 19, 1979, and charged with "antirevolutionary activities." In early 1980, he was released and immediately began preparations for his escape. On July 4, 1980, he made a 14-day cross-desert journey to the Sudan and subsequently journeyed to the United States.
3. For more on this denigration and destruction of the indigenous, see Ayittey (1991, chap. 11).
4. Even in the 1990s, one was still hearing some self-serving colonial arguments from African heads of state. For example, the colonialists also argued that authoritarian rule was needed to check Africa's constantly warring tribes. In 1990, such African heads of state as President Moi of Kenya and Bongo of Gabon were using the same arguments to disallow a multiparty system. Multiple parties, they argued, will degenerate into tribal politics. While there is some element of truth in this observation, as attested to by Nigeria's experience with party politics in the First Republic, for example, precautions and effective steps can be taken against tribal politics. These will be explored in a later section. But it was interesting to note that almost all those opposed to the multiparty system were heads of state and those demanding it were their people. The people could not always be wrong.
5. President Moi was wrong about African tradition. He seemed to have forgotten that in indigenous African political systems, it is the role of queen mothers to choose kings and chiefs.

# Chapter 6

## Quasi-Apartheid Regimes in Black Africa

African dictators are some of the most hypocritical leaders anywhere. They condemn oppression of black people by apartheid, yet they organize widespread massacres of their own black people. More than 2,000 Kenyans were killed in cold blood by Moi's security forces at the Wajir massacre in Kenya.

— Koigi wa Wamwere, former member of parliament in Kenya[1]

The degeneration of black African political regimes toward tyranny was so systematic that by the 1980s most were indistinguishable in character from the detestable apartheid system in South Africa. In fact, by 1990 the political regimes in Africa had become so bizarre that one could not describe them as African, Western, or even Eastern. The accompanying table classifies the political regimes in 52 African countries on the basis of indigenous African standards. The degree of repression is a function of the extent to which a regime has violated civil liberties and other freedoms.

Of these political regimes, military rule is the most alien and repressive. As we have already seen, militarists (*abongo boys* or military "fufu-heads" as Ghanaian peasants call them) did not traditionally rule Africans.[2] To disguise the character of their governments, some military dictators have added a layer of civilian authority to their regimes, as in Liberia and Zaire. Despite the presence of these civilian collaborators, I have classified these regimes as military dictatorships. I have also classified the regimes that characterize themselves as revolutionary, for example, Burkina Faso and Ghana, as military dictatorships.[3] Civilian dictatorships are also alien to African tradition.

Most of the political systems in Africa in the 1980s bore uncanny similarities to the apartheid system in South Africa. Hence, I refer to them as "quasi-apartheid regimes."

## POLITICAL CONFIGURATION OF AFRICA BY 1990

1. MILITARY DICTATORSHIPS (years of military rule/years of independence)

| BRUTALLY REPRESSIVE | VERY REPRESSIVE | REPRESSIVE |
|---|---|---|
| *Benin (27/30) | Burundi (25/28) | Central African Republic (9/30) |
| Burkina Faso (20/30) | Congo-Brazzaville (12/30) | *Chad (15/30) |
| *Ethiopia (16/—) | Equitorial Guinea (11/22) | *Mali (22/30) |
| Ghana (20/33) | Guinea-Bissau (10/16) | Nigeria (20/30) |
| *Liberia (10/—) | Guinea (7/32) | Gabon (23/30) |
| Mauritania (12/30) | Lesotho (7/24) | |
| Libya (21/39) | Niger (16/30) | |
| *Somalia (21/30) | Rwanda (17/28) | |
| Sudan (27/34) | Togoland (27/30) | |
| Uganda (15/28) | Zaire (25/30) | |

SUBTOTAL: 25

2. CIVILIAN DICTATORSHIPS (years of one-party rule/years of independence)

| BRUTALLY REPRESSIVE | VERY REPRESSIVE | REPRESSIVE |
|---|---|---|
| *Angola (15/15) | Cameroon (30/30) | Algeria (28/28) |
| Comoros (14/14) | *Cape Verde Islands (15/15) | Côte d'Ivoire (30/30) |
| Malawi (26/26) | Madagascar (18/30) | Djibouti (13/13) |
| Mozambique (15/15) | Kenya (27/27) | Egypt (20/—) |
| Zimbabwe (10/10) | *Sao Tome & Principe (15/15) | Seychelles (13/14) |
| | Tanzania (29/29) | Sierra Leone (29/29) |
| | Tunisia (34/34) | |
| | Zambia (26/26) | |

SUBTOTAL: 19

| MONARCHICAL RULE | WHITES-ONLY RULE | INDIGENOUSLY AFRICAN (CONSENSUAL DEMOCRACY) |
|---|---|---|
| Morocco | *Namibia | Botswana |
| Swaziland | South Africa | Senegal |
| | | Mauritius |
| | | The Gambia |

TOTAL: 52

Notes:
1. Asterisks indicate countries where changes in government occurred in 1990-1991.
2. Réunion (a French island off Madagascar) and Western Sahara (under Moroccan rule) have been excluded.

## CHARACTERISTICS OF QUASI-APARTHEID REGIMES

### *The Caste System*

After independence, two classes emerged from African society: the elites and the peasants. There were five subgroups within the elite, or educated, class. The first included professional politicians, represented by the head of state, cabinet ministers, party functionaries, and leaders of the opposition parties, if any. The second was the intelligentsia, members of professional bodies, vice-chancellors of universities, university professors, and lawyers. The third was the military. The fourth included bureaucrats—civil servants and chairmen of public corporations. The final subgroup, the lowest level of elites, included urban workers and secondary school and university students.

Although the peasant class constituted over 95 percent of the population, they exercised no political power. Of the 45 black African countries, only four—Botswana, Mauritius, The Gambia, and Senegal—gave their people the right to choose their leaders. Twenty-three were military dictatorships. The rest were "democracies" where only one candidate ran for president under a one-party system, always won the election, and declared himself president-for-life.[4] For example, in Zambia's presidential election of October 1988, Zambians had a choice of voting "yes" or "no" for the only candidate—Life-President Kenneth Kaunda, who had been in power for 24 years. Kaunda won 95.5 percent of the vote. After the election, his defense minister, Alex Shapi, issued a sharp warning to those who voted against Kaunda: "You will be found out. And how shall we regard you as a citizen? For me you will be regarded as an enemy!" (*New African*, Jan 1989; p. 43). Yet Kaunda called Zambia a democratic republic derived from African traditions. But as S. B. Tejan-Sie, a Sierra Leonian lawyer based in Freetown, observed, "If anything, a system which confines political power to only one political group is alien to our culture and traditions and has failed politically and economically for over a decade and a half" (*West Africa*, Apr 23-29, 1990; p. 663).

Decay of democratic institutions and the abandonment of constitutional rule were ubiquitous in Africa; in many places they never even had a chance to develop. One angry Nigerian, Henry Esomonye, wrote:

> It is only in Africa where you still find life-presidents in the twentieth century. People live in perpetual fear of their rulers, yet we call for unity against apartheid. African leaders portray their countries as flowing with milk and honey, yet an average African citizen today is on the verge of economic ruin.

Eating has become a problem and personal freedoms are eroded. How then do we expect to achieve black emancipation in South Africa?. . . How can we call for black freedom in South Africa when we only succeed in oppressing one another after independence? Our fallen pan-Africanists must not die in vain (*New African*, Oct 1988; p. 36).

During the 1980s not a single black African dictatorship was democratized, despite massive foreign aid, Western tutelage, and quiet diplomatic pressure, not to mention the numerous constitutions ostensibly drafted for this purpose. Rather, there were movements in the opposite direction as military dictatorships replaced civilian governments in Burkina Faso (1983), Burundi (1987), the Central African Republic (1981), Ghana (1981), Nigeria (1983), Guinea (1984), Guinea Bissau (1980), Lesotho (1986), and Sudan (1989).

Since 1957 there have been more than 150 African heads of state. Only six in the history of postcolonial Africa up to 1990 relinquished political power voluntarily: General Olusegun Abasanjo of Nigeria (after 1 year); El Hadj Ahmadou Ahidjo of Cameroon (after 22 years); Abdul al Dahab of Sudan (after 1 year); Julius Nyerere of Tanzania (after 23 years); Leopold Senghor of Senegal (after 20 years); and Siaka Stevens of Sierra Leone (after 14 years). The rest looted their treasuries and mismanaged their economies until they were overthrown in military coups.

After independence, when the ruling elites called for "people's power," they meant elite power to brutalize the people. When the elites called for food and houses for the masses, they really meant food and houses for the elites. They rejected capitalism as a "colonialist and imperialist tool" and preached socialism. But under this type of socialism, they used their governing authority to extract wealth from the productive masses and deposit it in Swiss banks or, in emulation of Western or colonial societies, spent it on extravagant projects or goods for themselves.

Indeed, the standards of living enjoyed by the elites far outstripped those of the peasants. For example, in Mauritania, while the elites—the Arabs—had access to subsidized supplies of tap water, the peasants, often black, paid from 7 to 40 times more for their water from sellers on donkey carts. In 1982, while the leadership in Zaire earned between $5,000 and $9,000 a month, a peasant was lucky to earn $50 a month (*Africa Now*, Mar 1982; p. 17). In 1985, Cameroon, with a per capita income of less than $1,000 a year, was the world's ninth-largest importer of champagne. In Angola the socialist system also channeled the richest benefits to the least needy:

Angolans who own cars can fill their tanks for less than a dollar, and international telephone calls cost only pennies. One local boasts of getting a round-trip ticket to Paris on Air France for the equivalent of two cases of beer. Luanda does not even pick up its own garbage; the job is contracted out to a foreign company using Filipino workers lured to Angola with fat paychecks, special housing and First World garbage trucks.

Of course, the chief beneficiaries of all this are the city's westernized elite and their foreign business bedfellows. Many of life's necessities, on the other hand, are not available at subsidized prices. For the poorest residents, survival is impossible without resort to *candonga*, or illegal trading (*Insight*, Oct 1, 1990; p. 13).

Living conditions rapidly deteriorated in Zaire after independence in 1960. Food became expensive. By 1988, a 50-kilogram bag of cassava cost up to Z40,000 (zaires)—the equivalent of a managing director's monthly salary in a state corporation. At the universities, educational facilities had sharply crumbled. Classrooms were often crowded. Over 750 students were often crammed into 250-seat amphitheaters. Students, as a rule, had to arrive at 4:00 a.m. to reserve a seat for an 8:00 a.m. class in an oven-hot room. In the dormitories, students slept five to a room. University clinics were filthy. Hospitals lacked essential supplies, including water.

In the face of these deplorable living conditions, in February 1989 students and lecturers organized a peaceful delegation to press for improvements. Troops from the Special Presidential Brigade, the Civil Guard, and the 31st Commando Brigade were sent to quell the demonstration. According to the opposition in exile, 38 students were killed and 300 others injured (*New African*, May 1989; p. 10). The people of Benin, Guinea, Kenya, and Zambia have also witnessed the deaths or disappearances of hundreds of those protesting government policy.

Although the elites coveted the trappings of Western materialism, they urged their people to shun such trappings, to drop Western names, and to adopt authentic African names. In Zambia, interracial marriages were frowned upon. Those Zambians who had married non-African wives (called "toothless bulldogs") were told, when their wives wore skimpy clothes, that "our culture in matters of dress is not to go naked." The wearing of miniskirts, wigs, blue jeans, and tight trousers was condemned. Members of Zambia's Youth Brigade cut off the hair of Africans who had straightened theirs. In Chad, under President N'Garta Tombalbaye, some Africans who insisted on attending Western churches were shot, buried alive, or put to death in other excruciating circumstances between 1972 and 1974.

### Brutal Intolerance of Opposition

In 1990 one had difficulty naming four black African countries where a group of citizens could demonstrate and express their disenchantment with government policies without having bullets rained on them. After independence, the strikes, boycotts, and demonstrations that nationalists had used to protest colonial rule became treasonable offenses subject to capital punishment. Although President Kaunda of Zambia declared that his party was "organizing to bring into being a government of the people, by the people, and indeed for the people," by 1972 he had banned all parties except his own and had exiled or jailed their leaders. Countless thousands of Africans have been jailed or executed on trumped-up charges of plotting to overthrow their governments, as we shall see in Chapter 9.

One feature of Africa's independence was the casualty rate of the nationalists who did not become heads of state; most disappeared for one reason or another. The other feature of postcolonial Africa was the noticeable dearth of African writers, philosophers, and thinkers. As of 1990 less than 200 of Africa's 560 million people engaged in these pursuits—a telling indication of the insidious repression that prevailed over much of Africa.

### Savage Repression of the Peasant Majority

In black Africa the repression of the peasant majority was as heinous as the South African repression of blacks. From the 1960s, Africans' native freedoms and rights steadily eroded. Brutalities were heaped upon the peasants by the elite minority. With no political rights, the peasants had no channels through which to seek redress of their grievances. The police and the army, which were supposed to protect them, instead perpetrated crimes against them. Uganda offers a classic example: There, more than 800,000 people perished at the hands of Idi Amin, Milton Obote, and Tito Okello—all former Ugandan heads of state. When Idi Amin was killing peasants at the rate of 150 a day, the Organization of African Unity did nothing. One Ugandan Anglican bishop, Festo Kivengere, was quite irate:

> The OAU's silence has encouraged and indirectly contributed to the bloodshed in Africa. I mean, the OAU even went so far as to go to Kampala for its summit (in 1975) and make Amin its chairman. And at the very moment the heads of state were meeting in the conference hall, talking about the lack of human rights in southern Africa, three blocks away, in Amin torture chambers, my countrymen's heads were being smashed with sledge hammers and their legs being chopped off with axes (quoted in Lamb, 1984; p. 106).

Nor did the United Nations protest Amin's barbaric atrocities. As OAU chairman, Amin addressed the U.N. General Assembly on October 1, 1975, in a speech that denounced the "Zionist-U.S. conspiracy" and called not only for the expulsion but also the extinction of the state of Israel. The U.N. General Assembly gave him a standing ovation when he arrived, applauded him throughout his speech, and rose to its feet when he left. The next day, the U.N. Secretary-General and the president of the General Assembly gave a public dinner in Amin's honor.

Amin's reign of terror and slaughter is well known. Less well known but equally infamous was the regime of President Francisco Marcias Nguema of Equatorial Guinea. In 1972, just four years after his country won its independence from Spain, Nguema declared himself president-for-life. Backed by Cuba, he pursued a policy of systematic extermination of anyone who stood in the way of his attaining absolute power. He expelled Nigerian cocoa farmers to destroy the country's main industry and sank the fishing fleet to prevent anyone from escaping. He declared himself the only god and the "Miracle and Strength" of Equatorial Guinea and demanded that his portrait be placed on every altar. When the Catholic Church refused, Nguema unleashed a campaign of annihilation against his people, who were predominantly (95 percent) Catholic. By the time he was overthrown in a 1979 coup, he had massacred an estimated 50,000 people, or one-seventh of the country's population.

Sadly, little has changed since the days of Nguema and Amin:

> In a sustained army campaign to deprive the rebel Uganda People's Army (UPA) of access to villagers, at least 50,000 civilians have recently been detained in camps in Kumi area. In one incident, troops arrested 32 men in the Kanyum area, demanding to know the whereabouts of the rebels. When the men said they did not know, 16 of them were lined up and shot. The remaining 16 were ordered to throw the bodies into the bush. They were then tortured for 5 days before being released (*Index on Censorship*, May 1990; p. 40).

Senseless wars and ruinous strife have ravaged at least 15 African countries despite the threat of famine. Peasants have seen their lives and livelihoods recklessly disrupted by "crocodile liberators," leaving carnage and human debris in their wake. More than 8 million of them fled their villages to escape generalized conditions of terror and violence in Ethiopia, Mozambique, Sudan, Uganda, and other African countries.

In Angola, Burundi, Ethiopia, and Mozambique Africans have had to contend with passbook laws that allow peasants to travel only in certain areas. In other African countries, peasants have had to face curfews and roadblocks.

Only the select few from the ruling class had the passes or permits to pass through roadblocks and avoid curfews. For the majority without passes, harassment and brutalities awaited. In many black African countries, road-blocks became points where uniformed bandits robbed innocent passengers of their belongings. By 1990 the extortion stations had multiplied with bewildering frequency across West Africa (*West Africa*, Sep 10-16, 1990; p. 2428). Fed up with such extortion, the people of Sierra Leone began boy-cotting private and public transport because the fares had been rendered exorbitant by, among other things, illegal taxes imposed by police buccaneers.

## Inequitable Systems of Justice

After independence, a bifurcated system of justice emerged in black Africa: a lenient one for the elites and a swift and more brutal one for the peasants. When peasants ran afoul of the law, punishment was severe. In Ghana, a circuit court sentenced a peasant woman to five years' imprisonment with hard labor for attempting to smuggle $4.36 worth of cocoa to Togoland to buy some soap. The same court "sentenced a 22-year-old farmer, Geze Rose Adzo, to six years' imprisonment with hard labor for allegedly attempting to export a basketful of cocoa valued at C100 ($36.36)" (*Daily Graphic*, Jul 3, 1980; p. 8). But when the Ghana Cocoa Marketing Board, through wicked negligence, caused the country "to pay over $31 million in foreign exchange as penalty for failing to fulfil its obligations to overseas buyers," none of its elite directors was jailed or even reprimanded (*West Africa*, Mar 8, 1982; p. 683).

The ruling elites also smuggled, embezzled funds, plundered state trea-suries, and illegally transferred their funds abroad. But when corrupt ministers were caught—if at all—the sentences tended to be lenient or nonexistent: forfeiture of the booty or dismissals or transfers from posts. For example, in Guinea "President Lansana Conte, after sacking the former Minister for Information, Culture and Tourism, reassigned him as Ambassador to Wash-ington. This is a man who is alleged to have used state funds to build five houses in record time" (*West Africa*, May 21-27, 1990; p. 832). Similarly, at Burkina Faso's corruption trials in January 1984, former President Sangoule Lamizana, who could not account for about $1 million he was charged with embezzling, was merely acquitted (*West Africa*, Jan 16, 1984; p. 133). Embez-zlement and gross abuse of office were also documented in Ghana, Nigeria, The Gambia, and Togoland.

## Economic Exploitation of the Majority

In black Africa the elite minority used various devices to exploit the peasant majority. As we saw, instead of allowing market forces to set prices, in accordance with African tradition, many African governments dictated the prices peasants could receive for their produce. Under a system of price controls, Africa's peasants came to pay some of the world's most confiscatory taxes. They faced stiff penalties and outright confiscation of their produce if they sold it at prices above the government-controlled prices.

In Ghana, cocoa farmers received less than 10 percent of the world market price for their produce in 1983. At the same time, peanut producers in Gambia received about 20 percent of the world market price. According to *West Africa*:

> On the average, between 1964/65 and 1984/85, the peasants of Gambia were robbed of 60 percent of the international price of their groundnuts! For 20 years, the Jawara Government "officially" took, free of charge, 3 out of every 5 bags, leaving the peasant with a gross of 2. With deductions for subsistence credit fertiliser, seeds, etc., the peasant would end up with a net one bag out of five... With these facts, it is simply wrong to say that the poverty of the peasant derives from the defects of nature—drought, overpopulation, laziness, and so on (Feb 15, 1989; p. 250).

In 1981 the government of Tanzania paid peasant maize farmers only 20 percent of the free market price for their produce. Meanwhile, the International Labor Organization found that "taxation levels in the agricultural sector in Sierra Leone averaged between 30 and 60 percent of gross income" (*West Africa*, Feb 15, 1982; p. 446).

When Zambian traders refused to sell their produce at government-dictated prices in 1988, authorities raided the markets. They arrested hundreds of people, took their money, tore down market stalls, and seized sugar, detergents, salt, maize meal, soft drinks, candles, flour, and clothing. Back in 1984 in Ghana, Mr. Kwame Forson, the Agona Swedru district secretary, urged "some unidentified soldiers who make brief stopovers at Swedru to check prices, and instead threaten and rob innocent traders, to desist from such acts" (*West Africa*, Jul 23, 1984; p. 1511).

## ARAB APARTHEID

In some parts of Africa there is a dominant Islam which allows practically no room for other religions . . . in other countries, there is a dangerous confrontation between Moslems and non-Moslems.

—Vatican Report, July 1990

For a long time in the postcolonial era, black Africans regarded Arabs as brothers and expressed solidarity with Arab causes and campaigns against Zionism. But of late, institutionalized racism by Arabs against black Africans has become a growing problem in Africa, especially in Mauritania, Sudan, and Tanzania. In Mauritania blacks have no political power and cannot vote. Like their counterparts in South Africa, they are persecuted and discriminated against by the Arabs. Ben Penglase of Africa Watch, a human rights group based in New York, wrote:

The ruling Arab-Berber Government of Mauritania, as a part of its continuing violence against black Mauritanians, arrested between 1,000 and 3,000 black Mauritanians during the last months of 1990 and the beginning of 1991, and held them in incommunicado detention. When this huge group of detainees began to be released in April 1991, details emerged of the deaths of at least 200 prisoners, most of them as a result of severe torture or extrajudicial execution...

Between 1989 and 1990, the Government forcibly expelled from the country into neighboring Senegal and Mali as many as 80,000 black Mauritanians, mostly members of the Halpulaar, Wolof, Soninke and Bambara ethnic groups.

Among the litany of abuses, the Government has burned and destroyed entire villages, and forcibly confiscated livestock, land and belongings of black Mauritanians . . . In addition, slavery persists despite its having been officially banned in 1980 (*The New York Times*, Jun 17, 1991; p. A14).

There is still slavery in Mauritania in this day and age. Africa Watch estimates that "there are between 100,000 total slaves and 300,000 part slaves and former black slaves in the service of Arab masters" (*Africa Report*, Sep-Oct 1990; p. 7).

On April 6, 1992, the *Washington Times* carried a story about Salkha Mint M'Bareck, a 14-year-old black slave girl, and the attempts to free her.

She told police she was given to a new master as partial payment for a car. She went to police after escaping but was ultimately forced back into bondage . . .

"These are people who are paid no salaries, have no rights and can be tortured and even killed by their owners with impunity," said Messaoude Ould Boulkheir, a former slave who leads the emancipation movement *El Hor* (the Free) . . .

The International Labor Organization, a United Nations agency, cites "continuing reports of forced labor, kidnapping of children and of torture meted out to slaves who try to escape."

Hundreds of people who work in factories and mines are also slaves, Mr. Boulkheir said. "Their wages are paid to their masters, who give them enough food to live on, clothe them, and that's it" (p. A9).

Similarly in Sudan Arabs enslave members of the Dinka tribe. According to *The Economist*: "Arab tribal militias formed and armed by the northern-dominated government are trafficking in slaves from the southern Dinka tribe. Dinka children and women seized in raids are either kept by the militias or sold north. In February 1988 a Dinka child could be bought for $90; so many slaves are available that the price has now fallen to $15" (Jan 6, 1990; p. 42).

The military regime of Lt. Gen. Omar Hassan Bashir of Sudan, who overthrew Sadiq al-Mahdi's elected civilian government in June 1989, has vowed to reimpose the *sharia* (Islamic law). Under this law theft is punishable by amputation of the right hand or, if there are more than three people or weapons involved, cross amputation: right hand, left foot. Defamation and drinking alcohol are punishable by flogging, as is adultery or, if both of the partners are married, by stoning to death. Apostasy, defined as the renunciation of Islam, is punishable by public execution with the body left on public display.

There is more to the *sharia* than amputations and executions, however. According to Abdullahi an-Na'im, a legal scholar, the *sharia* limits the rights of those who do not belong to the Islamic faith:

> Shari'a does not conceive of the permanent residence of unbelievers within an Islamic state. At best, unbelievers may be allowed to stay under the terms of a special compact which extremely restricts their civil and political rights. Believers who are not Muslims, mainly Jews and Christians, are allowed partial citizenship under *shari'a*.
>
> In exchange for being allowed to conduct their private affairs in accordance with their beliefs and customs while enjoying Muslim protection, these peoples, known in *shari'a* as *dhimmis*, must pay a special tax, *jiziah*, and are disqualified from holding any position of authority over Muslims. As such, *dhimmis* are disqualified from holding general executive or judicial office in their own country" (*Africa Report*, Sep-Oct 1990; p. 60).

Indeed, Kayango Lewis, an exiled Sudanese in Riyadh, Saudi Arabia, complained: "Most ministerial appointments since independence [in 1956] have been given to Muslim-Arabs from minority tribes in the north, neglecting the civil rights of the majority African tribes and in the end making them second class citizens" (*New African*, Oct 1990; p. 50). In addition, the Catholic Church has come under increasing attack, with southern Christians often being denied their right to worship, with the media disseminating anti-Christian propaganda, and with certain areas of Sudan being declared out of bounds for Christians. Former Sudanese Foreign Minister Francis Deng described the depth of discrimination against non-Muslims in his country: "A prominent person from a dominant religious sect intimated to me recently that they had been receiving letters from their followers inquiring whether killing a Dinka was forbidden or ordained by Islam" (*Africa Report*, Sep-Oct 1990, p. 61).

Abdelwahab El-Affendi (1992), a Sudanese intellectual and former diplomat, wrote:

Sharia can rule truly only when the community observing it perceives this as a liberating act, as the true fulfillment of the self and the moral worth of the community and each individual within it, for *sharia* can never be imposed. When it is imposed it is not *sharia*. When only coercion underpins *sharia*, it becomes hypocrisy . . . A despotic and illegal regime does not bestow legitimacy on subsidiary actions (cited in *New African*, Mar 1992; p. 33).

But Lieutenant General Bashir showed no signs of relenting in his move to impose the *sharia*: "My junta will destroy anyone who stands in the way... and amputate [the limbs of] those who betray the nation (*Africa Report*, Jan-Feb 1989; p.63)." Indeed, a prosperous merchant was hanged, despite diplomatic protests, for illegal possession of a small amount of foreign currency, and others were executed for foreign currency offenses. Amnesty International reported widespread torture and killings of civilians. In addition, "Lt.-Gen Omar Bashir himself is reputed to have a number of Dinka and Nuer slaves in his own home, from the time he was military commander in Muglad, south-west Sudan" (*New African*, Jul 1990; p. 9). *Al-Wafd*, an Egyptian opposition daily newspaper, reported that Bashir secretly visited Baghdad immediately after the invasion of Kuwait in August 1990 in support of Iraqi President Saddam Hussein. According to the report, that support was "apparently in thanks for a major shipment of [chemical] weapons . . . There have been unconfirmed rumors in the past, according to the *Guardian*, that Khartoum had used chemical weapons against non-Muslim rebels in the southern part of the country (*Africa Insider*, Aug 1990; p. 5).

In February 1992 the Bashir government drove 400,000 squatters—mostly black refugees fleeing the war in the south—out of Khartoum at gunpoint and into the desert, where temperatures can reach 120 to 135 degrees. At least a dozen squatters who resisted eviction were shot. "The scale of the callousness is hard to imagine . . . That the government wasted no time bulldozing the homes is matched in ruthlessness only by the official decision to send the displaced to campsites where water, food, sanitation, health facilities and adequate shelter are wholly insufficient or don't exist at all," wrote the *Washington Post* in an editorial (Mar 14, 1992).

Bashir's brutal treatment of non-Muslims was also evident in his use of food as a weapon. Despite the famine in 1990, the Muslim north deliberately blocked supplies to the south, where previous famines have hit hardest: "Trains and barges have been held up, surplus food stocks exported overseas and the Sudanese Air Force has even bombed relief sites, U.S. State Department officials said" (*Washington Post*, Oct 6, 1990; p. A22). In addition, in 1990 the Bashir regime exported 300,000 tons of sorghum, a staple food, to Libya and Iraq for the purchase of arms to use against rebels in the south. Nevertheless, in September 1990 Bashir attended the United Nations Summit for Children in New York and won applause when he claimed that his government's priority was children. As he spoke, his war planes were bombing civilian targets in southern Sudan and killing hungry black children.

Under an oppressive Islamic rule in Sudan, a wave of political terror claimed doctors, lawyers, journalists, poets, and trade unionists. Hundreds were detained and executed for the crime of dissent. Before Bashir seized power, Khartoum boasted of 40 newspapers and periodicals; its press was one of the freest on the continent. After the coup, Bashir gagged the press, abolished trade unions, and stripped political parties of their property. He entertained much grander designs: the spread of Islamic fundamentalism and the establishment of Iranian-style Muslim theocratic states in North Africa. Significantly, "Iranian President Ali Akbar Hashemi-Rafsanjani arrived for a state visit in Khartoum in Dec 1991, accompanied by more than 150 senior officials. Iran agreed to supply oil to replace the former shipments from Libya, as well as food and other economic assistance. In addition, Iran is supplying Chinese F-7 jet fighters, along with Chinese-made tanks, anti-tank missiles and armored personnel carriers" (*The Wall Street Journal*, Mar 16, 1992; p. A10).

The Islamic leadership in much of Africa has also been a failure. It is time the leadership in Africa—black, Muslim, and white—display a better sense of direction, tolerance and respect for Africa's immense cultural/ethnic diversity. Non-Muslims in Mauritania, Libya, and Nigeria have suffered oppression similar to that in Sudan. And in Kenya, among the Muslims, there is discrimination against members of the black Ismaili sect (*New African*, Mar 1990; p. 18). As we observed earlier, Islam is *not* indigenous to Africa. Even Muslim Ali Mazrui (1986) agrees, "In the seventh century A.D., Islam was brought to Egypt by Arab conquerors" (p. 46). Technically, then, there is no difference between the Arabs and the Europeans; both were colonizers in Africa.

Africa has always been hospitable to Arabs and other foreigners and will continue to be so as long as they respect the dignity and wishes of the African people. Islamic fanaticism and racism have no more place in Africa than apartheid has in South Africa or Marxism in Angola. By the year 2000 Islamic fundamentalism will collapse in Iran, just as communism bit the dust in the former Soviet Union. In May 1992 four days of rioting in the holy city of Mashdad in northeastern Iran were a sign of serious disaffection against the ruling mullahs. The riots followed disturbances in other centers such as Shiraz, Arak and Tabriz. "Asked to comment on the fruits of the [Islamic] revolution in Iran, a shopkeeper named Ali said it had 'brought nothing but corruption, the destruction of morale especially among the young and widespread drug-taking" (Financial Times, Jun 12, 1992; p. 4).

As we noted in Chapter 3, subsequent generations of Muslims, who ventured south of the Sahara, settled peacefully in black Africa. They made little effort to impose the sharia on Africans by force and showed a great deal of religious tolerance as well as respect for them and their cultures. For example, the Akans refused to accept Islam, yet they coexisted peacefully with Muslims in the Islamic empire of Ghana. But today's Arabs in Africa tend to be of a different breed. Islamic fundamentalism is tearing Sudan, Mauritania, and Nigeria asunder and threatens other African countries.

Africans have begun to urge the press to expose the intensity of the Islamic threat to freedom. Aloysius Juryit of Nigeria complained to the New African about Arabic racism: "Events in the Sudan and Mauritania (to mention only a few) have shown that the worst racists are Arabs, especially when it comes to dealing with blacks. It is the duty of the world press, especially New African, to expose all the atrocities being committed by independent African leaders against their citizens. Apartheid is bad, but apartheid should not be fought at the expense of freedom in independent African countries" (Mar 1990, p. 6).

B. Kontorfili of Nsukka, Nigeria, was even more irate: "Mauritanian history did not begin with the arrival of Arab tribesmen from the Arabian peninsula. The Soninke and other African people had civilizations which flourished long before the coming of the first Arab slave traders and conquerors. What the African people of Mauritania now demand, and which must receive the full and unconditional backing of the OAU and ECOWAS, is respect for their true dignity, not a repressive dose of Arabisation!" (West Africa, May 27-Jun 2, 1991; p. 865).

Of course, the Arabs themselves have also been victims of religious bigotry, in Chad. For example, French-educated Christian southerners governed Chad in the 1960s, discriminating against the northerners, mostly Arabs and Muslims. The northerners rebelled and civil war ensued. In Ethiopia, Muslims have long been persecuted, under both Emperor Haile Selassie and Comrade Mengistu Haile Mariam:

> In the Hararghe province, a number of Muslim community leaders, elders and religious teachers were tortured and killed in early Dec 1986 . . . Witnesses told how the men's tongues were cut out before they were shot in front of their students . . .
>
> A secret policy document (1981) noted it was 'necessary to employ new methods and tactics to destroy the Muslims' (*Index on Censorship,* Apr 1987; p. 33).

Furthermore, not all of Africa's Muslim heads of state have been religious bigots. For example, Presidents Abdou Diouf of Senegal, Sir Dawda Jawara of The Gambia, and Ali Hassan Mwinyi of Tanzania are among those leaders who demonstrated exemplary religious tolerance. In particular, President Mwinyi did not allow the Islamic faith of his ministers to shield them from disciplinary measures in the event of incompetence or corruption. In April 1990 Mwinyi told his ministers: "You have failed the party and the people. There is widespread corruption, there is no sense of responsibility and there is general laxity all around. You should resign today" (*New African,* May 1990; p. 19). He then dissolved the cabinet and demanded the immediate resignation of all 26 ministers, including premier Joseph S. Warioba.

There is only one solution, not only for Islamic-dominated African states but for all of Africa: removing religion—both Islam and non-Islam—from politics and government. In addition, Africa needs more heads of state like Mwinyi, regardless of their religion, ethnicity, or race. But if African heads of state can reshuffle their cabinets, the people must have the same right to reshuffle the heads of state. Most Africans are fed up with tyrannical leaders.

## COURAGEOUS AFRICAN VOICES

Many are troubled by parallels between postcolonial black tyranny or Arab apartheid and European colonialism or the apartheid system in South Africa. They argue that such comparative statements only serve to justify colonialism and apartheid. But if leaders in independent African nations—*both* black and Arab—condemn colonialism as evil and apartheid as an abomination, why should they act in ways worse than those of the European colonialists and the racists of South Africa? Must Africans or the world conceal this filthy disgrace and wash only the dirty linen of the whites in South Africa?

Others fear that exposing postcolonial African tyranny would divert attention from the inviolable cause of the blacks in South Africa. Still others believe that freedom must be granted to the blacks in South Africa before the world turns its attention to the plight of the 450 million blacks in independent Africa. While these various theses are understandable, they are fraught with inherent inconsistencies that for several reasons could exacerbate the crisis for all of Africa.

First, discriminating between which oppressed blacks to help—the 25 million in South Africa or the 450 million in black Africa—extends the very principle of segregation that the apartheid regime embraces. While the racists discriminate on the basis of color, the world seems to discriminate among oppressed black Africans on the basis of nationality.

Second, ignoring the heinous tyranny in black Africa passively condones black African tyranny as long as the tyrants are black. This insidious form of racism suggests that white rulers in Africa must be held accountable to a higher moral standard than black leaders face. Africans vehemently object to this treacherous double standard. To their dead compatriots, the color of the hand that killed them made little difference. Vehement denunciation of apartheid without a parallel condemnation of tyranny in black Africa serves only to perpetuate the myth of black inferiority and to accentuate the suffering of all black Africans.

Third, what many black African leaders do to their people has for years aided and abetted apartheid. Although apartheid is an *institutionalized* form of racism, when the issue is stripped of its emotional rhetoric there is really little difference between that system and black tyranny in independent Africa. The instruments of oppression are identical virtually everywhere on the African continent. Tyranny is tyranny, regardless of the race of the tyrant. Black-on-black tyranny is as ethically abhorrent as white-on-black oppression.[5]

Fourth, having African tyrants such as Idi Amin and Lieutenant Colonel Mengistu lead the campaign against apartheid impugns the legitimacy of the noble cause of black freedom in South Africa. How can those who do not understand freedom lead a battle to free others? How are the racists in South Africa supposed to react to demands for freedom for blacks when they see black African leaders of the north slaughtering their own people? Even some African leaders themselves see this problem. In a speech to the Organization of African Unity in 1986, President Yoweri Kaguta Museveni of Uganda said: "Africa's silence in the face of gross abuses by tyrants undermines its moral authority to condemn the excesses of others such as the regime in South Africa" (*Daily Telegraph*, Jul 30, 1986).

Fifth, the argument that freedom must first be won for the blacks in South Africa holds hostage the plight of blacks in independent Africa. Africans will never accept the position that, until a resolution is found to the apartheid problem in South Africa, they must resign themselves to wanton slaughter and oppression. Africans have waited since 1960 for a solution to the apartheid problem. In fact, for thousands of them, it is too late—they are already dead. And many of those living cannot wait any longer.

Sixth, a large number of Africans are now speaking out angrily against brutal despotism in independent Africa and the hypocrisy of its leaders on the apartheid issue. In a letter to the *New African* N. W. Awere wrote, "As a Ghanaian living in Transkei, South Africa, I wonder whether African leaders have any moral grounds to condemn South Africa. Which African country is a democracy in the true sense of the word?" (Nov 1988; p. 4). At the Nairobi All-Africa Conference of Churches in December 1987, Bishop Desmond Tutu was also forthright: "It is sad that South Africa is noted for its vicious violation of human rights. But it is also very sad to note that in many black African countries today, there is less freedom than there was during that much-maligned colonial period" (*The Wall Street Journal*, Jan 7, 1988; p. 18). Feeling betrayed, black Africans themselves are denouncing tyranny and demanding from their leaders the same political freedom, power-sharing, and right to choose their leaders as their brothers and sisters in South Africa. Does the world listen to cries for help from black Africans?

On April 12, 1987, the Right Reverend Alexander Kipsang Muge, Bishop of the Eldoret Diocese of the Anglican Church Province of Kenya, opened his sermon saying:

> People are the victim of threats, fear and tyranny. For how long will these injustices and humiliations continue in our country? What is the point of protesting against injustices in South Africa when there are worse violations of human rights at home? There is no difference whether a violation of human rights is committed by a white man or a black man, that is immaterial. The truth is, some of the violations of human rights in this country are no different from those of South Africa (*Index on Censorship*, Jul 1990; p. 21).

Pressure on South Africa has succeeded to some degree in improving conditions there. The pass laws have been abolished. A bill of human rights has been drawn up, and the apartheid regime has been making hesitant steps toward reform. Nelson Mandela has been released from jail after 27 years of incarceration, and bans on more than 30 political parties and antiapartheid

organizations have been lifted. Much more, of course, needs to be done in
South Africa.

If pressure on South Africa can achieve some results, the same pressure
on black African leaders should also achieve results. But where is this
pressure? In fact, *greater* pressure must be applied against black Africa since,
in the words of black American author Chancellor Williams (1987), "Black
Africa can never effectively deal with white-ruled areas until it deals with
Black Africa itself first" (p. 314).

When South Africa legalized more than 30 political parties, including the
Communist Party of South Africa, and released Nelson Mandela from jail,
Zambia's President Kaunda exclaimed: "What a glorious day!" Few noticed
that Zambia was a one-party state where all other political parties had been
outlawed and Life-President Kaunda did not entertain thoughts of sharing
power. One would have thought that African leaders who had been advocating a multiparty system for South Africa would themselves release the
political prisoners languishing in their jails and lift the ban on other parties.
But the standards to which they held others were not to be applied to
themselves.

Even more perverse was the hypocritical behavior of the Economic
Community of West African States (ECOWAS) in attempting to quell the
political turmoil, killings, and destruction of property in Liberia's tribal war.
Meeting in Banjul, The Gambia, the heads of state of ECOWAS proposed
an immediate end to the conflict by sending multinational troops from The
Gambia, Ghana, Guinea, Mali, Nigeria, and Sierra Leone to enforce a
cease-fire. In addition, ECOWAS adopted a resolution that the factions
should accept an early holding of free and fair elections with the participation
of all. According to *West Africa*, "Sources said ECOWAS has made it clear to
Mr. Charles Taylor that even if he wins the military war, he would forever
have lost the peace. They pointed out to him that he stands the best chance
of organizing a political party and he could go out to campaign *to gain
legitimacy* for his cause in restoring *constitutional democracy* to Liberia. The
sources said ECOWAS saw the present situation as one that could be used
to address the political ills in Liberia and Taylor could go down in history as
one who put Liberia on the right course (Aug 6-12, 1990; p. 2236; emphasis
added).

Few realized that what they were prescribing for Liberia was absent in
their own countries. Out of the 15 countries in the West African subregion,
only The Gambia and Senegal had constitutional democracy and allowed the
participation of all shades of political expression as well as free and fair
elections. As for the rest, what they advocated for others was not for them.

The Fanti of Ghana have a proverb: "Before you give somebody a piece of cloth, check to see if yours is all right."

In the summer of 1988, when the Reverend Jesse Jackson ran for the Democratic presidential nomination in a predominantly white country (the United States), he uplifted the hopes and aspirations of many blacks worldwide. Certainly, he could not have run in South Africa. But the shameful irony was that in 1990 he could not have run in 41 out of the 45 black African nations. A black man could not run for president in a black man's land! It is a disgrace that many blacks in their own black African countries have no voice or the right to choose their leaders.

---

## NOTES

1. In *Index on Censorship*, July 1990; p. 22.
2. "Fufu" is a Ghanaian dish and is prepared by pounding cooked cassava (manioc) into a pulp. It is served with soup—palm nut, groundnut or light soup.
3. Some scholars may express doubts about the classification of Senegal and Mauritius as democratic. It is often claimed that, although there are other political parties in Senegal, it is a de facto one-party state. Mauritius is a republic within the Commonwealth and recognizes the Queen of England as its head. Further, the government is formed by a coalition of political parties, which may sound similar to the union of the political parties in Zimbabwe.
4. One joke that was making the rounds in Africa recently went like this: Question: What's a life-president? Answer: A head of state who should be in prison for life!
5. Even in South Africa, this incapacity to apply the same standard has appeared. Escalating black-on-black violence has claimed more than 10,000 lives since 1984. Yet nobody wants to talk about this deadly factionalism.

# Chapter 7

## Military Regimes:
## Rule by "Uniformed Buzzards"

Any government which is not elected by the people will be crushed, no matter the number of people killed. Africans are fed up with coups and the one-party governments. The fall of dictator Doe is a clear warning to the dictators in Africa.

—Osei Tutu, a Ghanaian

The military should not get itself involved in politics. The sooner they leave the stage the better, or else the people may rise up against them.

—General Yakubu Gowon, former Nigerian head of state

The involvement of the military in African politics was gradual. In the first decade of independence, soldiers were barely seen in public, much less in politics. Traditionally, Africans were not used to military institutions. There were generally no standing armies in indigenous Africa, except in the Asante, Dahomey, Zulu, and Muslim states. For the rest of Africans—more than 2,000 tribes—the people constituted the army. In the event of imminent war the chief would summon young men of certain age-grades to his residence and lead them into battle. After the cessation of hostilities, the "peoples' army" was disbanded so that it did not act as a drain on the tribal economy.

Standing armies were introduced into Africa by the colonialists to enforce their rule and suppress African aspirations for freedom. Armies were thus viewed as agents of imperialism and instruments of oppression. Widespread discriminatory practices also compounded Africans' distrust and abhorrence of the military. For example, although Ghana had a relatively large educated elite in 1957, only about 10 percent of the army officers were native Ghanaians. In the Belgian Congo in 1960 the *Force Publique* had no African officers to lead its 24,000 recruits. Additionally, many African nationalists, such as Felix Houphouet-Boigny of the Ivory Coast and Julius Nyerere of Tanzania, opposed an expansion of the military establishment.

Changing circumstances, however, drew and accelerated the involvement of the military in politics.

## CAUSES OF MILITARY INTERVENTION

Four factors may be identified. The first was the increasing recognition of the role of the military in pan-Africanism that was directly attributable to Kwame Nkrumah of Ghana. He maintained that there was a need to establish an All-African Command Guard, not only to liberate the other African colonies, but also to fight the forces of imperialism and racism throughout the African continent. The small army he created continued to grow after independence. By the end of 1959 his army comprised one brigade and three battalions equipped with modern weapons. When the Congo crisis emerged in 1960, Nkrumah was the first to place his army at the disposal of the Congolese government to restore order.

However, the expansion of his army rankled many Africans within and outside Ghana. President Houphouet-Boigny asked, "Do you believe, my brothers, that Ghana's four battalions which have already cost our good friend Nkrumah millions . . . serve any useful purpose except his own false prestige?" (cited in Italiaander, 1961). Sylvanus Olympio, the prime minister of the neighboring Republic of Togo, was also apprehensive about Nkrumah's army since he, like Houphouet-Boigny, differed with Nkrumah on ideological grounds.

The second factor was the self-preservation of the elites in power. The popularity of postcolonial governments began to wane because of human rights abuses and suppression of civil liberties. To bolster their political legitimacy or add recognition and some credibility, the elites increased expenditures on the military and beefed up their presence in the political arena to intimidate or deter political malcontents. In Ghana, the opposition charged that the purpose of Nkrumah's army was to strengthen the one-party system and his own personal power.

The third factor that accelerated military intervention in government was the nationalists' generally lackluster and scandalous performance on the economic and political fronts. Virtually all of the nationalists who led the struggle for independence from colonial rule in the 1950s and 1960s subsequently became heads of their respective African states. But in practically every case, they led their countries down the path of economic ruin.

The political parties they established soon turned into patronage machines that doled out government largesse to their lackeys, and government administration discredited itself by engaging in venality, graft, gross mismanagement, and personal aggrandizement. Since power was concentrated in the hands of a single person or an oligarchy, schisms emerged within the government party and the country. In many countries, such as Nigeria, ethnic and religious undercurrents exacerbated the divisions, making national unity, administrative efficiency and open government impossible to achieve. The military, an institution dedicated to upholding these tenets, claimed it could not stand idly by. Therefore, it mobilized to save the country. Commenting on the proliferation of military regimes in Africa, the president of Mali, General Moussa Traore, observed, "The absence of institutions to build national unity is what brought about both the one-party states and military rule" (*Washington Times,* Oct 8, 1990; p. A8).

The fourth and final factor accounting for increasing military participation in African government was purely selfish—personal ambitions became dominant. Acting as any other politically vocal group, the military sought to increase its own share of government largesse through intimidation, blackmail, and the forcible takeover of the government itself.

The actual confluence of factors that provoked the military to seize power varied from one African country to another. In Upper Volta (now Burkina Faso) President Maurice Yameogo's extravagance at a time of austerity and his insensitivity to general suffering forced the military hand in a coup in 1966. In Togoland unemployment and widespread corruption were factors. In Ghana discontent over high prices, shortages of essential commodities, and the imposition of import controls ignited the 1966 coup. In Tanzania, Uganda, and Kenya, discontent within the military itself over salaries, promotions, and other amenities sparked mutinies. Similar motives also lay behind Col. Ignatius Kutu Acheampong's military takeover of Ghana's civilian government in 1972.

A spate of coups quickly swept across Africa in the early 1960s. The first occurred in the Belgian Congo on September 15, 1960, barely three months after independence. In West Africa the first coup occurred in Togo on January 13, 1963. Between 1963 and February 1966 there were 14 significant cases of military intervention in government. By 1968 there had been 64 attempted and successful interventions across Africa.

The first generation of coup leaders in the 1960s were professional soldiers, with little tolerance for inefficiency, government waste, and mismanagement. Most cleaned up the government house, injected discipline in the civil service, and retired to their barracks. These soldiers, whose purpose was to throw out the elite *bazongas* (raiders of the public treasury), were hailed as "saviors" and idolized by the people. But public adulation soon turned into terror when the soldiers unleashed brutalities against the people and continued with the same old misguided policies. For example, General Traore of Mali came to power in a 1968 military coup which overthrew a left-wing government that pursued policies of nationalization and embraced Soviet ideology. But Traore introduced no institutions to build national unity. In fact, he retained the one-party state system and won unopposed presidential elections in 1979, 1984, and 1989 for successive five-year terms.

The second generation of military rulers, who assumed control in the 1970s, turned out to be more corrupt, incompetent, and brutally tyrannical than the civilian administrations they replaced. They ruined one African economy after another with brutal efficiency and looted African treasuries with military discipline. Africans watched helplessly as they experienced yet another betrayal.

The next batch of military rulers was even more execrable, leaving wanton destruction and carnage in their wake. In fact Mokwugo Okoye, a Nigerian, saw no difference between these soldiers and the colonials:

> Any sober student of history must have observed a close parallel, in their undisguised paternalism and regimentation, between a colonial regime and a military junta. Both see the people as backward and therefore in need of some external agency to teach them the ways of civilisation. . . .
>
> The belief that the armed forces alone know all the answers to a country's multifarious problems—constitutional, economic, educational and political—obliges them to intervene even in fields in which they have little or no expertise until, like a bull in a China shop, they make a mess of most socio-political institutions of their country (*African Guardian*, Jul 30, 1990; p. 7).

Sierra Leonian clergyman Orishatuke Faduma probably had the military in mind when he classified men into two categories in 1919:

> The first class is composed of men with spiritual and ideal natures who look up and forward and are full of dreams and visions. They belong to the class anthropos. The second class is composed of those who are degenerates, animals in their relation to their fellow men. These belong to the class kantanthropos or kanthropos. Anthropic men are by nature and temperament constructionist. They love to put things together. They pick up fragments of thought and deeds and succeed in putting them to shape and use. They know instinctively the relativity of knowledge and action. Their work is that of the synthesis. Kanthropic men are by nature destroyers. They love to break to pieces what

others through much labour and tribulation put together. They are human buzzards, called in local parlance *gu-nu-gu*, and easily find out where offensive matter is. They do not, like buzzards, eat up and destroy what is malodorous but on the contrary love to scatter it among men and cause great injury thereby. They are not valuable scavengers like the well-known birds (cited by Langley, 1979; p. 73).

## PERFORMANCE OF MILITARY REGIMES

The soldiers who booted out the corrupt politicians considered it their professional duty to inject discipline into government administration and save their countries from naked mismanagement. They resorted to draconian measures and brutal tactics to establish an efficient administration. But how well did they perform?

The professional disciplinarians were themselves grotesquely undisciplined and ineffective. Flight Lt. Jerry Rawlings of Ghana offered this assessment of the performance of his own military regime, eight years after seizing power:

> Despite probes, Committees of Enquiry, dismissals and prosecutions of wrong-doers, despite restructuring exercises, new management, the provision of new equipment and capital, many of our organizations, state enterprises and corporations continue to swallow public money and fail to provide the services and goods which we expect of them, and also fail to pay their tax obligations, dividends and other expected revenues . . .
>
> Too many people in these outfits, from management to workforce, still steal, embezzle and cheat . . . They still do not care about waste, carelessness, inefficiency and lack of maintenance . . . There are innumerable abuses including the misuse of fuel, vehicles and even office stationery. In some public institutions and organizations, managements have developed a tendency to spend resources carelessly on frivolous and luxury office and residential furnishing (*People's Graphic*, Jan 6, 1990).

By the 1990s military rule in Africa had so deteriorated that it could be characterized as "rule by uniformed buzzards." Creating chaos and destroying lives across Africa, the soldiers became the scourge of the region, squandering its resources and severely impeding its development. In fact, they proved to be grossly ignorant of their own basic purpose in society, let alone being competent to manage the functions of other institutions. They turned their guns on the very people they were supposed to defend, in

Ethiopia, Ghana, Nigeria, Liberia, Somalia, Uganda, Zaire, and other African countries.

The basic function of the military and the police is to protect the territorial integrity of the nation as well as the lives and safety of its citizens. But many of Africa's soldiers and policemen could not even do battle with a disorganized band of armed robbers, much less fight off a well-organized brigade of foreign invaders. Writing in *West Africa* (May 27-Jun 2, 1991; p. 865), Peter Worae chastised:

> It is now the norm in Africa, especially in West Africa, that whenever there are civil disturbances, demonstrations or protests, the soldiers are called in to kill. So much is spent on defense, yet whenever our countries face an external threat, we call in the so-called friendly countries to fight the enemy—not our soldiers.
>
> After being high-handed on student demonstrations which resulted in some deaths, when dissidents tried to overthrow his government in 1986, President Eyadema called in French and Zairean soldiers to fight the enemy, not the Togolese soldiers. Early last year (1990) when pro-democracy demonstrators went on the streets to demand a multiparty system, President Houphouet-Boigny sent in his soldiers, which resulted in the death of two protesters. In Doe's Liberia, the situation was no better. It was common for soldiers to storm the university, rape women, kill and maim others.
>
> Now President Joseph Momoh is joining in. After his heavy expenditure on defense, we should expect the soldiers to defend the nation against external aggression. It is absurd for the president to call in the so-called friendly countries. He would have sent his own men to take up arms against any pro-democracy or student demonstrators on the streets.

A retired Nigerian army chief, General Hassan Usman Katsina, also complained: "The problem with the armed forces today is their lack of dedication to duty and the duty of professionalism. Perhaps no profession is as abused" (cited in *Africa Report,* Jul-Aug 1990; p. 52). Could they even fight a war? According to Brigadier Benjamin Adekunle, a retired general, "Nigerian soldiers of today are so inexperienced that they are scared of war" (*New African,* Jul 1989; p. 58). The police in Africa were no better at protecting lives and property (*New Africa,* Apr 1989; p. 35). Their comparative advantage has been in extorting bribes.

Africa's truly brave revolutionary leaders are its indigenous chiefs. They carry no weapons except ceremonial swords on special occasions. Yet they can meet their people face to face, on an equal footing. African chiefs do not surround themselves with a platoon of armed bodyguards as do its military rulers. Peter Madakson of Nigeria observed:

The role of the African chief, which I am sure most Africans appreciate, is that he is the social and spiritual father of his people. He is there for them at all times. He helps them to solve material or marital problems; he fights with them against drought and starvation; he eats with them; and he works with them. In my area, the chief went from village to village to stay with the villagers for days, to listen to their problems and give help where needed. Where in the Western world did this concept of leadership ever exist? (*West Africa*, Apr 24-30, 1989; p. 658).

That question should be rephrased to read: Where in modern Africa does such leadership exist at the national level? Most African heads of state, including the military, are afraid to go near their own people, let alone to eat with them or to listen to them. The true measure of power, popularity, and authority is the extent to which a leader does not require an arsenal of offensive and protective gear. The most effective form of protection is that offered by the people, not by a collection of bazookas and tanks. In fact, the very presence of such weapons is the leader's tacit acknowledgment of his weakness and of the illegitimacy of his authority.

After assassinating all his political opponents, Idi Amin declared, "Well, there is nobody to hand over power to." Other military dictators, bent on clinging to power at all cost, insist that it is the civilians who must be educated and prepared for civilian rule. In Nigeria, for example, a Center for Democratic Studies (CDS) was established expressly for this purpose. According to *West Africa*:

> Aspiring politicians will have to pass two examinations for certificates leading to "competence in the Nigerian constitution" before they can hold public office.
>
> The director-general of CDS, Professor Omo Omoruyi, who made this disclosure, said the first assessment would be made after short term workshops, seminars and conferences organized by the Center. The second assessment was to inculcate democrative values in prospective political office holders. "They must be a way of ascertaining whether (prospective politicians) know how Nigeria is governed," he added (Dec 18-24, 1989; p. 2122).

There were no provisions requiring comparable certificates for aspiring military heads of state, despite the fact that the military has held power for 20 out of 30 years of Nigerian independence.[1] Who then needed the political education?

In Liberia, the military regime of the late Samuel Doe resorted to savage barbarism, often including dismemberment, the mutilation of bodies, and cannibalism. For example, when students at the University of Liberia protested the arrest of a professor in August 1984, troops from President Doe's Executive Guard stormed the campus to quash the demonstration and fired indiscriminately into the crowd of students. After a failed coup attempt in December 1985, Doe's army cut up the body of the coup leader and ate it (*West Africa*, Dec 23-30, 1985). After another abortive coup attempt in December 1989, Doe's soldiers unleashed savage retribution that resulted in the massacre of over 500 innocent civilians and sent over 120,000 refugees pouring into the Ivory Coast and Guinea. The villages of Kahnplaye and Butuo, for example, were completely destroyed, and large parts of the Liberian countryside in Nimba province were virtually depopulated. Military barbarism gripped the country.

## FLAGRANT HUMAN RIGHTS VIOLATIONS

Although virtually all African governments have carefully crafted bills of human rights and have signed the United Nations' Declaration of Human Rights as well as the African Charter of Human Rights drawn up by the Organization of African Unity, respect for human life and private property is non-existent. The repression is most severe under military regimes. Military brutality, vandalism, arbitrary rule, constant harassment and arrests of civilians are now the norm. And how do the soldiers, who proclaim efficiency to be their professional imperative, run Africa's prisons?

In Liberia, under Doe's military regime, prison conditions at Belle Yallah and Post Stockade were appalling. Many cells had been "befouled through lack of proper sanitary facilities," according to a 1988 U.S. government human rights report on Liberia. "In many cases, prolonged detention of persons without charge occurs as a result of judicial inefficiency and administrative neglect." Reports often surfaced that the judicial system had either forgotten or did not know the number of those imprisoned.

In Togoland, near Lome at the Ghana-Togo border, Dr. Kofi Kodzi operated a remote clinic at Be Kpota. On September 29, 1985, he crossed the border to visit friends at Vakpo in Ghana. He was arrested and accused of having treated Ghanaian dissidents at his clinic. He did not deny the charges. Medical ethics, he asserted, forbade doctors' turning away patients because of their political activities or beliefs. He pointed out that even on battlefields, doctors sometimes treat wounded enemies. But Ghanaian military authorities were unyielding. They imprisoned him without a trial and denied him necessary medical treatment for three years (*New African*, Apr 1989; p. 18).

When a national conference stripped Togolese dictator Gen. Ghassingbe Eyadema of power and chose Joseph Kokou Koffigoh as the new prime minister, soldiers went berserk. They killed about 20 pro-democracy activists and seized the television station on November 28, 1991. They broadcast this message: "The armed forces of Togo demand one more time of the head of state [Mr. Eyadema] that he name an effective man to form a new government. If not, the entire town [of Lome] will be reduced to ashes. The sooner the better" (*The Washington Times*, Nov 29, 1991; p. A11).

In Nigeria, Africa's most populous nation, the allegedly efficient military allowed thousands of prisoners to die of scabies and other diseases. According to *West Africa*, "food meant for prisoners was often diverted for private use by the prison officials" (Apr 23-29, 1990; p. 2073). One prison official in the southeastern state of Anambra, Nigeria, estimated that at least two prisoners die in city jails every day because of poor prison conditions (*New African*, Sep 1988; p. 32).

Lagos prisons are said to be the worst in Africa. Ibrahim Jarma, Nigeria's controller of prisons, disclosed that a total of 273 prisoners died in 1989 in Lagos prisons alone because of the "acute shortage of drugs, lack of vehicles to convey inmates to hospitals and overcrowding" (*West Africa*, Apr 23-29, 1990; p. 660). The Ikoyi prison had the highest toll with 132 dead, while the Kirikiri medium and maximum security prisons accounted for 25 and 54 deaths, respectively. The Ikoyi prison was the most congested, with 2,184 inmates in a space designed for 800. The Kirikiri medium and maximum security prisons both exceeded their 704 and 956 capacity by 800 and 539 inmates, respectively. Conditions in these prisons were atrocious: "Lack of potable water and primitive methods of disposing of human faeces pose horrible health hazards to the crowded inmates . . . Compounding the lack of hygiene is the inadequate medical provision. Each prison has only two nurses and all five [prisons] overall are supervised by only one doctor. The clinics are grossly short of not only drugs but ordinary disinfectants, and it is anybody's guess how they cope with an established attendance rate of 500 inmates daily" (*West Africa*, Apr 23-29, 1990; p. 660).

As long as they had their guns and armored personnel-carriers, the Nigerian military did not care about the welfare of the rest of the population, let alone that of prison inmates. Nor was the human rights picture any better in other African countries ruled by the military.

In August 1988 two Belgians, Paul Staes and Jef Ulburghs, catalogued the military's horrifying human rights abuses in Zaire. According to their report, the Zairian Green Berets killed several peasants and merchants in the Northern Kivu (Eastern Zaire) region during the summer of 1988. In addition, the army went on a rampage, plundering and looting the area and the Kibali-Ituri region. The Roman Catholic bishop of Kataliko (Northern Kivu) implored Field Marshal Mobutu to keep his troops inside the barracks. According to *New African*, rape was commonplace: "The two Euro MPs also gave details of rape involving three schoolgirls . . . by six soldiers in the town of Lumee. There were reports indicating that two other schoolgirls were raped by soldiers in Goma and Bulera-Vuhovi. According to the same sources, 88 women who participated in a women's demonstration on April 19 in Kinshasa suffered the same fate" (Sep 1988; p. 22).

A Zairian exile, Lucien Naki, reported:

> The beating and murdering of civilians is declared a security matter. Even murder in Mobutu's cabinet is classified as a state secret . . . Mobutu is a thoroughly unbalancing and destructive force for Africa and for the rest of the world. For too long the world has laughed him off, for too long the world has excused him. Too many exiles have been frightened into silence by the fear that he could wreak terrible revenge on friends and relatives remaining behind in Zaire. I know that by speaking out I risk more lives, but I also know that my silence will guarantee nobody's safety . . . Thousands of Zairian students, on whose training the government had spent millions of dollars, don't come back after their studies abroad. More of Zaire's professional talent lives out of the country than inside. Mobutu is worse than Botha and his apartheid (*New African*, May 1989; p. 41).

On May 10, 1990, several Lubumbashi University students from Mobutu's Gbande tribe were caught on campus in possession of walkie-talkies, handcuffs, weapons, and various instruments of torture. They were severely beaten, and one of them confessed to taking part in the abduction and killing of 23 Lubumbashi students in the past. Fellow students lynched three of the alleged Gbande student-spies, one of whom was the son of General Baramoto, commander of the civil guard and a relative of President Mobutu. Retribution was merciless:

> A special commando force of 250 "red berets," most of them from Mobutu's own tribe, were flown to Lubumbashi from Kinshasa. Disguised as civilians, the commandos attacked the Lubumbashi campus at 11 pm on May 11, 1990.
>
> First, they cut water and electricity to the campus, then separated the students from Mobutu's Equator Region from the rest, and proceeded to beat and slit the throats of students from other parts of the country, especially those from the Kasai and Bandundu regions, well known for their hostility to Mobutu. Unofficial sources say between 50 and 150 students were slaughtered that night (*New African*, Jul 1990; p. 16).

On September 24, 1991, Zairean soldiers, angry at not being paid, rioted and looted businesses and private homes. The stolen goods, including television sets, video recorders, bicycles, rowing machines, and cars, were brazenly sold at an open market at Camp Kokolo. "Camp Kokolo is proof not only that the military is completely out of control but that the senior officers are afraid of their own soldiers," said Albert Moleka, a member of the opposition party Young Republicans (*The New York Times*, Nov 4, 1991; p. A6).

In Burundi in August 1988 the military government, run by the Tutsi minority, massacred an estimated 20,000 Hutus—a number far greater than the official count of 5,000. U.N. officials at refugee camps near the border with Rwanda told of soldiers chasing, machine-gunning, and bayoneting fleeing Hutus. The scale and barbarity of the military carnage shocked many Western aid officials. "Why are we here?" asked one European diplomat. "Morally, we should get out and slam the door."

Civil wars and final offensive campaigns now provide military regimes with an excuse to perpetrate heinous atrocities against innocent peasants. In "Denying the Honour of Living: Sudan, a Human Rights Disaster 1986-89," Africa Watch noted:

> The Bashir government has embarked on the repression of political opposition in Khartoum on a scale never seen before. In a direct attack on the institutions of civil society, the RCC has purged the judiciary, the army, and civil service, banned trade unions and any form of protest, silenced the press, and detained several hundred political prisoners, including doctors, politicians, journalists and trade unionists. It has set up a new and unofficial security agency which has tortured and humiliated detainees in secret detention centers . . .
>
> [Africa Watch] lays down 8 tough recommendations to the government, from releasing all political prisoners and abolishing the military-run kangaroo courts where defendants are denied lawyers, to disarming the militia and enforcing the law against slavery (*Africa Report*, May-Jun 1990; p. 24)

In Ethiopia on May 12, 1988, ex-president Lt. Col. Mengistu Haile-Mariam's army entered the town of She'eb in northeastern Eritrea and rounded up about 400 men, women, and children, including the elderly, the disabled, and the blind. Accusing them of collaborating with the Eritrean People's Liberation Front, the soldiers drove two tanks over the people and fired machine guns at those trying to escape. According to *New African*: "Eighty thousand people escaped from She'eb that day. All the shops were looted and burned by the Ethiopian army, who also slaughtered 10,000 sheep, goats, cattle and camels, putting some of the carcasses down the town's only well, thus polluting it forever" (Oct 1988; p. 24).

These brutalities drew a protest from Goshu Wolde, Ethiopia's foreign minister: "I cannot, in good conscience, continue to serve a government whose shortsightedness and rigidly doctrinaire policies are leading the country and the people into misery and destruction . . . I have watched with helplessness as my country slipped further and further into authoritarianism and absolute dictatorship." He subsequently defected.

In neighboring Somalia the story was the same: pillage and carnage. After seizing power in a coup on October 21, 1969, the military regime of Siad Barre sank deeper and deeper into depravity. In May 1988 it dropped bombs on its own citizens when they demonstrated against Barre's 20-year despotic rule. Adam Egeh, a Somalian, charged:

> Torture, mass detention, execution, human rights violations, confiscation of private properties and the prohibition of all political parties became widespread. In all parts of Somalia, the military regime of Mr. Barre has the ultimate *carte blanche* to either detain or execute any Somali citizen the regime is not satisfied with. In fact, for the past 20 years, hundreds of thousands of innocent people were put to death or imprisoned without going through the legal court procedures. Many politicians, businessmen, religious leaders and young students disappeared and their whereabouts are not known to date. The number of prisoners of conscience is quite enormous in Somalia and international journalists were long banned from reporting on such situations (*African Letter*, Apr 16-30, 1990; p. 3).

Indeed, one of Barre's own military intelligence officers confessed in an article to *New African*:

> I, Cali Selebaab Suuleed (Huube), am a former Intelligence Officer of the National Security Service of Somalia (NSS), and can confirm the inhuman and oppressive measures instituted in Northern Somalia, in general, and in northwest Somalia, in particular. In the last few years NSS forces have conducted massive lootings, kidnappings, rapings, killings and the harsh imprisonment of innocent people, without trial. For example, here follows a list of people arbitrarily killed in Burao, subsequent to the May 1988 incident (Jul 1989; p. 22).

He went on to list 68 names.

Somalian church leaders were not spared from these inhumane acts. Bishop Salvatore Colombo, the Papal Nuncio and a man committed to human rights, was mysteriously murdered. In July 1989, in the early hours of the *Iid*

*Al Adba* day, a Moslem holy day, government forces swooped down and arrested six prominent imams after the morning prayers. *New African* reported:

> Military units, already deployed, showed as little respect for human life as they had in Hargeisa and Burao in the north. Whole sections of the crowd of worshippers were gunned down. Innocent people were rounded up in the hundreds and many were murdered and buried on the Jasira beach.
>
> *New African* has the names of 144 persons seized from their homes in the Wadajir (Madina) quarter of Mogadishu, on the night of July 16, 1989, who were killed in Danane prison and on the beach.
>
> As the diplomatic corps looked on in horror, arrests continued . . . Even the *Times of London* called for the demise of the unpopular and discredited regime of General Siyad Barre. Research by *New African* has revealed that . . . over 1,000 died (Nov 1989; p. 11).

In March 1990 Africa Watch issued a report entitled "Somalia: A Government at War with Its Own People". It charged the regime with "responsibility for the deaths of 50,000 to 60,000 civilians since hostilities broke out between the government and rebels from the Somali National Movement, while half a million have fled to neighboring countries" (*Africa Report*, Mar-Apr 1990; p. 10). In hundreds of interviews with refugees, the human rights group described in chilling detail how the government, frustrated in its attempts to defeat the rebels, turned its guns against the civilian population. According to the report, the army engaged in systematic violence toward Isaak clan members in northern Somalia by burning and bombing their villages and detained hundreds for suspected association with the Somali National Movement. Originally confined to the north, the abuses soon spread to the southern and central parts of the country. "Entire regions have been devastated by a military engaged in combat against its own people, resembling a foreign occupation force that recognizes no constraints on its power to kill, rape or loot," Africa Watch reported. Siad Barre fled Mogadishu on January 26, 1991, leaving the country in total ruin.

Similarly, Uganda was ravaged by military plunder, barbarism and carnage. Soldiers roamed the Ugandan countryside to pillage and rape. Even the urban areas were not safe. Soldiers relieved drivers of their cars and other possessions at gunpoint. Even diplomats lost their vehicles this way (*New African*, Oct 1988; p. 17). *The Economist* reported that in northern Uganda "the army has destroyed grain stores, burned huts—sometimes with villagers inside—shot civilians and taken thousands of prisoners. Lots of people have run away. About 100,000 displaced villagers are encamped in Gulu alone, with 50,000 more in the surrounding area" (Jul 8, 1989; p. 45).

In November 1989 Major Okello Kolo, a former member of President Yoweri Kaguta Museveni's ruling National Resistance Council and the National Resistance Army (NRA) High Command, broke his silence and spoke out to *New African*: "Incidents of rape, looting, slashing of food crops, razing of homes and food stores, theft of livestock have been going on unabated at the hands of the troops of the NRA . . . Already 150,000 people in the north and east have perished at the hands of the NRA and over 4,000 have been forced into exile" (Nov 1989; p. 23).

Major Kolo also testified to seeing armored personnel-carriers running over unarmed villagers to kill them. Barely three months after that exposé, Major Kolo was found murdered near his village.

It is difficult to make any sense out of the killings in Uganda, especially after its people suffered so much under the tyranny of Idi Amin. The tragedy is particularly shocking in view of President Museveni's rhetoric when he seized power on January 15, 1986. Many Africans applauded when he lambasted other African leaders for their hypocrisy and failure to condemn the flagitious abuses of human rights in the past in Uganda and elsewhere in Africa. He promised to hand over power in four years—1990. But he turned out to be as power drunk as those he had condemned. When his announced term of office expired in January 1990, he demanded a five-year extension. "Democracy is a must for Africa," said Museveni. But he refused to submit himself to a democratic election.

In February 1990 the NRA deployed thousands of troops to launch a final offensive against rebel soldiers in the eastern Uganda district of Kumi. As usual, the real victims were innocent peasants caught in the crossfire who had nothing whatsoever to do with the military barbarians on either side of Uganda's senseless civil war. The operation began in earnest when army trucks invaded villages and ordered the people to leave for special concentration camps. According to *New African*: "The people were simply dumped there and told to fend for themselves by building makeshift huts to live in. It is estimated that over 100,000 people are now cramped into camps where they are without water or latrines. Relief organizations are often denied access and the people are underfed sometimes near to starvation. At Kidongole camp, a Red Cross team was beaten up by the camp commander who refused them access to the starving people" (May 1990; p. 18).

By June 1990 over 1,000 villagers, half of them children, had perished from various types of diseases associated with overcrowding. By August, discipline in the NRA had completely broken down. According to a BBC report: "Sixteen people were herded into a hut in Ogerai Village and burnt to death on suspicion of harboring rebels" (Focus on Africa, Oct-Nov 1990;

p. 23). Finally, the military government of Uganda adopted a measure to help its citizens. *New African* reported: "The exercise of repatriating over 100,000 people crowded into about 13 camps started on June 30. Over 7,000 people in the Mukura camp near the railway station, where some 69 youths were suffocated to death when they were locked up in a disused train wagons in July 1989, were told by government officials to go home. The following Saturday another 8,000 people who had been living in a camp at Kapir on the main Kumi-Soroti road were also sent home" (Sep 1990; p. 24).

Military lawlessness is still widespread in Africa, however. In Benin, Burkina Faso, Ghana, Liberia, Somalia, and many other countries, the people cannot argue with soldiers over civil liberties, freedom of expression, and private property rights. Even in Ghana "reports in the state-owned media have confirmed the popular suspicion about the role of some military, police and Civil Defence Organizations personnel in the increasing number of armed robberies" (*West Africa*, Aug 1, 1988; p. 1390). The situation was the same in Mozambique: "Ragged government troops and a shadowy guerrilla army take turns terrorizing villages and stealing their meager crops. Entire units have degenerated into banditry. 'The gun for many people has become a source of income,' says an official sadly . . . Mozambican soldiers have been known to hire out their weapons to criminals for a fee or a piece of the loot" (*Insight*, Oct 1, 1990; p. 17).

In the 1970s the military in Africa professed to be waging a crusade against corruption and mismanagement in government. But in the 1980s the military became more obsessed with political power itself. The least sign of opposition to military rule was squelched with brutal abandon. Africa's military dictators widely used kidnapping and murder by "road accidents" to frighten their people and to maintain power.

One victim of such an "accident" was Roman Catholic Father Silvio Sindambiwe of Rwanda, who died on November 7, 1989, along with two passengers, when a truck struck his car. From September 1979 to January 1986, the priest had been the director of the *Kinyamateka-Hobe*, a Catholic weekly. He was a courageous journalist, exposing corruption in state corporations and human rights violations in Rwandan prisons. These exposés incurred the displeasure of the military government of Gen. Juvenal Habyalimana. Members of the state security force hounded and intimidated Sindambiwe. *New African* chronicled his harassment:

> In June 1986 he was involved in a motor cycle accident. Several months later he was told that this was his "last warning." Shortly before his death he participated in the 15th World Congress of the International Catholic Press Union which

took place in Ruhpolding, West Germany. It was his performance there and his contacts with international journalists and Rwanda political exiles, which upset the Habyalimana regime. In 1988 he wrote a critical book. The government was so worried it sent security agents to West Germany to try and abduct him and the West German police had to give him protection (Feb 1990; p. 16).

At about the same time, the military regime of Mobutu Sese Seko of Zaire was reaching outside the country to kidnap political opponents in exile. A July 21, 1989 confidential document from the United Nations High Commission for Refugees charged that a number of Zairian refugees in neighboring countries had been kidnapped by agents of the Zairian *Agence Nationale de Documentation*. Anselme Kabongo, a political opponent, was abducted in Apr 1989 from Bujumbura, Burundi. Lambert Mende, a spokesman for Msaada, a Belgian organization that supported development projects in western Uganda, reported other kidnappings:

> Zairian agents tried to kidnap a Mobutu opponent in exile in Arua earlier in 1989. But they found his pregnant wife Fatuma who was seized and taken to Bunia in Zaire. The woman's 3 million Uganda shillings were stolen by the security agents . . . Fatuma was sighted in October, 1989, at the Makala Prison in Kinshasa.
>
> In that same prison is another Zairian refugee, James Mundoni, an MNC-Lumumba [political] activist, who was kidnapped in Uganda in 1967 by Mobutu's security men (*New African*, Dec 1989; p. 19).

Kidnappings and military brutality were commonplace in Nigeria as well, but the increasing level of barbarism there was alarming. *New African* reported that stories of military vandalism were almost a daily occurrence (Apr 1988; p. 10).

Elsewhere in West Africa, abductions and brutality by military savages were the norm. In July 1988 Ghanaian soldiers punished teachers who were late for school by shaving their heads, lining them up for the students to ridicule, and locking them up in a military guardroom until evening (*West Africa*, Aug 1, 1988; p. 1413). In December 1988 Victor Mintah, the past president of the Ghana Institute of Chartered Accounts, died in custody. According to *West Africa*: "Mr. Mintah, 55, was taken from his home by agents of the Bureau of National Investigations (BNI) on July 18, 1988. At the time of his death, no charges had been preferred against him, and according to informed sources, he had not even been questioned during his six months of detention . . . The BNI is reportedly still using his two private cars . . . which they allegedly took from his home when they arrested him" (Jan 30-Feb 5, 1989; p. 164).

Ironically, these acts were viewed as an improvement in military-civilian relations in comparison with the cruelties Ghanaians suffered during the revolution in 1982, when *West Africa* reported: *"The Pioneer* [newspaper] has lamented the fact that certain uniformed men think the revolution has given them a carte blanche to terrorize civilians on the flimsiest excuse" (Jan 13, 1983; p. 295). In addition, during Ghana's enforcement of price controls over the 1981 to 1983 period, the military confiscated and destroyed a great deal of private property. For example, markets were burned down in Accra, Kumasi, and Koforidua.

The reign of terror in Ghana has continued into the 1990s. In November 1991 George Naykene, editor of the *Christian Chronicle*, was arrested and detained for suggesting in an article that all members of the Armed Forces Revolutionary Council (AFRC), which ruled Ghana in 1979, benefited from an illegal loan obtained by the People's National Party (PNP) from an Italian businessman.

At Naykene's trial, Lt. Col. (retired) Mensah Gbedemah, a former AFRC member and secretary of state for the National Development Commission in the ruling regimes, was called to testify:

> The court, which has a capacity of 120 people, was overfilled with some 400 people who jeered when Lt. Col. Gbedemah threatened one of the defense lawyers with a series of remarks, the final one being: "I will blast off your head," as he stood up . . .
>
> On March 13 when the court resumed the crowd had grown thicker and when the accused, Mr. George Naykene appeared they gave him a 30-minute ovation amidst shouts of order in court by the clerk.
>
> Before proceedings began, Mr. Ray Kakrabah-Quarshie drew the court's attention to the witness's behavior at the last sitting and stated that this contempt should have been dealt with immediately, no matter the status of the witness...
>
> Surprisingly, the judge, Mr. Justice Tetteh, told the court that he did not hear the exact words uttered by the witness in the three-minute confrontation because 'I had then bent my head down' and the crowd burst out in laughter (*West Africa*, Mar 23-29, 1992; p. 514).

Were these the professional soldiers that Africa inherited from the colonial era? Atta Poku of Kumasi, Ghana, did not think so. In a letter to *New African* he wrote:

> Africa today has been turned into the world's largest military zone by African soldiers, and one wonders if this is more neocolonialism. That no military regime has ever succeeded in building any viable economy anywhere in the world, can

best explain why Africa is so undeveloped. Under the pretext of revolution, African soldiers turn their countries into fertile grounds for all sorts of unworkable Marxist theories, blinding the people with all sorts of socialist jargons.

The paradox of the African soldier is that they always begin as socialist revolutionaries and end up in the West as one of the bourgeois class they had condemned at the peak of their revolutions. Why these revolutionaries refuse to live their exile in Soviet-bloc countries baffles me. The day African soldiers will realise that a soldier's place is at the barracks and not at the state house, mother Africa would begin to write a progressive report (*New African*, Aug 1989; p. 6).

## THE MILITARY AND ECONOMIC DEVELOPMENT

While Africa's infrastructure and public services disintegrated, African dictators found the wherewithal to spend more and more on themselves and the military. Whitaker (1988) noted, "The proportion of African funds going to equip and pay the military has been steadily rising, reaching for example over 40 percent in Ethiopia, and 25 and 20 percent respectively in drought-ravaged Mauritania and Mali" (p. 43). Libby (1987) added:

The Zairian armed forces have been a continuous drain on the economy largely through misappropriation of funds and food supplies for the personal enrichment of senior officers. One illustration of this is General Eluki, the former state secretary for national defense. In August, 1979, General Eluki along with former Minister of Agriculture Tepatondele were convicted of embezzling government funds. Eluki's wife was reported stopped at a roadblock and found to be in possession of 17 suitcases of money, and a search of Eluki's home resulted in uncovering US $2 million and an additional 2 million zaires. An indication that Eluki was simply a scapegoat among hundreds of other offenders who were not arrested is the fact that General Eluki's 20-year prison sentence was set aside, and he assumed the position of commander of Shaba region (p. 274).

Military expenditures by developing nations have soared over the past two decades. In its 1990 Report on Human Development, the United Nations Development Program deplored the fact that "arms imports in developing countries skyrocketed from only $1 billion in 1960 to nearly $35 billion in 1987. Three-quarters of the global arms trade involves exports to developing countries. Some of the poorest and least developed countries spend far more on their military than on their education and health" (cited by the *Washington Times*, May 25, 1990; p. A9). "Developing countries have 8 times more soldiers than physicians and the ratio of soldiers to teachers in some cases is as high as 5 to 1," according to the same U.N. report.

Indeed, Sammy Kum Buo, director of the U.N. Center for Peace and Disarmament, lamented that "Africa spends about $12 billion a year on the purchase of arms and the maintenance of the armed forces, an amount which is equal to what Africa was requesting in financial aid over the next 5 years" (*West Africa*, May 11, 1987; p. 912).

Military spending by African countries, according to the U.S. Center for Defense Information, reached $16.9 billion in 1983, up 400 percent from $3.8 billion in 1973. Sixteen African countries spent more on arms than they received in aid. Libya topped the list with $1.9 billion in arms purchases against $52 million in aid. Angola, hard hit by drought, spent $525 million on arms and received $502 million in aid. Nigeria and Mozambique spent $430 million and $260 million, respectively, on arms and received $48 million and $242 million, respectively, in aid.

Angola spent more per capita on the military ($892) than on education ($310) and health ($115). Many other African countries also spent more on the military than on health: Gabon ($88 versus $49); the Congo ($45 versus $25); Mauritania ($31 versus $6); and Zimbabwe ($52 versus $17).

Top arms suppliers to Africa in the 1980s were the Soviet Union (50 percent), France (11 percent), Italy (5 percent), West Germany (5 percent), and the United States (3 percent). The Warsaw Pact countries accounted for 58 percent of arms sales and NATO 31 percent.

The rising level of military expenditures in Africa has begun to attract wide attention. The World Bank, which characteristically has refrained from political commentaries, expressed alarm: "Military spending has diverted enormous resources from southern Africa's development, and has consumed nearly 50 percent of government expenditures in the countries experiencing the worst destabilization" (World Bank, Nov 1989; p. 23). Moreover, *West Africa*, which historically has avoided criticizing African governments, also began to complain:

> During the 1970s, arms importation by African countries grew faster than any other region in the world, doubling between 1970-77. Since the beginning of the 1980s, this trend has tailed off, due as much to the saturation of military inventories, as the continent-wide economic crisis. But in most African states, defence still consumes an excessive share of the national budgets, easily outstripping social spending. One million dollars could provide 1,000 classrooms for 30,000 children, and yet it is the cost of a modern tank. The price of a single helicopter is equivalent to the salary of 12,000 schoolteachers. The policy choice

of more tanks means less classrooms, with inevitable consequences for economic growth and social development . . .

Theoretically, an efficient military institution is an investment. It ensures stability and maintains the stability necessary for economic growth. But all too often in the African setting they are part of the problem. African armies modelled on the Western example, as opposed to Frelimo in Mozambique and the NRA in Uganda, are not productive; they simply consume. There is also a very high probability that the tanks and armoured cars bought for the defence of the country's frontiers will be used to surround the radio station for the announcement of a military coup, which is statistically likely to be followed by a countercoup (Mar 27-Apr 2, 1989; p. 508).

Two former Nigerian heads of state have joined those calling for a reevaluation of the role of the military in African governance. Retired General Olusegun Abasanjo urged cuts in soaring military expenditures to facilitate economic development (*African Letter*, Apr 1-15, 1990; p. 6). General Yakubu Gowon, in a lecture at the Oxford and Cambridge Club entitled "Charting Nigeria's Path to Democracy in this Decade and Beyond," charged:

Nigeria's problems started shortly after independence because the army allowed itself to be polluted and politicised, hence the incessant coups and countercoups. The military intervention in politics in 1966 started a chain of reaction whose deleterious effects are still relevant in our national life even today, so many years after the ill-advised putsch . . .

The military should not get itself involved in politics. The sooner they leave the stage the better, or else the people may rise up against them (*West Africa*, Jun 11-17, 1990; p. 993).

The African story is indeed a tragedy of one betrayal after another. When black Africa asked for its freedom and independence from white colonial rule, it did not ask black neocolonialists and military despots to impose another alien rule on Africa that would destroy its indigenous institutions and slaughter its people. Nor did it ask "Swiss-bank socialists" to plunder its treasuries. Africa's experience proves unequivocally that military solutions to political and economic problems do not work. In fact, they exacerbate the problems. More Africans are now awakening to the ineffectuality of military solutions. Nigerian journalist Pini Jason wrote: "It is a damning indictment of the military that coup after coup and regime after regime, the very ills they set out to cure go from bad to worse. We now have a worst case scenario where the military which boasts of being the only surviving national institution is badly threatened by religion, partisan politics and ethnicity within its ranks" (*New African*, Jul 1990; p. 34).

These concerns were echoed elsewhere. R. M. Yamson of Legon, Ghana, wrote: "It is high time we learn from our mistakes. We should learn a little from what has happened in Liberia. Africa is fed up with military dictatorships (*West Africa*, Oct 8-14, 1990; p. 2604).

Even the military is beginning to acknowledge the deleterious effect of military expansion in Africa. Retired General Abasanjo of Nigeria has been foremost. In a keynote address at a meeting of the Africa Leadership Forum, hosted by the Organization for Economic Cooperation and Development, he remarked:

> While Africa may have ceased to be a pawn in the Cold War, there is the paradoxical and real danger that individual African leaders and small African countries with perceived and real security concerns may feel compelled—or induced—to build up their own military establishments.
>
> I submit that, in the interest of promoting the development of their societies, African leaders must refrain from pursuing—often instinctively—this unproductive path. No matter how many weapons they will be able to accumulate, they will always lose: either to a superior adversary or to the distraction from their real task of development and nation-building . . .
>
> With the prospects for peace and democracy being firmly established in Africa, it is to be hoped that the African struggle for democracy that is bound to be intensified and radicalised will force undemocratic African regimes to reduce considerably their defence spending and increase the budgetary allocation to the social sector (*West Africa*, May 7-13, 1990; p. 763).

Abasanjo was not alone. In fact, former Nigerian chief of staff Lt. Gen. Theophilus Yakubu Danjuma was more insistent. In a commencement address at the University of Liberia in March 1990, he accused military governments in Africa of corruption and mismanagement of resources. Danjuma "urged military governments to 'drastically cut defence budgets' and pay more attention to social welfare, health, and education . . . The internal wars being waged by various African governments against dissident groups do not themselves justify such an arms build-up" (*West Africa*, Mar 5-11, 1990; p. 389).

At the national conference on democracy in Benin in February 1990, the head of the armed forces, Colonel Vincent Guezodje, also stressed that soldiers should remain apolitical and should be required to leave the army if they planned to enter politics (*West Africa*, Mar 5-11, 1990; p. 389).

Even military strongman Mobutu Sese Seko of Zaire has come to realize that reform is necessary. After a three-month "consultation with the people," Mobutu admitted in a televised speech: "The people have told me that the public institutions, the schools, the hospitals, are in terrible shape. People are demanding change" (cited by *The Economist,* May 5, 1990; p. 56). In Ethiopia, Lt. Col. Mengistu Haile-Mariam admitted in his May Day speech: "The mood of the people is no longer as militant as it once was [and] the bid to build socialism has failed" (*The Economist,* May 5, 1990; p. 56). Major General Joseph Momoh, the ex-head of state of Sierra Leone who was ousted on April 29, 1992, confessed that he was a failure:

> In his own admission in public, Maj. Gen. Joseph Momoh stated that after 5 years in office, he had achieved nothing. This confession is particularly correct. Under his leadership, Sierra Leone deteriorated immeasurably, but Momoh amassed considerable wealth in real [estate] property and cash, both locally and overseas. This ugly truth about Momoh equally applies to his political acolytes—ministers, party functionaries, heads of parastatals, his close political advisers, some high commissioners and ambassadors, and others too numerous to mention. Knowingly and shamelessly, Momoh headed a corrupt regime and, morally weak, was unable to take appropriate action against any of his ministers for corruption (*West Africa,* May 18-24, 1992; p. 840).

It is admirable and commendable for the military dictators to admit failures, but admissions alone are not enough. If the military cannot solve the problem, it should clear out of government and return to the barracks. After all, an African country does not belong to the military or to one person. Retired Nigerian chief of army staff General Gibson Jallo aptly concluded: "The army has no moral justification to rule this country [Nigeria]" (cited in *Africa Report,* Jul-Aug 1990; p. 52).

As to what to do with the military, some Africans, fed up with military lawlessness, have been calling for the total disbandment of the military once and for all. All it takes is to put the question in an open referendum to the peasants. In Ghana, restrict the vote to the Makola women traders. They are still waiting for their market to be rebuilt. Back in the late 1970s, General I. K. Acheampong sent his troops to Makola Market to enforce price controls. The traders used womanly wiles to disarm the troop; then they beat them thoroughly. Ask only these market women to vote in a referendum to decide whether Ghana needs a military. Costa Rica has no army, these Makola women will point out, yet its territorial integrity has not been violated.

According to T. Paine, a Ghanaian exile in Los Angeles, "Many Ghanaians are of the opinion that the Armed Forces of Ghana should be phased out by the end of the decade. Such Ghanaians fail to be convinced that we need not only an army but an air force and navy as well" (*West Africa*, Jun 3-9, 1991; p. 892). Other Ghanaians have some interesting suggestions:

> Mr. Danso-Boateng suggested: 'The numerical strength of the military must be drastically reduced, the army reduced to one regiment, the air force reduced by half, with all their rockets, bullets and jet fighters confiscated by the civilian-president. The navy could be maintained at present strength because ships cannot come onto the land to be used for coups.' An even more interesting suggestion came from Wilson Blay: 'Lock up all the armories and, let the civilian president keep all the keys.' Kwamena Nyanzu called for the disbanding of the entire armed forces. Mr. Thomas Osei insisted that the armed forces should concern themselves with their traditional role of defense and keep off politics (*West Africa*, Nov 26-Dec 2, 1990; p. 2901).

Obviously, the military is out of control in Africa, butchering its people and squandering resources that could be used for development. The people of Chad have already taken action: "The ruling *Mouvement Patriotique du Salut* (MPS) is speeding up the reorganization of the military, which should see the army halved from 50,000 to 25,000" (*West Africa*, May 18-24, 1992; p. 852).

In the following chapters we shall explore in detail the insidious march from independence to tyranny and military barbarism in Africa.

---

### NOTES

1. In Benin, the Congo, Ghana, Somalia, Togo, Uganda, and Zaire the military has also ruled for much longer periods than civilians.

# Chapter 8

## *The March toward Tyranny*

The preceding chapters reviewed the tyrannical regimes that had been installed in much of Africa at the dawn of the 1990s. This chapter describes the evolution of the culture of political repression in selected countries after independence in the 1960s. Africa has experienced one-party civilian or military dictatorships in both pro-Eastern countries such as Ghana and Zimbabwe and pro-Western countries such as the Ivory Coast, Kenya, and Liberia. But despite professed ideological leanings, the same measures of oppression were employed against the African people. Ideology, therefore, is irrelevant as a determinant of the political plight of the people.

Greater focus is placed on Ghana because Ghana was widely acknowledged to have started the African liberation struggle in the 1960s. Furthermore, Ghana's charismatic leader, Dr. Kwame Nkrumah, influenced the course of many political and nationalist events in Africa.

### GHANA: WHERE IT BEGAN

The unreserved idolisation of Dr. Nkrumah's domestic and foreign [policies]. . . should not go unchallenged.

New Nkrumahism is beholden to Dr. Nkrumah's politics inasmuch as Nkrumah was one of the vigorous political thinkers of our time. Apart from that, the old Nkrumahism should apologise to Ghanaians for betraying their trust in it. Old Nkrumahism imprisoned political opponents, forced opponents into exile, outlawed the rule of law and ousted competition and free enterprise.
—Robert Kwao Glah in *West Africa* (May 4-10, 1992; p. 744).

When Ghana achieved its independence in 1957, Dr. Kwame Nkrumah became its first black prime minister. His background was that of a man of

modest upbringing, which starkly contrasted with his subsequent performance as head of state. He was born on September 21, 1909. His father was
a goldsmith in the village of Nkroful in Nzima in the southwest of Ghana.
His mother was a market trader. Both parents were private entrepreneurs,
not government or state employees.[1]

In 1935 Nkrumah went to the United States to study economics and
sociology at Lincoln University, near Oxford, Pennsylvania. He subsequently declared a major in theology and graduated in 1942 with a bachelor's
degree. In 1943 he secured a master of arts degree in philosophy from the
University of Pennsylvania. He enrolled in the Ph.D. program and began a
thesis on logical positivism but then left for Britain. (He never completed the
thesis; however, in 1951 Lincoln University awarded him an honorary doctor
of laws degree.

From 1945 to 1947 Nkrumah served as the general-secretary of the
Pan-African Congress and published a monthly paper called the *New African*.
The first issue (March 1946) preached African unity and nationalism and
attacked imperialism and the unjust laws of the colonies. A prolific writer,
Nkrumah authored many books to propagate his ideas and to condemn
colonialism. Among his works were: *Towards Colonial Freedom* (1940); *Education
and Nationalism in West Africa* (1943); *What I Mean by Positive Action* (1950); and
*Ghana: An Autobiography* (1957).

On December 29, 1947, Dr. J. B. Danquah founded the United Gold
Coast Convention (UGCC), the country's first nationalist party. Danquah
offered the post of general secretary of the party to Nkrumah. For two years
they organized and built up the UGCC. But differences in temperament
eclipsed further progress. On June 12, 1949, Nkrumah broke away and
founded his own party, the Convention People's Party (CPP). This party was
broad-based since, according to Nkrumah, "a middle-class elite, without the
battering ram of the illiterate masses, can never hope to smash the forces of
colonialism" (cited in Italiaander, 1961; p. 242). In addition to the peasants,
many market traders supported the CPP.

In the elections of 1951, Nkrumah developed a six-point program for his
party. Among them were:

1. To fight relentlessly by all constitutional means to achieve full
   "self-government now" for the chiefs and people of the Gold Coast.
2. To serve as the vigorous conscious political vanguard for removing
   all forms of oppression and for establishing a democratic government.
3. To secure and maintain the complete unity of the chiefs and people
   of the Colony, Ashanti, Northern Territories, and Trans-Volta.

4. To work for a proper reconstruction of a better Gold Coast in which the people shall have the right to live and govern themselves as free people.

Nkrumah stood for positive action and called for "the adoption of all legitimate and constitutional means by which we could attack the forces of imperialism in Ghana. The weapons were legitimate political agitation, newspaper and educational campaigns and, as a last resort, the constitutional application of strikes, boycotts, and noncooperation based on the principle of absolute nonviolence" (cited in Italiaander, 1961).

In 1949 Nkrumah's party demanded immediate self-government. "If we get self-government, we'll transform the Gold Coast into a paradise in ten years," Nkrumah declared. To press for self-government, he initiated a series of strikes and boycotts that provoked the colonial authorities to arrest him and his associates and to sentence them to three years in jail in January 1950. After Nkrumah's party received 95 percent of the votes in the elections of February 8, 1951, however, the British governor-general, Sir Charles Noble Arden-Clarke, pardoned him and asked him to form a government in the colonial legislature.

Nkrumah worked within the colonial administration to propose independence for Ghana. With the solid support of his party behind him, he won elections with overwhelming majorities in an effort to convince the colonial authorities that the people of Ghana resolutely sought freedom. On March 6, 1957, the colonialists granted Ghana its independence. Nkrumah thereupon became Ghana's first prime minister, with Lord Listowel as the governor-general. Although Listowel had the right to veto any legislation in Ghana—as did the governor-general in other British Commonwealth countries—he seldom exercised it. He was more content to serve as an overseer of orderly government. When Nkrumah became the prime minister, Dr. Danquah, the leader of the opposition, commented wryly, "It is a great opportunity for testing Mr. Nkrumah's ability for statesmanship" (*West Africa,* Jan 11, 1982; p. 86).

At independence, Nkrumah and his Convention People's Party faced a number of challenges and dilemmas. First, freedom had been achieved. The colonial infidels had been ousted. How could he maintain the momentum? He had raised the people's expectations to unrealistic levels and those who had supported him in the struggle were impatient for their rewards. How could he make good on his promise of a paradise in 10 years? Failure to deliver could erode his support. Second, he faced regionally based opposition parties. Opposition to Nkrumah during the 1950s had been strongest in the

Ashanti region, under Dr. Kofi A. Busia and Dr. J. B. Danquah. A resurgence of Ashanti nationalism and threats of secession briefly erupted in the late 1950s. Similar tendencies emerged in other parts of the country as well. The Ewes, split by the Ghana-Togo border, threatened to secede and join their kinsmen in Togo. In the north there were similar rumblings. Third, Nkrumah wanted to build a modern nation-state, but to do this he felt he needed uncontestable authority. To ensure this authority, he had to provide at least a glimpse of the paradise he had promised by creating jobs and demonstrating some economic progress. He had to accomplish all this when the world cocoa market was soft.

Clearly these were formidable tasks for any politician. In hindsight, it was precisely at this juncture in 1957 that Nkrumah should have bowed out of politics. Had he done so, his place in history would have been secure. He had made many personal sacrifices to win independence for the people of Ghana. Ghanaians would have been forever grateful to the hero and father of their nation. By staying on to lead the country, however, he made a grievous error.

There was a vast difference between the skills needed to fight the forces of colonialism and imperialism and those needed to develop an economy successfully. Battling the forces of colonialism required agitation, strikes, boycotts, highly charged emotional rhetoric, and unrelenting activism to call world attention to colonial injustice. To run an economy or a government, skills such as patience, diligence, and a willingness to compromise were needed.

It is true that Nkrumah initially lacked capable administrators. He could, however, have enlisted the expertise of economists, administrators, and teachers who held no political affiliation. Bankole (1981), a Nigerian, argued that Nkrumah feared the possible political rivalry of intellectuals and there-fore surrounded himself with lackeys:

> Though he did not have capable and experienced men in his camp, it was nevertheless his responsibility to form a competent body of advisers on various aspects of Government functions. The country had a number of economists, experienced administrators, educationalists, etc., divorced from party politics, from whom Nkrumah could have drawn up an advisory planning committee. But because he was afraid of possible political rivalry from such men of learning, he surrounded himself with time-servers, job-hunters and sycophants; in other words, "yes-men" who were out for personal gains and favors. Because of this fear, treatment meted out to intellectuals in Nkrumah's own party assumed the form of either persuading them to leave the country and take up appointments

abroad or systematic vilification or removal from the Central Committee of the party. Even intellectuals who had been consistently loyal to the party were denied responsible posts (p. 280).

Many other nationalists lacked administrative expertise. For example, Kenneth Kaunda, Julius Nyerere, Ahmed Sekou Toure, and others had also won the political battles for independence at great personal cost and sacrifice. Their people were grateful. They too should have left the economic battle to those who possessed skills to manage the economy. But in choosing to stay on and run their economies according to their own vision, they entered a competitive arena for which they were ill-equipped. In the process they bloodied themselves, tarnished their images, and risked all that they had achieved for their countries by way of independence from colonial rule.

History shows that most of the nationalists who took over the controls of their countries' economies failed in their efforts to generate development, disgraced themselves, and ruined millions of African lives in the process. Tarnishing their own record of courageous struggle for independence, most of these nationalists fell, with monotonous regularity, from grace to grass to the grave. The case of Nkrumah was perhaps the most pathetic. He was overthrown in 1966 while headed for Hanoi, where he said he intended to find a solution to the Vietnam War. Ghanaians furiously tore down the statue he built for himself, charged him with extortion and corruption, and sent his photograph to 60 member countries of Interpol. According to Lamb (1984), "[i]t was an inglorious ending for a man who once held such hope as a leader of global stature, a man whose gravest error may have been that in the final years he began believing he was really all the things he said he was" (p. 287). In fact, Colonel Akwasi Amankwa, one of the leaders of the 1966 coup, wrote: "Nkrumah could have been a great man. He started well, led the independence movement and became, on behalf of Ghana, the symbol of emerging Africa. Somewhere down the line, however, he became ambitious, built a cult of personality and ruthlessly used the powers invested in him by his own constitution. He developed a strange love for absolute power" (cited in Lamb, 1984, p. 287).

After a brief stay in Romania, Nkrumah settled in exile in Guinea, where he died of cancer. Sadly, the man who won independence for Ghana was not even honored with a state burial as a final tribute. The state constructed a mausoleum in his village, Nkroful, where his remains were quietly laid to rest. But the mausoleum in 1990 was overgrown with weeds.

Nkrumah's method of dealing with the colonialists was confrontational, but that method was inappropriate for developing domestic policy. Conciliation and accommodation were far superior in view of the need for national unity. Impatient to transform Ghana into a socialist state, Nkrumah had no time for compromises and conciliation. The opposition, he charged, deliberately filibustered to waste time. Ghana could not afford such luxury. He declared, "We must achieve in a decade what it took others a century," (Nkrumah, 1957; p. 398). In his quest for uncontestable power, he sought the elimination of the opposition—the first step in his march toward dictatorship.

Within a year of Ghana's independence, Nkrumah's parliament had introduced the 1957 Avoidance of Discrimination Act, which banned various ethnic organizations, allegedly to promote national unity. This act caused the opposition parties to coalesce into the United Party, which rapidly grew throughout the country. In response to this development, in July 1958 Nkrumah passed the Preventive Detention Bill, which gave the government sweeping powers to "imprison, without trial, any person suspected of activities prejudicial to the state's security." The government-owned media charged that Nkrumah's opposition was divisive and bent on sabotaging Ghana's construction efforts. But Nkrumah's *Autobiography* exposed a more selfish motive for attacking the opposition: "It has always been my conviction that after any political revolution, nonviolent or violent, the new government should, immediately on coming into power, clear out from the civil service all its old leaders. My own experience taught me that by failing to do so, a revolutionary government risks its own destruction" (cited in Italiaander, 1961; p. 244).

Accordingly, Nkrumah abolished the regional assemblies and proscribed opposition activities. Some opposition leaders, the same men who had fought alongside him for Ghana's independence, were arrested. Obetsebi-Lamptey and Dr. J. B. Danquah died in prison. Others, such as Dr. Busia, fled into exile. In the summer of 1959 Busia settled in Holland. There he charged: "From the day of independence, Nkrumah banned all regional parties. About 100 members of the Opposition were in jail, their families lived in poverty, and their children had to leave school, as the Opposition leaders—just like their parties—were without funds. Every hope for democracy in Ghana was lost. Nkrumah had destroyed the basis for it" (cited in Italiaander, 1961; p. 246).

Recall that the colonialists had weakened the authority of traditional African rulers. Instead of restoring their authority, Nkrumah stripped the chiefs of much of what remained. Without membership in his party, they had no effective role to play in government. Nkrumah did create a House of Chiefs, but it had only advisory functions.

Not content with the British governor's veto power over his policies, Nkrumah introduced a republican constitution that abolished the governor-generalship in July 1960. This enabled Nkrumah to become the head of state with the power to rule by decree. With the opposition bludgeoned to extinction, he had an automatic majority in parliament.

Next, the newspapers and the news media came under the complete control of Nkrumah's Convention People's Party. Censorship was imposed. Any opposition to Nkrumah's dictatorship was brutally suppressed. Finally, in January 1964 a plebiscite was held to decide whether Ghana should be a one-party state. It was a meaningless exercise since there was nobody left to oppose the idea—all the opposition members were in jail or in self-imposed exile. The people approved the measure by a 2,773,920 to 2,452 vote (Boahen and Webster, 1970).

Each treacherous step Nkrumah took toward despotism was defended in pursuit of socialism. He asserted that "[The] Convention People's Party is the state and the state is the party. . .The Party has always proclaimed socialism as the objective of our social, industrial and economic programmes. Socialism however will continue to remain a slogan until industrialization is achieved" (Nkrumah, 1973; p. 190). He spelled out the economic content of the ideology: "Let me make it clear that our socialist objectives demand that the public and cooperative sector of the productive economy should expand at the maximum possible rate, especially in those strategic areas of production upon which the economy of the country depends" (Nkrumah, 1973; p. 191).

At times, Nkrumah seemed indecisive or unclear about his choice of the socialist ideology. Nor did he clearly define the goals of socialism. At one point he stated, "This choice is based on the belief that only a socialist form of society can assure Ghana of a rapid rate of economic progress without destroying that social justice, that freedom and equality, which are a central feature of our traditional way of life" (*Seven-Year Development Plan*, Government of Ghana, 1963; p. 1). At another point, he asserted that the socialist transformation would "eradicate completely the colonial structure of our economy." According to Nkrumah:

> Ghana inherited a colonial economy and similar disabilities in most other directions. We cannot rest content until we have demolished this miserable structure and raised in its place an edifice of economic stability, thus creating for ourselves a veritable paradise of abundance and satisfaction. Despite the ideological bankruptcy and moral collapse of a civilization in despair, we must go forward with our preparations for planned economic growth to supplant the

poverty, ignorance, disease, illiteracy and degradation left in their wake by discredited colonialism and decaying imperialism (1973; p. 185).

Nkrumah was constantly haunted by the specter of imperialism and neocolonialism, which he claimed "is only the old colonialism with a facade of African stooges." He believed that only socialism could effectively check the evil machinations of neocolonialism and felt himself obliged to enlighten his fellow African heads of state.

In sum, for Nkrumah, socialism would initiate a rapid social transformation of Ghanaian society, would create a "veritable paradise of abundance and satisfaction," would check the "evil machinations of imperialism and neocolonialism," would foster "economic independence" in an adverse colonial heritage, would serve "in the vanguard of the revolutionary struggle," and would liberate the oppressed continent of Africa.

He imposed a bewildering array of legislative controls and regulations to assure state participation in the economy. There were controls on imports, capital transfers, industry, minimum wages, the rights and powers of trade unions, prices, rents, and interest rates. Although some of these controls had been introduced by the colonialists, Nkrumah retained and expanded them. He nationalized private businesses and set up many state enterprises with little planning or projections of cost. For example, when the sugar factory at Asuatuare was completed, it stood idle in 1964 for more than a year because someone forgot to include a water supply system in the construction plans. Thus Nkrumah began his massive industrialization effort under the impetus of socialism.

The plethora of controls brought in its wake two interrelated and pernicious problems: bribery and corruption. By imposing price controls that required producers to charge prices lower than the free-market prices, the Nkrumah government caused shortages of commodities as producers cut output. State enterprises that were supposed to make goods available to ease the shortages failed in their tasks; they produced only small quantities of goods. Because supply did not meet demand, the government resorted to rationing. To obtain more than their allocated share of ration coupons, some people offered officials bribes, and some women offered sexual favors. Government officials allocated to themselves extra chits that they could give to party lackeys, wives, and girlfriends. Wives of ministers reaped huge profits reselling on the black market commodities purchased at the lower, government-controlled prices. Thus was born a practice Ghanaians called *kalabule* or profiteering.

By 1963 corruption was so pervasive that Ghanaian society appeared to be beyond redemption. One member of the National Assembly, M. Archer (MP-Wawa East), berated the Nkrumah regime:

> Anytime I stand and say that people are corrupt, Members in this house think I am joking. I am not joking at all. I say that with all seriousness. What we saw and what we listened to during the deliberations of the Public Accounts Committee is evidence of the fact that people in this country—in fact, many of them—are corrupt. One thing that I should like to say is that many people in this country think that it is only politicians who are corrupt. . .But those who are corrupt are civil servants and people in the public corporations. . .Only Heaven knows how much we are losing in this country through the practice of corruption (quoted in LeVine, 1975; p. 50).

Nkrumah responded to the charges of corruption in his government by setting up Commissions of Enquiry to investigate the charges and submit recommendations. In effect, they allowed the government to shirk responsibility and delay adopting effective remedial action. In fact, since 1957, Ghana has set up more than 109 of such commissions; but corruption is still rampant.

Although Nkrumah's parents were private entrepreneurs and although peasant farmers, market traders, and chiefs supported his struggle for independence, Nkrumah gave these groups very little assistance. His voluminous *Seven-Year Development Plan* devoted only two paragraphs to peasant agriculture. In fact, to Nkrumah peasant agriculture was an inferior form of economic activity. Unofficial comments indicated that he referred to cocoa farming as "poor nigger's business" (Killick, 1978; p. 63, fn. 97). Instead, Nkrumah favored industrialization: "Industry rather than agriculture is the means by which rapid improvement in Africa's living standards is possible. There are, however, imperial specialists and apologists who urge the less developed countries to concentrate on agriculture and leave industrialization for some later time when their population shall be well fed. The world's economic development, however, shows that it is only with advanced industrialization that it has been possible to raise the nutritional level of the people by raising their levels of income" (Nkrumah, 1957; p. 7).

Nkrumah saw great surpluses in agriculture that he could appropriate to finance his massive industrialization effort. His Convention People's Party took control of the Cocoa Purchasing Company, a subsidiary of the Ghana Cocoa Marketing Board. The function of the Cocoa Purchasing Company was to purchase, store, sell, or deal in cocoa and to make advances or loans to facilitate its purchase, but the company quickly became a huge patronage machine. Without membership in the party-sponsored United Ghana

Farmers Council, farmers were not entitled to sell their cocoa to the Cocoa
Purchasing Company or to receive loans from that body. Nkrumah would
not assist independent cocoa farmers because he maintained that assistance
would have encouraged the growth of the bourgeoisie. He was highly
suspicious of such a class in the midst of the socialist state he was building
for Ghana. He was quite explicit on the subject: "We would be hampering
our advance of socialism if we were to encourage the growth of Ghanaian
private capitalism in our midst" (National Assembly Debates, Mar 11, 1964;
cited by Killick, 1978; p. 63).

As for the peasant farmers and traders without whose support his struggle
for independence would have collapsed, their reward came in the form of
price controls. Those farmers and traders who violated the controls were
jailed and their produce confiscated by the state. Of course, the imposition
of price controls was in blatant disregard of indigenous African economic
tradition. In traditional African village markets, chiefs did not set prices. They
were determined by bargaining. Why then should an African government
impose such alien measures on its people?

By 1966 Ghanaians were fed up with Nkrumah and his rhetoric. He was
ousted in a military uprising. His socialist experiment was a miserable failure.
When Ghana had gained its independence, its foreign exchange reserves
stood at $400 million. In 1966 Ghana had a foreign debt of $858 million.
Only three out of the 64 state enterprises Nkrumah established were financially viable. More hopeless were the state farms he established (amid
pompous fanfare) with mechanization as their guiding principle. In 1965 the
state farms barely produced enough food to feed their own workers, let alone
the nation. After only three years of operation these government farms had
accumulated losses of over $15 million. Between 1960 and 1966 local food
prices doubled as a result of these shortages. The reaction of the Nkrumah
government to rising food prices was one of paranoia. Instead of acknowl-
edging the shortfalls in food production, Nkrumah blamed neocolonialist
agents and economic saboteurs.

On the industrial front Nkrumah's leadership was also a failure. Actual
manufacturing output was a mere 20 percent of capacity in 1966. The Paper
Convention Corporation at Takoradi operated at only 3 percent of installed
capacity.

When Nkrumah was overthrown, there was much jubilation in the streets
of Ghana. But the tragedy of Ghana was that, up to 1983, successive heads
of state after Nkrumah never had the sense to dismantle the huge government
interventionist behemoth that he had erected. Apart from Dr. Kofi Busia,
who made feeble attempts to cut the size of the grossly inefficient govern-

ment sector, almost all the Ghanaian heads of state retained Nkrumah's socialist apparatus and even expanded its role. In 1972 a military version of Nkrumah appeared: Col. Ignatius Acheampong. He even spoke like Nkrumah. His regime was also a failure, and he was ousted by a military coup and executed.

Nkrumah's legacy is the greatest obstacle facing Ghana today. But to many Ghanaians, other Africans, and black Americans, criticizing Nkrumah is sacrilegious because they revere him for his crusade against Western colonialism and imperialism. Admittedly, Nkrumah had a few economic successes. The Akosombo Dam stands as a towering achievement that cushioned the impact of the 1973 and 1979 oil price shocks. Tema Harbor was another Nkrumah success. But his general economic and political failures were so massive that they dominated his successes. Moreover, Ghanaians resoundly rejected his socialism and rejoiced at his overthrow.

Some African intellectuals rather unfortunately misinterpret criticism of Nkrumah as an attack on socialism. Indeed, the objectives of socialism—equity and justice—may be laudable. Moreover, questioning the method of achieving socialist goals does not mean that one opposes the ideals of socialism. The objectionable aspects of Nkrumah's socialism were the inefficient methods he used to reach the goals and his resultant drift toward personal dictatorship.

True socialism is practiced by the people themselves; it is not imposed upon them by a government. Nkrumah's socialism became an instrument to oppress and exploit Ghanaians. While Nkrumah preached socialism, his ministers were importing luxury items for their personal use and living lavish lifestyles.

In 1962 a member of Ghana's National Assembly, B.E. Kusi, excoriated these professed socialists:

> Many children go about in the streets because they cannot get accommodation in secondary schools, while those Ministers who are in charge of the money send their children to international schools and to University. Most of them ride in Mercedes-Benz (220s) and yet call themselves socialists. This is very bad.
>
> If we want to build a socialist country, then we must let the President know that we are serious about the use of public funds and that we do not pay mere lip service to socialism (quoted in LeVine, 1975; p. 12).

Nkrumah, however, cleverly justified almost all his repressive measures as vehicles to achieve his socialist objectives. He thus shielded himself and his measures from being criticized as dictatorial. In fact, a criticism of Nkrumah automatically meant the critic would be portrayed as procolonial or even worse, an African stooge of imperialist forces. Nkrumah's success with this strategy was due less to his ingenuity than to his opposition's failure to develop an effective counterstrategy. Instead of charging the man who had been a hero with despotism, the opposition should have praised the goals of socialism while insisting that there were better ways of achieving them.

The success or failure of Nkrumah's leadership still evokes heated debates. In international circles he was without question a man of enviable stature. He was a source of inspiration to the oppressed in Africa. He won freedom and political independence for Ghana. Everyone would agree. But what counted most was his acceptance among his own people. In Ghana, Nkrumah was a miserable disaster politically and economically. His political failures become more glaring in the wake of the collapse of one-party state systems in Eastern Europe and Africa.

*West Africa* concluded that Kwame Nkrumah should have retired after Ghana gained its independence:

> The consequences of what Nkrumah did when he acquired executive power are painfully visible in Ghana today where the moral standards of public life have been so sadly lowered, where a spoils system seems to have been institutionalized, and where politics seems to be treated as a personal pecuniary opportunity rather than a civic and neighbourly duty. Certainly, the exodus of educated people has contributed to the slenderness of Ghana's managerial resources. One big question is why did Nkrumah permit the deterioration of Ghana which followed in his wake? What was his tragic flaw? Was it that he found practical administration and responsibility uninteresting and preferred simply campaigning, thus caring little for what was happening domestically so long as he was able to use Ghana as a platform for his United Africa campaign? Was it that he had lost interest in politics but did not know how to retire gracefully from the hurly burly without it seeming to be some form of defeat? Perhaps had he been able to withdraw honourably from the scene the history of much of Africa over the past two decades might have been different by virtue of his example (Jan 11, 1982; p. 87).

But Nkrumah did not retire after Ghana's independence. He enjoyed much influence in Africa. Tragically for Africa, one country after another, with deadly consistency, followed in his footsteps: Guinea, Mali, Congo-Brazzaville, Tanzania, Zambia, and a host of others. Predictably, in each country tyranny followed, economies were ruined, and the nationalists were ousted by the military. Incredibly, 25 years after the failure of Nkrumah's socialist experiment, Zimbabwe was charging obstinately along the same disastrous lines. This is of particular relevance to South African blacks. While

Nelson Mandela has made enormous personal sacrifices and suffered greatly in his struggle to bring freedom to South Africa, great care and precautions must be taken to prevent his transformation into another Nkrumah.[2] In Zimbabwe it is probably too late.

## ZIMBABWE

In Zimbabwe, socialism means what is mine is mine but what is yours we share.

—A minister in Robert Mugabe's cabinet

Zimbabwe, formerly Northern Rhodesia, won its independence after a bitter struggle. At the time, the black majority outnumbered the tiny white population by a ratio of almost 20:1 or 8 million to 250,000. Yet under Prime Minister Ian Smith, the whites had refused to share power with the black majority, despite pressures from Britain—the colonial power—and from African leaders. To block any hopes of freedom for the blacks, Ian Smith unilaterally declared Rhodesia independent of Britain in 1965. Britain denounced the move as illegal, initially imposed mild sanctions on Rhodesia and gradually broadened them. In 1968 the United Nations imposed comprehensive sanctions.

In response, Smith introduced many repressive measures. These included controls on foreign exchange transactions to stem capital flight and on imports and exports. In addition, he set up a vast security apparatus to suppress black agitation for freedom and declared a state of emergency under which the white racist government could detain any suspected nationalist indefinitely. Civil liberties were suspended. Blacks were routinely subjected to arbitrary arrests, detention without charge, unwarranted searches and seizures, and summary killings by the hundreds. Torture was commonplace. Police powers were virtually unlimited.

The struggle for black freedom was waged on two fronts. In December 1961 the Zimbabwe African People's Union (ZAPU) was formed under the leadership of Joshua Nkomo. But disagreements over the pace of the struggle led to a breakaway of the Zimbabwe African National Union (ZANU), formed under the leadership of Ndabaningi Sithole. Both ZAPU and ZANU were banned completely in 1964 and most of their leaders were imprisoned.

Following the unilateral declaration of independence (UDI) in May 1965, both ZANU and ZAPU opted for a strategy of armed struggle. Robert Mugabe, a Shona who received his training and taught at a secondary school in Ghana in the 1950s, replaced Sithole as leader of ZANU. He also became the leader of ZANU's armed wing, the Zimbabwe African National

Liberation Army (ZANLA). ZAPU's guerrilla movement—the Zimbabwe People's Revolutionary Army (ZIPRA)—was led by the aging and venerable Joshua Nkomo, an Ndebele. These two forces waged a guerrilla campaign that at one point in the 1970s was costing the Smith government $1 million a day or 40 percent of its budget. The war was marked by extreme savagery. An average of 500 people were killed each month, mostly blacks.

The cost of this guerrilla campaign forced the intransigent Ian Smith to agree to a meeting with Henry Kissinger and Premier Balthazar Vorster of South Africa to discuss Rhodesia's independence. Smith signed an agreement, declared an amnesty for the nationalists, and scheduled elections for 1980. Both ZANU and ZAPU nominated candidates. ZANU won the elections, and Robert Mugabe became Zimbabwe's first black prime minister. As in Ghana, Zimbabweans would find that they had won their independence but not their freedom.

The first task of the new black government was to integrate the existing Rhodesian armed forces with the two guerrilla armies to form a new national army and then to reduce the forces to a manageable size. Not surprisingly, the new army consisted primarily of Mugabe's forces, drawn mainly from his tribe. Many of the former ZIPRA guerrillas, who fought and suffered in the bush for more than five years, suddenly found themselves rewarded with unemployment. The biased selection process sowed the seeds of terror and instability.

The disaffected former ZIPRA guerrillas refused to give up their guns and began a campaign of terror to destabilize the Mugabe government. The New York-based Lawyers Committee for Human Rights reported: "Since 1982, several hundred people have been killed by the dissidents in Matabeleland and to a lesser extent in the Midlands, including more than 1000 ZANU officials and roughly 40 white commercial farmers or their relatives. Fearful white farmers have abandoned over 500,000 acres of productive commercial farmland since 1981" (Zimbabwe: Wages of War, 1986; p. 7).

There was no question that Zimbabwe had a problem with dissidents. But by using excessively harsh methods to deal with the problem, Mugabe demonstrated poor judgment. Although the dissidents numbered less than 9,000, Mugabe demanded extraordinary powers and imposed draconian measures that caused great injury and alienated those who had nothing to do with the dissident problem. Worse, with all the firepower at his disposal and with all the North Korean military advisers at his command, for 10 years Mugabe could not bring the problem under control because he failed to consider using negotiations to resolve it.

Although during the first six years of majority rule in Zimbabwe Mugabe made progress in dismantling the machinery of racism and assuring white Rhodesians that they had a future in Zimbabwe, he maintained the machinery of state security forces. In addition to the army, the police, and a domestic intelligence agency, he reinstituted the state of emergency in 1980 (repealed after 10 years on July 25, 1990) and thereby retained and even strengthened the same repressive measures the white colonialists had introduced to quell black aspirations for freedom. His excuse for the semiannual renewal of the state of emergency was the guerrilla war in Mozambique and destabilization attempts by South Africa.

Mugabe's emergency powers regulations effectively suspended constitutional protections ranging from personal liberty to freedom of speech and association. They also granted the authorities broad powers of arrest and detention without charge or trial. These powers paved the way for large-scale abuses of human rights and terrorism of innocent civilians who had nothing to do with dissident activity. The rule of law was seriously undermined, and because the emergency powers suspended freedom of association, there were official and quasi-official campaigns to intimidate opposition supporters.

Because the dissidents were originally ZIPRA forces, who were mostly drawn from the Ndebele people, Mugabe launched a systematic attempt to suppress the Ndebele people and to wipe out the main opposition, ZAPU and Nkomo. In late 1980 nine senior ZAPU officials were arrested and detained. From 1981 wide-ranging raids were conducted throughout Matabeleland, the principal source of Nkomo's support. In March 1983 Nkomo was arrested and detained for eight hours without reason. Upon release, he fled to London. Another ZAPU high-ranking officer, Makhatini Guduza, fled to Botswana.

By resorting to authoritarianism rather than conciliation, Mugabe deeply disappointed his international supporters and admirers. Remember that to put down some of his own political opponents as well as suspected saboteurs and foreign agents, Mugabe relied upon the very emergency laws and powers that Ian Smith had used to repress black activists during the struggle for independence.

For about a year, Mugabe's government placed a strict curfew on the Ndebele people. It also withheld vital food shipments to the area during a drought to starve them into obedience. He did not distinguish between dissidents and innocent Ndebele people. Ndebele villagers told of executions and torture. After returning from London, Nkomo sent Prime Minister Mugabe a 24-page letter protesting the brutal treatment of his people.

Nkomo concluded, "[T]oday Zimbabwe is defenseless because the people live in fear, not of enemies, but of their own government."

The oppression of the Ndebele has been brutal. Since 1980 Mugabe and his Shona tribesmen have slaughtered more than 43,000 Ndebele tribesmen, although the total number of dissidents was only 9,000. At one point in March 1985, Nkomo's stronghold of Bulawayo was sealed off as Mugabe's soldiers and police searched for dissidents and weapons. More than 50 of Nkomo's leading supporters disappeared during the raids, and more than 1,300 were arrested and detained for questioning. Government workers sent to Matabeleland to register new voters would only accept those who professed allegiance to Mugabe's party, and only a ZANU membership card guaranteed people their freedom from police harassment. Without a ZANU card, no Zimbabwean was safe. The campaign of terror was also waged against Bishop Muzorewa's United African National Conciliation Party (UANC). In February 1985 five UANC officials were shot to death in the western coal-mining town of Hwange by members of Mugabe's Youth Brigade.

In the July 1985 elections Mugabe could not conceal his contempt for the Zimbabwean constitution. He referred to it as "that dirty piece of paper." The elections took place amid relative calm, but when they were over, mobs of ZANU supporters rampaged through the suburbs of Harare to brutalize supporters of the opposition. Homes were raided, and furniture and household possessions were thrown out into the streets. The thugs declared the houses to be ZANU property. As the violence intensified, victims were beaten and pummelled to the point of unconsciousness, their belongings were stolen, and their houses were set on fire. More than six people were reported killed. A defeated ZAPU candidate, Simon Chauruka, was gruesomely hacked to death with axes when a mob of ZANU supporters attacked his home in the Dzivarasekwa suburb. Another ZAPU candidate, Kenneth Mano, who had just been released from detention, was stabbed three times. More than 200 ZAPU officials, including members of parliament, were detained without charge under the emergency powers after the July elections.

Afterwards Mugabe made peace overtures to the opposition party by presenting various arguments for the need for a unity party. In 1987 Nkomo joined Mugabe to form one united political party. That merger created the illusion of unity and tranquillity to outsiders. But many Africans were not fooled by such appearances.

In June 1987 Makhatini Guduza, a senior member of ZAPU who fled to Botswana in 1983, was "forcibly returned to Zimbabwe and [was] held at Chikurubi Maximum Security Prison in Harare on a charge of unlawfully leaving the country. It [was] thought that his detention might be the result of his ZAPU position" (*Index on Censorship*, Jul 1987; p. 41). On September 22, 1987, the minister of home affairs ordered the offices of ZAPU throughout the country to be closed. On September 30, ZAPU's secretary-general, Welshman Mabhena, was arrested by plainclothes security men.

On January 21, 1988, the state of emergency, which had been renewed every six months since 1980, came up for renewal. The country's parliament, dominated by ZANU lackeys, voted unanimously for its renewal. Those members of parliament who granted Mugabe the emergency powers would have a taste of those powers when they fell out of line with Mugabe. The Fanti of Ghana have a proverb: *"Abaa na wodze boo Takyi no, wodze bobo wo so."* ("The stick used to beat your enemy, Takyi, will be the same one used to beat you too.")

Criticism of Mugabe became illegal:

> The Central Intelligence Organization (CIO) routinely harasses Zimbabweans who criticize the government, particularly if their attack is aimed at Robert Mugabe. A young playwright, Denford Magora was detained by the CIO after his work, *Dr. Government*, was performed in Harare. The CIO officers quizzed Mogaro about whether he had based his satirical play on Mugabe . . . CIO officers have been charged with abduction and possible murder of Rashiwe Guzha, a young woman who was taken into custody by CIO officers and never seen again (*Africa Report*, Mar-Apr 1992; p. 53).

Mugabe openly stated his determination to make Zimbabwe a one-party nation and his ZANU party "a truly Marxist-Leninist party to ensure the charting of an irreversible social course and create a socialist ideology." Indeed, in December 1982 all 57 ministers and deputy ministers in Mugabe's cabinet arrived at the Harare airport to greet visiting Ethiopian leader Mengistu Haile-Mariam—black Africa's archapostle of Marxism-Leninism. (Any wonder why Comrade Mengistu fled to Zimbabwe in May 1991?)

Steadily and insidiously, freedom of expression eroded in Zimbabwe as Mugabe's government took over the country's newspapers. Shortly after independence in 1980, the Zimbabwe Mass Media Trust was set up to buy out the country's five main newspapers. Mugabe argued that the newspapers were owned by the South African Argus newspaper group and that the news was racially biased. Nathan Shamuyarira, the minister of information, declared that the purchase was motivated with a "view to getting the right news through to the consumer." Who could challenge that objective? As in Nkrumah's Ghana, each repressive measure in Zimbabwe was dressed in either anticolonialist or antiracist garb. In 1981 the editor of the *Umtali Post* was dismissed on Mugabe's order after she raised questions about the presence in Zimbabwe of North Korean military instructors. Nor could journalists or even members of parliament investigate allegations of corruption in high echelons of the government.

After 1982, a wave of corruption scandals began to sweep the country. For example, at the Ministry of Education phantom teachers were added to the government payroll, and their salaries were collected by teachers already on the payroll. *New African* reported the extent of the corruption:

> Civil servants at all levels, workers in parastatals and private organizations and bank tellers have been appearing in court with monotonous regularity for dipping their hands in the kitty . . . Government critics point fingers at the leadership of the country for the malaise saying that a lot of Ministers are the ones, who, through their "get rich quick" tendencies started the "each one for himself and God for us all" survival syndrome. The critics point to the massive wealth which many Ministers have amassed in the seven short years of independence. It is a common secret that several leaders have thrown the country's avowed policy of socialism to the winds and have used their positions to acquire wealth in the form of hotels, houses for rent, ranches, farms, buses and stores" (Dec 1987; p. 58).

As early as 1982, Edgar Tekere, a maverick and also a nationalist who fought alongside Mugabe for Zimbabwe's independence, decided to fight against this incipient "Swiss bank" socialism. He declared: "We all came from Mozambique with nothing; not even a teaspoon. But today, in less than two years, you hear that so-and-so owns so many farms, a chain of hotels and his father owns a fleet of buses. Where did all that money come from in such a short period? Isn't it from the very public funds they are entrusted to administer?" (*New African*, Mar 1989; p. 21).

For this attack on corruption, Mugabe expelled Tekere from the ZANU party, although his constituency returned him to parliament. University students also protested, saying that Zimbabwe's revolutionary heroes had been betrayed by corrupt and ideologically bankrupt leaders (*New African*, Dec 1988; p. 23).

Zimbabwe's military was also tainted by corruption. In March 1989 Captain Edwin Nleya threatened to expose what he called a "big scandal in the army." He alleged that some senior army officers were extremely corrupt, including some who were engaged in smuggling. He also alleged that some members of the army, operating under orders, had shot rare black rhinos in the Zambezi Valley. Corruption was serious in the Army's Signals Directorate in Harare and in the elite Sixth Brigade, according to Captain Nleya. In July 1989 Nleya "was brutally killed and his decomposed body later found on a mountain near the coal-mining town of Hwange. The officer had earlier told his wife that he was being followed by suspicious men in dark glasses who had threatened to get his head" (*New African*, Jul 1989; p. 16).

The Rev. Ndabaningi Sithole, an exiled former nationalist, complained about the rampant corruption in an open letter to Mugabe that was dated July 10, 1989:

> The exposure of the gross corruption of your most senior ministers and other government officials raises several questions regarding the ability of the present government to run the country. The whole episode causes one to wonder whether we have a government or merely a gang of the most unscrupulous ministers ever to be entrusted with the running of our country. Even in colonial or white settler days nothing matched this corruption and the misuse of public funds. It is inconceivable to a logical mind that your most senior ministers conducted these corrupt deals for months, and you were not privy to these deals. It is equally inconceivable that you were not privy to the constant diversion of foreign aid to the pockets of your very close relatives who have today acquired large farms and businesses by the most unorthodox methods. It has become common knowledge among the members of the public that all your senior ministers have acquired large farms by unorthodox methods which have shocked and amazed our people and undermined the integrity of the government . . . It is common knowledge that the Premier himself and several of his ministers—for example, Chidzero, Kadunqure, Muzenda, Shamuyarira, Kanqai, Munyaradzi and Nkomo keep large bank accounts abroad as if they had no confidence in the country which they themselves run! Nothing can undermine the confidence in their own country more than that their own senior ministers find they have to keep their own funds outside the country (*New African*, Jul 1989).

Journalists who set out to investigate corruption scandals were brutalized and threatened with job terminations and transfers. A scandal that surfaced in the early 1980s drew much attention. Zimbabwe has only one car assembly plant, Willowvalle Motor Industries in Harare. Owing to a shortage of foreign exchange created by a combination of import, export, and exchange controls as well as the refusal of Mugabe to deal with South Africa, a chronic shortage of vehicles developed. Government officials who used their excessive allocation of chits to purchase automobiles later resold them on the black market at three times their purchase price. In October 1988 *The Chronicle*, owned by the government itself, set out to expose this racket. The editor, Geoffrey Nyarota, was himself an ardent supporter of Mugabe and a member of ZANU. He published the names of the ministers who had obtained vehicles. Soon after the publication of the names, insults and accusations were hurled at the editor. The most heady clash was with Defense Minister Enos Nkala, who was masterminding the car racket. When Nyarota's deputy, Davison Maruziva, attempted to question the defense minister further about the scandal, the minister issued threats: "I will lock you with your editor. Where did you get that information? That information is supposed to be with the President and the police. I want that information here in my office. I will use the army to pick you up, then you can ask your questions. I do not care!" (*New African*, Feb 1989; p. 34).

Mugabe demoted and transferred Nyarota. One member of parliament, Bryon Hove, protested, "If someone differs with us, let alone on corruption charges, and he is thrown into the sea, it serves to show how much we condone corruption." Sydney Malunga, an outspoken ZAPU member, charged, "The transfer of Nyarota marks the beginning of a totalitarian state" (*New African*, Apr 1989; p. 36).

Pressure finally forced Mugabe to set up the Sandura Commission of Enquiry to investigate the "Willowgate" scandal. One minister who appeared before it, Maurice Nyagumbo, admitted using his influence to obtain over 36 vehicles for friends, relatives, and contacts within his constituency (*New African*, Apr 1989; p. 36). Mugabe forced five ministers implicated in the scandal to resign. But he spared ministers from his own tribe. Maurice Nyagumbo, who had been the number three man in Mugabe's party and the government's senior minister of political affairs, felt so dishonored that he later committed suicide in April 1989.

Although Mugabe must be given some credit for taking action against corruption, the car racket was not an isolated incident. Nor was the transfer of Nyarota the only evidence of reprisals against journalists. Other editors have lost their jobs for stepping on the toes of the government. Among them were Willie Muserurwa (formerly of the *Sunday Mail*), Henry Muradzikwa (*Sunday Mail*), and Alexander Mahlangu (*Sunday News*). Mahlangu had published an article by one of his travel correspondents that suggested that the races lived more harmoniously in South Africa than in Zimbabwe. Mahlandu admitted he made an error but was nevertheless replaced.

For much of the 1980s jungle law prevailed in Mugabe's Zimbabwe. Joshua Nkomo could have done much to save Zimbabwe, but he sold off his principles and conscience after being implicated in the corruption scandals. In 1987 Edgar Tekere appeared as the one person with sufficient credibility to lead Zimbabwe. He formed a new political party, the Zimbabwe Unity Movement (ZUM), which opposed corruption and supported a multiparty state and economic growth. He asserted, "Democracy in Zimbabwe is in the intensive care unit and the leadership has decayed before it is dead" (*New*

*African*, Dec 1988; p. 23). Although some find Tekere's mannerisms and militant rhetoric offensive, he deserves support from Africans and the world community in his crusade against the tyranny in Zimbabwe that sanctions the oppression of political opponents. Indeed, attempts have been made on Tekere's life. According to *New African*: "There is now strong speculation that the army truck that killed Senator William Ndangana when he was driving to Mutare was intended for Tekere whose own vehicle was just behind that of the late senator. Tekere was the first witness of the accident" (Dec 1989; p. 20).

It is a disgrace to see a professional army covering up murder by making it look like an accident. More maddening, approval for such diabolical acts came from high government officials—those who should respect the laws they expect ordinary citizens to obey. But most of Mugabe's ministers showed not only contempt for the law but uncouth disregard for the rights of others. The worst offender was the defense minister, Enos Nkala, who, intoxicated by the exercise of power, was often given to vituperative utterances and erratic behavior. The Lawyers Committee for Human Rights' *Report on Human Rights in Zimbabwe, 1986* disclosed the minister's intention to crush Nkomo and ZAPU:

> In November 1980, barely six months after independence, Nkala told a rally in Bulawayo, "I will crush Joshua Nkomo." It was ZANU's main task, he said. . .In a series of speeches in September, 1985, Nkala spoke of his intention to crush ZAPU: "Let me assure the nation that the policy of reconciliation toward ZAPU has been withdrawn," he told the Senate on 18 September. "Nkomo should take note—in the next few weeks you'll be seeing fire . . . We want to wipe out the ZAPU leadership. You've only seen the warning lights. We haven't yet reached full blast. I don't want to hear pleas of mercy . . . My instinct tells me that when you deal with ruthless gangsters you have to be ruthless. I have locked up a few honourable members [of Parliament] and I think they will have a rest for a long time to come before they reappear to continue their dissident activities" (p. 53).

In March 1990 Mugabe held general elections to seek a mandate from the people to establish a one-party state. He won 94.5 percent of the vote, but only 54 percent of registered voters bothered to cast their ballots, a number far less than the 95 percent voter turnout for the 1980 and 1985 elections. The *New York Times* reported that urban voters were dissatisfied with economic conditions, government corruption, and violence directed against Mugabe's opponents:

The [election] campaign has been marked by allegations of intimidation and violence. Last weekend, in Gweru, an opposition candidate, Patrick Kombayi, was campaigning against ZANU's vice president, Simon Muzenda, when he and five other opposition members were shot. The opposition asserted that the shootings were carried out by Mr. Muzenda's bodyguards, who are members of the Government's Central Intelligence Organization.

The Gweru shootings prompted the Catholic Commission for Justice and Peace to declare that "the rising incidence of violence and intimidation is calling into question the freedom and fairness of the general election."

The commission suggested that the shootings were carried out by Government officials, stating that "the use of firearms against political opponents in the presence of uniformed police was a most shocking development. The shootings were a gross misuse of state machinery for intimidation purposes. We look forward to the arrest and trial of those responsible" (Mar 29, 1990; p. A6).

Nevertheless, Mugabe misinterpreted the outcome of the election as "a mandate for all our policies including a one-party state." Before establishing a one-party state, however, he disclosed at a news conference that "he would like to 'seek out' the more than 400,000 people who voted for the opposition leader Edgar Tekere" (*New African*, May 1990; p. 16).

Mugabe has been adept at political survival, but he may be woefully deficient in reading political signs. Opposition to a one-party state has been growing, and the people have become increasingly fed up with his rhetoric. *New African* reported: "On Africa Day, only about 8,000 people went to listen to President Mugabe deliver a speech at Rufaro Stadium in Harare. Within hours after the stadium was cleared, 40,000 people paid to watch soccer at the same stadium . . . People have reasons to be apathetic. They complain of high taxation, unemployment, corruption among government and party officials and price hikes" (Dec 1989; p. 20). In fact, at the December 18-22, 1989, National People's Congress, Byron Hove, a member of parliament from Mugabe's party, objected to the one-party state idea. For this criticism, he was ejected from the congress. Eddison Zvobgo, the minister of state for political affairs and ZANU-Patriotic Front chairman in Masvingo province, also opposed the single-party system. In Zimbabwe's *Moto* magazine (Sep 1989) he asserted: "A one-party state is not the panacea to the problems which Zimbabwe faces. Personally, I am against a one-party state. I do not believe that a one-party state, despite the fact that it embodies some democratic trends, is the best system of democracy . . . I do not believe in a one-party state brought about by legislation" (cited by *Africa Report*, Mar-Apr 1990; p. 56). Dumiso Dabengwa, ZANU party chairman of Bulawayo province and a member of the central committee, opposed a Marxist-Leninist state. According to *Africa Report*, Dabengwa "said his province wanted to see references to Marxism-Leninism dropped from the Constitution, as that ideology was foreign to Zimbabwe" (Mar-Apr 1990; p. 56). Other prominent Zimbabweans were also unhappy. *New African* noted:

President Robert Mugabe's long cherished goal of turning Zimbabwe into a one-party state appears to be faltering as he has stumbled into fierce opposition from his powerful politburo.

At a meeting of the ruling ZANU party's top executive body on August 2, the 26-member politburo opposed every move to turn the country into a one-party state, taking leaf from the events of Eastern Europe and some parts of Africa (Mozambique, Tanzania, Zambia, etc.) where prodemocracy and multi-party politics have won the day . . .

[But] the President was quoted recently as saying he was aware of the fact that some of his "comrades" were back-tracking on the issue but that he would work single-handedly to see his long cherished dream come true.

He has warned that if his politburo members were chickening out of the idea, he would be forced to act above their heads and call another congress to decide the future of the country (Oct 1990; p. 58).

Not only are the vestiges of freedom eroding in Zimbabwe, but the economy is markedly declining. Corn production dropped sharply from 2 million tons in 1981 to 620,000 in 1983. Zimbabwe, once a food exporter, is rapidly becoming a food importer. Shortages of commodities and foreign exchange are becoming rampant. "The cost of living has risen astronomically since independence in 1980. Inflation is running around 20 percent per annum and most people are having to dig deeper into their pockets to survive" (*New African*, Dec 1987; p. 58). The unemployment rate is now 50 percent in the urban job market.

Zimbabwe is following the same treacherous path, in deadly lock-step rhythm, toward tyranny and censorship that Nkrumah led in Ghana. Of course, to win international sympathy Mugabe will blame the lackluster performance of Zimbabwe's economy on dissident activities and the spillover effects from the South African situation. But he has made the same errors Nkrumah made. In fact, it would be wise for Mugabe to retire now, after running the country for 10 years, rather than to stay on to fall from grace to grass.

In council elections in Bulawayo in September 1989, a candidate for Mugabe's ruling party was trounced by a white candidate who received the black vote. The defeat upset ZANU officials. Addressing a central committee meeting, a sober President Mugabe lamented: "We now have to admit that we are reaping the bitter fruits of our unwholesome and negative behavior. Our image as leaders of the party has been tarnished. The people are crying for our blood and certainly are entitled to do so after watching our actions" (*New African*, Dec 1989; p. 20).

During a speech in August 1991, Mugabe was heckled by a black citizen who stood up and yelled: "Ian Smith was better!" According to the *Washington Post*, "Some listeners cheered the bold heckler as he was bundled off to jail on charges of 'insulting' the president" (Sep 9, 1991; p. A20).

The only rational course of action is for Mugabe to exit before the people "get his blood."

## KENYA

It is better to die on one's feet than to live on one's knees.

—Dedan Kimaathi, Mau Mau leader hanged by the British on February 18, 1957,
on the slopes of Mount Kenya

Kenya offers a sad story and a scenario too often repeated in many African countries. Kenya used to be highly respected by other African nations. It was one of the rare African edifices of prosperity, order, and stability—an enviable exception to the cupidity, mismanagement, and violence that have afflicted much of the continent.

Of all the black African regimes of the postcolonial period, the Kenyan government served its people best. A nation of 20 million, Kenya was long considered the United States' strongest ally in Africa. More important, it was also one of the few former African colonies in which the transition from white colonial rule to black rule was marked by conciliation and peaceful coexistence of the races. Its tourist industry and safaris were world-renowned. The award-winning film *Out of Africa* was filmed in Kenya.

In the 1960s and 1970s Kenya enjoyed robust economic growth. Its average growth rate of 6 percent was the envy of Africa. But all this progress is in danger of being aborted, not so much because of defective economic policies but because of the increasing paranoia of the Daniel arap Moi regime and a rapidly deteriorating political situation.

U.S. corporations have begun pulling out of Kenya because of its uncertain political future and increasing repression. From 1982 to 1989 the number of U.S. subsidiaries in Kenya fell from 140 to 115 (*South*, Jun 1989; p. 29). Firestone, Mobil Oil, and the First National Bank of Chicago are among the transnationals that have withdrawn from Kenya. This disinvestment is not yet a major trend but is likely to grow as the political crisis deepens.

Relations with the United States began to turn sour in the early 1980s amid growing reports of rampant human rights abuses and police torture. U.S. aid to Kenya shrank from $111 million in 1984 to $53 million in 1986. In 1987 events came to a head. Moi's visit to Washington was abruptly cut short after his request for increased U.S. aid met with firm refusal.

Kenya's prominent position in Africa began to erode after the death in 1978 of Jomo Kenyatta, its first president, who served for 14 years. His appointed vice-president, Daniel arap Moi, served as acting president for 90 days in accordance with the country's constitution. Moi was never elected and had no popular base. But after the interim period was over, Moi simply declared himself president. There was no election. In addition, on November 3, 1978 he promulgated the Preservation of Public Security Act by executive order without ratification by the Kenyan parliament. This act instituted a state of emergency under which hundreds of political dissidents, university professors, students, and journalists have been jailed. In 1980 Moi's close friend, Charles Mugane Njonjo, Kenya's attorney general for 17 years, appointed himself minister of constitutional affairs.

On June 17, 1982, Kenya became a one-party state through an amendment to the constitution engineered by Njonjo. Citing a growing security threat along its borders, parliament passed the amendment after only 20 minutes of debate, and the Kenya African National Union (KANU) became the sole legal party. To be eligible to vote, citizens were forced to pay to register as KANU members, under threats to their jobs and personal security. To work for the Kenyan government, one had to be a KANU member.

During 1981 and 1982 the Moi government banned various trade and professional unions, including the Union of Civil Servants and the University Staff Union, and brutally suppressed strike actions by doctors, bank employees, industrial workers, and students. The government also reinstated detention without trial.

On August 1, 1982, an attempted coup by disaffected soldiers failed. Moi's reprisals were brutal. Over 1,000 members of the armed forces were court-martialed and sentenced to long prison terms, and hundreds more were detained without trial. About 80 university students were arrested. In the early months of 1983 the political arrests continued. Moi's government tried people from all walks of life, including newspaper vendors, for various charges of seditious intent. Among them was Ajama Oginga Odinga, a former vice-president of the country, who was placed under house arrest for seven months. Many university lecturers, journalists, students, former members of parliament, and others fled into exile.

Paranoia and hysteria prevailed during the early 1980s. The government silenced churches, proscribed academic discussion in schools and universities, and monitored or denied access to certain literature. The paranoia stemmed from the activities of an underground movement, Mwakenya (*Muungano wa Wazalendo Kukomboa Kenya*—the Union of Nationalists to Liberate Kenya). Moi accused this movement of being run by fanatical socialists. Any alleged connection with this movement warranted arrest. Over 40 people were apprehended for associating with the group.

All these repressive measures were taken despite the fact that Sections 78 and 79 of the Kenya Constitution protect the freedom of every Kenyan to receive and hold ideas and beliefs without interference. Section 79 of the constitution also outlaws discrimination against any Kenyan on grounds of political opinion. But these guarantees were insidiously removed through various constitutional changes. Two of Kenya's most prominent attorneys, Gibson Kamau Kuria and Paul Muite, complained that "since 1978, Kenya has witnessed constitutional changes which . . . enable the political leadership of the day to wield unlimited power . . . The weakening of the independence Constitution has been mainly through dilution rather than the abolition of institutions. This weakening of the institutions results from the removal of the legal protection which an individual or an institution requires in order to function properly in a democracy. Every person or institution is now expected to act the way the Executive or another institution wants him or it to do" (*The African Letter*, Apr 16-30, 1990; p. 18).

Even parliament began to voice Moi's views. The speaker of parliament is generally expected to be independent of the head of state. But in Kenya under Moi, he is a *nyayo*. The word *nyayo* literally means "footsteps" but has now come to mean following closely in *Moi*'s footsteps. Koigi wa Wamwere, a former member of parliament who was detained twice (from August 1975 to December 1978 by the Kenyatta government and from August 1982 to December 1984 by the Moi regime), explained:

For a speaker to be *nyayo* means having no mind or views of his own. It simply means a parrot, as Moi put it in a speech on September 13, 1984 after his return from Addis Ababa. According to the *Nation* newspaper: "I call on all ministers, assistant ministers and every other person to sing like parrots. During Mzee Kenyatta's period, I persistently sang the Kenyatta tune until people said: This fellow has nothing to say, except to sing for Kenyatta. I said: I did not have ideas of my own. Who was I to have my own ideas? I was in Kenyatta's shoes, and therefore, I had to sing whatever Kenyatta wanted. If I had sung another song, do you think Kenyatta would have left me alone? Therefore you ought to sing the song I sing. If I put a full stop, you should put a full stop. This is how the country will move forward. The day you become a big person, you will have the liberty to sing your own song and everybody will sing it" (*Index on Censorship,* Jul 1990; p. 17).

Accordingly, measures were taken to force government officials to do exactly that: sing like parrots. In 1986, for example, a change in the constitution deprived the attorney general and the auditor general, who oversees government expenditures and reports directly to parliament, of security of tenure. In 1988, following another constitutional amendment, senior judges and the Public Service Commission, which is responsible for the appointment and discipline of civil servants, saw their functions abrogated.

After 1986, the political situation began to deteriorate more rapidly. The Moi government apprehended more than 200 Kenyans in a new wave of arrests, detentions without trial, and disappearances. The police tortured dozens of political dissidents to force confessions. According to Amnesty International, methods of torture in Kenya included: "beatings on various parts of the body including sexual organs; electric shocks; being held naked for a lengthy period in a cell flooded with water; confinement in a small cell without light; and death threats" (*Torture in the Eighties: An Amnesty Report,* London, 1984; pp. 115-116). After July 1986, Kenyan journalists were forbidden to report the arrests, trials, and conditions of detainees. The percentage of Kenyans imprisoned has come to be the highest in the world, rivalling that of South Africa. Kenyan prisons are overcrowded and have deplorable facilities. Contaminated water and cholera killed five inmates at Kodiaga Prison, Kisumu, in May 1986.

Democracy was further diminished when the Moi government introduced a queuing system into the electoral process in 1986. After being vetted by the local branch committee, prospective candidates would put their pictures in the voting areas, and the local Kenya National Union (KANU) members would line up behind the candidates they wished to see elected. Any primary candidate who managed to win over 70 percent of the vote automatically became the member of parliament. If no one gained over 70 percent, the top three scoring candidates went on to the general election. Moi himself was exempt from this system, of course. For the candidate to qualify for the election, he had to be a life member of KANU, Kenya's sole legal party and had to pay KANU K Sh3,000 (Kenyan shillings—about $1,000) as sponsorship money. Another K Sh1,000 was paid to the government. Voters had to line up behind their chosen candidates from noon to 6:00 p.m. Those not wanting to line up had to stay 1000 meters from the venue. The government claimed that this system would eliminate ballot rigging and election violence. But the system effectively disenfranchised non-KANU members. The secret ballot was gone. Those who stood behind losing candidates risked retaliation by the winning candidates. Moreover, teachers, lawyers, and other professionals were unable to leave their work for six hours to stand behind their candidates. The Catholic Bishops of Kenya complained in a letter to President Moi in November 1986: "We can envisage situations where professional people, businessmen and even the humblest worker would be faced with the choice of compromising their means of livelihood or abstaining from exercising their right to vote" (New African, Apr 1988; p. 22). Moi responded by asking the bishops to stay out of politics.

In the fall of 1986, U.S. Rep. Howard Wolpe, then chairman of the House Subcommittee on Africa, visited Kenya and requested meetings with Kenyan authorities to discuss human rights violations. The meetings were cancelled by the government without explanation. Said Wolpe: "This . . . shows that human rights and democracy in this country are fast deteriorating. But it is not too late. Kenya is a sovereign state and if anybody is prepared to listen the trend can be corrected for the better" (New African, Apr 1987; p. 18).

The first few months of 1987 boded ill for Kenyans believing in liberty. The government imposed unprecedented sanctions against religious and nongovernment organizations, foreign diplomatic missions, politicians, and civil servants. For example, so heightened was President Moi's concern for security that religious organizations' funds were audited to see whether they included support from dissident groups such as Mwakenya. Moi made several speeches upbraiding and accusing organizations of engaging in activities detrimental to the national security of the state. Then he introduced measures to control these groups. Licenses for radio equipment were withdrawn from some organizations because their transmitters "were too powerful for their legitimate purposes." But he did not stop there. Consumed by paranoia, the Moi regime suspected almost everyone, including its ally, the United States, of providing support to Mwakenya.

Editors, newspapers, and magazines soon came into Moi's line of fire. In March 1988 his government banned Beyond, a magazine published by the National Christian Council of Kenya, after it published detailed accounts of election rigging. In April 1989 Financial Review was banned for criticizing many of the government's economic and political initiatives. In June 1989 Development Agenda, a monthly business journal that had published only two issues, was banned. On June 28, 1989, reporters from the Nation Group of newspapers, the largest group in the country, were barred from covering parliamentary proceedings for more than four months after *The Daily Nation* criticized the poor quality of parliamentary debate.

Meanwhile, the Moi regime harassed exiled politicians' families in Kenya and accused foreign political representatives of consorting with criminals. In September 1986 the wife and two sons of Koigi wa Wamere (the former MP) were prevented from boarding an Air France flight to Norway. Their passports were impounded by immigration authorities although the trip had been sanctioned by the Norwegian government. After this incident, Moi announced on January 22, 1987, that "no government officer and members of parliament, including ministers, would be allowed to visit foreign embassies or high commissions without permission from the foreign office." Even the foreign minister and his secretary had to obtain Moi's permission.

*The Economist* expressed concern about the increasing repression:

> Mr. Moi has strengthened the overweening power of the sole legal party. He regards even mild criticism as disloyalty, and spies conspiracy everywhere, blaming all dissent on a shadowy left-wing organization called Mwakenya. Amnesty [International] thinks that since March 1986, 75 people have been illegally held incommunicado before pleading guilty in perfunctory court hearings, to such offences as "neglecting to report a felony." This means not telling the police that you suspect somebody else of being a Mwakenya member, and earns 15 to 18 months in prison. "Taking an unlawful oath" to join Mwakenya earns six years in prison, even where no acts or advocacy of violence are alleged. In the same period, ten academics and lawyers, all open critics of the government, have been detained without trial for alleged links with Mwakenya. None was said to have advocated violence; one, a well-known lawyer, had defended Mwakenya suspects. Some suspects have been tortured, and at least three have died in custody. Hundreds more have been unlawfully detained, then released (Jul 25, 1987; p. 36).

On March 21, 1988, Moi scheduled elections. In a bizarre bid to influence them, he released nine detainees on the same day that he announced the elections and invited the detainees to the state house for tea. According to *New African*: "The President finished his meeting with them by saying that they ought to return to society and become involved in 'nation building.' He also said that he hoped there would be no need to detain anyone again. Instead of immediately returning to building the nation they held a press conference detailing how they had been tortured. They talked of beatings and suffering the 'swimming pool,' whereby the cell is filled with two inches of water for several days" (Apr 1988; p. 22).

UKENYA, an exiled political movement for "unity and democracy in Kenya" based in London, issued a lengthy list of complaints and accusations against the Moi government. The movement demanded "'the return of land,' the unbanning of political parties and associations, the rule of parliamentary 'democracy,' a more even spread of wealth, justice, cessation of murder and torture and the release of political detainees. The details of misdemeanors of both the ex-colonial masters in Kenya and the present African 'stooges' was extensive" (*New African*, May 1987; p. 41).

Koigi wa Wamwere noted a grotesque irony about Kenya: "While the [colonial] governor could be criticised by the British government, the president of Kenya is above criticism. He is almighty and without accountability to anybody" (*Index on Censorship*, Jul 1990; p. 18). Within KANU itself, the slightest appearance of criticism was not tolerated. When long-serving cabinet minister Kenneth Matiba complained about election rigging, he was immediately expelled from the cabinet and the party. His call for competitive politics elicited a strange reaction from party stalwarts. He was placed in detention.

In an interview with *Africa Report*, Maina wa Kinyatti, a former lecturer in history at Kenyatta University who is now living in exile in the United States, described the repression that developed from Moi's paranoia:

Moi sees enemies everywhere. You see, there are two options in our country. Either you sing to the tune of *nyayo* or you keep quiet. And even that silence can be a problem. You can't say anything against the president, he cannot be criticized because he tells the truth all the time. So what you find is that even those liberal MPs who are members of the party but who are very critical of some things like the queuing policy become an enemy. Then the police follow you all over the place. . .

Kenya's courts have become kangaroo courts where the president has all the power to appoint and dismiss the judges, and of course, to dictate what the judges are going to do. Now the courts are being used as a tool to suppress democracy and justice. There is no longer such a thing as a just court. Judges are no longer independent, so the judiciary has been really killed.

You find the same thing with Parliament. Whatever Moi says goes because he has put all his people in Parliament who will not question him. Now they are all "yes men." So he has killed Parliament as well. We no longer have an independent Parliament. It has become a rubber stamp for the president. Moi has transferred power from Parliament to the party. And the party is a tool to be used by Moi to fight those people who are critical. He is killing democracy, he is killing the national constitution, and he is killing Parliament (Jul-Aug 1989; p. 58).

After the collapse of communist dictatorships and one-party state systems in Eastern Europe, the Rev. Dr. Timothy Njoya suggested that African leaders should reconsider the one-party rule in light of those events. He prophesied that Kenya was headed for a major disaster unless the government removed corruption, injustice, road accidents, abuse of power, and other evils, which in the 1980s had become matters of course. Njoya added, "The Church may not avoid suffering, 'road accidents,' inflation, shortage of essential drugs... detentions, imprisonments, torture, oppression and deprivations as other members of society, but she has a hope of surviving the crisis through the power of the cross" (*New African*, Mar 1990; p. 16). The reaction of KANU officials was predictably vitriolic. "Absolute madness and folly!" fumed Peter Oloo Aringo, the national chairman. Elijah Mwangale, minister for livestock development, called for Njoya to be detained.

Of the numerous political assassinations in Kenya, the case of Dr. Robert Ouko, a former foreign minister, serves as a reminder of the danger of concentrating excessive power, without checks and balances, in the hands of a single party or government. In Kenya, there are no assurances of safety once an individual falls out of step with the party or government. Ouko was brutally murdered on February 13, 1990, and his body was burned in a cover-up. Kenyan security men have been widely implicated. According to *New African* (May 1990; p. 18), a week before his death Ouko and President Moi had attended the American Annual Congressional Breakfast Meeting in Washington, D.C., where Ouko delivered an address to American journalists about the political situation in Kenya. Shortly after he returned to Kenya, security personnel apprehended him.

The Moi government claimed that Ouko's death was a suicide. Questioning how a person could shoot himself in the head and then burn himself, University of Nairobi students demonstrated and called for a full independent inquiry. Immediately afterward, circulars went out from departmental heads of government ministries instructing employees to desist from rumormongering on pain of losing their jobs. At least 40 people were arrested and interrogated in connection with such rumors, but most were freed after a few hours without being charged. The Rev. Lawford Ndege Imunde was not so fortunate. For noting in his desk diary that the murder of Dr. Robert Ouko was carried out with the connivance of the government, he was convicted of sedition under Sections 56 and 57 of the penal code for printing and possessing seditious publications "exciting disaffection against the President or the government of Kenya" and was sentenced to six years in jail (*The African Letter*, Apr 1-15, 1990; p. 1).

More detentions and arrests related to the Ouko case followed. *New Africa* reported that by May 1990 "almost every critic, opponent, or past enemy of the government has been swept up in the police net" (May 1990; p. 17). At Ouko's home town, Kisumu, over 56 demonstrators were arraigned in court and charged with illegal demonstrations and another 60 were held in detention for "spreading malicious rumors over the death of Ouko."

Finally, in July 1990, a team of Scotland Yard detectives, who had assisted Kenyan authorities in their investigation, concluded that Ouko had been murdered. Their report, published in the United Kingdom's *Sunday Correspondent* (Jul 22, 1990), claimed that the killing of Ouko "was prompted by his investigation into corruption among his fellow Cabinet members." Members of President Moi's cabinet could be implicated in the murder.

Prominent Kenyans are now demanding change from the one-party system that gives rise to such abusive acts. Anglican Bishop Henry Okullu has called for the abolition of the one-party state and a maximum of two terms in office for any future president. Two former cabinet members, Kenneth Matiba and Charles Rubia, have demanded an immediate repeal of the 1982 constitutional amendment that made KANU the only legal party. In a joint statement they said: "Twenty-seven years of experiment are enough. Only those with vested interests can turn a blind eye to the obvious need for change. We believe our single-party system is the major single contributory factor and almost solely the root cause of the political, economic and social woes we now face (*Washington Times*, May 11, 1990; p. A8).

An incensed President Moi described Matiba and Rubia as "dictators," "traitors," and "tribalists." He repeated the now-familiar refrain that a multi-party system would divide Kenya along tribal lines. According to *The Economist*, "[t]hose asking KANU to relinquish its monopoly of power were accused of being colonialists and tribalists working for foreign masters" (Jun 23, 1990; p. 39).

According to the June 19, 1990, issue of Zambia's *Daily Mail*, "Moi ordered an end to debate on whether or not Kenya should adopt a multiparty system . . . President Moi said that the debate was over and that the people should now concentrate on development." In Moi's support, Vice-President George Saitoti denounced the advocates of the multiparty system as "puppets of foreign masters, out to cause trouble in Kenya" (*Washington Times*, May 11, 1990; p. A8). President Moi promised to hunt them down "like rats" (*New York Times*, Oct 10, 1990; p. A22). Indeed, security agents soon began following Kenneth Matiba around Nairobi. *The Economist* (Jun 23, 1990; p. 39) reported that they broke into his house and severely beat his wife and daughter. Matibia and Rubia were subsequently arrested.

On November 18, 1991, KANU called for the expulsion of 10 foreign diplomats, most of them from the United States, for aiding dissidents. Secretary-General Joseph Kamotho said they had "interfered in the running of a *free* country" (*Index on Censorship*, Mar 1992; p. 37).

Moi's fear of the mere mention of multiparty democracy is significant. Economically, signs of disintegration have begun to appear in Kenya. Official corruption is widespread; public wealth is being diverted into the private hands of those in power. The closing of several financial institutions in June 1986 threatened the stability of the monetary system. Living standards have started to decline. Kenya's population is growing at a rate of 4.1 percent annually, one of the highest in the world. A joint UNICEF/Kenya Bureau of Statistics Report (1985) observed that the majority of Kenyans live below the poverty line—defined to be $125 a year. According to Koigi wa Wamwere:

> In Kenya, the gap between the people and the leaders is great. Leaders are fat and well-fed, the people are thin and ill-fed. Leaders look at life with satisfaction and hate changes. People are fed up with life, cry for changes, and in their absence dream about heaven liberating them from their hell on earth. Leaders live in the exclusive former European residential areas that are built on the high forested grounds of Kileshwa, Karen, Muthaiga, Lavington and elsewhere, while the people continue to live in former "native" or African quarters on the dusty grounds below, which are aptly named *Kivumbini* [in the dust], *Land Panya* [the land of rats] and *Korogosho* [rattling] (*Index on Censorship*, Jul 1990; p. 20).

In 1963 Tom Mboya, the Luo secretary-general of KANU and the expected successor to Kenyatta, who was assassinated in 1969, asserted that the KANU party and the government of Kenya were safeguards against dictatorship: "Anyone who knows Kenya will realize that there is enough constructive cut and thrust within Kenya African National Union (KANU) party to dispel any fears of dictatorship. Furthermore, there are better safeguards for democracy than a frustrated opposition. The Kenyan government believes in the rule of law, in the independence of the judiciary. We respect the rights of the press, of the trade unions, of employers' organizations and of other pressure groups" (*The New Leader*, Sep 30, 1963; p. 24).

But precisely the opposite is the case. Kenya has been betrayed. As Koigi wa Wamwere lamented: "If Kenya is the African model for economic development and political stability, there can be little hope for Africa" (*Index on Censorship*, Jul 1990; p. 22).

## THE IVORY COAST

> Colonialism was a good thing for Africa. Thanks to it, we have one united Ivorien
> nation, rather than 60 tribes who know nothing about each other.
>
> —President Felix Houphouet-Boigny

In 1960 President Felix Houphouet-Boigny of the Ivory Coast and Kwame
Nkrumah of Ghana made a wager. Nkrumah had chosen a socialist road and
Houphouet-Boigny a capitalist route to development. They were to assess
their records a decade later to determine who had been most successful.
Houphouet-Boigny won handily. By 1966 Nkrumah had been ousted in a
coup, and by 1970 the economy of Ghana was in a shambles.

In the 1960s and 1970s the Ivory Coast enjoyed robust economic growth,
averaging 6 percent annually—one of the highest growth rates in Africa. The
country also enjoyed remarkable stability and peace under the leadership of
Houphouet-Boigny. But the political tranquillity began to fade in the 1980s.

For 30 years, until November 1990, the Ivory Coast was a one-party state.
The sole legal party was the Partie Democratique de Côte d'Ivoire (PDCI).
In 1985 Houphouet-Boigny was elected to his sixth consecutive five-year
term at the age of 79, having polled, according to official figures, 100 percent
of the votes cast. He retained responsibility for all policy decisions.

Mechanisms for some degree of consensus government did exist, but they
were largely ineffectual. The PDCI's supposedly supreme decisionmaking
body was the political bureau. But its 60 members met only occasionally—
usually to endorse presidential decisions. Below this, there was the 210-mem-
ber directorate, whose theoretical function was to draft proposals for
approval by the political bureau. Then there was the 13-man executive
committee or council of ministers. According to *West Africa*: "All members of
the executive committee are ministers, underlining the considerable overlap
between party and government. Ministers have little real power. Weekly
cabinet meetings consist of little more than a lengthy presidential monologue
about the 'conspiracies' allegedly being mounted by Western commodity
speculators. There is little discussion — and no dissent" (May 1-7, 1989; p.
676).

The National Assembly must formally endorse laws approved by the
council of ministers before the laws can be implemented. The assembly's 175
members were vetted members of the PDCI. Until 1980 there was only one
candidate for each assembly seat. During the 1985 elections, however, the
government introduced a measure of democracy by allowing more than one
candidate to run for each post in the assembly and in the party's regional

offices. But to be eligible, all candidates had to be screened for their militancy and morality. In addition, a bevy of laws were passed imposing severe sanctions on anyone advocating foreign ideologies—measures used to silence those who deviated from the party line.

There was also an advisory Economic and Social Council, whose members, in theory, represented all ranges of opinion in the country. In reality, however, all members were nominated by the president. Therefore, diverse opinions were unlikely.

The press was tightly controlled by the government and faithfully reflected the party line. All civil servants were party members. Even the women's movement, the *Association des Femmes Ivoiriennes*, was affiliated with the PDCI. Registered workers had to belong to the central trade union federation, *L'Union Generale des Travailleurs de Côte d'Ivoire* (UGTCI). Its secretary-general, Akido Niamkey, reiterated that the UGTCI was a responsible federation that followed party dictates. Only the teachers' unions were not members of the federation, but strenuous efforts were being made to incorporate them into the party.

Article Seven of the 1960 constitution provided for the "freedom of establishment and action" of "parties and political groups." Although the constitution clearly permitted the establishment of a multiparty system, Houphouet-Boigny traditionally justified his one-party regime on the grounds that, with 60 different tribes in the country, open competition between parties would fan ethnic rivalries. Such rivalries, according to Houphouet-Boigny, would seriously hamper economic development. But his critics questioned the extent of freedom of expression (*West Africa*, May 1-7, 1989; p. 676).

The influence of the party was so pervasive that dissidents or anyone outside the party had little chance of being heard. Over the years, opposition to the regime was squelched by a combination of carrot-and-stick techniques—the distribution of economic largesse or government jobs, and, less frequently, by overt suppression. These techniques were the same ones used by Mobutu of Zaire, although Mobutu was also well known for frequently shuffling his cabinet to neutralize internal dissent.

Professor Laurent Gbagbo has been the most outspoken critic in the Ivory Coast of the Houphouet-Boigny regime. He is the founding leader of the underground opposition party, *Le Front Populaire Ivoirien* (FPI). Gbagbo's political agenda is unclear but he has attracted extensive attention with his frontal attacks on corruption in the PDCI. In 1985, when he tried to organize a political party, he was driven into exile. Publication of a political book he wrote in exile describing Houphouet-Boigny as a "reckless rogue, criminal and a big thief" was followed almost immediately by a wave of arrests and detentions under the emergency regulations and the summary removal from office of six senior and two middle-level officers of the security services. The first to be detained were 21 teachers and 16 students believed to be connected with the publication and distribution of a clandestine leaflet, *The Patriot*, which had been highly critical of the government.

In 1988 President Houphouet-Boigny offered general amnesty to all political opponents and exiles. Professor Gbagbo accepted the offer and returned to the Ivory Coast in October. His pardon did not last long, however. Gbagbo was detained and subjected to intense government pressure to disband his organization after convening a clandestine party congress near Abidjan in November 1988. According to *New African* (Jun 1989): "Felix Houphouet-Boigny personally received the man he once described as 'his number one enemy in the country' and dashed [gave] him 50 million CFA for resettlement. But just two months after his arrival, Laurent Gbagbo was put under house arrest in a military camp for 28 days because, in the words of a security curse, 'he undermined the security of the State' " (p. 19).

Initially, the government denied rumors that Professor Gbagbo had been detained, but it subsequently confirmed that he was indeed confined for security reasons. The authorities would only say that he was helping in the "investigation of a political problem" and that the security services wanted to get to the bottom of the whole affair.

Asked why he wanted to lead the Ivory Coast, the university professor replied: "I take inspiration from President Houphouet-Boigny. Everything he does is what we should NOT do. Look around Abidjan and you have the Houphouet-Boigny stadium, the Houphouet-Boigny bridge, the Houphouet-Boigny maternity center. . .What we need is decentralisation. That is when people can take their own affairs into their own hands" (*New African*, Jun 1989; p. 19).

Another leader of the FPI was arrested when he returned from the party congress Gbagbo had convened in November 1988. Kobena Anaky, a wealthy businessman, was held for 12 days at Houphouet-Boigny's Abidjan residence before being transferred to the headquarters of the internal security police and later to Yopougon jail. He was not formally charged until December 19, 1988. The main charge was that Anaky's firm, Intertransit, had exceeded its credit ceiling with the customs authorities by CFA 142 million ($454,000). Although it was established that Anaky had no intention of defrauding the customs authorities, at a rushed trial in Abidjan in March 1989 he was convicted and sentenced to a 20-year jail term and fined CFA 7 billion ($23 million). In addition, all of Anaky's possessions and Intertransit assets were seized. Anaky's lawyers charged that his detention and trial were politically motivated. The government, they argued, feared that Anaky was funding the FPI.

Houphouet-Boigny showed increasing intolerance for opposition. Even possession of an opposition tract or association with an opposition party could invite severe penalties and sanctions. For example, on April 13, 1989, Bamba Monfere, one of the eight vice-presidents of the Ivorian National Assembly and dean of the faculty of pharmacy at Abidjan University, was arrested at Abidjan airport, after returning from a trip to Paris. Airport security had found in his suitcase a copy of the manifesto of the Movement for Democracy and Justice (MDJ), a clandestine opposition group based in Paris. He was stripped of his office in the Assembly and placed under surveillance (*West Africa*, May 15-21, 1989; p. 811).

In addition to political pressure, Houphouet-Boigny's government began to experience economic problems in the 1990s. The Ivory Coast's economy, long a model of free-market success, faced a crisis in part precipitated by falling commodity prices for cocoa on the world market. Houphouet-Boigny blamed the declining market on Western commodity speculators. To help resolve the crisis, he asked all public sector employees, students, and teachers for a solidarity tax—cuts in wages and allowances. Viewing the vast basilica Houphouet-Boigny was building for himself at Yamassoukrou and taking a cue from the dramatic developments in Eastern Europe, the workers opposed the tax. They took to the streets in February and March 1990 to vent their anger at the government for demanding austerity but doing nothing to punish an increasingly corrupt ruling elite. According to the *Washington Post*, "The opposition had accused Houphouet-Boigny and some of his powerful government ministers, past and present, of having hidden away in Europe sums said to exceed the foreign aid that Western donors have poured into Ivory Coast" (Mar 26, 1990; p. A17).

Houphouet-Boigny's forces responded to the protests with tear gas, stun grenades, and truncheons. Schools were closed and 120 teachers were arrested (*West Africa*, Apr 2-8, 1990; p. 558). Synares, the lecturers' union, issued a statement on February 22, 1990, signed by Professor Marcel Ette, a professor of medicine and the union's secretary, that declared that the unrest reflected "the deep malaise afflicting the Ivorian society." It condemned the government's economic policies and demanded "the repatriation of the immense sums illicitly acquired and placed abroad" (*West Africa*, Mar 5-11, 1990; p. 364). Referring to the heavy-handed reaction of security forces, Synares commented: "The contradiction is a flagrant one. In a country which promotes dialogue, how can one not become indignant when the expression of the most minor grievance prompts a systematic recourse to brutal force?" (*West Africa*, Mar 5-11, 1990; p. 364).

Houphouet-Boigny steadfastly rejected the protesters' demands for multiparty democracy. He claimed that "tribalism was still the main obstacle to the achievement of national unity—the prerequisite for a change in the status quo" (*Africa Report*, May-Jun 1990; p. 16). But too many of the African leaders who loudly denounce tribalism are the very same ones who often surround themselves with members of their own tribes.[3] Henri Konan Bedie, the speaker of the National Assembly and groomed since 1960 by Houphouet-Boigny as a possible successor, is from the president's Bauole tribe. So, too, is Defense Minister Jean Konan Banny, another strong contender to succeed the president.

Houphouet-Boigny, however, is far more enlightened than the more brutal African tyrants. "Not one drop of human blood has been spilled in this country since I've been president," he has often asserted. While that may be true, it seems that the days of even the benevolent dictator are over in Africa.

On May 4, 1990, about 400 people attended a press conference given by Laurent Gbagbo at a hotel in central Abidjan. They chanted, "Our Bastille has fallen!" Three months later, however, Houphouet-Boigny was still entrenched in power with the political situation undergoing further deterioration. This prompted the Ivory Coast's 13 bishops to issue a pastoral letter. Noting that "the Ivorian 'miracle' was over and it was more appropriate to speak of an 'Ivorian malaise' that was economic, social, political, moral and spiritual, they asserted that 'society no longer functions in accordance with the principles of equity, but is governed by individual interest and corruption'" (*West Africa*, Aug 6-12, 1990; p. 2251).

Mounting pressure—through strikes and demonstrations—and the refusal of France to send troops to prop him up forced Houphouet-Boigny to legalize other political parties and to hold multiparty elections in November 1990. But Houphouet-Boigny handily won a seventh term in a presidential election generally regarded to have been rigged. Although the Ivory Coast may have pursued the right economic policies, the concentration of political power in the hands of one person proves that there are limits even to benevolent dictatorship.

## LIBERIA: RULED BY MILITARY SAVAGES, 1980-1990

Liberia [is] a country whose fate and progress have been placed in the hands of many idiots.

—Ellen Johnson-Sirleaf, former minister of finance

Liberia, like the Ivory Coast and Kenya, is another close U.S. ally. It was founded in 1847 by freed U.S. slaves and received about $67 million a year in U.S. aid in the mid-1980s. On April 12, 1980, a group of young enlisted men, under the command of Samuel Doe, a Krahn tribesman, stormed Liberia's executive mansion in Monrovia and overthrew the regime of William Tolbert. Tolbert's rule had been marked by despotism, corruption, and an extreme concentration of wealth. The initial jubilation in Monrovia did not last long, however.

The coup was accompanied by acts of savage brutality. Tolbert was murdered as he lay in bed. The soldiers disemboweled the dead leader and gouged out one of his eyes with a bayonet. They displayed his mutilated body for two days at the John F. Kennedy Hospital morgue and then buried him with 27 others in a mass grave. Colonel Harrison Pennue, a close associate of Doe, openly boasted that he had disemboweled Tolbert.

In the ensuing days and weeks, the soldiers, heady with their new-found power, killed an estimated 200 people in a spree of looting and barbaric reprisals. High government officials of the deposed regime were perfunctorily tried and then executed by a drunken firing squad. The chilling spectacle was televised nationwide. The half-naked corpses were then dangled from a row of telephone poles on the beach outside Barclay Training Center. Liberians who had initially welcomed the coup became alarmed when the flow of blood became torrential.

In the early years of Doe's administration, the soldiers sought consultations and partnerships with intellectuals. But this union came to an abrupt end in 1981 when Doe decided to purge the government of radicals and ordered the execution of vice head of state Thomas Weh-Syn. Most other intellectuals were demoted or dismissed; others fled into exile. Dr. Togba Nah-Tipoteh, the former minister of economic affairs and planning who went into exile, reported: "Very early on, people began to observe the nature of Doe's regime; this took the form of executions in an atmosphere where there was a complete absence of any fair trial" (*West Africa,* Apr 16-22, 1990; p. 612).

On August 22, 1984, the arrest of Dr. Amos Sawyer, a popular professor who had played a prominent role in the drafting of a new constitution, triggered spontaneous student demonstrations on the campus of the University of Liberia. A detachment of about 200 soldiers of the executive mansion guard, acting on direct orders of President Doe, stormed the campus to suppress the demonstrations. The soldiers fired indiscriminately into the unarmed crowd, stripped students naked, flogged them with rattans, beat them with rifle butts, extorted money from them, and raped female students. The soldiers later looted dormitories and classrooms. When the military barbarism was over, more than 50 students had been killed and scores were arrested. Many were injured and hospitalized.

Doe's government fired the entire university administration and teaching staff and made reappointment conditional on one's holding views that were either progovernment or apolitical. Testifying before the U.S. Congress' Subcommittee on Foreign Relations on February 12, 1985, Dr. Patrick Sayon, former vice-president of the University of Liberia, pleaded with the U.S. government to halt military aid to the government there. He indicated that the aid enabled Doe "to oppress, suppress and repress the people so that they are denied their fundamental rights" (*West Africa,* Apr 16-22, 1990; p. 613). But the United States was unresponsive.

In October 1985 Doe held general elections that were generally regarded as the most brazen fraud in recent African history. When Doe appeared to be losing, the vote count was suddenly halted and the ballot boxes were trucked to an army barracks, where the votes were tallied and Doe was declared the winner. The U.S. Department of State described the elections as "generally fair although marked by a few irregularities." But several events leading to the elections pointed to a massive election fraud.

First, months before the vote, the Doe government banned the two most popular opposition parties. These were the United People's Party (UPP), under the leadership of Gabriel Baccus Matthews, and the Liberian People's Party (LPP), under the leadership of Dr. Amos Sawyer, a professor at the University of Liberia. Doe's reason for banning them was their alleged advocacy of foreign ideologies, namely socialism. Justice Minister Jenkins Scott contended: "Baccus Matthews is an avowed socialist. What are his sources of support? When an individual living in a capitalist society tells us he is an avowed socialist, and we're capitalists, should he be permitted to run?" (*West Africa,* Jun 4-11, 1989; p. 763).

Second, Doe issued Decree 88A, which banned criticism of the government. It became a criminal offense to "create disharmony, spread rumours, lies and disinformation" and it became a felony to accuse a public official of any unlawful conduct if the intent of the accusation was to "injure the official or other individual in his reputation to undermine his official or personal status."

Third, the newspapers, the *Daily Observer* and the *Sun Times*, were closed to prevent coverage of election campaigning. Soon after, opposition leaders were detained. Among them was Ellen Johnson-Sirleaf, a former finance minister now in exile in the United States. According to the Lawyers Committee for Human Rights: "On a trip to the US in July 1984, Mrs. Johnson-Sirleaf made a speech in Philadelphia in which she was harshly critical of the military government's handling of the Liberian economy; at one point she assailed the 'many idiots in whose hands our nation's fate and progress have been placed.' Upon her return to Monrovia, she was promptly placed under house arrest and accused of sedition; she was later detained in the Post Stockade" (*Liberia: A Promise Betrayed*, 1986; p. 113).

Her arrest caused an international uproar. The U.S. Congress finally passed a resolution suspending aid to Liberia until Johnson-Sirleaf and other political prisoners were released. As a result, the Reagan administration suspended $25.5 million in aid. Eventually Doe released Johnson-Sirleaf and other detainees.

A month after the elections, Thomas Quiwonkpa attempted a coup on November 12, 1985. The coup failed, Quiwonkpa was captured, and his body was chopped up and cannibalized. Hundreds of others were also executed in that abortive plot—some Liberians placed the number at 3,000. An unknown number of civilians who were seen celebrating in the streets on the morning of November 12 were dragged from their homes in the afternoon, shot, and ferried off to beaches outside the capital for burial in mass graves. Witnesses saw truckloads of corpses rolling through the streets of the capital and out along the airport road.

A soldier who was detained at the executive mansion gave this testimony to the Lawyers Committee for Human Rights:

> There were dead bodies all around. The soldiers were in a jovial mood as if they were conquering heroes, as if they had just won a war. They were openly smoking marijuana, openly drinking. They had bottles of gin. The thing was out of control. The commander had lost control . . . It became a tribal war. Most of the soldiers were Krahn soldiers. If you were anything else but Krahn or Loma then you had a problem . . .
>
> I was in handcuffs. We were waiting for the truck to take us away. But the truck was filled with bodies. I saw the soldiers, about six soldiers—they were in a jovial mood. They identified one man as of the enemies. Even though he was already dead, they were cutting his body apart. They took the bayonet, and

opened his stomach, and cut his testicles off . . . The soldiers were vicious. They
were not like human beings . . . They were reopening the bodies. They were
cutting out people's eyes, even though they were already dead. These were the
things I really saw (*Liberia: A Promise Betrayed*, 1986; p. 51).

A civilian who spent two weeks in detention, including nine days in the
executive mansion, described in gruesome detail to the committee how the
soldiers forced their prisoners to eat the flesh of dead prisoners (*Liberia: A
Promise Betrayed*, 1986; p. 53).

Perhaps the most galling case was that of Charles Gbenyon, the 29-year-
old editor-in-chief at the Liberian Broadcasting System (LBS) television
station. His crime was in filming scenes of the coup attempt in its initial
stages—the arrests of officials of Doe's regime and crowds celebrating in the
streets—and broadcasting this footage. When the coup failed and Doe's
forces regained control, Gbenyon was seized by security forces, stripped
down to his briefs, handcuffed, and thrown into an army jeep. He was never
seen again.

Doe asserted that Gbenyon accidentally shot himself while struggling
with soldiers over a pistol he had in his possession. But a soldier who was
detained at the executive mansion claimed that Gbenyon was bayonetted to
death. "I actually saw his body," the soldier said. "He was a friend of mine, a
personal friend. I saw his body. He had been bayonetted in the neck. They
had actually ripped his head off with a bayonet. The skin of his neck was just
holding his head on his body. I didn't see any other stab wounds" (*Liberia: A
Promise Betrayed*, 1986; p. 60). The Lawyers Committee for Human Rights
described executions between 1980 and November 1985 as "by far the worst
spasm of summary killings in recent memory."

By 1985 Liberia's economy was in a shambles. Systematic looting, profligate government spending, and the squandering of more than $375 million
in U.S. aid between 1980 and 1985 forced that country into a receivership
on May 2, 1986, for the fifth time since 1971. A team of 17 operational
experts drawn from the World Bank, the International Monetary Fund, and
the European Economic Community were called in to manage certain activities of the Ministry of Finance and the Central Bank of Liberia. These
included expenditure control, check signing, and tax collection. But control
was illusory. "Millions of dollars went missing from ministries, with the figure
put at up to $3 million for 1988 alone" (*Africa Report*, Jul-Aug 1990; p. 49).
Frustrated by unrelenting official corruption, the team gave up midway
through the project and left in 1988. Commercial banks, including Citibank,
threatened to pull out. Liberia was about $120 million in arrears in debt
payments to the International Monetary Fund and to the U.S. government.

As *West Africa* reported: "According to Dr. Togba Nah-Tipoteh, the government had only $5 million in its coffers on the eve of the December coup, foreign debt stood at $700 million and there was only a week's supply of rice left. An unofficial source also estimated that unemployment was at 50 percent. And despite having received $500 million in US aid—more, it is said, than all the previous Liberian governments put together—over the last ten years, Liberia has accumulated an external debt of $1.7 billion" (Apr 16-22, 1990; p. 613).

Most Liberians believed that unconditional aid to Liberia only perpetuated instability, since Doe and his army represented primarily the interests of a single minority tribe, the Krahn. Indeed, in 1987 the United States withheld about $10 million in economic support funds and $5 million in military aid from Liberia. When Sen. Edward Kennedy sponsored a bill to cut off U.S. aid to Liberia, Doe responded by making overtures to Romania.

For years Liberia was rife with talk of revenge. All factions conceded the possibility of massive reprisals against the Krahn if Doe was removed. The Krahn themselves lived in fear. A Gio scholar from Nimba County who was detained for two weeks and flogged by Krahn soldiers in Yekepa averred, "I'm afraid that if they allow this man [Doe] to be killed, it will be recorded in history that there was once a tribe called Krahn in Liberia" (*Liberia: A Promise Betrayed*, 1986; p. 23). The only feasible solution for the Krahn was to remove Doe themselves and make amends to the other tribes or face extinction. Unfortunately, they neglected to do so.

After 1985 there were at least eight coup attempts against Doe. But observers believed that most were fabricated by the government to justify a crackdown on political opponents. Worsening economic conditions, however, prompted another, more credible coup attempt—this one led by Charles Taylor, a former civil servant, on December 24, 1989. As we noted earlier, that coup attempt also failed, and the Doe regime unleashed savage reprisals. Doe's army, using scorched-earth tactics, engaged in indiscriminate killings and atrocities. Refugees gave harrowing accounts of "the army using tanks and mortars, burning homes, and killing women and children, as well as several people praying in a mosque" (*Africa Report*, Mar-Apr 1990; p. 8).

By July 22, 1990, President Doe was a virtual prisoner in his oceanfront executive mansion with a 500-member presidential guard composed of soldiers from his Krahn tribal group. Doe believed that he was invincible inside the eight-story stronghold, which was jammed with ammunition and explosives.

Doe had been asked to resign even by his own government delegation to the peace talks with the rebels that had been held in Sierra Leone. The

July 21, 1990, statement, signed by Information Minister Emmanuel Bowier, revealed that the delegation "had advised President Doe, in the supreme interest of our nation and people, to make the supreme political sacrifice in order to save Liberia from further destruction of lives and properties and to ensure his personal safety" (*Washington Post*, Jul 23, 1990; p. A15).

Doe refused, insisting that he was still president, although 98 percent of the country was out of his control. That took the concept of personal rule to new heights of folly. On September 12, 1990, he was killed by rebel leader Prince Yormie Johnson, plunging the country into chaos. Several individuals claimed the presidency of Liberia. Reprisals were taken against the Krahn, famine appeared and by December 1990 over a third of Liberia's population of 2.5 million, mostly those of Krahn ethnicity, had fled into exile. Sadly, there were several Does in Africa in 1990.

As we have seen, political ideology is not particularly relevant in analyzing oppression in Africa. Regimes of the left have been as brutal and despicable as those of the right. For example, socialist or Marxist countries, such as Ethiopia, Somalia, Zambia, and Ghana, have records of repression that are as deplorable as those of Malawi, Liberia, Uganda, and Zaire, which are staunchly pro-West nations. Therefore, one cannot accuse the United States or the West of propping up tyrannical regimes in Africa without leveling the same charge at the Soviet Union and its allies. In any case, the institution of repression in either system has followed exactly the same pattern.

First, a member of the elite assumes power either through the barrel of a gun or the ballot box. He manufactures a coup plot, a security problem, a dissident problem, an imperialist conspiracy, or some other imaginary problem and demands sweeping powers to deal with it. Since the government's goals are ostensibly laudable and necessary, the means to achieve them, however draconian, are seen as justified.

Accordingly, constitutions are suspended, civil liberties held in abeyance, and the press gagged. Criticisms of government policies in any quarter are outlawed. The society becomes polarized—either one supports the government or opposes it. The slightest criticism of the government makes one an enemy who must be repressed. That invariably entails exile, assassination, or mysterious disappearance.

Meanwhile, despite all the resources and power the government appropriates to solve the problem, it worsens. Suddenly, the government is overthrown amid charges of corruption and incompetence. The new leader comes to adopt the same methods of oppression as his predecessor, only he modifies them to be even more repressive. He wastes much time and effort hounding and prosecuting officers of the old regime. Meanwhile, the problems fester, and suddenly the new government is overthrown by another leader wielding a bigger bazooka. And on and on the cycle repeats itself—a point well noted by Bright E. Okogu, a Nigerian:

> I join millions of Africans in congratulating President Soglo and the people of Benin Republic for the peaceful transfer of power after their long (17) years in the woods.
>
> This, however, is equally the time to remind the new President that the world once rejoiced with other African leaders at the dawn of their reign, after they in some cases had just succeeded repressive "presidents-for-life." But no sooner were they in power than they clamped all formal and informal opposition groups in jail, and proscribed whatever democratic process that brought them to government (*West Africa*, Apr 29 - May 5, 1991; p. 640).

---

## NOTES

1. Most other African nationalists were also raised and nurtured by market women, due to the traditional division of labor among the sexes. Raising food-crops and trading of foodstuffs were female avocations in indigenous African societies.
2. Indeed, this author suggested that: "When apartheid is finally dismantled, Mr. Mandela and the other nationalist leaders, both black and white, should retire and make way for new leaders" (*The Wall Street Journal*, Mar 28, 1990; p.A15).
3. For example, Samuel Doe with the Krahn, Mobutu Sese Seko with the Gbande, Moi with the Kalenjin, Biya with the Beti, Barre with the Marehan clan, Banda with the Chiwe, Babangida with Muslims, and Rawlings with the Ewe.

# Chapter 9

*Repression of Freedom of Expression*

It is high time the official, controlled, censored, muzzled or partisan news gives way in Africa to news based on the diversity of opinions and ideas, with free access to the various sources of official and unofficial information . . . The one-party states always want to control information.

—Auguste Mpassi-Muba, Congolese director of the Pan-African News Agency.

Ironically, it's [South Africa's] black liberation movements—or their supporters—which are now gagging the press, which should be one of the cornerstones of the free society they claim to be fighting for.

—Fred Khumalo, a black reporter.[1]

## THE EROSION OF FREEDOM OF EXPRESSION IN AFRICA

Traditionally, Western governments assumed that human rights were mostly synonymous with such civil liberties as freedom of assembly, the right to a fair trial, and the right to humane treatment; while in the former Soviet Union they meant having enough to eat, a place to live, decent health care, and education. But the one freedom that is critical and indispensable for the existence of all other human freedoms is freedom of expression—the freedom to express one's thoughts, wishes, and criticisms by words and actions without fear of reprisal. Two Yoruban proverbs underscore the importance of freedom of expression: "Only the millipede knows how and when to move its legs," and "Only the organism knows what is good for itself." How can the people, those being governed, tell the government what is good for them if they are denied the freedom to express themselves? To expose corruption, human rights violations, economic mismanagement, and abuse of political power, freedom of expression is vital. Gara LaMarche, executive director of the Fund for Free Expression, wrote:

> Of all the rationales for censorship of governments—national security, protection of public morals, curbing racial and ethnic hatred—perhaps the predominant real reason is *preventing exposure of corruption*. That's why Kenya's President Daniel arap Moi has shut down newspapers and outlawed all political parties except his own, and why Zaire's President, Mobutu Sese Seko, has been desperate to retain the absolute power that enabled him to accumulate a fortune estimated at [$10 billion] . . .
>
> Those in power fear disclosure of their foreign bank accounts, their real estate and business empires, because it can undermine their control. They see the example of democratic societies where awareness of corruption can unravel political power, as in the 1989 election defeat of India's Congress Party after independent publications showed a cover-up of kickback payments in a $1.4 billion arms deal with a Swedish company.
>
> Freedom of expression is not an abstract concept that must take a back seat to economic development. In all too many countries top officials plunder the treasury because the press is not free to bring the story to light (*The New York Times*, Dec 3, 1991; p. A22. Emphasis added).

At the 42nd New Year School's symposium at the University of Ghana, Legon (January 1991), the conferees adopted this resolution: "Freedom of speech is a prerequisite for national development." This view was echoed by Catholic Bishops in Malawi in a March 8, 1992 pastoral letter:

> [The strength] of any society resides in recognising the gifts of all and allowing these gifts to flourish and be used for the building up of the community. *"Mutu umodzi susenza denga"* [One head cannot carry a roof]. No one person can claim to have a monopoly of truth and wisdom. No individual—or group of individuals—can pretend to have all the resources needed to guarantee the progress of a nation. *"Mtsinje wopanda miyala susunga madzi"* [A river without rocks does not hold water]. The contribution of the most humble members is often necessary for the good running of a group. *"Wopusa anaomba ng'oma wochenjera nabvina"* [The fool beat the drum to which the clever one danced] . . .
>
> Real progress can only be attained when the true problems and the real needs are identified and all resources are channelled towards solving them" (*Index on Censorship*, May 1992; p.17).

Political freedom requires people to have access to competing ideological views so that they can debate the relative merits of each and thereby make an intelligent choice about what is good for them. But in many African countries, the people cannot make this assessment. For example, "Political discussion among Sudanese has two distinguishing features: a swift glance over the shoulder and a conspicuous lack of interest in the head of state, Gen. Omar Hassan Bashir . . . 'They (the National Islamic Front) have extended their tentacles in all directions—into the army, the university, the business community and they have got the people cowed' " (*The Washington Post*, Mar 21, 1992; p. A20).

The importance of freedom of expression can also be gleaned from the fact that societies that advance economically are invariably those that permit large measures of freedom of expression. Quite often there is no one permanent solution to a social or economic problem; there may be several alternative solutions. Only through an open, free debate of the alternatives can the optimal solution emerge. Society must engage in a dynamic process to find a solution that meets certain criteria. Even when found, a feasible solution does not remain sacrosanct because circumstances change. Therefore, what may have been an optimal solution at one point in time may prove ineffective or even disastrous at another. Consequently, solutions to problems must constantly be reviewed, modified, or even abandoned in favor of more appropriate ones. Such is the case with political solutions. Obviously, many of the ideas and proposals espoused by such African nationalists as Kenneth Kaunda, Kwame Nkrumah, and Julius Nyerere to deal with 1950s problems have become woefully obsolete. Yet some African intellectuals still rigidly cling to them.

Clearly, a solution that is not freely debated and critically reviewed in the face of changing circumstances will progressively lose its effectiveness and could even aggravate the problem it was intended to solve. Freedom of expression is essential to this review process.[2] It should come as no surprise that the worst human rights violators and the worst economic performers in Africa are those countries that deny their people freedom of expression. Although this freedom is anathema to most autocratic regimes, irrespective of their ideological predilections, military regimes have been the worst offenders. Not surprisingly, the African countries considered to be in the most severe economic decline in 1990 were ruled by military dictators: Benin, Burkina Faso, Burundi, the Central African Republic, Chad, Congo, Ethiopia, Guinea, Guinea-Bissau, Liberia, Libya, Mali, Mauritania, Niger, Nigeria, Rwanda, Somalia, Sudan, Togo, Uganda, and Zaire. (In 1990, the World Bank classified Ethiopia as the world's poorest nation.)

Only in an atmosphere supporting the free exchange of ideas can the people find internal, self-reliant, native, and efficient solutions. The absence of intellectual freedom prevents the search for and development of internal solutions. This, in turn, has two pernicious ramifications. First, it perpetuates the offensive notion that Africans are incapable of devising their own solutions to their problems. Second, it forces the adoption of externally generated solutions. Unfortunately, there are many difficulties associated with foreign solutions to African problems. For one, the foreign experts who devise these solutions may be sincere in their desire to help Africa overcome its problems, but they lack an understanding of the complexity of those problems and their interplay with cultural, historical, and political factors. The excessive number of "black elephants" eloquently attests to the failure of many foreign solutions in Africa. For another, Africans will never demonstrate their intellectual capabilities if they must always rely on foreigners to do the thinking for them. For Africans to develop their problem-solving skills, they need the freedom to experiment and to present their ideas to the people. The government should support and encourage their endeavors by providing an environment conducive to free expression.

This freedom is not alien to Africa. Williams (1987), the black American who conducted 16 years of research and field study covering 26 African nations and 105 language groups, asserted that one of the indigenous and fundamental rights of the African people was "the right to criticise and condemn any acts by the authorities or proposed new laws. Opposition groups, in some areas called 'The Youngmen,' were recognized by law" (p. 174). Consensus was the most cardinal feature of the indigenous system of government, and freedom of expression was crucial for reaching a consensus. Ordinary tribesmen participated in the decisionmaking process by sitting in on the council of elders' deliberations, where they could voice their opinions. Further, they attended village assemblies or meetings, where they could debate various positions until a consensus or unanimous decision was reached.[3] Busia (1967) observed, "The traditions of free speech and interchange of views do not support any claim that the denial of free speech or the suppression of opposition is rooted in traditional African political systems" (p. 29).

Once a consensus was reached, no further debate or criticism was allowed. Those who were fervently opposed to decisions reached by consensus had two options. First, they could quietly, not publicly, seek to persuade the elders or councilors to have a policy changed. Such lobbying activities were conducted during visitations with councilors in the privacy of their homes. The second option, if the first failed, was to exercise the right to leave the community without fear of reprisal. Indeed, the history of Africa is replete with such migrations.

When the European colonialists discovered the African institution of consensus-building, they belittled it as backward because they did not see a parliament or official recorders. But the most serious transgression was committed by African nationalists and elites. They too denigrated the indigenous and grievously failed to erect any institution capable of building a national consensus. For such a national consensus to be possible the people required a forum in which to meet, channels through which they could present their views and participate in government—either directly through the media or indirectly through representatives they selected—and the guarantee of freedom of expression. But the nationalists and the elites provided none of these at the national level after independence. Considering the parliament building left by the Europeans a colonial institution and failing to understand its purpose, some nationalists closed down these buildings. Where the parliament was allowed to continue to exist in independent Africa, it was transformed into a den of corrupt lackeys, ever ready to approve government policies. This was inevitable as parliament had representatives from only one party. Those who did not belong to that party were excluded.

Nor could a national consensus be reached. Policy was determined by one individual, usually the head of state, and imposed on the whole country. There were hardly any parliamentary debates. The rest of the people in the government were too timid or servile to offer constructive criticisms. For example, Koigi wa Wamwere, a former member of parliament in Kenya, complained:

> The level of debate in Kenya's Parliament is lowered by the fear that reigns among both highly educated and illiterate MPs. Fear of detention and expulsion from the party and parliament imposes censorship on MPs who dare not criticise the president, or the police. There are also crimes of thought for which people are detained and imprisoned. For example, you may not imagine, think or talk about the death of the president even if it is as imminent as tropical rain. Even if the president is sick or mad, MPs dare not think about it, as it is high treason. In 1976, when Kenyan politicians were debating Kenyatta's succession, the then attorney general, Charles Mugane Njonjo, announced: "It is a treasonable offense punishable by a mandatory death sentence for anyone to encompass or even mention the possible [change] of the head of state." Freedom of thought is as absent from Kenya's political life as freedom of expression . . .
>
> There was a KANU parliamentary group meeting in which Moi talked about MPs who claim to have personal opinions.
>
> "There are MPs who think that they have some personal opinions that are very dear to them. Let me now tell you this. As a KANU MP, you have no ideas

or opinions of your own. Your opinions are those of the party. Those who think
they have ideas of their own are free to quit the party. But you can't be in the
party and have your own ideas. Just remember that" (*Index on Censorship*, Jul 1990;
p. 17).

President Mobutu once boasted that "Zaire's one-party state system is the
most elaborate form of democracy." In fact, a democratic one-party state is
an oxymoron. It is a despicable fact that most African heads of state generally
do not tolerate alternative viewpoints or allow input from their own citizens
into the decisionmaking process.

The danger is that a mistake by one individual could lead an entire nation
with millions of people into economic ruin. Indeed, many African heads of
state have not shown themselves to be competent at managing their economies. They rule their countries as if they were their own personal property.
African heads of state need to be reminded of this elementary fact: An African
nation does not belong to any one single individual or group. Even the
traditional chiefs seldom acted as if the whole tribe belonged to them and
stifled all dissent.

The most crucial of all human rights, freedom of expression is the most
difficult to protect. It can be curtailed explicitly by censorship, but far more
pervasive in Africa are the indirect and insidious forms of control. Threats,
intimidation, detention, and violence can banish freedom of expression. A
government may by its brutal acts so cower the people that they may become
too frightened to speak, even though there may be no expressed laws against
free expression. Said a Libyan: "All the people are afraid. They can't talk. If
they are afraid to talk, how can they do anything? Life is paralysed . . . The
people have no dreams. They are waiting for a change. Any change. They
are waiting for anything" (*The Washington Post*, Feb 15, 1992; p. A24).

## CENSORSHIP OF THE PRESS

I don't censor. Let them [Nigerian journalists] write what they want to write. But
if anybody does anything that is against the national interest that person will
have to answer questions. To criticize Nigeria is to criticize God.

—Alex Akinyele, Nigerian Minister of Information.[4]

Since independence there has been a systematic strangulation of the means
available for Africans to express themselves. African leaders took over the
foreign-owned newspapers on grounds that they were used to advance
colonial policies. Here again, they descended on a colonial institution
without understanding its purpose. Nor did they create or tolerate the

creation of substitute means for the people to express their viewpoints and thereby participate in the decisionmaking process.

In most African countries, the opposition was decimated. Anyone not in the government's party was necessarily a dissident, and any newspaper editor or journalist who published the slightest criticism of an insignificant government policy was branded a foe of the government and jailed or killed. Journalists who for years praised government measures suddenly found themselves in detention when they erred by expressing criticism. According to Richard Carver, a research director at Africa Watch, "President Banda is now in his 80s—although in Malawi you would be locked up for suggesting such a thing" (*Africa Report*, Jul-Aug 1990; p. 59). The same journal reports that "when the presidential motorcade passes, Malawians are obliged to go to the nearest window or sidewalk and wave to it. It is forbidden to mock or criticize the president. It is forbidden to make a photocopy of a newspaper photograph of the president. And any reference to him must employ the full title: His Excellency the Life President Ngwazi Dr. H. Kamuzu Banda (*Africa Report*, Mar-Apr 1992; p. 59).

Many nationalists could not distinguish between progovernment, antigovernment, and strictly neutral or independent newspapers. Nor can modern African heads of state distinguish between constructive criticism and subversion. Any critic is an enemy. President Moi of Kenya viewed even the possession of certain cassette tapes as subversive.[5]

Newspapers that have lavished praises upon the government have been closed for carrying an occasional critique. Lamb (1984) documented the declining number of newspapers in Africa:

> In the mid-sixties, according to the London-based International Press Institute, there were 299 daily newspapers in Africa. That figure included about 40 papers in the Arab States, mostly Egypt, and about 30 in white-ruled areas of southern Africa. By the early 1980s, only about 150 dailies were left on the continent, and the shrinkage had occurred almost exclusively in black Africa. Nine countries had no newspapers at all.
>
> The combined daily circulation of the papers in Africa fell during that period from well over 3 million to 2 million. Thus, the circulation on a continent of 455 million people is only about two-thirds of what a single London newspaper, *The Daily Mirror*, sells in a day (p. 247).

A. Mensah of Tema, Ghana, reported, "The grip on freedom of speech is such that not even a school magazine can now be published in Ghana without a licence (*West Africa*, Oct 15-21, 1990; p. 2648).

African leaders crave praise even when their tails are on fire:

Balinagwe Mwambungu, a sub-editor with the government-owned *Daily News* in Tanzania, was summoned to the office of Horace Kolimba, secretary-general of the Chama Cha Mapinduzi (CCM) party after telling a symposium in Dar-es-Salaam on Dec 5, 1991 that government leaders in the country interfered with journalists' work and loved to be praised, and appealing to the authorities to allow journalists to operate freely. *Daily News* editor, Joseph Mapunda, was also summoned. At the meeting, the CCM boss apparently told them that with such opinions Mwambungu had insulted and belittled the entire government leadership (*Index on Censorship*, Mar 1992; p. 40).

The leadership needs to be reminded that criticism can be useful. African leaders love to criticize but childishly do not want to take criticism. The credo of the Gikuyu of Kenya is unequivocal: *"Kanya gatuune ne mwamokanero,"* which means "give and take [criticism]." The Asante of Ghana also have a proverb: *"Funtummireku denkyemmireku won afuru bom sno wodidi a na wo ko,"* which means "Funtummireku and Denkyemmireku are two crocodiles with one stomach; yet when they eat, they fight." Thus, there can be disagreements over a common goal; unity does not mean blind allegiance to the dictates of another. In fact, this proverb is symbolized on the Asante *adinkra* cloth by two crocodiles crossed at the stomach. It is a symbol of unity in diversity and of democracy. Diversity of opinion is not permitted in much of Africa, however. Of the total of 52 African countries, including South Africa, only Botswana, Senegal, Mauritius, and arguably Nigeria tolerate criticisms of government policies. Under the colonial system, Africans could not speak out freely against oppressive policies. Today, after gaining their so-called independence and freedom, they are still muzzled by modern "liberators."

Currently the rule in Africa is to follow the party line or engage in a debilitating exercise of self-censorship. The slightest deviation from the official line elicits sanctions, often fatal, against writers, journalists, and intellectuals. As a result a national consensus becomes impossible to reach since alternative viewpoints are not tolerated. Creativity is lost and initiative stifled. Sensible, internal solutions elude policymakers. Writers, journalists, and professors languish.

The information media in much of Africa have been monopolized by the state and turned into propaganda organs for the party elite. In Ghana, the editorial of *The People's Graphic* was actually written or dictated from the castle—the seat of government. Angola boasted that *Jornal de Angola* was the "voice of the people." But its daily total print run until December 9, 1989, when a new printing press was added, was 60,000 for a population of 9.2 million. Nor did the copies reach the rural areas. Most copies were circulated in Luanda, and it was impossible to obtain a copy even one mile away from the city center.

The official press characterized the freedom-fighters of UNITA (*Uniao Nacional pela Independencia Total de Angola*) as a group of terrorists, bandits, and puppets. Shortly after Angola's President Jose Eduardo dos Santos and UNITA leader Jonas Savimbi shook hands at a peace summit, however, these designations had to change. The official media was directed by high-ranking government officials to describe UNITA members as rebels and misguided fellow Angolans who would at some future date be integrated into Angolan national life under the continuing rule of the MPLA (*Movimento Popular de Libertacao de Angola*). Joao Pokongo, a senior journalist at *Jornal de Angola*, described the layers of state censorship: "You have to remember that information is a monopoly of the Party. Every year the MPLA draws up a directive on propaganda to determine editorial policy. On top of that there is day-to-day control. In any case, every journalist knows, and has a duty to know, the essential Party line—he has to know that first so that his writing is in line with it" (*Index on Censorship*, May 1990; p. 22).

Maria Luiza Fancony, program director at Radio Nacional de Angola, admitted: "We learned our trade with help from Cuban, East German and Soviet broadcasters, so naturally we learned their style of making propaganda" (*Index on Censorship*, May 1990; p. 24). According to Roberto de Almeida, the MPLA party secretary responsible for overseeing the ideological soundness of all the information propagated in Angola, censorship was necessary because "his fellow Angolans are not yet intellectually mature enough for the news to be reported as it happens" (*Index on Censorship*, May 1990; p. 22). Was the Angolan government "intellectually mature" enough to accept diversity of opinion?

To compound the problems, the censorship guidelines in most African countries are ill-defined. A journalist does not know where the limits are until he crosses them. He does not even know what sort of questions he will be allowed to ask an African head of state at a press conference. For example, on January 30, 1990, at a press conference at the end of Zambian President Kenneth Kaunda's state visit to Uganda, members of the press asked him the following questions:

Alfred Okware, associate editor of *Newscast* magazine: "When you look around you today, leaders of your generation are gone. Don't you think your continued stay in power is inhibiting your Zambians from taking up the challenge of running their country?"

Festo Ebongu, a journalist working for the government-owned newspaper, *New Vision*: "Why is there a secret trade between Zambia and racist South Africa?"

Hussein Abdi Hassan, BBC's Swahili service correspondent: "Why is your son alleged to have murdered a woman [his former girlfriend] still free [in the United States]?"

Uganda's head of state, Yoweri Museveni, angrily protested that such questions were a gross affront to another head of state. *New African* reported that the police arrested the three journalists and charged them with "defaming a foreign dignitary." In addition, "the Ministry of Information in a statement broadcast over state-owned Radio Uganda announced the cancellation of all permits to foreign journalists working in the country or Ugandans working for foreign-based media" (May 1990; p. 21).

Although African governments insist that there is no direct censorship and that journalists are, in theory, free to publish within the usual professional constraints—legal, ethical, or otherwise—the exercise of this freedom can lead to transfers or dismissals. For example, "The editor of the international section of *Jornal de Angola*, Mr. Graca Campos, was transferred to another desk for having given too much coverage to the events in Eastern Europe" (*Index on Censorship*, May 1990; p. 24). Jose Catorze, the director general of Mozambique's official *Noticias* until the end of 1989, was not so fortunate. He "was summarily dismissed on the grounds that he had used the newspaper to air distorted Western views of the transformations taking place in Eastern Europe" (*Index on Censorship*, May 1990; p. 26).

Justice Annan, a member of Ghana's military government, wisely observed, "Without free discussion on national issues, progress will be slow and ineffective" (*West Africa*, Jan 23-29, 1989; p. 124). Two months later, however, the Ghanaian government revoked the registration of all newspapers and magazines published in Ghana and required all publishers to reregister after submitting a copy of their last published issue for review. The government alleged that this measure was spurred by "public concern about the indecent content and unethical standards of some publications" (*West Africa*, Apr 10-16, 1989; p. 548). The government also required the publications to disclose the names and addresses of the editors and publishers and sources of financial support.[6]

It was difficult to believe the Ghanaian government's assertion that its newspaper licensing regulation of 1989 was not intended to muzzle the independent press. Indeed, the first casualty of that regulation was *The Independent*. Its editor, Kabral Blay Amihere, asserted, "I would really like to see an independent paper of real substance with in-depth analysis of issues and events." He called upon Ghanaian journalists to come out into the open, put off fear and set up newspapers to present the other side of national issues. He did not get his license.

The Ghanaian government also engaged in censorship after sponsoring public debates on the political future of the country in August 1990. A number of groups, one of which was the Movement for Freedom and Justice (MFJ) under the chairmanship of Professor Adu Boahen, held press conferences in Ghana's cities to air their views.[7] *New African* reported that the government set up a committee to monitor the MFJ and apprehended its top leaders for "conspiring to publish false information likely to injure the reputation of the state" (Oct 1990; p. 20). The "false information" referred to the MFJ's press conference statement on October 1990, which, among other things, denounced the state of repression and flagrant violations of human rights in Ghana. In particular, the statement demanded the repeal of "repressive laws," which allowed the government to detain people without due process of law.

The governments of Kenya, Sierra Leone, and Uganda used the same methods to muzzle editors and journalists. In a treacherous attempt to silence the *Nairobi Law Monthly*, the Kenyan government charged its editor, Gitobu Imanyara, with the technical and criminal offense of failing to register the magazine and filing official returns to the Registrar of Books and Newspapers in April 1990. As the *African Letter* complained: "This action against the *Nairobi Law Monthly* is but the latest in a series of crackdowns against freedom of the press and the right of Kenyans to free expression" (Apr 16-30, 1990; p. 18).

In Sierra Leone the government hastily promulgated a Newspaper Amendment Act on April 25, 1990. A radio announcement stated that the licenses of five newspapers had been cancelled. *The New Shaft, Weekend Spark, For Di People, Vision,* and the *Globe* were ordered to stop publishing immediately. All newspapers, according to the new act, were required to renew their registration with an annual fee of Le 1,000 ($16). The act also empowered the minister of information to refuse registration or to cancel or suspend registration already granted if a paper carried "defamatory and libelous" articles. The real motive for the hastily enacted law was the embarrassment of senior officials exposed for their corrupt dealings. Two days before the new law was announced, the *New Shaft* had carried photographs of the minister of information, V.J.V. Mambu and a house he had under construction. The caption read: "Barely three years in parliament, former Works Minister, now Minister of Information, is building himself a palace. When will these men start serving the nation?" (*West Africa,* May 8-14, 1989; p. 772).

The ban was lifted in May 1989 after the Sierra Leone Association of Journalists, concerned citizens, and the affected editors appealed to President J. S. Momoh. But a month after the lifting, the security service raided the Bo-based *Chronicle* and the home of its editor-in-chief, K-Roy Stevens, in search of subversive documents. Stevens was then taken to the Freetown headquarters of the Criminal Investigation Department for questioning (*West Africa*, Jun 19-25, 1989; p. 1030). Subsequently, Franklin Bunting-Davies, the editor of the *New Shaft*, was given "an ultimatum to furnish the Ministry of Information and Broadcasting with copies of his professional certificates and other documents relating to his practice as editor or cease publication with immediate effect" (*West Africa*, Mar 5-11, 1990; p. 387).

While the government of Sierra Leone engaged in these repressive acts against the press, President Momoh hosted three press luncheons "at which he appealed to journalists to help in eradicating indolence, indiscipline and corruption from society" (*West Africa*, May 21-27, 1990; p. 840). The situation in Sierra Leone was even more perfidious, however, in view of the fact that Sierra Leone was the birthplace of an active free press in black Africa. It was here that the first newspapers in the colonial territories were founded.

In Uganda journalists had to be cleared by the Internal Security Organization. *New African* noted that some journalists reported that the Ministry of Information denied them accreditation on the advice of the intelligence arm of the government (May 1990; p. 21).

Nigeria also harassed journalists. When the principal officers of the Nigerian Civil Liberties Organization published a report on human rights violations in Nigeria on December 10, 1988, they were arrested and charged with subversion. In an irate editorial, a Nigerian paper, the *Daily Sketch*, excoriated: "We claim to be a civilized country but we do not really respect free speech, even when it is responsible. Those who do not hold the same views with government are regarded as traitors, people to be harassed and thrown into jail without trial. It is in the interest of government that those who hold views different from its own are allowed to air them. Nobody knows best. The person regarded as an enemy may have the better perspective" (Feb 1, 1989).

In another case, after Nigeria's abortive coup attempt on April 22, 1990, Ibrahim Babangida's regime indiscriminately harassed and detained journalists. *West Africa* reported that "the Nigerian Union of Journalists said journalists in the Federal Radio Corporation of Nigeria (FRCN), the News Agency of Nigeria (NAN), *Punch, Concord*, and *Vanguard*, newspapers are under siege" (*West Africa*, May 7-13, 1990; p. 777). A month later, the government intensified its crackdown against the press. On June 8, 1990, the state security force sealed off the premises of *Newbreed* magazine, apprehended its publisher, Chief Chris Okolie, searched the premises, and seized all the latest editions of the magazine. "According to the news editor, the men claimed they were looking for 'subversive undertones,' and were acting on 'orders from above' " (*West Africa*, Jun 18-24, 1990; p. 1043). On the following day, the government closed the *Daily Champion* and the *Vanguard*. The editor of the *Daily Champion*, Emmanuel Ifeanyu Agu, appeared before a Lagos magistrate's court and was charged with publishing a seditious editorial in the June 8 edition. Several journalists and editors were detained for more than a month (*West Africa*, Jun 18-24, 1990; p. 1043). "You cannot be a government that advocates human rights and attack people who are defending those very rights," said an angry Olu Onagoruwa, a lawyer defending Beko Ransome-Kuti (chairman of Campaign for Democracy and who was in detention)" (*Washington Post*, Jun 16, 1992; p. A16).

In Rwanda, President Juvenal Habyarimana ordered the prosecution of journalists publishing false information or inciting the people against the government (*New African*, Apr 1990; p. 17). Following this order, the Rwandan state security head, Augustin Nduwayezu, threatened journalists who had written allegedly subversive articles. Journalists such as Anastase Seruvumba of *Iwacu* and Father Andre Sibomana and Felicien Semusambi of *Kinyamateka* have been detained or placed under house arrest. One journalist, Sylvio Sindambiwe, met his death in a mysterious car accident. He had been an independent, uncompromising journalist who had been repeatedly threatened by the security forces.

Hundreds of other editors, journalists, writers, poets, scholars, and professors have also mysteriously vanished in many parts of Africa. Others still languish in jails.[8] Today, African writers lay their lives on the line for every sentence they write and publish or for every view they espouse in public. The magazine *South* deplored the censorship of writers in Uganda: "Uganda was once one of Africa's most literary countries—Kampala was stocked with bookshops. Makerere University had a well-established drama troupe and Oko p'Bitek's poems were widely read. But economic collapse and political terror silenced the writers and emptied the bookshops. Many of Uganda's best writers are dead: Okot through drink; playwright Byron Nawada on the orders of Idi Amin; playwright and novelist Robert Serumaga, mysteriously while in exile in Kenya in 1980" (Jan 1989; p. 88).

The irony is that this intellectual repression was being meted out by the same African nationalists who protested vigorously against the denial of free expression during the colonial era. Back in September 1958 delegates to the Pan-African Freedom Movement of East and Central Africa had met in

Mwanza, Tanzania, where they adopted a Freedom Charter that called upon "the Government of East and Central Africa to remove legal restrictions against the freedom of the press and particularly condemn[ed] the unjust prosecutions and convictions which [had] taken place in some of these Territories against the African Press in particular" (cited in Langley, 1979; p. 780). Indeed, Boahen and Webster (1970) reported that in British West Africa the colonialists had accorded African elites a degree of free expression to criticize colonial policies:

> Political associations could be formed without permission from the British and newspapers could operate on the whole free of interference . . . African elites moved freely from one colony to the other in the course of their work . . .
>
> In British West Africa the press was the most important single element in the birth and development of nationalism. The press kept a constant eye upon British officials, was quick to point out oppression, kept African claims to advancement and dignity alive, stimulated creative writing and never allowed the British to forget that their ultimate aim was to develop self-governing states. The press brought before West Africa the issues of the larger world, especially the black world extending from Africa to America and the West Indies (pp. 275-276).

After independence, however, Africa's new leaders tolerated no such watchdogs and independent presses. In response to the perceived bias of the Western media's coverage of Africa, the new African heads of state established a Pan-African News Agency. By 1988, however, even its Congolese director, Auguste Mpassi-Muba, objected to the bias caused by African state censorship: "It is high time the official, controlled, censored, muzzled or partisan news gives way in Africa to news based on the diversity of opinions and ideas, with free access to the various sources of official and unofficial information. . .The one-party states always want to control information" (*World Development Forum*, Jan 1988; p. 3). Lamb (1984) documented various African states' often brutal repression of journalists: "President Hastings Banda of Malawi jailed virtually the whole nongovernmental press corps in the mid-seventies. President Kenneth Kaunda appoints and fires newspaper editors in Zambia; in Uganda and Zaire, journalists shuttle in and out of jail so regularly that their wives don't even ask where they have been when they reappear after an absence of several days. Equatorial Guinea's president Marcias Nguema Biyogo went one step further: by the time he was overthrown and killed in 1979, all journalists of note had been executed or were in exile" (p. 246).

The repression of African journalists continues. For example, in Malawi the Banda government tortured journalist Osborne Mkandawire to death in

November 1988 and imprisoned and tortured several other journalists and writers "whose work was interpreted as critical of the government of Life-President Kamuzu Banda (*New African*, Apr 1989; p. 37). In September 1989 agents of the Malawian government assassinated exiled Malawian journalist Mkwapatira Mhango in Zambia. Mhango was an official of the exiled Malawi Freedom Movement (MAFREMO). His crime was publishing an article in the foreign press critical of Malawi government policies. The *African Letter* reported that Mhango's brother, a veterinary surgeon, has been a political prisoner since 1987, apparently in reprisal for Mkwapatira's writings (Nov 16-30, 1989; p. 18).

Fed up with repression in their country, the Catholic Bishops of Malawi wrote in a pastoral letter (March 8, 1992): "Human persons are honored— and this honor is due to them—whenever they are allowed to search freely for the truth, to voice their opinions and be heard, to engage in creative service of the community in all liberty within the associations of their own choice. Nobody should ever have to suffer reprisals for honestly expressing and living up to their convictions: intellectual, religious or political" (*Index on Censorship*, May 1992; p. 17).

This intellectual barbarism has reared its ugly head in South Africa, where black liberation movements have shown themselves viciously intolerant of reporting by black journalists. Sandile Memela, a political reporter for the *City Press*, a Johannesburg-based weekly, received death threats after being accused of writing "anti-ANC stories." His offense was a story in which he stated that, since its unbanning, the Pan-African Congress (PAC) was gaining more support. But it is not only the ANC which is guilty of intimidating black journalists:

Supporters of AZAPO (Azanian People's Organization) have been equally brutal in their attacks against reporters. One Soweto reporter, at that time an AZAPO member, had to flee his home after he heard that he was going to be attacked as it was suspected that he had changed political allegiances.

The conservative Inkatha Freedom Party has been most direct when dealing with black journalists: it shoots them if they seem to question too much.

A newspaper reporter, Sithembiso Sangweni, survived by the skin of his teeth when a volley of shots thundered behind him as he fled Inkatha supporters in the south coast township of KwaMakhutha. His crime: a series of stories exposing the unfair allocation of building sites by councilors who are members of Inkatha...

Kaizer Nyatsumba, a political correspondent for *The Star*, says: "I fear for the freedom of the press. It seems to me we are headed for a situation similar to that experienced in other African countries, where you can write what you like as long as you do not criticize the government. As you can see now, all the organizations are very sensitive to criticism. No magic wand is likely to suddenly strike them when they come into power for them to change those attitudes" (*New African*, Feb 1992; p. 9).

Khaba Mkhize, the editor of *Echo* in the Natal Province of South Africa, tirelessly championed the cause of peace among warring black factions. For that, he earned death threats. To survive, he frequently changed his car, swapping with friends (14 times in an 18-month period) and taking unplanned vacations abroad.

## DEVELOPMENTAL CONSEQUENCES OF REPRESSION

The intellectual barbarism of Africa's educated leaders has seriously impeded Africa's economic development. In 1990, 24 of the 36 poorest nations in the world were in black Africa, despite its tremendous wealth of natural resources. But its leaders continue to slaughter those who offer different solutions to its problems or otherwise disagree with them. This is not to suggest that African journalists and writers are without fault. Indeed, as *West Africa* observed, "There is a great need for more educated journalists who will report truthfully, fairly, accurately, and objectively, with maturity and professionalism" (May 21-27, 1990; p. 840). But detaining or killing journalists for "inaccurate reporting" is senseless. How are journalists supposed to learn from their mistakes if they are killed? And if people must pay for their mistakes with their lives, how many of Africa's incompetent leaders would be left?

Botswana is an example of an African country that affords its people freedom of expression and enjoys a relatively prosperous economy. Commenting on the political process in Botswana, Professor Patrick Mulotsi, a lecturer in sociology at the University of Botswana, said: "If you look at the prerequisites of liberal democracy, the rule of law has been highly respected. A lot of people can say a lot of things with relatively little fear. There has been a lot of response by the ruling party to debates with the opposition" (*New York Times*, May 16, 1990; p. A6).

Botswana can find solutions to its economic problems because it permits free debate and freedom of expression. The growth rate of Botswana's economy has averaged 8.8 percent in per capita terms for the 20 years since independence. In 1990 its foreign exchange reserves stood at a record $2.7 billion, which on a per capita basis was the highest in the Third World.

The Botswana example shows unequivocally that, given the freedom to express themselves, publish their ideas, and search for solutions, Africans are quite capable of engineering economic miracles. The barbaric governments set in place by most educated African leaders deny their people the freedom to enjoy a prosperous economy. The situation is even more confounding considering the fact that most African nations have signed or ratified the Organization of African Unity's (OAU) African charter on Human and Peoples' Rights. For example, Cameroon did so in 1987, Ghana in 1989, and Malawi in February 1990. Article 6 of the charter states clearly: "No one may be arbitrarily arrested or detained." Article 7 guarantees "the right to a fair trial in an independent court with a defense lawyer." Article 8 advocates "religious tolerance" and freedom from religious persecution. More important for the subject at hand, Article 9 of the charter guarantees "the right to free expression." Apparently, however, most African governments do not comprehend the significance of subscribing to the terms of such a document.

Moreover, all African countries are members of the United Nations. Article 19 of the U. N.'s Universal Declaration of Human Rights asserts that freedom of expression is a universal human right: "Freedom of expression is not the product of any political system or ideology. It is a universal human right, defined and guaranteed in international law . . . Everyone has the right to freedom of opinion and expression; this right includes freedom to hold opinions without interference and to seek, receive and impart information and ideas through any media regardless of boundaries."

When members of Ghanaian Professor Adu Boahen's Movement for Freedom and Justice held their first press conference on August 1, 1990, they called for an end to repression of the media and for an independently organized national referendum on the future of Ghana:

> We of the MFJ believe that the local mass media should be liberated from the grip of the PNDC. The atmosphere of fear, suspicion and intimidation and the existence of the culture of silence caused by the ready application of such oppressive laws as the Preventive Custody Law cannot make for a free and fair debate . . .
>
> We consider as highly dangerous to the political health of our country and to the national development effort that decisions affecting a whole country are not subject to the will of the people and that a group of individuals who have no mandate and are accountable to no one wields the powers of government and are free to take policy decisions in the name of the people . . .

The only way to find out what the true views and feelings of the people are is through a genuine national debate culminating in a National Referendum organized by an independent body.

Under the prevailing political climate of the country, however, it is neither possible to ascertain what Ghanaians truly think about the future political system of our country nor arrive at a national consensus on this vital question. In order to create an atmosphere which permits and guarantees free and open national discussion of the country's political future, we demand the repeal of all repressive laws, especially:

- The Preventive Custody Law (Provisional National Defence Council Law 4) under which individuals can be detained indefinitely,
- The Habeas Corpus Amendment Law (PNDC Law 91) under which an individual can be jailed without charge,
- The Newspaper Licensing Law (PNDC Law 211) by which a newspaper critical to government policies can be denied a licence,
- The sections of the Public Tribunals Law (PNDC Law 78) which deal with executions of political offenses.

Iron-fisted control of the media allowed the PNDC government of Ghana to conceal its economic failures and permitted selective manipulation of news consumed by Ghanaians. For example, when teachers went on strike on February 28, 1991, to demand basic trade union rights and a long-denied review of their salary structure and conditions of service, the state-owned media did not cover it. Said the *West Africa* (Apr 22-28, 1991): "Throughout the strike, no state-owned media agency carried any statement by the Ghana National Association of Teachers explaining the position of the teachers and their reasons for their strike. Nor was there any news report of the fact that a general strike of teachers was on. On the other hand, there was a lot of commentaries, editorials, threats and denunciations in the media about an event they had not reported" (p. 597). One Ben K. Ansah bemoaned this state of affairs:

The stranglehold of the PNDC administration in Ghana on the media houses will surely be a topic for a study in deception and oppression of a nation through media management and manipulation in the years to come.

On May Day, Ghanaian television viewers tuned in to watch the rallies held during the day at various centers in the country. I tuned in 20 minutes after the programme had started, hoping they would have finished with Rawlings! But lo and behold, he was still in view, finding scapegoats in the trade practices of the Western world for his economic failures.

Eventually they showed bits of celebrations in other centers as far apart as Sunyani, Ho and Koforidua. Then the surprise came. The newsreader, with a sly smile exposing her own embarrassment, said there were celebrations at Tema when the regional secretary Col. Thompson (a still of his was shown on the screen) spoke. But no coverage on the Tema event was screened! And Kumasi was not mentioned at all!! Tema is 18 miles away from Broadcasting House—could it not be covered? It was later learnt through residents there that the Tema celebrations were *against* PNDC rule and the present TUC leadership (*West Africa*, May 27-Jun 2, 1991; p. 865).

The solutions to most of Africa's problems lie in Africa itself—not in the corridors of the International Monetary Fund (IMF) or the inner sanctum of the Soviet Presidium. But solutions cannot be found when Africans do not have the freedom to devise and debate them.

One disgraceful development in 1991 was a $240 million program, sponsored jointly by the World Bank, the United Nations Development Program (UNDP) and United States Agency for International Development (US AID), for "intellectual capacity building in Africa." Are Africans intellectually deficient? The ostensible purpose was to rebuild Africa's universities and other institutions of higher learning, which have been neglected by years of budgetary cutbacks. But that was only a small part of the problem.

More fundamental has been the pervasive incidence of intellectual repression. Maina wa Kinyatti, a former senior lecturer in history at Kenyatta University (Kenya), complained: "Lecturers and intellectuals are arrested because of their ideas. You cannot comfortably teach because the police is planted in the classrooms. Whatever you teach is taped, and if you eventually say something critical against the president, you are detained. Censorship is so tight that even KANU [government] people are scared of what to write because they know that the police can come to their houses and take them away (*Africa Report*, Jul-Aug 1989; p. 58). Any "intellectual capacity building" program is bound to fail in an atmosphere of barbaric intellectual repression. It is this which has been the primary cause of Africa's brain drain. According to the World Bank, about 100,000 highly educated Africans have left Africa for the United States and Europe (*The Chronicle of Higher Education*, Jun 5, 1991; p. A30). This emigration necessitates the employment of "almost over 100,000 expatriate advisers working in Africa, who are paid $4 billion out of donor funds, a World Bank chief of mission in East Africa, Mr. Stephen O'Brien said recently. Mr. O'Brien termed the scenario a scandal" (*African Mirror*, Feb-Mar 1992; p. 34). In 1990 the government of Mozambique alone hired about 3,000 foreigners at an annual cost of about $180 million, which was nearly three times the country's regular government payroll of 100,000 workers (*The Chronicle of Higher Education*, Jun 5, 1991; p. A30).

There are other reasons why freedom of expression is vital to the African states. For example, by eliminating intellectual repression, African states will enjoy greater stability. In an editorial, *West Africa* noted that "in general, those countries which allow some freedom of expression find that it serves as a safety valve, a vehicle whereby rulers may better know the ruled. Likewise, where this openness is suppressed for whatever reason, these factors of stability are removed" (Nov 20-26, 1989; p. 1919).

The irony is that banning an organization and arresting or harassing its leaders does not achieve the intended objective. In fact, such acts achieve precisely the opposite result. A government ban of a book or a newspaper leads people to read it because they suspect that it contains some truth the government wants to hide. The ban merely piques their curiosity. In addition, the ban tends to draw more attention to the victim or the author. In fact, the persecution of an author or journalist by a hated and oppressive regime might well transform him into a martyr or a hero because what is evil in the eyes of the devil must be good. One Ghanaian, K. Danso-Boafo, wrote: "By preventing the Movement for Freedom and Justice (MFJ) from using the premises of the Teachers' Hall for a symposium, and holding and questioning its deputy national secretary Mr. Kwesi Pratt, (Ghana's) PNDC functionaries are making 'political martyrs' out of the MFJ and its leadership—something any astute politician would want to avoid. The political history of Africa is replete with such political miscalculations" (*West Africa*, Jun 3-9, 1991; p. 892).

One such miscalculation was made by President Kenneth Kaunda, whose socialist United National Independence Party, the sole legal party, had been in power for 27 years. In July 1990 he released several key members of the Movement Multi-Party Democracy (MMD) (Goodwin Mumba, Edward Shamwana, and Christon Tembo) from jail. They were immediately hailed as heroes. A perplexed Kaunda fumed, "I release the criminals and now they are called heroes" (*African Letter*, May 1-15, 1991; p. 1).

Nigerian writer Peter Ezeh averred:

> There is one basic truth governments which stifle the press need to know, and that is that only good work on the part of the government, inspired by the sincere desire to satisfy the great majority of the governed, can effectively frustrate a bad press where such actually exists. People are intelligent enough to be a good judge. To paraphrase de Rivarol, "In the long run, one always loses when one attacks ideas with bullets. Only ideas can successfully attack ideas." Censorship

leaves the impression that the censor has something to hide (*Index on Censorship,* Aug 1988; p. 18).

It is not the business of government to ban publications. If a publication has nothing to offer, the people will reject it. Nor is it the business of government to ban organizations. They have various viewpoints to propagate in the marketplace of ideas. If these viewpoints have no merit, again the public will reject them. By banning newspapers or organizations, an "evil" government sanctifies their ideas or agenda. These ideas by themselves may not necessarily be sacrosanct. But the very fact that they have been banned enhances their value and status. The ANC of South Africa, UNITA of Angola, Mwakenya of Kenya, and many other groups and newspapers have been banned. But they did not die.

As one specific example, the Kenya government of Daniel arap Moi persecuted and repeatedly jailed Gitobu Imanyara, editor of the *Nairobi Law Monthly.* His offence was to publish in 1990 a series of articles on constitutional reform and to advocate multi-party democracy. He was thrown into jail and his magazine *retroactively* banned. Pressure by international human rights groups forced his release. He was immediately given the "Golden Pen of Freedom" award (by International PEN) in the United States. On his return to Kenya, he was re-arrested, despite his failing medical condition. The charges read:

"You have been involved in subversive activities aimed at undermining and overthrowing the government of Kenya as by law established.

"You are the editor or proprietor or publisher of a Nairobi magazine known as the *Nairobi Law Monthly* in which you have repeatedly written and published articles which denounce, ridicule and discredit the government of Kenya, its activities and its established constitutional leadership. You have given lectures or speeches at Limuru Theological College on diverse occasions and on subjects which constitute or amount to downright subversion against the government of Kenya as by law established.

"You have aligned yourself to and associated with known anti-government characters and personalities, such as Kenneth Matiba, Charles Rubia and others, and have worked in concert with them to lay groundwork for the formation or creation of another political party contrary to the provision of the Constitution of the country.

"You have participated with the same said characters, in a series of illegal meetings in Nairobi and at these meetings, you, together with those characters, have discussed, promoted and mapped out plans and strategies to overthrow the government of Kenya by unlawful means including use of violence.

"You have conducted yourselves in total disregard and disrespect of the Head of State and have participated in activities calculated to create disaffection, discontent, ill-will, hatred and hostility amongst the people of Kenya.

"Now, therefore, because of these anti-government activities and in the interest of preservation of public security your detention has become necessary" (*Index on Censorship*, Apr 1992; p. 22).

What happened to his magazine after all this persecution? According to *Africa Report*:

His magazine has enormously increased on last year's readership of 5,000 and now sells over 15,000 copies. Just after the ban was overturned, a taxi driver buying *The Law Monthly* said it had become the most popular magazine in Nairobi—" because the editor is a brave man." This is despite the fact that some of its issues are virtually impenetrable to the layman in its legalistic style of scholarly and elitist discourse.

The magazine has, above all, become important as a symbol of defiance and progress. More recently, however, the government *inadvertently* popularized it—and politicized it—by linking its fate with the poorest section of the population, the hawkers and vendors (because) the Special Branch had harassed and threatened the street sellers, confiscating thousands of issues in a city sweep on Feb 29, 1991 (May-Jun 1991; p. 52).

African leaders must learn that the atrocities of banning books, silencing writers and journalists, and exiling, imprisoning, torturing, and murdering dissidents are counterproductive. Worse, they have silenced millions of Africans who are terrified of expressing alternative viewpoints. A "culture of silence" now grips Ethiopia, Ghana, Liberia, Uganda, Zaire, and many other countries. This fear has made it virtually impossible for Africans themselves to come forward with their own solutions to their problems. The inevitable consequence has been the absence in Africa of a free marketplace for ideas and home-grown solutions to the continent's problems. As a result, solutions to African problems must come from abroad, and this perpetuates the myth that Africans cannot think for themselves and devise solutions to their own problems. Worse, the foreign solutions often prove unsuitable for Africa's unique socioeconomic conditions and usually results in wasted foreign exchange expenditures.

Sahabu Wakilu, a lecturer, summed up the frustrations of Ghanaians with the economic effects of repressing free expression in their country:

The political environment prevailing in Ghana today can best be described as "a culture of terror" and not "a culture of silence" as the Head of State Flt.-Lt. Jerry Rawlings wants us to believe.

What does it pay for a brave Ghanaian to criticise the government only to be made a scapegoat while 14 million Ghanaians made up of cowards and opportunists look on helplessly and unconcerned?

If Rawlings is genuinely concerned with the "culture of silence," why did his government make attempts on the life of Professor Adu Boahen after the Professor had made his views known on the current political happenings in Ghana?

The clandestine killing of Ghanaians considered to be opponents of the government is now an open secret. Therefore the current indifference of Ghanaians to the government's educational, economic and political reforms is a manifestation of general discontent with the government. If Ghanaians are not talking today, it is because we know it is of no use talking. I know we have enough guts left to ask the government: Why waste 6 billion cedis on an election of district assemblymen who would be responsible to the government alone—when they could have been appointed? Why can't the 6 billion be judiciously used to repair our roads or even build new houses for the suffering workers of Ghana?

May I also use this opportunity to appeal to foreign diplomats on visits to Ghana to refrain from making statements hailing the "success" of the economic recovery program. If it were, why the Program of Action to Mitigate the Social Cost of Adjustment and Development?

Ghanaians know how to assess the merits of the PNDC Government. If it has achieved nothing at all, it has succeeded in making our currency worthless by persistent doses of weekly devaluations through the auction system (*New African*, Jan 1989; p. 56).

Africa must be freed from intellectual barbarism by rising to the call of Wole Soyinka, the Nobel laureate. At the Lagos Conference on African Literature on May 2, 1988, he called for African dictators to set a date by which they would desist from denigrating their people:

Today, I seize the occasion to invite the *writers* of this continent to join me in a complementary endeavour. The "divine right of kings" which ended with the decapitation of crowned heads of Europe several centuries ago, has—need I state the obvious?—been replaced by the "divine right of the gun" on this continent. We must now invite all our dictatorships, under no matter what camouflage, and however comparatively civilianised and domesticated they are - to set a definite date within this century for the abandonment of this denigration of our popular will. I urge my fellow writers to use their skill and exploit whatever strategies can be thought of for ending the uncertainty of social existence which is innate to the condition of the forcibly governed (published in *Index On Censorship*, Aug 1988; p. 8; emphasis added).

Give Africa back to its traditional rulers. Often denigrated as "illiterate and backward," these rulers often showed intellectual maturity far superior to that of many educated African heads of state. These chiefs not only tolerated but also solicited alternative viewpoints. In so doing, they availed themselves of options that they might otherwise have overlooked. When the people presented an idea to a chief, he would examine it very carefully, even if it differed radically from his own. If the idea made sense, the chief would thank the people for it. Commenting on the public debates Ghana's military government held in August 1990 to determine the country's political future,[9] native African chief Osagyefo Kuntukununku stressed the need for freedom of expression to reach consensus: "Future governments would do well to encourage a dialogue between themselves and the populace, confront contrary views with well reasoned arguments rather than intimidation and detention. Suppression of dissent and the denial of the right to express contrary views can only encourage sycophancy and opportunism. There must be a free press to enhance dialogue, efficiency and accountability and to champion the cause of victims of governmental vindictiveness and arbitrariness (*West Africa*, Aug 27- Sep 2, 1990; p. 2372).

The chief displayed far more political wisdom than many educated African leaders. His thoughts were echoed by Nobel laureate Bishop Desmond Tutu in a speech at Oxford University in June 1990:

I should confess to our shame that on the whole we in modern Africa have not been able to accommodate differences of opinion.

When you differ from someone . . . if you don't agree four-square at every point with him, that is taken to mean that you are his enemy. But that is not traditionally African.

In traditional Africa, a chief was a good chief because he could work out a consensus, and the consensus arose because people had different points of view. I have to confess, that is a fundamental weakness that we have at the present time (*New African*, Aug 1990; p. 35).

The intolerance of alternative viewpoints on the part of many educated African leaders is the root of the continent's problems. S.M. Khalid observed:

Most traditional rulers arrived at decisions through exhaustive debate involving the entire group and only after a consensus had been reached to satisfy all parties, not through imperious personal decree.

The problem in Africa, as elsewhere, is that without a channel for dissent or public debate, opposition groups that have inevitably emerged will be forced to seek redress through political violence.

The African continent is replete with many such bloody examples, innumerable coups bringing worse military governments to power and civil wars raging in Sudan, Ethiopia, Angola, Mozambique, Somalia and Liberia. Settlements of all these conflicts will hinge on the inclusion of political pluralism by different groups (*Baltimore Sun,* Jul 22, 1990; p. 3E).

The media is particularly vital in the struggle against oppression. *New Internationalist,* comparing India and Sudan, wrote:

Although one of the poorest countries in the world, India's relatively free press ensures that the Government cannot easily hide failures in food distribution. By comparison, the absence of a free press in Sudan means food shortages are disguised until it is too late and famine has already struck . . .

Television and radio are powerful allies to the people in pushing for human rights. Thanks to monitoring by human-rights groups like Amnesty International and Human Rights Watch, images and reports of atrocities can be flashed across the world within minutes of the abuse being committed. Remember that single student standing courageous in front of a row of Chinese tanks in Beijing? Or those heart-rending pictures of the Kurds freezing to death in the mountains after the Gulf War? (Mar 1992; p. 5).

Get control of the media out of the hands of incompetent and corrupt African governments. This is exactly what the Christian Council of Ghana said in a December 1990 memorandum to the ruling PNDC regime: "We recommend that the country's press and media be privatised, to operate independently of the Government's involvement and control. The Government shall, therefore, neither own, nor run any newspaper in the country. Where the Government desires to inform, or to advertise to the general public, it shall do so through its own Gazette, press releases and conferences, and periodic bulletins."[10] Without a free media, respect for freedom of expression and a climate that admits intellectual pluralism, Africa will never solve its problems.

## NOTES

1. See *New African*, Feb 1992; p. 7.

2. Of course, there is no guarantee that the institution of freedom of expression alone would suddenly produce an end to all problems. A feasible solution to a problem may be found through debate and exchange of ideas, but a *lack of political will* may prevent its implementation. Regardless, freedom of expression is needed to find the optimal solution. Whether it is implemented is a different issue. We should note, however, that the issue of political will is irrelevant in autocratic regimes. A military regime that holds itself accountable to no one cannot be said to be constrained by the political feasibility of its policies.

3. The tradition of a community's meeting to debate policy options before agreeing on a decision is still alive in some parts of Africa. In rural Ghana in 1982 the villages of Boabeng and Flema raised funds from voluntary contributions by the villagers and fund-raising activities for development. The chiefs, prominent members of the community, and ordinary villagers met to determine the best use of the money. Proposals included a health post, a post office, road pavement, electrification, pipe-borne water, and a day nursery. The people thoughtfully considered and heatedly debated each proposal and eventually ruled out all of them. Then "a stranger by colour and language" told the people about bee farming. The people adopted the project, and it became successful (*West Africa*, Nov 1, 1982; pp. 2818-2819).

4. *New Internationalist*, May 1992; p. 30.

5. The cassettes confiscated included: the *Speeches of Jomo Kenyatta*, initially released in 1978 when the late president of Kenya died; *Let's Praise the Lord*, which touched on the 1975 assassination of the former member of parliament for Nyandarua North, Josiah Mwangi Kariuki, the mysterious death of the former member of parliament for Dagoretti, Dr. Johnstone Muthiora, and the mysterious disappearance of Kenyatta's detainee colleague, Kung'u Karumba. Another cassette was *The Tribulations of the Poor People of Muoroto*, which referred to the May 25, 1990, eviction of the Muoroto squatters in which many died. Other seized cassettes were *Who Killed Ouko?*, *Matiba's Tribulations*, *Big Fish*, and *Who Is with Us?*

6. The newly established procedures closely resembled measures instituted by the apartheid government in South Africa to control the press (*Index on Censorship*, May-Jun 1989; p. 5).

7. The choice of the organization's name is significant because Ghana's official motto is "Freedom and Justice."

8. The appendix provides a country-by-country documentation of these arrests and detentions.

9. The debates were a classic example of how an African government can pervert a good idea. When the military government of Ghana embarked upon a program of instituting "grass-roots democracy," it consulted no one. It employed the services of a pre-1989-revolution Bulgarian expert. After spending C 2 billion (or about $10 million) on the district assembly elections, the government set up a National Commission for Democracy (NCD) to hold seminars in the major cities of Ghana to collect views on the country's political future. The debates should have preceded the district elections. In addition, the debates were not entirely free from intimidation. Senior officials, including the head of state himself, were always present. This led the Tema District Council of Labor to demand "a reconstitution of the National Commission for Democracy to exclude government officials. It also proposed the creation of a Constituent Assembly that would be responsible for collating views from the NCD-organized seminars on the country's future and from other organizations and individuals" (*West Africa*, Sep 3-9, 1990; p. 2408).

   Several prominent individuals added their voices to the call to exclude government officials as there was clearly a conflict of interest. The Association of Nurses, in particular, deplored the fact that the debates were being held in an atmosphere of "intimidation and arbitrariness."

10. The full text can be found in Appendix D of a June 1992 report prepared by the International Foundation of Electoral Systems (IFES) in Washington, DC. The report is titled "Ghana: A Pre-Election Assessment Report, June 1, 1992."

# Chapter 10

## The Looting of Africa

If you steal, do not steal too much at a time. You may be arrested. Steal cleverly (*yiba na mayele*), little by little.

> —President Mobutu Sese Seko of Zaire in an address to party regulars

Every franc we give impoverished Africa comes back to France, or is smuggled into Switzerland and even Japan.

> —*Le Monde*, March 1990

In 1988 there was much outrage over the discovery of toxic waste dumps in Africa. Since this waste came from both the East and the West, the issue was immediately couched in a North-South paradigm. Headlines screamed, accusing the North of turning the South into a dump site. Of course, irresponsible and unethical disposal of deadly chemicals anywhere should be condemned, and Africans had a right to be incensed. But what most African radicals ignored was the fact that foreign companies, whether of Eastern or Western origin, could not dump hazardous materials in Africa *without* the knowledge and cooperation of some of its leaders and officials. Indeed, when Benin accepted radioactive nuclear waste from France, President Ahmed Kerekou "decided that waste will be buried on the outskirts of Abomey, one of the centers of opposition to Kerekou" (*West Africa*, Jun 20, 1988; p. 1109).

In March 1989 Francois Roelants du Vivier, president of the European Environment Alliance, disclosed that the Angolan government had signed an agreement with a Swiss businessman, Arnold Andreas Kunezler, that would allow the dumping of five million tons of toxic waste in Angola. According to *Africa Report*, "[t]he $2 billion contract reportedly calls for waste from Western countries to be stored in a 19,300 square-mile semi-desert area, about 125 miles north of the coastal town of Namibe in southern Angola. The 4-year deal is allegedly due to start in March, 1989" (Mar-Apr 1989;

p. 5). It was easy for African radicals to accuse Western countries of environmental racism. But were African leaders blameless?

On many other issues, such as the Third World debt crisis, one encounters similar diatribe. Africa's total foreign debt had reached a staggering $270 billion in 1991, exerting a drag on its rate of development and frustrating efforts to alleviate widespread squalor and poverty. But nobody talked about helping to repay Africa's foreign debt by repatriating the loot corrupt African elites had stashed abroad.

For decades, African radicals railed against colonial plunder, American economic imperialism, the avaricious propensities of Western banks, the predatory practices of multinational corporations, and the tight-fisted International Monetary Fund as the causes of Africa's economic crisis. For example, it was incessantly argued that Western banks, acting as monopolists, cornered credit markets and callously extracted exorbitant interest charges from destitute, problem-plagued African countries that could ill afford to pay them.

To be sure, the practices of some foreign commercial banks were of a questionable nature, and one could justifiably draw up a lengthy list of charges and dubious financial transactions. For example, overzealous Western bankers routinely neglected checks on creditworthiness, financial controls, and supervision in extending loans. Moreover, the international financial system, dominated by Western banks, can be said to have operated to the pernicious disadvantage of many Third World countries. Further, the collapse of the oil and copper markets and the slump in the prices of cash crops imperiled government finances in a number of countries. But unethical practices by foreign banks and defects in the international economic system and other *external factors* alone are insufficient to explain Africa's economic crisis. Nor could foreign companies exploit African economies without the connivance or active encouragement of corrupt government officials.

## CORRUPTION: THE EVIDENCE

An investigation of the causes of Africa's financial crisis cannot be complete without a consideration of the behavior of the other party to a financial transaction—the borrower, in this case African governments. While a lender seeks the maximum return possible, it is the borrower's responsibility to seek the best possible terms for the loan. In the majority of cases the African borrowers were the educated elites. Thus, it is unrealistic to argue that these government officials did not know or understand the loan agreements they were signing. Vincent Mensah, a Ghanaian, placed the blame exactly where it belonged:

> Some Ghanaian intellectuals still cling to the notion that our current problems are the deliberate attempts by imperialism to thwart our efforts at development. The "imperialism and neocolonialism" rhetoric belongs to the 1950s and 1960s. The real problem is the way we run our own affairs. At the 25th anniversary of Ghana's independence, ironically, J. J. Rawlings said: "Ghanaians must be their own masters." We have been our own masters, mismanaging our affairs for 25 years, that is why he is now Ghana's head of state, purportedly to "correct things."
>
> Corruption inevitably results as people try to circumvent the controls and regulations, and take advantage of the loopholes. The ruling class, comprising the exploitative capitalists, and the corrupt public servants (more often than not including our soldiers of "fortune") emerge as the winners.
>
> Our myopic intellectuals then supply the rhetoric to divert the people's attention from the class struggle, and blame imperialism and aliens who, they claim, cheat us and sign dubious contracts with us. No foreigner can exploit us without the cooperation of some Ghanaians (*West Africa*, Jun 21, 1982; p. 1657).

Another factor to consider in determining the cause of Africa's economic crisis is to what use the foreign loans were put. The painful truth is that African governments squandered, wasted, and consumed many of the loaned funds. Thus, there is little to show for the enormous African debt.[1]

True, there was colonial exploitation in the past but today the real exploiters and oppressors of the African peasants are often the African elites. It is common knowledge that highly placed African government officials extort commissions on foreign loan contracts and deposit them in overseas banks. The very people who are supposed to defend and protect the peasants' interests have instead been responsible for the institutionalized looting and capital flight that have plagued the African economy.

An estimated $15 billion—more than what Africa receives in foreign aid—flees Africa annually. In 1988, for example, France sent $2,591 million in aid to Africa, but in the same year, according to the *Independent*, "[n]early CFA 3.5 billion—47 percent of the total issue—was exchanged in Europe by the Bank of France, some of it exported in suitcases" (Jun 19, 1990). Kenyans alone have stashed more than $5 billion abroad, an amount which is greater than their country's foreign debt of $4 billion (*South*, Jun 1989; p. 30). *The Economist* asked: "What Arab country has $50 billion in private savings stashed abroad? Where do customers fight over Mercedes sports cars that sell for $400,000? . . . This is not some gilt-edged petro-sheikhdom. It is Egypt, a country of 58 million people whose foreign debt of $35 billion nearly equals its Gross Domestic Product, where a typical monthly wage is $50, and rubbish is collected by small dirty children in rickety donkey-carts" (Jan 18, 1992; p. 42).

Some of this capital flight from Africa represents wealth legitimately earned by Africans who have no faith in their countries' futures because of economic and political instability. But the rest is booty, wealth illegally acquired and transferred by the African elite. Shamefully, educated African officials amass their wealth by stealing it from the labor of poor peasants.

Corrupt African officials looted billions of dollars from their countries in the late 1970s and early 1980s, and the financial drain continues. In Algeria a "former prime minister, Mr. Abdelhamid Brahimi, said recently that officials of the ruling *Front de Liberation National* had pocketed $26 billion in bribes and commissions on foreign contracts. The present prime minister, Mr. Mouloud Hamrouche, called the charge 'grossly exaggerated' but did not deny its gist" (*The Economist*, Apr 14, 1990; p. 51).

Libya should have one of the highest per capita incomes in the world with a population of only four million and vast oil wealth estimated at $10 billion in 1990. But "mismanagement and corruption so eroded the country's economic base that Libya sometimes fails to pay its foreign bills on time and some government employees go without a paycheck for months" (*The Washington Post*, Feb 15, 1992; p. A23).

In November 1988 The Gambia launched a presidential inquiry into allegations of corruption and embezzlement against the telecommunications minister and other high government officials (*West Africa*, Nov 28, 1988; p. 2264). In Guinea President Lansana Conte admitted that "generalized corruption, incessant embezzlement, laxity in implementing budget estimates and malfunctioning of our administrative system have created a situation that has finally paralysed all the recovery programs that have been launched" (*West Africa*, Oct 17-23, 1988; p. 1974).

In Mali former head of state, Moussa Traore, looted the country to amass a personal fortune worth over $2 billion—an amount equal to the size of Mali's foreign debt. This was the gist of a January 1992 article entitled "Le Sang des Pauvres" (The Blood of the Poor) written by Swiss MP Jean Ziegler, in the French newspaper *Liberation* (cited in *West Africa*, May 4-10, 1992; p. 746).

In Sierra Leone scores of ghost workers were added to the government payroll and their salaries collected by workers, defrauding the government of millions of leones. "In one government department 75 percent of the staff were found to be nonexistent" (*West Africa*, Sep 5-11, 1988; p. 1648). In almost all cases such practices are indicative of corruption at the top. Indeed, in

March 1989 Dr. Shamsu Mustapha, the former minister of state in the Ministry of Economic and Development Planning, was charged with financial impropriety. That brought to three the number of ministers charged with such offenses (*New African*, Apr 1988; p. 36). In 1992, according to *West Africa*, "The Criminal Investigation Department (began) examining documents pertaining to a $500 million loan contract entered into by former foreign minister, Dr. Abdul Karim Koroma and the Sierra Leone ambassador to Saudi Arabia on behalf of the government, and arranged by an oil company in Houston, Texas, on the understanding that the company would be paid a consultancy fee of $12 million" (Dec 16-22, 1991; p. 2115). (The Houston firm complained it never received its fee, fueling speculation as to what happened to the $12 million.) One irate African in Kano, P.F.U. Taylor, wrote:

> Any observer who knew Sierra Leone two decades ago can bear witness that it has been reduced to a country where there is virtually no medical facility; a country where potable water is a rare luxury; a country where pothole-free roads only exist in history; a country where a monthly salary is not sufficient to feed oneself.
>
> Given the present economic state of the country, which is considered as one of the poorest in the world, I refuse to believe that a national can contemplate an act that is, to say the least, worse than trading in slaves. Because while slave traders sold human beings who were not related to them, those under investigation, if guilty, have knowingly sold the whole population, including their own relations, generations yet unborn and the country itself . . .
>
> Those who rip off an African country should be put in the zoo. That is where they belong! (*West Africa*, Mar 16-22, 1992; p. 444).

Outlining his reasons why he overthrew the Momoh regime in Sierra Leone on April 29, 1992, Captain Valentine Strasser declared:

> The nation as a whole was in a state of virtual collapse. Corruption, indiscipline, mismanagement, tribalism, nepotism, injustice, and thuggery were rampant. Members of government were engaged in the plundering of the state's resources to enrich themselves . . .
>
> To indicate the depth to which our country had declined under the APC (All People's Congress) misrule, only 22 percent of all classes of roads are motorable; only one-third of cash crops were exported in the last few years.
>
> Infant and under-5 mortality rates are among the highest in the world. Life expectancy of 42 years is among the lowest in the world. Health services and infrastructure have been in a state of decay for a prolonged period. Recording

exports of diamonds are now only a fraction of what they were a decade ago (*West Africa*, May 18-24, 1992; p. 840).

The Liberian government initiated a number of probes to recover public funds expended for personal use by several officials in both the private and public sectors. The managing director of the National Ports Authority, his deputy, and the acting controller were dismissed for reportedly embezzling $1.5 million (*West Africa*, Apr 12, 1982; p. 969). In April 1986 the government's own newspaper, *New Liberian*, reported that "$13 million had allegedly been stolen through manipulation of customs receipts. The paper linked several top finance ministry officials with the scandal, including a deputy minister, a deputy commissioner of customs and an assistant minister" (*West Africa*, Apr 28, 1986; p. 908). The World Bank estimates that every year $60 million are diverted from state corporations to private pockets. In 1988 $3 million in U.S. aid funds simply vanished. That same year President Samuel Doe "fired the entire staff of the government's cheque printing and general auditing bureau for alleged corruption" (*West Africa*, Mar 21, 1988; p. 529).

Declaring corruption as the scourge of Ghanaian society, the military government of Ghana embarked in 1982 on a crusade against corruption. After eight years of imposing stiff sentences and executing the guilty by firing squad, the government learned that it could not even clean up its own house. Top government officials were found to have fraudulently purchased equipment (*West Africa*, Dec 4-10, 1989; p. 2036), to have demanded and collected bribes (*West Africa*, Apr 5-15, 1990; p. 598), and to have embezzled government funds (*West Africa*, Apr 9-15, 1990; p. 598).

In Togo the manager of the National Agricultural Fund was sentenced to 20 years in prison for embezzling $8.7 million (*West Africa*, Mar 28, 1988; p. 569). In the following year the former minister of justice and his associates were charged with involvement in swindling approximately CFA 15 million from Togo's lottery. In addition, the former minister of commerce was removed from office and fined because he had continued to draw his salary as a managing director of the Union of Togolese Banks (*West Africa*, Apr 17-23, 1989; p. 622). But the worst offender was the head of state, Gen. Gnassingbe Eyadema, himself:

Mba Kabassema, who was Minister of Trade and Transport in Eyadema's government in 1977, alleged that Eyadema pillaged the country's resources with the connivance of a Moroccan adviser, Maurice Assor.

Another delegate [to the national conference] alleged that Eyadema's personal fortune was 800 billion CFA francs ($2.8 billion) most of which has been put into foreign banks. He said that the Nangbeto dam project which was costed at CFA 8 billion, was then increased to CFA 48 billion, so that funds could be "diverted" into the wrong pockets. Eyadema spent CFA 50 billion to build a chateau at Pya his home town in northern Togo.

When Togo's phosphate mines were nationalized in 1974, Kabassema alleged that Eyadema had diverted 150,000 tonnes of phosphates valued at CFA 2.05 billion into the account of his adviser Maurice Assor. He also gave Assor exclusive monopolies on the export of 12 agricultural crops and later established SONACOM a central procurement agency for the purchase of imports. SONACOM became the conduit for all kinds of deals masterminded by Assor on behalf of President Eyadema. He bought Presidential jets, a Fokker 28, Grumman helicopters, a DC-8, various Boeing jets and an arsenal of arms. The construction of Niamtougu airport in the north and Hotel 2 Fevrier were also handled by Assor.

On all these deals, Kabassema alleged, there were massive kickbacks banked overseas. The price of the Hotel 2 Fevrier jumped from CFA 17.5 billion to CFA 35 billion and yet the hotel only reached 26 floors high, compared with the 35 storeys originally specified (*New African*, Oct 1991; p. 12).

In 1988 Benin was rocked by a series of corruption scandals involving its military ruler, Mathieu Kerekou, and his cronies (*New Africa*, Mar 1988; p. 14).That same year President Paul Biya of Cameroon decided to wage a merciless war against corruption and the misappropriation of funds in his government. Although 115 high-ranking officials were arrested (*New African*, Nov 1988; p. 43), the government's investigators made little progress, and corruption increased. Minister of Public Service and State Control Haman Garga Adji "reported funds missing totalling CFA 357 million ($1.3 million) owed by top level civil servants and politicians" (*New African*, Jan 1992; p. 18).

State firms in Kenya were similarly looted. In 1990, for example, the auditor of state corporations reported that "fraudulent behavior in the management of Kenya's parastatal organizations caused a loss of $25 million; the losses were due to gross mismanagement and embezzlement of public funds" (*The African Letter*, Dec 16-31, 1991; p. 9).

In Angola, theft of the country's wealth by members of the ruling MPLA administration accelerated in 1992, after peace accords were signed in May 1991 to end the country's civil war:

The law banning possession of diamonds [was] revoked to allow senior members to take stolen and smuggled diamonds out of the country.

The proceeds of the sale of a 10-percent share in an oilfield which President Eduardo dos Santos said raised $312 million have apparently disappeared. Many diplomats in Luanda think much of the money has gone into private pockets. Several of the leaders of the MPLA, particularly those who have been in the oil sector, now own property in Europe and the United States (*The Independent*, London, Feb 19, 1992).

Even socialist Tanzania suffered from corruption. Prime Minister Joseph Warioba was moved enough to speak out with scathing frankness: "Everywhere you go even in hospitals and schools, corrupting and corrupt people seem to rule the day." Corruption has become institutionalized at the top among those who handle big money. As *New African* reported: "Ordinary Tanzanians are complaining bitterly that they have been let down by their leadership. Even essential services such as education, hospitals, and police are up to their necks in corrupt practices. People who use government hospitals expect to have to bribe doctors and nurses before they can be treated" (Apr 1990; p. 16).

In Zimbabwe top government officials used their influence to buy trucks and cars at the artificially low official price from the state-owned vehicle assembly company and quickly sold them on the black market for enormous profit (*Africa Report*, Jan-Feb 1989; p. 37). Meanwhile, in Zambia President Kenneth Kaunda, the architect of Zambia's socialist ideology of humanism, dismissed as "a big lie" recent allegations that he had transferred $6 billion in state funds to personal bank accounts abroad (*New York Times*, Aug 15, 1990; p. A6). Civil servants who had retired ten years earlier from Zambia's Ministry of Power, Transport and Communications were found to be drawing their salaries on a regular basis. "A snap survey carried out on various public service departments found that 3 percent of the names on the government payroll were counterfeit . . . It was estimated that the government was losing 500 million kwachas ($12.5 million) a year in fraud of this kind (*New African*, Dec 1991; p. 33).

What follows is a more detailed examination of corruption in selected African countries. Since data on the subject are hard to obtain, I have relied largely on published newspaper accounts and on reports of commissions of inquiry set up by African governments.

## THE IVORY COAST

President Felix Houphouet-Boigny once admitted being interested in the creation and multiplication of wealth rather than in its distribution. He described this economic philosophy as "state capitalism." Indeed, it has long been alleged that many of his associates have enriched themselves enor-

mously under his watchful patronage. Professor Laurent Gbagbo, a vocifer-
ous critic of President Houphouet-Boigny who spent seven years in exile,
alleged that corruption in the Ivory Coast was rife: "We are the country with
the most millionaires, which means we have the most thieves. The more
Houphouet ages, the more his collaborators sense an end to the regime, and
the more they steal" (*West Africa*, Apr 3-9, 1989; p. 536). "The central bank
calculates that some CFA 130 billion [or $456 million] are spirited out of the
country illegally each year" (*Africa Report*, May-Jun 1990; p. 14).

World Bank figures suggest that the distribution of wealth in the Ivory
Coast is more skewed than in almost any other African country. A confidential United Nations report revealed that the government had extracted large
surpluses from small-holders (peasant farmers). Indeed, President
Houphouet-Boigny admitted in his 1988 New Year's address to the nation
that the country's farmers had over the years parted with four-fifths of the
value of what they produced to enable the government to finance economic
development. Much of this money went to the State Marketing Board.
Nevertheless, the development that took place was concentrated in Abidjan
and other urban areas and thus bypassed the rural peasants. Large sums were
also channeled into the creation and maintenance of unwieldy and unprofitable parastatal corporations. The president's protégés used the rest of the
peasants' money for self-enrichment.

*West Africa* reported, "The number of financial scandals involving top
political figures which have come to light in the past decade give some
indication of the extent to which self-enrichment is tolerated" (May 1-7,
1989; p. 677). These included Henri Konan Bedie, the current chairman of
the National Assembly and, in constitutional terms, Houphouet-Boigny's
heir apparent, who committed "misdemeanors relating to ambitious but
ill-fated plans for the expansion of the country's sugar industry," and Bedie's
arch-rival, Emmanuel Dioulo, the former mayor of Abidjan who fled to
Europe in March 1985 to avoid criminal charges of embezzlement and fraud.
Allegedly, his company, COGEXIM, "had failed to repay loans worth $58
million to the Banque Nationale de Development" (*West Africa*, May 1-7,
1989; p. 677). In addition, in April 1989 Dr. Theodore Kouba, an executive
member of the ruling Partie Democratique de Côte d'Ivoire (PDCI), was
charged with extorting CFA 6.8 billion ($21.8 million) from executives
working for the Abidjan-based Continental Bank, the African Development
Bank, the World Bank, and from some 800 Ivorian teachers under the pretext
of building estate houses for them. During the trial anonymous pamphlets
denounced "the selfish power and the scandalous mismanagement of the
economy, the waste of billions of dollars of commercial loans over the last

28 years. . .and the greedy hoarding of power by the President and his party"
(*New African*, Apr 1989; p. 20).

Houphouet-Boigny himself is reputed to hold a vast personal fortune. In
1983 he declared, "I do have assets abroad. But they are not assets belonging
to Côte d'Ivoire. What sensible man does not keep his assets in Switzerland,
the whole world's bank? I would be crazy to sacrifice my children's future in
this crazy country without thinking of their future" (*La Croix* (Paris), Mar 13,
1990). According to *Africa Report*, one anonymous tract estimated the
president's fortune to be CFA 3,353 billion ($1=CFA 285 in April 1990)
(May-Jun 1990; p. 14). In the *Guardian Weekly* (London) Paul Webster claimed
that Houphouet-Boigny "was siphoning off French aid funds to amass a
personal fortune as high as 6 billion pounds sterling" (Jun 17, 1990; p. 9).

While Houphouet-Boigny was amassing his fortune abroad, he reduced
the official price paid to growers of cocoa and coffee by 50 percent for the
1989 to 1990 growing season. In the early 1980s he also froze the nominal
incomes of most Ivorians while inflation raised the cost of living. By 1990
prices had gone up some 50 percent without any compensating adjustment
in wages.

Houphouet-Boigny's argument that Western commodity speculators
were responsible for the collapse of the markets rapidly lost credence in the
face of estimates of his personal wealth and extravagance. Although he was
allegedly personally financing the construction of the basilica at
Yamassoukro (at a cost of over $360 million), Neil Henry, a foreign service
correspondent, reported that "demonstrators calling for more political parties
demanded the president's resignation and specifically derided the basilica as
a paramount example of his failed leadership. Many protesters charged,
'Houphouet-Boigny is a thief!' and accused the ruler of misappropriating
public funds to construct the basilica, a charge the government has denied"
(*Washington Post*, Jul 5, 1990; p. A23). And in the marketplace at Abobo-Gare,
an unemployed worker addressed a crowd of fellow unemployed workers, all
aged around 30: "We don't have work," he shouted. "We can't pay our debts.
Houphouet, with your basilica at Yamassoukrou, you can certainly repay all
the country's debts" (*La Croix*, Mar 13, 1990).

The people have been calling for the prosecution of the *grotos*—the
Mercedes-Benz and BMW owners. When Houphouet-Boigny insisted that
there were no billionaires in the Ivory Coast, a tract revealed that Minister
of Primary Education Odette Kouame, appointed in 1985, owned a castle on
Boulevard Latrille in Cocody and another in her own village. "You get rich
quick," said Houphouet-Boigny, "and leave politics to me" (*La Croix*, Mar 13,
1990). Accordingly, "[s]ome people, after a quarter of a century, are enjoying

the benefits of their situation and belong to the Ivorien billionaires club" (*La Croix*, Mar 13, 1990).

## KENYA

On June 15, 1987, Martin Shikuku, Kenya's member of parliament for Butere, stormed into parliament to accuse wealthy Kenyans of siphoning billions of shillings out of the country and depositing them in foreign banks. *New African* reported that "he produced a copy of *Finance and Development*, a publication of the International Monetary Fund (June 1986) which showed that funds held by Kenyans in foreign banks amounted to Ksh 930 million in 1982, Ksh 870 million in 1983 and Ksh 830 million in 1984. It amounted to Ksh 43.396 billion [*sic*], a figure he later told the *New African* 'might not represent the aggregate total but it very well illustrated the kind of money held outside, when the country is passing the hat around for aid'" (Oct 1987; p. 45).

*South* reported that since Kenya gained its independence in 1963, the amount of capital wealth that residents have stashed abroad exceeded $5 billion. This is "more than the total amount of Western investment and aid" (Jun 1989; p. 30) and exceeds Kenya's total foreign debt of $4 billion. In other words, Kenya would have no foreign debt problem if its citizens returned the capital that they have accumulated abroad.

One often hears the argument that corruption is rife in Africa because the African people are inexperienced and incompetent in management. This argument derives from the inability to distinguish between the real people of Africa—the peasants—and the elites. Detailing the corruption of the elite in Kenya, Koigi wa Wamwere, a former member of parliament, asserted that "[t]he educated use their knowledge to advance corruption, which is more difficult to fight [because] the powerful . . . are protected." He pointed out that in each instance the corrupt acts by top government and corporate officials were motivated by greed and were not the result of mismanagement or incompetence. He concluded that President Daniel arap Moi "has privatised power and property to serve his personal ends. President Moi acts as if what belongs to the state is his. This is why African presidents like Moi are richer and more powerful than the governments they lead (*Index on Censorship*, Jul 1990; p. 19).

The pervasiveness of corruption is only possible when those at the very top are actively engaged in it. Corruption emerged in Kenya soon after independence and got progressively worse: "The first President of independent Kenya, Jomo Kenyatta, and his family amassed a large fortune in land, precious gems, ivory and casinos during his rule from 1963 to 1978" (*The New York Times*, Oct 21, 1991; p. A9). After Daniel arap Moi took over from Kenyatta, corruption became institutionalized.

According to U.S. officials, four Kenyan government officials (three of whom were relatives of Moi) had greatly enriched themselves at the expense of Kenyan citizens. These officials were: Mr. Moi, Energy Minister Biwott, Vice President George Saitoti, and the Permanent Secretary in the President's Office for Internal Security, Hezekiah Oyugi.

President Moi sits at the apex of a growing empire of graft. He is worth at least $3 billion. As he has tightened his authoritarian control of political life, he has continued his conspicuous acquisition of personal wealth and built an economic empire of vast fortune. His business interests are reported to include $100 million worth of prime real estate in Nairobi, a transport corporation, the oil company (Kobil) that bought out Mobil's interests in Kenya, and a cinema chain with monopoly control over movie distribution in Kenya. His numerous business concerns always manage to win huge government contracts and charge the state exorbitant fees and prices. He is "believed to be a partner in an oil refinery in Puerto Rico with an Israeli businessman and has a share in a Nairobi casino and a hotel in the Masai Mara game park" (*The New York Times*, Oct 21, 1991; p. A9).

Kiptiuiu Investment Corporation, with its head office in the City Hall Annex, Nairobi, for example, imports fertilizer. Moi forces the state-run Kenya Tea Development Authority and another government-owned agency, Kenya Planters Cooperative Union, which grows coffee, to purchase the fertilizer at inflated prices, often running 300 percent higher than elsewhere.

Another Moi company, Trans-World Importers, headquartered in the State House in Nairobi and headed by Abraham Kiptanui, the comptroller of the State House and principal private secretary to Moi, imported so much sugar in mid-1987 that the Kenya National Trading Corporation (KNTC) could not buy even half of it. Worse, the importation occurred when Kenya had a sugar surplus and was having difficulty finding storage space for it. Because of the dumping of sugar on KNTC and Moi's insistence on immediate cash payment, KNTC could not accept any more sugar from millers, and many went unpaid for 14 months. In another example, Moi received a " 'seven-figure commission when Kenya bought two airplanes from the European consortium Airbus Industries in the late 1980s.' He also profited from the sale of wheat from Saudi Arabia. The Saudi government, as part of its aid program, 'provides wheat to Kenya at $145 a ton. Traders acting for Moi then resold it to the Kenyan Government grain agency for between $207 and $220. The profit on one such deal was $16 million' " (*The New York Times*, Oct 21, 1991; p. A9).

It is a clear conflict of interest for the president of a country to run businesses and to force the government to make purchases from these businesses. Ministers should guard against and condemn such practices. But many of them were Moi's friends and clients, who had also amassed fortunes from their political positions. For example, Nicholas arap Biwott, Moi's most trusted ally in government, was embroiled in a huge corruption scandal to which Moi, of course, turned a deaf ear. According to Edward Odoi Abuor, a Kenyan reporter with the *Standard* newspapers, in 1987 the government invited bids for a $400 million agricultural project and Turkwell Gorge Dam in the Elgeyo-Marakwet district. Initially, a Chinese and later a French firm won the contract. But when they declined to pay a Ksh 75 million ($5 million) bribe Biwott demanded, he cancelled the contract and reopened the bidding process. The construction contract was eventually awarded to the French firm Spie Batignolles, and French companies were also selected to supply turbines, generators, and transmission equipment. After paying the bribe, the company doubled the cost of the project to recoup, according to journalist Abuor.[2] This was confirmed in an interim memorandum drawn up by Mr. Achim Kratz, then European Commission delegate to Kenya (*Financial Times*, Nov 27, 1991; p. 4).

Subsequently, in March 1989 Moi sent Biwott to Britain to inquire about purchasing 12 new Hawk 2000 fighter jets that the military had requested. British Aerospace refused to offer a personal bribe but instead offered £100,000 (pounds sterling) to move personnel to patrol Kenya's game parks and to protect elephants and rhinos from poachers. An angered Biwott left London for Paris, where he visited the French aeronautical firm, Marcel Dassault Preguet. He found that the French fighter jets cost twice as much as the British ones, but the French offered to give Moi a free presidential jet. Subsequently, Moi flew to Paris to sign a contract to purchase 12 Mirage fighter jets and 60 Panhard automatic guns at a hefty price of $637 million.

Koigi wa Wamwere, a former MP, who was detained for three years (1975-1978) and subsequently fled to Norway in 1986, gave a trenchant insight into the workings of the corrupt Moi regime:

> When a former chairman of the National Bank of Kenya took over 300 million shillings from the Bank, that was robbery, not incompetent management.
>
> When the Kenya Chemical and Food Corporation in Kisumu cost 1.3 billion shillings instead of 540 million shillings and then hired MPs to defend it in

parliament in return for personal rewards, that was theft, not incompetent management. (*Weekly Review*, Feb 19, 1982).

When in March 1982 Joseph Kamere, an attorney general, and Titus Mbathi, a minister for labor, received three million and one million shillings respectively to cover up illegal foreign repatriation by the bank of Baroda, that was corruption. When government ministries engaged in the employment of 85,397 bogus employees that allowed government officers to receive from the government nearly 85,397,000 shillings every month in the form of fake salaries, the creation of such a hole in government coffers was corruption. (*Weekly Review*, Apr 26, 1985).

On January 24, 1986, the Kenyan Minister for Finance, Professor George Saitoti, officials of the French government and representatives of a consortium of Paris-based banks, under the leadership of the *Banque de l'Union Europeenne*, signed a contract with the French contractor Spie Batignolles, to finance the Turkwel Gorge Hydro-Electric Project at a price that was more than double what the Kenyan government had budgeted for by international tender—despite warnings by the European Commission in Kenya. It was not lack of competence but greed for gain and lack of patriotism.

According to a confidential European Commission report by Mr. A. Katz, 'the Kenyan government officials who are involved in the project are fully aware of the disadvantages of the deal . . . but they nevertheless accepted it because of high personal advantages' . . .

When Kenyan politicians and top civil servants form an alliance with foreigners to take billions in hard currency abroad while knowing that the country is dying for lack of foreign exchange for the import of drugs, and other essentials, that is outright war against one's own country and people (*Index on Censorship*, Aug 1990; p. 19).

Nicholas Biwott, a member of Moi's Kalenjin tribe and considered to be President Moi's closest political confidant, was paid an official salary of Ksh 21,033 but was worth "hundreds of millions of dollars, chiefly in offshore holdings" (*The New York Times*, Oct 21, 1991; p. A9). He "amassed large interests in construction, petroleum distribution, aviation and property. He first entered the business world in 1975 in partnership with Mr. Moi in a company called Lima Ltd. Lima became the bedrock of a business empire which expanded into Lima Finance, which in turn acquired large holdings in the prominent Kenyan private companies, Trade Bank, Trade Finance and Prudential Assurance" (*Financial Times*, Nov 27, 1991; p. 4).

Biwott and two other cabinet ministers demanded kickbacks from BAK, a Swiss-based consultancy firm, in return for a multi-million dollar contract to rehabilitate a molasses plant in the late Robert Ouko's constituency. Ouko "clashed with Biwott during a trip to the U.S. over foreign accounts Biwott and other government ministers held in other countries" (*Financial Times*, Nov 27, 1991; p. 4). Ouko was brutally murdered on his return to Kenya. Mr. John Troon, the British detective who investigated, named Biwott and one other senior government official as prime suspects. Biwott was arrested by Moi and later released "for lack of evidence."

In June 1991 a quarrel broke out between Kenya's Energy Minister, Nicholas Biwott, and Terry Davidson, managing director of Citibank in Nairobi. As the *New York Times* (Oct 21, 1991) reported: "The trouble arose when Citibank sought to collect on $14 million in loans to some of Mr. Biwott's companies. Western diplomats said Mr. Biwott's lawyers went to Kenya's High Court and got an injunction that blocked the bank from collecting on the loans, of which $11.2 million worth was secured by letters of credit in a Swiss bank account of Mr. Biwott . . . Western diplomats added that an employee of Mr. Biwott cautioned the managing director of Citibank, Terry Davidson, to be prepared for *strange car accidents* and fraudulent foreign currency transactions" (p. A9; emphasis added).

This escalating greed—along with the increasingly arbitrary and oppressive character of Moi's rule and the growing economic problems of unemployment and rural and urban landlessness—threatens Kenya's tradition of stability. As the decay and repression deepen, the prospect that change will come not through gradual political liberalization, but rather through abrupt and violent military intervention, increases.

## MALAWI

If my people don't want me, I will go back to Britain.

—President Hastings Kamuzu Banda

Dr. Hastings Kamuzu Banda openly and proudly stated that capitalism was the only course his impoverished country should follow. He once told his parliament, "We do not suppress the acquisitive and possessive instinct here. Instead, we encourage it." This was a broadside directed at Julius Nyerere, who denounced the "individual acquisitiveness of the capitalist system." President Banda, a strong believer in teaching by personal example, proceeded to demonstrate how a Malawian adequately endowed with acquisitive instincts should go about acquiring a vast financial empire. The most conspicuous part of his empire is Press Holdings Ltd., in which he holds 4,999 of 5,000 shares. The remaining share is reportedly held by Aleke Banda, who is not related to the president and has been in jail since 1980. His crime was to question "Banda's withdrawal of 6 million Malawi kwacha ($3.3 million) from the Press Holdings bank account (*Africa Report*, Mar-Apr 1992; p. 59).

The status of Press Holdings baffled many economic analysts and vexed international financiers. Although it was legally a privately owned firm, it generally enjoyed all the privileges of a parastatal organization. Dr. Banda himself confused matters further by treating the corporation as his personal property, while claiming that he held it in trust for the people of Malawi. The genesis of Press Holdings dated back to the time of the struggle for independence. The company was started in the 1960s as part of Malawi Press, which was owned by the ruling Malawi Congress Party (MCP). For Malawi Press to have access to financial resources, such as banks, it had to be incorporated and financially detached from the party. The solution was to establish Press Holdings, the shares of which were divided between Banda, as the party chief, and Aleke Banda, as editor of *Malawi News*. The source of the original Malawi Press was not clear. Nevertheless, the two Bandas became the legal owners of what once belonged to the MCP, and by 1988 Press Holdings was an economic octopus with tentacles in every branch of the Malawi economy. Although it was virtually impossible to obtain information on the extent of the conglomerate's activities and financial status, Malawi's telephone directory and reports of other companies in which Press Holdings had shares suggested the vastness of the financial octopus. The telephone directory listed 14 Press Companies. In addition, there were other subsidiaries that did not have "Press" in their names but that are known to belong to the conglomerate. One such company was the People's Trading Center, with department stores, supermarkets, and mini-marts in almost every district of the country. There was also General Farms, reputedly one of the largest individually owned tobacco handling companies.

Dr. Banda's empire is vast. It encompasses breweries, distilleries, food processing industries, textiles and metal products manufacturing, tourism and hotels, and wholesaling and retailing. How the life-president amassed this vast fortune is still a mystery to his impoverished countrymen, because when he came to what was then Nyasaland some 30 years ago, after 40 years of self-imposed exile in Great Britain, the United States, and the Gold Coast (Ghana), he brought virtually nothing with him except his three suits. The Nyasaland African Congress paid all his expenses, including his house rent, food, transportation, and a monthly allowance of $590.00.

The octogenarian president routinely announces the profits of his farming activities to parliament. Recently, he boasted of profits of more than K 3.5 million from tobacco alone. Usually he accompanies these announcements with appeals to his lackeys to emulate his acquisitive capacity. Since Malawi attained independence in 1964, Banda has been Minister of Agriculture and Natural Resources. This position has given him unlimited access to the ministry's technical and research services. He sees no conflict between state interests and his personal ones. When insurgent ministers accused him of running the country as his personal farm, Banda disarmingly admitted doing so and said that he was proud of it.

A more glaring example of the relationship between Banda's personal interests and those of the state is a curious figure in the annual financial reports of the state agency Agricultural Development and Marketing Corporation (ADMARC). For a number of years now, more than K 35 million have been included as unsecured loans to Press Holdings Ltd. It is clear that no other Malawian capitalist could even dream of having such a line of credit.

ADMARC is the linchpin of the Malawi government's relationship with the peasants. The corporation enjoys a monopoly on the purchase of virtually all marketable peasant produce. The rich farmers, on the other hand, have direct access to the world market through the auction floors. ADMARC buys crops from the peasants at very low prices and sells them at higher prices on the world market to earn large profits. Between 1983 and 1987 profit margins on crop trading averaged 32 percent of net sales. In some years the profit margin has been as high as 42 percent. These profits have not been invested in the peasant sector, but instead have been invested in estate agriculture and industry. In addition, some of the profits have been channeled into unsecured loans to Banda. According to *New African*, "The President's use of his profits is a tale in itself. He has made lavish 'gifts' to the nation. He built the elitist Kamuzu Academy at the estimated cost of K 25 million. He has built expensive houses for members of the women's league who have excelled in dancing and praising him. He has even purchased planes to ferry dancing and singing troupes of women to his meetings" (Oct 1988; p. 20).

In a country plagued by unprecedented poverty, malnutrition, and acute unemployment, it is disgraceful that the available resources are allocated to the pet projects of one man.

## NIGERIA

In Nigeria corruption has grown alarmingly over the past two decades. During late colonial rule and the period of the first republic, corruption ran rampant first at the local and then at the regional and federal levels. It was perhaps most serious in the cocoa-rich Western region, where investigators found that the activities of a small clique of ruling-party politicians and businessmen had drained the Region's Marketing Board of more than 10 million naira, essentially bankrupting it in seven years. (One *naira* at that time was equivalent to approximately $1.35.) Throughout that period, government contracts, purchases, and loan programs were systematically manipulated to enrich political officials and the politically well connected. Public disgust with the growth of this venality figured prominently in the downfall of the republic.

After the 1975 coup that toppled the regime of General Yakubu Gowon, a commission of inquiry found 10 of the 12 state governors guilty of corruption and the misuse of funds totalling over 16 million naira. But those amounts were small in comparison with the levels of corruption during Nigeria's oil boom in the 1970s, which saw a "frantic grab of the well-placed for easy wealth" and "hideous displays of affluence" amidst appalling poverty, according to Hoover Institution scholar Larry Diamond (1989).

In the late 1970s favorable market conditions yielded oil revenues at a level of $29 billion a year. From 1979 through 1983, scandals involving billions of dollars dominated the headlines. These included: the illicit auction of much of the $2,500 million annual allocation of import licenses; the arrest of several top officials of the Federal Capital Development Authority in Abuja over an alleged $20 million fraud; and the revelation by a federal minister that Nigeria was losing $50 million a month to ghost workers and other forms of payroll fraud.

Thereafter, the newspapers continued to publish exposés of gross corruption, something much more than business as usual. In 1983 alone these included: a press report from London of fraudulent import-export transactions exceeding $6 billion; the disappearance of millions of naira worth of building materials from the warehouse of the Nigeria National Supply Company; the acceptance of large bribes by legislators deliberating on the renewal of a monopoly contract to a Swiss firm; and the rumored apprehension at customs in London of a Nigerian governor trying to smuggle several million naira in cash into Britain. None of these charges was ever punished in court, but this failure only deepened the sense that things were out of control.

Theft of public resources was not only rampant but destructive. Mysterious fires razed buildings housing important government agencies that had become enmeshed in scandal, including the Ministry of External Affairs and the Development Authority in Abuja. In January 1983 fire broke out at the 37-story headquarters of the Nigerian External Telecommunications, a state agency in Lagos. The building was the pride of Nigerian architecture, and the fire, described by the government-owned *New Nigerian* as "a calculated act, planned and executed to cover up corruption and embezzlement in the company," visibly quickened the pace of political decay. To both ordinary Nigerians and the country's intelligentsia—students, intellectuals, professionals, and military officers—it symbolized the rapaciousness of the ruling elite. Students quickly took to the streets in Lagos and several state capitals to call for the return of the military, which obliged when Maj. Gen. Muhammadu Buhari booted out the Shagari government in a December 31, 1983 coup.

In May 1984 the Buhari regime set up various tribunals to try corrupt former ministers, governors, and politicians. Chief Bisi Onabanjo, the former governor of Ogun state, was charged along with three others for soliciting side payments. The charge read:

> Being public officers, to wit: Governors of Ogun, Ondo and Oyo states, respectively, between July 5 and 9, 1983 at Lagos did corruptly enrich a person, namely the United Party of Nigeria, by causing to be paid as "kick-back" to the said United Party of Nigeria (UPN), a sum of 2.8 million *naira*, an amount representing 10 percent of the contract awarded to Bouygues Nigeria Ltd. for the construction of the Great Nigeria Insurance Co. Ltd. headquarters building and therefore committed an offence contrary to the provisions of the Recovery of Public Property (Special Military Tribunals) Decree (*West Africa*, Jun 11, 1984; p. 1205).

The other governors were acquitted, but Chief Onabanjo was sentenced to 22 years in prison. *West Africa* subsequently detailed several other convictions with stiff penalties (Jul 2, 1984; pp. 1349-1351). Nigerians considered the penalties excessive for what they regarded as petty corruption and called for the government to take action against high-ranking government officials guilty of *gross* corruption.

On July 5, 1984, the Buhari regime clumsily attempted to correct the situation by pursuing the larger targets. One was Alhaji Umaru Dikko, the Transport and Aviation Minister in the Shagari government who had fled to Britain. He was alleged to have amassed a fortune of over $1 billion during barely three years in office. A bungled attempt to kidnap him in a crate from London caused a diplomatic uproar in Britain. Another target was Maitama Yussuf, the Minister of Commerce and Industry in the Shagari regime. He was arrested in April 1986 and jailed when he tried to enter Nigeria clandestinely.

In August 1985 the Buhari government was overthrown and Maj. Gen. Ibrahim Babangida took control. The various tribunals set up to recover public assets had been left in abeyance. They were, however, reconstituted. Justice Sampson Uwaifo's tribunal reported that it recovered over 200 million naira in cash, real estate, and vehicles and more than 35 million naira from politicians, public officers, and contractors (*West Africa*, Jun 9, 1986; p. 1234). Precisely how much Nigeria lost during Alhaji Shehu Shagari's civilian rule will never be known, but the amount is reckoned in the billions of dollars. Leading figures in the government were known to have accumulated vast fortunes abroad in bank accounts, mansions, and precious assets, including a solid gold bathtub (*New York Times*, Jan 20, 1984). Wealth exported by top government officials was unofficially estimated by Western diplomats at $5 billion to $7 billion during the short-lived second republic, the most corrupt in Nigeria's history. But a 1986 Nigerian government investigation also estimated that at the height of the oil boom in 1978, corrupt politicians were transferring $25 million a day abroad. Much of that oil windfall was also squandered by the ruling elites and wasted on prestigious projects such as a brand new capital at Abuja at a hefty cost of $18 billion. As if the oil bonanza was not enough, a $32 billion foreign debt was also racked up. The Morgan Guaranty Trust Company estimated that Nigeria's foreign debt of $32 billion would have been only $7 billion had there been no capital flight (*Business Week*, Apr 21, 1986; p. 14). To this day the Ministry of Petroleum cannot account for some 4 billion naira (or $1.5 billion) in crude oil sales between 1980 and 1986. By 1989 corruption had penetrated virtually every agency in the public sector. *West Africa* reported, "The Nigerian Ports Authority has failed to account for the sum of 4.6 million naira provided by the federal government in 1987 to pay the salary arrears of dockworkers" (Jul 31-Aug 6, 1989; p. 1266).

Unsubstantiated rumors have been rife about corruption and illicit enrichment by President Babangida and other members of the government. These rumors led Uchendu Egbezor to suggest that "a panel be set up to investigate the accounts of the President of Nigeria, Vice Admiral Augustus Aikhomu, and other members of the AFRC" (*West Africa*, Jul 31-Aug 6, 1989; p. 1264). In April 1989 the Christian Association of Nigeria revealed that more than 3,000 Nigerians held Swiss bank accounts and that Nigerians were near the top of the list of Third World patrons of Swiss banks (*West Africa*, Apr 10-16, 1989; p. 570). As if to confirm this, Chief Olu Falae, secretary to the federal military government, announced after a debt verification exercise that "over 30 billion *naira* (or $4.5 billion) of Nigeria's external debt was discovered to be 'fraudulent and spurious' " (*West Africa*, Sep 25-Oct 1, 1990; p. 1614). In other words, it was added on, and payments went into the pockets and overseas bank accounts of corrupt officials. Indeed, the Lagos *National Concord*

(Aug 16, 1990) reported that the staggering sum of $33 billion owned by Nigerians in foreign bank accounts was equivalent to Nigeria's huge foreign debt.

The Babangida regime did not account for the $10 billion in oil windfall occasioned by the Gulf War in January 1991. When the Lagos correspondent of the *Financial Times*, William Keeling, charged a misuse of this bonanza in August 1991, he was promptly deported from Nigeria with less than 24 hours notice. Of course, "shooting the messenger" did not solve the problem of endemic corruption. "For all the promises of probity, the military elite [has been] as corrupt as any regime that preceded it, taking kickbacks on contracts and diverting government funds" (*Financial Times*, May 22, 1992; p. 6).

An irate reader wrote this to the BBC's *Focus on Africa*:

> You need to know that: 6 Nigerians are billionaires; 6,000 are multimillionaires; 55,000 are millionaires; 22 million Nigerians earn less than 10 *naira* a day; and around a million Nigerians earn less than 5 *naira* a day.
>
> You also need to know that Nigeria is a country that has petroleum but has a scarcity of petrol. You also need to know that over 70 percent of Nigerian land is arable, but less than 5 percent is cultivated.
>
> You also need to know that we Nigerians have the potential for revolution (Dec 1989; p. 66).

## ZAIRE: THE EPITOME OF AFRICAN KLEPTOCRACY

> Zaire under Mobutu has become almost a caricature of an African dictatorship, its government autocratic to a fault, its resources shamelessly squandered and mismanaged.
>
> —Chris Simpson of *West Africa* (May 7-13, 1990)

Mobutu Sese Seko's paternalistic, absolutist state has relentlessly bankrupted a nation endowed with great natural wealth. The line between private and state property was almost nonexistent. Embezzlement, fraud, theft, illicit economic ventures, including widespread smuggling and export-import swindles, were pandemic. External efforts by the World Bank and the International Monetary Fund to control them all failed.

The amount of revenue lost or diverted equaled roughly 60 percent of each annual operating budget. Much went to fatten the salaries of Mobutu's cronies. In 1975, for example, the Shaba Regional Commissioner reportedly grossed $100,000 a month, of which only 2 percent was his salary. Also in 1975, a prominent general drew a monthly salary of 45,000 zaires plus numerous informal payments, including 8,000 zaires a month paid to him out of a special account in the Banque de Kinshasa.

Each newly appointed member of the political bureau or executive council received a 17,000 *zaire* settling-in allowance to allow the purchase of the "essentials" needed to maintain the life-style expected of a high member of the political aristocracy.

Presiding over this empire of graft and venality, President Mobutu bragged in a 1984 CBS "60 Minutes" profile that he was the second richest man in the world with more than $8 billion in a numbered personal account at a Swiss bank. Mobutu's fortune has variously been estimated to be between $3 billion and $10 billion. Eight billion dollars would seem to be a reasonable figure, since the 1981 estimate was $5 billion:

> President Mobutu's fortune approached $5,000 million in a Swiss Bank account, a fortune larger than Zaire's $4,400 million foreign debt. . .The President's official salary alone amounted to 17 percent of the annual budget, while the country's foreign debt amounted to 70 percent of the GNP (*West Africa*, Nov 30, 1981; p. 2881).

At an interest rate of 10 percent compounded annually for nine years, this fortune, if all kept in a Swiss bank, would have grown to $11.7 billion. Of course, the percentage of the fortune that Mobutu kept in liquid assets can only be a matter of speculation.

At any rate, together with his close family and friends, Mobutu owned more than 26 extensive properties in Belgium, France, and elsewhere around the world. They included a 15-acre beach resort, a plantation of orchards and a huge vineyard in Portugal, a 32-room mansion in Switzerland, and a sixteenth-century castle in Spain.

When Mobutu traveled, he took along a plane load of government-paid lackeys to ensure a warm reception. The airport at his ancestral village, Gbadolite, was lengthened to accommodate the supersonic Concorde he often chartered from Air France. *Africa Now*, in its March 1982 issue, ran an investigative report on the Mobutu clan's practice of looting the treasury. From 1977 to 1979, for instance, Mobutu acquired 4 billion Belgian francs (BF) and his uncle, Litho Moboti, received 486 million BF in transfers from the central bank alone ($1 = 65 BF). Nguza Karl Bond, Mobutu's former prime minister, reported that before Mobutu left Zaire in April 1981, he asked the central bank to transfer $30 million in Belgian francs to his personal account and arranged to export and sell 20,000 tons of copper and an unknown quantity of cobalt and diamonds, the proceeds of which he would deposit in his personal accounts abroad.

Mobutu's income came not only from illegal business deals but also from his budgetary allocation as president. He gave no account of these monies, and much of it left the country in foreign currency. In 1980, for instance, he received 530 million BF. Other budgetary items for that year included an exceptional 58.3 million BF item for the allegedly unforeseen celebration of 20 years of independence and 260.5 million BF for the visit of Pope John Paul II. On that occasion, 30 million BF were spent on 51 new Mercedes-Benz cars, which, according to the *New Internationalist*, were the "enduring symbol" of Mobutu's social stratum (Jun 1990; p. 19).

In 1981 Mobutu's budgetary allocation was nearly trebled to 1.48 billion BF. That was not enough; the 1981 budget had a section for the president's personal expenses amounting to another 600 million BF. For comparison, the entire province of Shaba had a budgetary allocation of 535 million BF for the year. By 1989 Mobutu was receiving almost $100 million to spend as he wished. "This is more than the Government spends on education, health and all other social services combined," noted the *New Internationalist* (Jun 1990; p. 18).

Nor was Mobutu's family neglected. The budget assigned funds for a roving ambassador—a post recently occupied by Mobutu's son, Niwa. For that post he received 1.5 million BF a month. The top group that ruled Zaire were: Mobutu; Litho Moboti, his uncle; Seti Yale, his security adviser; Gen. Bolozi Gbudu, head of military intelligence and married to two of Mobutu's relatives; and Moleka Liboko, his nephew and a businessman. All come from two clans originating from Mobutu's father's village, Gbandolite (home of the Gbande tribe), on the northern Ubangi River in Equateur province. The predatory instincts of that "Gang of Four" rivaled those of the colonial plunderers. "When he died sometime in the 1980s, Litho was known to have about $1 billion in a Swiss bank account" (*The Washington Post*, Oct 3, 1991; p. A38).

One reporter observed that besides Mobutu and his family, only 80 people in the country were important. "At any one time, 20 of them are ministers, 20 are exiles, and 20 are ambassadors. Every three months, the music stops and Mobutu forces everyone to change chairs" (cited by Steve Askin in *New Internationalist*, Jun 1990; p. 18).

Mobutu's philosophy was one of "authenticity," by which he meant establishing a form of government distinctly "African." But this proved to be a farce. He accumulated a personal fortune while advocating that others would be better off poor and hungry than wealthy slaves to colonialism. Indeed, some 50 prisoners starved to death in his jails in 1983, according to Amnesty International. That torture, brutality, and economic mismanagement were Mobutu's hallmarks was confirmed by Pierre Davister, a Belgian, who had been one of Mobutu's closest confidants. In a March 1982 interview with *Africa Now* (London), Davister explained:

"I am asked why I have changed my policy from supporting Mobutu to condemning him. I reply it's not me but his regime that has changed. At first I admired this man for what he was doing; then I changed for I realized that this country, so rich in resources, has been impoverished and is now starving. It is also important to remember that he is incapable of administering the country. Furthermore, he tortured his opponents, and I couldn't support a regime that allowed that" (p. 22).

In the early 1970s Mobutu expropriated foreign enterprises worth $500 million and expelled the Asian merchants who had kept his economy running. He also expelled most of the Belgian plantation owners, technicians, and businessmen. Mobutu awarded the businesses he confiscated to his friends and clan, who also took over the export and marketing of Zaire's products. Mobutu and his son Niwa retained the bulk of the shares in Zaire's three largest industrial diamond mines, which are the largest in the world.

Throughout much of the 1980s an estimated 1.32 billion BF worth of diamonds were illegally taken out of Zaire. The proceeds of their sales were deposited in a Swiss bank account. To ensure greater access to the profits, Mobutu took over control of the sale of diamonds from a subsidiary controlled by de Beers. Gold from the Kilo Moto mine was sold by Mobutu's nephew, Moleka, and the Simeki gold mine was placed in the hands of his uncle, Litho.

Much of the black marketing of cobalt was done through "an air transport system controlled by Mobutu's clan. His son, Niwa, had his own air transport company. Some of the cobalt went direct by charter aircraft to the USSR" (*Africa Now*, Mar 1982).

In the early 1970s, with copper commanding record prices on the world market, Zaire found itself riding the crest of an economic boom. The response of President Mobutu was "to go on a spending orgy that made economists' heads whirl. He built palaces, eleven in all, and linked some of them to the capital with 4-lane highways. He dedicated monuments to himself and constructed stadiums in which to address his people" (Lamb, 1984; p. 44).

In 1976 Mobutu set up SOZACOM to market the country's copper in Belgium. But most of the proceeds never reached Zaire. In a 1982 confidential report the World Bank expressed alarm that SOZACOM was draining money from copper sales. "Diplomatic, banking and mining industry sources also suggest that government and SOZACOM officials were skimming off tens of millions of dollars in proceeds for themselves" (*Wall Street Journal,* Oct 2, 1984; p. 16). "Officials of both the World Bank and the U.S. AID said that in 1988, about $400 million in revenues from Zaire's mineral exports disappeared and was never accounted for" (*The Washington Post,* Oct 3, 1991; p. A38).

Management of Zaire's coffee plantations was placed in the hands of Mobutu's clique, which is also deeply involved in the smuggling of coffee. In 1977 Zaire's coffee crop was valued at $400 million. Because of smuggling and underinvoicing, only $120 million was returned to Zaire's treasury. The rest ended up in foreign bank accounts held by Mobutu and his Gbande colleagues.

Everyone was on the take, and in Zaire one needed to know only two things to survive: "Whom do I see and how much will it cost?" (Lamb, 1984). Even postal workers and telephone companies often refused to provide service unless they received bribes. At hospitals, sick patients had to pay hospital guards before they were admitted and then bribe the nurses to ensure that they would be looked after. Workers had difficulty making ends meet with worthless zaires. According to *Africa Report,* "Real wages in Kinshasa are 6 percent of what they were prior to independence. The 1 percent growth in Zaire's GNP has not been able to sustain a 3 percent population growth rate. Analysts have also voiced concern that the president has been using the printing press to pay government bills, causing the *zaire* to drop to 30 percent below the official rate on the black market" (Jul-Aug 1990; p. 9).

Development projects did not escape Mobutu's megalomania. "I know my people. They like grandeur. They want us to have respect abroad in the eyes of other countries," he once declared. Consequently, half of Zaire's total foreign debt (now $4.5 billion) was incurred by building two big dams, the Inga-Shaba power line, and a $220 million double-deck suspension bridge over the Congo River. One level is for a railroad that does not exist.

In September 1981 Nguza Karl I. Bond, the former prime minister and foreign minister of Zaire, testified before the U.S. House of Representatives' Foreign Affairs Committee. He charged that a military program whereby Zairian officers were trained in the United States and other Western countries and sent back to improve the fighting efficiency of the Zairian military, was pointless: The officers were immediately forced out of the army and blocked from any position of influence and sometimes experienced worse treatment. The C-130 transport planes given by the United States routinely engaged in private black marketeering. The air force with its C-130 planes simply became an import-export forwarding company that was exempted from customs taxation and worked for the head of state, his family, and the top commanding officers (to ship building materials, coffee, latex, and hemp). One C-130 plane crashed when landing at Kindu airport because it carried an excessive cargo of rice for the officers. In addition, the military chiefs often diverted communications equipment to their villages and plantations instead of delivering it to the units that needed it. Medication and spare parts were handled in the same way (*Africa Now*, Mar 1982; p. 18).

By 1980 Zaire had become an economic cripple. At Mama Yemo General Hospital, named for Mobutu's mother, unattended patients died because there were no bandages, no sterilization equipment, no oxygen, and no film for X-ray machines. The dead often remained in the intensive care unit for hours before being removed because there was no room for extra bodies in the morgue (Lamb, 1984). The health clinics at the university campuses in Kinshasa and Lubumbashi had shut down because the medicines intended for use there had been diverted to the black market. Agricultural produce intended for market often rotted on the ground because the transportation system had broken down. Zaire had 31,000 miles of main roads at independence in 1960; in 1980, only 3,700 miles were usable.

By 1980 Zaire's foreign debt had soared to $4 billion with little to show for it. The government's news agency closed down for lack of paper. Two of Air Zaire's planes, a Boeing 747 and a Douglas DC-10, were repossessed. In desperation Mobutu turned the running of his country over to foreigners. The Belgian businessmen, whose firms were expropriated in the 1970s, were invited to return to Zaire. Moroccan guards were brought in to provide his security. The International Monetary Fund was running the central bank, and the Belgians were operating the finance ministry and customs department.

Despite Mobutu's excesses, the West supported him. The United States asserted that Zaire was economically and strategically important. It was the only noncommunist supplier of cobalt. Furthermore, Zaire was a counterbalancing force to the growing Soviet influence in central Africa, and Mobutu, a staunch anticommunist, should be supported regardless of his shortcomings. In the late 1970s Zaire received nearly half of all the funds Jimmy Carter's administration allocated for black Africa. Until 1989 Zaire received some $70 million annually from the United States in economic and military assistance.

Mobutu endeared himself to Ronald Reagan's administration when he agreed to serve as a conduit for arms to be channeled to Jonas Savimbi's UNITA forces in Angola. Subsequently, the Gbadolite Summit he convened in Zaire, at which Manuel dos Santos and Jonas Savimbi shook hands for the first time since 1975, won high marks in Washington. Although the peace accords collapsed shortly thereafter, Mobutu was viewed as a peace-maker and a promoter of regional stability. But was Mobutu really promoting African interests? Chris Simpson, in an article in *West Africa*, suggested that Mobutu's dealings with the United States actually heightened tensions in Africa:

> The suspicion inevitably lingers that Mobutu is merely playing Washington's game. Mobutu will never be able to shake off the stigma of a long association with the CIA—possibly preceded by a relationship with the Belgian *Surete*. He was instrumental in obtaining US support for his long-time ally Holden Roberto, during the Angolan civil war, and the US-Zairian axis has frequently militated against the kind of regional cooperation which Washington professes to want to encourage in southern and central Africa. The Carter Administration's knee-jerk support for Mobutu over the two insurgencies in Shaba Province—formerly Katanga—in 1977 and 1978, heightened regional tension (*West Africa*, May 7-13, 1990; p. 753).

U.S. aid hardly made a dent in improving the standard of living for Zairians: "Of every dollar coming into Zaire, whether it was in the form of a foreign aid grant or a business contract, Zairian officials took twenty cents off the top for their personal cut" (Lamb, 1984; p. 44). Furthermore, much of the military assistance Zaire received in the form of training and materiel went to waste. In 1983 the International Monetary Fund drew up a structural adjustment program. The zaire was floated in February 1984. The country's foreign debt of $4.5 billion was rescheduled in March 1986 in Brussels. These measures proved only temporary in the face of pervasive looting.

Mobutu's fortune alone could have paid Zaire's entire foreign debt and then some. But instead of paying the debt, he accused Western lending governments of greed and claimed that they were using the International Monetary Fund to keep poor countries in a state of dependency. He contended that creditor governments were making "money-grabbing demands totally irrelevant to the excellent political and diplomatic relations they have with Zaire" (*African Letter*, Jun 1-15, 1988; p. 13).

When U.S. Rep. Mervyn Dymally asked Mobutu about his personal wealth, he responded, "Yes, I have a fair amount of money. However, I would estimate it to total less than $50 million. What is that after 22 years as head of state of such a big country?" (*World Development Forum*, No. 9, 1988; p. 3). His query made the real motives of many of Africa's leaders abundantly clear: to impose themselves on their people and loot their countries' treasuries for deposit in foreign banks. It may be noted that these were the same leaders who virulently denounced colonial exploitation and plunder.

Pierre Davister observed somberly: "Zaire is like a pear tree with only one pear left on it— shake the tree and it falls. The Americans say it is up to the Zairians to shake the tree; the Zairians say it is up to the West to do it" (*Africa Now*, Mar 1982; p. 20).

For years, the pear dangled tantalizingly as the two sides haggled. Pragmatism would have suggested a cooperative effort and a sharing of the fruit. Otherwise, some other group, probably the communists, would have plucked it.

Finally, there were some stirrings in the West. In December 1988 the Belgian press suggested that the 70 million pounds sterling given as aid to Zaire each year went into President Mobutu's pocket. Mobutu was furious. He ordered all 15,000 Zairian residents in Belgium to sell their assets and return home. State companies were directed to withdraw their deposits from Belgian banks. Belgian officials sent Foreign Minister Leo Tindemans to placate Mobutu with an offer to partially cancel Zaire's debt to Belgium. That diplomatic move misfired. Mobutu's government announced in January 1989 that it was abrogating the two treaties of friendship with Belgium and halting repayments on its 670 million pounds sterling debt to Brussels. The Belgian airline, Sabena, was told to cut its four weekly flights to Kinshasa to two, and the Air Zaire office in Brussels was moved to Paris. Brussels responded by threatening Zaire with legal action for a breach of an international airlines agreement. The diplomatic row escalated when the Zairian transport minister threatened to withdraw all landing rights granted to Sabena and to ban Air Zaire from flying to Belgium.

In response the Belgian cabinet convened on January 14, 1989, and decided to drop its former attempts at diplomacy and to prepare for an offensive. Prime Minister Wilfred Martens announced that his government would fund no new development projects in Zaire. Mobutu's government responded by announcing its intention to publicize Belgium's exploitation and pillage of the Congo until independence in 1960. When Belgian television aired an American documentary detailing the extravagant life-style of President Mobutu in February 1989, an incensed Mobutu demanded that the broadcast be canceled. Brussels refused. Then a Belgian financial daily, *Financieel Ekonomische Tijd*, published documents from the Belgian Ministry of Finance that showed that Mobutu had not paid taxes on his Belgian properties since 1984, and a tax controller issued an order to seize his assets. In addition, the Belgian press published accounts of Mobutu's imports of luxury items for his palace while the Zairian economy was collapsing, the Belgian parliament examined the foreign exchange taken by Mobutu and his close relatives from the Bank of Zaire, and the Belgian Ministry of Finance detailed the properties

Belgium registered in Mobutu's name and in the name of his late uncle, Litho Moboti Nzayombo.

Why was Mobutu so furious when the Belgian press and parliament publicized how he squandered public money when he had often been criticized for the same transgressions in French, British, Swiss, and American newspapers? According to *New African*:

> One theory is that he is simply trying to draw international attention to the plight of his country. He is already in difficulties with the World Bank and the IMF over his economy, but he wants to show that Zaire is really in desperate straits. He wants to publicise his much repeated threat "It's either me or chaos . . ."
>
> But if that is his intention, he has actually achieved the opposite. He has turned the world's spotlight onto his own corruption and nepotism. In the words of one World Bank official "Zaire suffers from fraud and muddle in public administration." How can an economy run properly if it is run as one man's private fiefdom, when he seems more interested in salting money away than in sorting out economic priorities at home? (Mar 1989; p. 19).

Unfortunately, Belgium finally capitulated. It agreed to cancel Zaire's entire public debt of 730 million pounds sterling on July 15, 1989. According to *West Africa*, "Belgian Foreign Minister, Mr. Mark Eyskens, said that one third of Zaire's commercial debt was also wiped out, and the interest on the remaining amount could be paid in Zairean currency into a fund that is earmarked to finance development projects in Zaire" (Jul 24-30, 1989; p. 1230).

It is disheartening that foreign countries that profess to be friends of the African people lack the moral fiber to stand up for the principles they espouse. It is even more distressing that these countries buckle and scamper at the vitriol of African tin gods. Zairians will never forget how the Belgians abandoned them.

By April 1992 there was nothing in Zaire: hospitals and schools were closed, no safe drinking water, government ministries had ceased to function. Incredibly, Mobutu was still blaming his problems on the West. Kitenge Yesu, the Communications Minister, said: "Our opposition are the Western embassies. It is the West that is trying to force a solution" (*The Washington Post*, Apr 1, 1992; p. A28).

Sadder still was the fact that there were virtually no credible forces for change inside Zaire, except possibly in the military. Under pressure from the United States, Mobutu created a parliament, the National Legislative Council, in 1977. But he muzzled it in February 1980 when it asked too many questions about government policies and finances.

In the aftermath of the political uprisings in Eastern Europe, a worried Mobutu began making concerted efforts to improve his image. On May 20, 1989, on the 23rd anniversary of the founding of the ruling MPR, certain detainees' sentences were reduced by one year. But those convicted of "embezzlement of public funds" were not included (*West Africa*, Apr 24-30, 1989; p. 666). Mobutu also retained the law firm of Van Kloberg and Associates in Washington, D.C., for a fee of $17,000 a month.[3] But that expenditure was a waste as Mobutu's reputation was beyond salvation through a public relations campaign.

After visiting Kinshasa in April 1990, a U.S. congressional delegation led by Rep. David R. Obey requested that the United States suspend aid to Zaire because President Mobutu Sese Seko was corrupt and did not respect human rights. According to *Insight*, Obey, a member of the House Appropriations Committee, said, "No bill bearing my name will include any money destined for that idiot" (May 14, 1990; p. 37). Nevertheless, the Bush administration allocated $53 million for Zaire in 1991.

The Zairian government had a fatuous response to charges regarding its abysmal human rights record. Tatanene Manata, Zaire's ambassador to the United States, contended that Zaire's difficulties in protecting human rights stem from its not having "the resources necessary to properly establish the mechanisms for the maintenance of the rule of law and to create the framework for a democratic government" (*Washington Post*, Oct 4, 1990; p. A2).

## POSTSCRIPT ON CORRUPTION

Corruption is certainly not a social vice unique to Africa or the Third World. Corruption prevails in one form or another in practically all countries, Western and communist alike. Nevertheless, there are several reasons why we must not discount the grave consequences of corruption in developing countries. First, corruption has detrimental effects on economic development. It decreases the efficiency of the civil service and its ability to formulate and implement government development policies, and it robs the country of vast sums of foreign exchange needed for investment. Second, the seriousness of corruption is relative. Developed countries can afford the embezzlement of a sum that would spell economic disaster for a developing country. Third, it is relatively easy for corruption to get out of control and become self-reinforcing because the administrative, political, and constitutional institutions of a developing country may possess insufficient checks to deal with the problem effectively. Witness the African political system whereby a president can confer upon himself such titles as "president-for-life," can manipulate the constitution, and can embezzle millions of dollars for deposit in Swiss bank accounts with impunity. Fourth, a corrupt government loses its legitimacy and its subjects' respect, making it difficult to elicit the sacrifices, initiatives, and enterprise necessary for development.

Africa's experience shows that a corrupt government is incapable of efficient economic management. It would be a great disservice to minimize the seriousness of the corruption problem in Africa. It would also be economically irresponsible to advocate that Africa needs more external assistance when there is the clear possibility that corruption can render such assistance useless. So insidiously endemic is corruption in many African countries that even neutral observers now entertain serious doubts about the ability of many of these countries to extricate themselves from their economic miasma. It is important to note that corruption is not peculiarly innate to indigenous African political culture. Corrupt chiefs and kings were deposed (Ayittey, 1991). What breeds corruption, bribery, and other types of malfeasance in modern times is the system of pervasive state controls, regulations, concentration of economic and political power, the institution of one-party state systems which lack accountability, and the muzzling of the press to expose corruption and wrongdoing. Obviously it is useless to rail against corruption and still keep in place the very system which breeds it.

This is not the appropriate place to propose a reform of the "system" to rid an African country of corruption. However, a corrective system must have what I call O-IDEA: Organization, Incentive, Discipline, Efficiency, and Accountability. With respect to accountability, in particular, freedom of expression and freedom of the press are necessary for citizens to demand an accounting of public monies appropriated by officials and for the press to expose malpractices.

Finally, the following development should be of interest to African kleptocrats:

> On May 4, 1991, Switzerland announced that it will lift the 57-year-old iron-clad secrecy that enshrouded its "Form B" bank accounts. This designation allowed clients to conduct bank transactions through a lawyer, notary or trust administrator without ever revealing their own identities. At the end of 1989, Swiss banks held 30,000 "Form B" accounts holding about $135 billion. Most of those accounts are owned by Western tax evaders, drug money launderers and corrupt Third World dictators, including African. After September 30, 1991, the ac-

counts will be replaced with a written statement on the identity of the real owner (*Washington Post*, May 4, 1991; p. A20).

The Swiss have actually gone beyond disclosing the identities of real owners of these accounts:

> The Swiss Justice Ministry extradited to Russia a former Soviet citizen accused of embezzling 85 million rubles from Soviet companies and banks between 1988 and 1990.
>
> Gregory Lerner, a 40-year-old financier, who became an Israeli citizen after emigrating from the Soviet Union in 1989, was arrested at the request of Soviet authorities during a visit to Switzerland in 1991. He lost an appeal to the Swiss Supreme Court (*Washington Times*, Apr 6, 1992; p. A2).

Africans will be making similar requests. As Ekoue Teko demanded: "It is time the West helped Africa to retrieve the money our politicians have stashed in Western banks. If this is done, Africa will cut down on the requests for Western loans. Everyone will be happy—the West will have some peace of mind, we will have enough to live on without borrowing (*New African*, Dec 1991; p. 43).

---

## NOTES

1. Proposals for resolving Africa's debt crisis as well as other crises, such as food shortages, inflation, budget deficits, and the foreign exchange crisis, are presented and discussed in detail in my forthcoming book *Africa's Economic Crisis: Indigenous Solutions*.
2. For this exposé, Abuor was hounded by Kenyan security agents. He fled to Tanzania in July 1988 and with the help of U.S. Embassy officials immigrated to the United States via West Germany.
3. Van Kloberg also represents Romania, Iraq, Cape Verde, and Surinam. The people of Africa will be closely watching Van Kloberg and Associates.

# Chapter 11

## *External Props of*
## *Tyrannical Regimes in Africa*

There's no doubt that many people here blame the United States for keeping Mobutu in power for so long. The anti-American sentiment has recently become a lot worse because many people still can't understand why the U.S. is still supporting his regime.

—Etienne Tshisekedi, leader of Zaire's biggest opposition party, in March 1992.

Various actors, groups, institutions, and factors contributed to the entrenchment of tyranny in postcolonial Africa. In some instances this role was indirect, benign, or inadvertent, while in others, support for despotic African regimes was more blatant and active. We discuss the external props in this chapter and the internal props in the next.

The external props were many. These included activities of foreign governments, institutions, groups, and individuals that conferred respectability or recognition on the tyrannical regime: for example, outright diplomatic recognition, cultural exchanges, expressions of solidarity with the ruler, the provision of economic development assistance or military aid, economic or military pacts or alliances. Additionally the cold war and the intellectual environment in the West played to the advantage of African despots while blacks in diaspora unwittingly aided and abetted tyranny in Africa.

### COMPETING IDEOLOGICAL INTERESTS IN AFRICA

After independence in the 1960s, African nations gained admission to the United Nations and for the first time ever could participate in international diplomacy. Simultaneously, various foreign interests competed for the African nations' allegiance and proffered aid: the Western bloc, led by the United

States; the socialist bloc, led by the Soviet Union; and an emerging Third World nonaligned bloc, in which no country was dominant, although India, China, and Yugoslavia were prominent.

The geopolitical and strategic importance of Africa increasingly attracted the attention of the superpowers. With its rich supply of important minerals and its large potential market for foreign goods, Africa became a terrain on which the Western and Soviet blocs and other foreign powers competed for access, power, and influence—often by playing one country against another. African leaders also benefited enormously from the cold war game. They touted their ideological importance to both sides and played one superpower against the other to extract concessions and aid. African leaders also competed among themselves for the largesse of a particular foreign bloc or superpower. The continent thus became a theater of blunders and miscalculations in almost every quarter: "The Russians with paid Cuban assistance, the Americans with paid French, Belgian, Moroccan and Saudi assistance, laid the continent open" (Calvocoressi, 1985; p. 83).

## France

France did not equate decolonization with retreat or accept the notion of the relative unimportance of Africa in world affairs. The official French attitude was one of eccentric paternalism. As former colonial rulers, the French felt morally obligated to protect the newly independent African nations from the rapacious excesses of America. A presence in Africa was imperative. In addition, the French wanted the African people to be assimilated into a worldwide French community.

Accordingly, France created a sister franc CFA (*Communauté Financière Africain*) for the former French colonies. A Department of Cooperation was set up to provide them with financial aid, tariff concessions, and support for their currencies. The department had an African aid budget five times greater than that of Britain. In 1988, for example, France spent $2,591 million in aid to Africa; Britain spent $516 million.

France left hundreds of officials in Africa as advisers. Behind the doors of many key ministries in the Ivory Coast and Senegal or Gabon, discreet but powerful French officials kept a close eye on policy.[1] The French also sent teachers to Africa and brought African students and civil servants to France for training. France's primacy as an external actor in central and western Africa thus continued largely unabated after colonialism. In return, France secured the right to maintain a heavy military presence in Africa. In 1989, for example, France had a significant number of military advisers in 16 African countries and permanent *Forces d'Intervention* in 7. Total strength of French troops in Africa exceeded 12,000 in 1990. In France itself, the *Forces d'Action Rapide*, numbering 47,000, could be mobilized in less than 48 hours for action anywhere in Francophone Africa. These forces played an economic policing role and backed up French diplomacy and paternalism. They supported "approved" Francophile governments such as those of Leopold Senghor of Senegal and Felix Houphouet-Boigny of Côte d'Ivoire.

After 1960 the French intervened on many occasions to prop up unpopular African regimes against internal dissatisfaction and disorders. The most notorious such occasion was in Gabon in 1964, when French troops were used to reinstate President Mba after a coup. Noting that the French did not intervene to save President Youlou in Brazzaville in 1963, critics charged that intervention was predicated on mineral wealth. (Gabon is rich in oil.)

By the beginning of the 1990s, however, two areas of French influence in Africa began to show signs of weakness. The CFA Zone was beginning to crumble in the advent of European monetary union in 1992. In addition, the cultural link was beginning to weaken. In North Africa it was slowly ceding to Arabic. In the Sahel—or Francophone—countries bordering the Sahara, African languages such as Hausa were gaining ascendancy. The military link remained the sole tool at the disposal of France to protect its cultural empire, but by July 1990 even the military link was being questioned in France.

## The United States

From 1960 to 1974 the United States was not an active force in Africa, although it entertained various strategic concerns and commercial interests. In the early 1960s the United States maintained space tracking stations in Nigeria, Zanzibar, South Africa, and Madagascar and communications and intelligence-gathering bases in Nairobi (Kenya) and later in Mogadishu (Somalia).

The United States was also interested in Africa's minerals. From South Africa came uranium (20 percent of U.S. imports from 1957 to 1961); amosite, used for high-temperature insulation (100 percent); chromium (44 percent); thorium (72 percent); germanium (23 percent); and gold (Dickson, 1985; p. 14). South Africa also exported manganese, platinum, antimony, vanadium, and asbestos to the United States. Another mineral source for the United States was the Congo, which in 1960 provided three-quarters of the cobalt imported into the United States and one-half of the tantalum. Both minerals had strategic uses in aerospace production. Cobalt also came from Zambia. Thus, the United States was almost totally dependent on Africa for cobalt. In addition, 80 percent of the industrial diamonds—as well as copper and tin—came from the Congo. Gabon provided manganese, and Nigeria furnished columbium.

Before 1957, U.S. policy toward Africa was one of benign indifference. According to Dickson (1985), only Liberia and Ethiopia "provoked curiosity in government circles" (p. 2). Liberia, founded in 1847 by freed U.S. slaves, became increasingly dependent upon the United States for economic and financial assistance. Ethiopia attracted U.S. attention when the Italians invaded the country in 1935; the U.S. Congress responded by barring the export of arms to the adversaries.

After World War II three developments forced a change in U.S. policy toward Africa: the march of the British and French colonies in sub-Saharan Africa toward independence, beginning in 1955; increasing U.S. tensions with its allies, as demonstrated by the split over the Suez invasion in 1956; and the growing Soviet economic and political presence in Africa by the mid-1950s.

The Eisenhower administration's reaction to these events was to send Vice-President Richard Nixon to eight African states in February and March 1957 to ascertain appropriate policy responses. Nixon recommended increasing U.S. consular representation, cautiously committing to decolonization, and enhancing both private and government aid.

To handle African affairs, Congress authorized a Bureau of African Affairs with its own assistant secretary in July 1958. Loans and grants to Africa, appropriated under the Mutual Security Act, were increased. These had totaled $120.3 million from 1953 to 1957, but in 1958 alone Africa received $82.4 million, and in 1960 this figure rose to $169.7 million. By the late 1950s an assortment of U.S. governmental agencies were expanding their activities in Africa.

By the end of the Eisenhower administration, a discernible American approach to sub-Saharan Africa was emerging. The policy was based on three chief premises. First, the United States would limit the presence of the Soviet bloc in Africa to the minimal extent possible. Second, the United States would continue to keep the level of physical and human resources committed to Africa low relative to levels committed to other countries. Finally, the United States would continue to adjust its African policy in deference to European positions on African issues. For example, the United States did not assertively advocate decolonization until the French, British, and Belgians were devoted to this process and it appeared irreversible (Dickson, 1985; p. 7).

The noncomplementarity of the three premises underlying U.S. African policy undermined its success. The U.S. ambivalence or cool reception toward the struggles for independence rankled many African nationalists and caused many of them, especially Kwame Nkrumah, to become virulently anti-American. Moreover, preventing Soviet bloc encroachments required providing more resources than U.S. policy authorized and adopting policies that conflicted with those of the Europeans. Such an orientation, according to Dickson (1985), "rendered the achievement of American goals in Africa difficult, and in some instances impossible" (p. 7).

Despite the weak U.S. African policy, until 1974 the East-West ideological conflict in Africa was low-keyed, centered on the Congo (Zaire), and later extended to Ghana, Mali, and Guinea. In 1965 a pro-Western Mobutu was in power in Zaire after socialist Patrice Lumumba had been assassinated in a plot in which the American CIA was implicated. A secession movement in Katanga, in southeastern Zaire, led by Moise Tshombie had been crushed with the aid of Western troops. By the late 1960s Soviet hopes in Africa had crumbled. Kwame Nkrumah of Ghana and Modipo Keita of Mali had been overthrown in coups. The Soviets turned their attention elsewhere.

The second phase of U.S. involvement in Africa began in 1974 when a coup in Portugal and a revolution in Ethiopia opened the door to regimes with stronger Marxist credentials. In the late 1970s and early 1980s, Western reverses in Iran and Afghanistan served as the chief impetus for a new American presence in Africa, although Soviet inroads were also a factor.[2] Southern Africa increasingly became the focus of American attention. Angola and Mozambique had won their independence in 1975 but rabidly Marxist governments had been installed, and opposition to these regimes had erupted into civil wars. In Rhodesia, Marxist guerrillas, under the leadership of Robert Mugabe and Joshua Nkomo, were battling Ian Smith's white minority regime. In 1980 Rhodesia gained black majority rule and became known as Zimbabwe with Robert Mugabe (who was virulently anti-U.S.) as its first black head of state.

Since the mid-seventies, U.S. African policy has lacked coherence. Muddled objectives and inconsistent policy reversals eroded U.S. credibility, particularly in southern Africa. In the late 1970s, the Carter administration made human rights a top priority, coupled with high-visibility official trips to Nigeria and Senegal. South Africa came under intense scrutiny and censure. But the election of Ronald Reagan brought about a near-complete policy reversal. The "Reagan doctrine" placed greater emphasis on geopolitics and ideology.

Though the system of apartheid was denounced by the Reagan administration, it sought "constructive engagement" with South Africa, arguing with some merit that active engagement, investment, and trade with South Africa, rather than sanctions and ostracism, would accelerate the collapse of that evil system.

To check the spread of Marxism in this region, the United States sought and nurtured alliances with "pro-West" regimes (Kenya, Malawi, South Africa, and Zaire) and guerrilla groups (UNITA in Angola). Substantial American investment poured into these countries and military support was covertly supplied to UNITA while at the same time the U.S. government attempted to woo socialist/Marxist regimes in the region (Madagascar, Mozambique, Tanzania, and Zambia). But the nemesis of U.S. policy in southern Africa was its own application of conflicting standards to different countries in the region. The inconsistencies were sharpest in Angola and Mozambique.

In Mozambique, U.S. policy initiatives in the 1980s were still wedded to the "old thinking" of the 1960s and 1970s. The Marxist FRELIMO regime—ensconced unilaterally in power since 1975—was viewed by the U.S. State Department as a nationalist force that simply turned—for reasons of expediency—to the Soviet bloc for the duration of the anti-colonial struggle. Therefore, the FRELIMO adherence to communist ideology was relatively superficial, it was argued, and with a bit of aid and military assistance the regime could easily be enticed away from the Soviet bloc. It was hoped, in the process, the regime also would become a useful piece on the broader southern African chessboard.

In Angola, the MPLA (Popular Movement for the Liberation of Angola), the FNLA (National Front for the Liberation of Angola), and UNITA (National Union for the Total Independence of Angola) waged a liberation struggle against the Portuguese colonialists. On independence day, the MPLA, the dominant resistance movement reneged on a promise of free elections and invited Soviet and Cuban troops to back its usurpation of power. A 15-year civil war ensued. Thus, one had a near-identical situation in both Angola and Mozambique: Marxist regimes in power and an ongoing civil war. Yet U.S. policy responses were dramatically different.

The U.S. refused diplomatic recognition of the MPLA regime in Angola but sought to woo the Marxist FRELIMO government in Mozambique. Further, the U.S. provided covert military aid to UNITA but distanced itself from RENAMO (National Resistance Movement) in Mozambique. As Robin Birley, chairman of the London-based Mozambique Institute, complained: "This lumpen-realpolitik has failed miserably, even by its own dim lights. No

Soviet Bloc any longer exists from which to detach Mozambique . . . This muddled-headed thinking has rendered a disservice to the people of Mozambique" (*Washington Times*, Jun 21, 1992; p. B4).

In South Africa, "constructive engagement" did not appear to be working toward the demise of apartheid. African leaders in the region, with the possible exception of President Hastings Banda of Malawi, formed a united front and intensified their campaign against apartheid. By 1985 sufficient support had been garnered in the United Nations for the imposition of worldwide sanctions against South Africa. In the U.S. itself, domestic pressure had been building. So intense were the domestic calls for divestment that the Reagan administration was forced to concede that "constructive engagement" had not been successful. Some sanctions were imposed against South African exports and, by 1988, scores of American companies pulled out of South Africa. This setback in U.S. policy in Africa, however, was temporary.

In 1989 the Berlin Wall came crashing down, sparking a revolution in eastern Europe that culminated eventually in the collapse of communism and the disintegration of the Soviet Union. The effects on socialist/Marxist regimes in southern Africa, as elsewhere in Africa, were profound and lethal. Angry Africans demanded multiparty democracy. Mugabe renounced Marxist-Leninism, Kenneth Kaunda, life-president of Zambia, was tossed out in free elections in October 1991. One-party socialist Tanzania was opening its political system.

It is difficult to determine how much credit the United States or the West should be accorded for these changes in Africa. First, most Africans do not see the changes occurring in Africa as direct tribute to a successful U.S. foreign policy in Africa but rather as a product of the worldwide winds of change occasioned by the collapse of communism in eastern Europe. Second, American and African perspectives differ. The United States may have won the ideological battle in Africa, but ideology has not been particularly relevant to most Africans. Their struggle has been for *freedom* since "pro-West" regimes have been as brutally repressive as their Marxist counterparts in Africa.

### The Former Soviet Union

The former Soviet Union also had client states in Africa, which included Angola, Benin, Ethiopia, and Mozambique. The Soviets also courted Zambia and Zimbabwe. In the 1950s the Soviets responded to American imperialism by building a special university in Moscow named after Patrice Lumumba.

Students from developing countries received scholarships to study in the Soviet Union. By the end of 1981, 34,805 African students had been trained in the USSR.

The Soviets had no pressing need for Africa's minerals. Africa only had strategic and perhaps ideological significance if Africans could be persuaded to stop mineral exports to NATO countries. To help sever African countries' ties with the West, the Soviet Union provided some economic aid and tutelage, which increased dramatically during Nikita Khrushchev's regime. Soviet aid to Africa, however, was not substantial. In fact, since the early 1960s the Soviet Union rejected any moral obligation to provide assistance to Africa. Soviet official Grigori Rubinstein maintained that "the true causes of Africa's plight. . .are colonial and neocolonial exploitation by the Western powers and the transnational corporations" (cited in *West Africa*, Dec 12-18, 1988; p. 2320).

Consequently, the bulk of Soviet aid was in the form of military advisers and equipment. Angola, Ethiopia, and Mozambique all received substantial amounts of Soviet military hardware. For example, Mengistu Haile-Mariam of Ethiopia received more than $11 billion in military weapons between 1975 and 1990. Angola received at least $2 billion annually in military assistance from the Soviet Union in the 1980s (*The Independent*, London, Feb 19, 1992).[3]

The economic aid the Council for Mutual Economic Assistance (Comecon) provided to sub-Saharan Africa in 1985 was $300 million. Of this, Ethiopia received by far the most (57.9 percent). Next were Mozambique (13.8 percent), Egypt (6.6 percent), Madagascar (4.2 percent), Angola (2.8 percent), and Tunisia (2.1 percent) (*West Africa*, Dec 12-28, 1988; p. 2320).[4] The $300 million aid was only 5 percent of total Comecon bilateral disbursements and only 3 percent of the total aid flow to sub-Saharan Africa.

Furthermore, the little Soviet economic aid that did flow to Africa had strings rigidly attached. Loans and trade credits supplied could only be spent in the Soviet Union and Comecon countries. In addition, the Soviets supplied the technical personnel and the equipment for project construction. Repayments of loans were often by barter, but to the decisive advantage of the Soviet Union. For example, in Guinea, Soviet help in building a bauxite plant at Kindia was to be repaid with deliveries of two million tons of bauxite ore a year for 30 years. Interestingly, when an American company, Agripetco, tried to reach a similar agreement in Ghana in 1980, it met with an uproar and charges of American exploitation.

Barter arrangements also hurt Soviet clients in Africa in a different way. For example, repayments of loans Nkrumah of Ghana took from the Soviet Union were to be made in kind with exports such as cocoa. But the Soviet

Union had little use for Ghana's cocoa. Reexport of cocoa by the Soviet Union helped depress the world market price of cocoa in the mid-1960s.

In addition to these problems, much Soviet aid was used for highly visible, low-return public infrastructural projects, such as roads and stadiums. Moreover, the Khrushchev regime rigidly stressed the need for a planned economy dominated by the state sector. The Soviets believed that only a strong state sector could check the machinations of Western capitalists in Africa. Thus, the main motive for their aid to Africa "was to disrupt Western links with the continent and to buy influence with the newly installed nationalist governments" (Lawson, 1988).

The Soviet Union's African policy was no more successful than the U.S. African policy. According to Calvocoressi (1985): "The Soviet Union has done little to draw Africa to its side. Much of what it has attempted has been ill-conceived and ill-executed, half-hearted and meanly meager, or plainly conditioned by non-African considerations" (p. 88). *West Africa* reached a similar conclusion: "[Soviet] policy was short-lived and ineffective because the gains in political influence were insignificant in comparison to the amount of money spent. Two major blows to Soviet influence in Africa came with the fall of Nkrumah in Ghana and Keita in Mali" (Dec 12-28, 1988; p. 2320).

Initially, Moscow was exceptionally ignorant about Africa because it lacked information about the continent from traders, missionaries, explorers, and colonial administrators. In addition, the new African leaders favored the West because they were familiar with Western languages and customs and needed Western aid. Although the Soviet Union tried to exploit the fact that it had not been a colonial power, it generally had a great deal of difficulty penetrating Africa, even ideologically. With a chance to build a position on what may broadly be called the left-wing ground in Africa, the Soviet Union failed to do so. According to Calvocoressi (1985), "[t]o Africans the Soviet Union appears a cynical great power, not a warm socialist friend" (p. 91). Even racism was a factor. In buses, trains, taxis, and bars in the Soviet Union, a black African was referred to as *abisyan* (monkey).

The Soviet Union also had ideological misgivings about an alliance with Africa. In the 1960s many Russian writers and scholars detested the African intellectuals' notion that African socialism differed from other kinds of socialism. Ultimately, to the Russians, there was only one true socialism— Marxist and scientific (Calvocoressi, 1985; p. 93). Finding no true socialists in Africa, Moscow was forced to work with the nationalist socialists or coalitions of progressive or noncapitalist forces. One was Nkrumah of Ghana. Although "[i]n Soviet eyes he was a typical product of the wrong section of the bourgeoisie who had won power by his readiness to do a deal with the British and whose sympathies therefore were more than half in the wrong camp" (Calvocoressi, 1985; p. 95), Moscow was willing to work with Nkrumah because he was truculently anti-American. Similarly with Sekou Toure of Guinea.

In all, Moscow's dividends in Guinea, Ghana, and Mali were meager. Sekou Toure turned against the Soviets by expelling their ambassador for complicity in a "communist-inspired conspiracy" and refusing them the use of a Soviet-built airport during the Cuban missile crisis. Kwame Nkrumah was booted out in a coup. In Mali, Modibo Keita languished and was also eventually ousted by a coup.

Elsewhere on the African continent, Soviet designs suffered similarly. In Rhodesia the Soviet Union supported the wrong leader: Joshua Nkomo instead of Mugabe, who later became president of Zimbabwe. In Angola it stopped helping Agostinho Neto and the MPLA (Popular Liberation Movement of Angola) and resumed aid only in time to recover some credit with the ultimate winners. As Calvocoressi (1985) put it, "Africans were unimpressed" (p. 90).

These failures caused the Soviets to revamp their African policies in the late 1960s and early 1970s. Since then, there has been an ever-growing shift in emphasis from politics to economics. According to *Izvestia*, the new Soviet approach was based on "genuine equality, complete respect for national sovereignty, noninterference in internal affairs and mutual benefit" (cited in *West Africa*, Dec 12-28, 1988; p. 2321).

Although the Soviet Union did not have much to show in the way of economic and political accomplishments in Africa, it won the propaganda war and consequently the hearts of many Africans. The main reason was that the Soviet bloc was officially strident in its demands for African independence and provided military support to the nationalist struggle. The West, except France after Algeria, offered resistance, while the United States waffled.

### China

China, an active player in Africa, sought to win adherents to the Chinese brand of socialism. Zhao Ziyang, China's foreign minister in the early 1960s, reminded African leaders of the presence of Chinese coolies in Africa. (Britain had rounded up more than 60,000 coolies at the beginning of the century to work in South African mines. Ten years later, when their labor was no longer needed, they were deported with little or nothing to show for their suffering.)

As members of the Third World, united in poverty, China and Africa were identical, Ziyang once declared.

China's conception of the world was tripolar: the United States, the Soviet Union, and the Third World. In the postcolonial era China viewed the Third World as an adjunct of the West. China competed with the Soviet Union to recruit the allegiance of the African nations by supporting their liberation movements. In the early phases, China was the more aggressive, revolutionary force. The Chinese trained and armed liberation movements in both colonial and independent African countries. At the same time, denouncing Moscow as reactionary and revisionist, China also strove to provide Africa with more nonmilitary aid than the Soviet Union offered. Like the emerging states of Africa, China was a Third World country, and its revolution was a model for all Third World revolution, Ziyang claimed.

Lin Biao, Mao's designated successor, noted that China's revolution was won when the Communist Party mobilized the peasants of the rural areas to encircle the cities of China. Similarly, he viewed the Third World as rural areas, and the West, to which it was attached, as the cities. The Chinese global revolutionary strategy was to mobilize these rural areas to encircle the cities. In reality, however, the driving forces behind China's engagements in Africa had little to do with Africa. As Calvocoressi (1985) asserted:

> Like Moscow's, Peking's interests in Africa were primarily extraneous to Africa. The first of these concerns was to seek international recognition for Mao's communist regime and, more specifically, votes at the United Nations which would be cast in favor of the transfer of the permanent Chinese seat in the Security Council from Taiwan to China proper.
>
> A second concern, which arose when Sino-Soviet friendship turned into Sino-Soviet rivalry, was to make trouble for the Russians. The conflict between Peking and Moscow, unlike the [ideological] alliance between them, could be furthered in Africa (p. 100).

China's perception was that Moscow, not Washington, was its principal enemy. Its strategy was therefore to weaken "social imperialism at the expense of monopolistic capitalism" (Snow, 1988; p. 54). *West Africa* observed that "in Africa, China increased assistance to old friends such as Tanzania and Zambia. The 2000km Tan-Zam railroad was meant to overshadow the Soviet-built Aswan High Dam in Egypt. China also made friends with old enemies such as Mobutu, helping him during the Shaba uprising in 1978-79; in 1980 they helped him build a naval base at Kinkuzu in southern Zaire to threaten Angola" (Aug 15, 1988; p. 1473).

China's fortunes in Africa quickly turned into mirages, however. At first, China's anticolonial stance was welcomed by African liberation movements. But as independence was gained, China's emphasis on subversion and its intense enmity toward the Soviet Union became less and less appealing or relevant to Africans. In fact, as early as 1963 Julius Nyerere of Tanzania complained of a new scramble for Africa between the Soviet Union and China. Because their actions were anti-Soviet rather than pro-African, the Chinese themselves did not achieve much by way of influence.

Furthermore, China was no less immune to blunders than the Soviets. Less wisely than the Soviets, China meddled in Burundi ethnic feuds. In 1963 China backed the Tutsi expedition by training a number of Tutsi in guerrilla warfare in China. The subsequent massacres in Burundi earned China much opprobrium. China also supported the Biafran secessionists in Nigeria's civil war (1967 to 1970) simply because Moscow backed the Federal Government of Nigeria. Similarly, in Angola, China supported the FNLA (National Front for the Liberation of Angola) because Moscow was backing the ruling MPLA.

In Mali and Congo-Brazzaville, China made some headway. But a spate of military coups brought to power new rulers distrustful of China. Only in Tanzania did China achieve some diplomatic and ideological success. China agreed to fund and build the 1,200-mile Tan-Zam railway line at a cost of 166 million pounds sterling, free of interest. The railway was both an engineering and a political achievement. It was completed two years ahead of schedule and was much touted as a model of what foreign aid could do for Africa. But it was one thing to build the railway and quite another to run it efficiently. Maintenance was poor, services degenerated, and the Dar es Salaam terminal became chronically clogged to the point of immobility. Although the Chinese had nothing to do with these shortcomings, their reputation suffered.

## THE DISMAL FAILURE OF WESTERN POLICIES IN AFRICA

By 1990 each bloc had failed to attain its policy objectives in Africa. But the rout of Western policy initiatives in Africa was far more dismal and devastating than Soviet failures, for several reasons. First, the West was quite aware of Soviet designs and strategies—the establishment of one-party Marxist-Leninist states through revolutionary means. Yet the West failed to develop appropriate responses and active policy initiatives tailored to regional or local conditions. Instead the West generally contented itself with reacting to rather than preventing Soviet expansion. Furthermore, containment implied disengagement when there were no signs of Soviet expansionary activity. An African country was "neglected" if there was no Soviet presence in that country. Worse, in some cases the West descended to the use of crass and deplorable Soviet tactics such as fomenting turmoil through subversive activities, propaganda, and assassination plots.

Second, what the West gained in Africa was not commensurate with the resources it spent there. Third, the West had the opportunity to learn from its debacles in other parts of the Third World, yet it repeated the same mistakes with uncanny regularity in Africa. The West was often seduced by the charisma and the euphonious verbiage of Third World despots, providing them with substantial aid in Iran (under the Shah), Nicaragua (under Somoza) and the Philippines (under Marcos). But the West gained little in return. Heavy Western investment in such strongmen, often blatantly corrupt and brutally repressive, drew the ire of the people. The subsequent overthrow of these dictators often unleashed a wave of intense anti-American or anti-Western sentiments. Tensions rose even further when these corrupt ex-leaders almost always managed to escape to the West with their booty.

Similarly, in Africa the West often obliged and supported pro-capitalist African dictators, despite their hideously repressive and neocommunist regimes. Gerhard Hohnle, a West German, speculated that the West supports such leaders to acquire Third World wealth: "The rich countries of the world want to get the goods of the Third World, especially Africa, at all costs. And what is easier than to deal with a dictator. A democratic system would complicate the transfer of the goods" (*New African*, Sep 1990; p. 36).

For geopolitical, economic, and other reasons, the West propped up tyrants in Cameroon, the Ivory Coast, Kenya, Liberia, Malawi, Zaire, and other African countries to the detriment of democratic movements.

"There's no doubt that many people here blame the United States for keeping Mobutu in power for so long," said Etienne Tshisekedi, leader of Zaire's biggest opposition party. "The anti-American sentiment has recently become a lot worse because many people still can't understand why the U.S. is still supporting his regime . . ."

A poll taken by the Zaire Institute of Public Opinion in Feb, 1992, found that 73.3 percent of those asked had a poor opinion of American policy toward Zaire...

"It is not the virulence of the stories appearing in the local press that concern me," said Melissa Wells, the United States Ambassador, "but the comments of longtime American residents, including many missionaries, who say they have never known this extent of anti-American sentiment. And I hear such comments day after day after day" (*The New York Times,* Mar 30, 1992; p. A5).

Similarly, in Liberia the United States offered little assistance to the people to free themselves from the military barbarism of President Samuel Doe. The United States was more interested in protecting its Voice of America relay station and Omega satellite navigational tracking system in Monrovia. Because he received no aid from the West, Charles Taylor, the leader of Doe's opposition, sought aid from Libya. In this way the West drove many freedom fighters into the communist camp by default. It was not that communism appealed to these opposition leaders, but that the communists were willing to help the liberation struggle. Tragically, the West failed to understand this. As Calvocoressi (1985) noted:

> For most Africans anticolonialism was a program rather than a concept or ideology. It was something that had to be done, and although the program found more sympathy with the left than the right in the Western world, the left-right pattern was largely irrelevant. There was nothing particularly odd about the fact that nearly all Britain's acts of decolonization were performed by Conservative governments. In spite of Western fears, there was no recourse to the Soviet Union by anticolonial movements except in those few cases where, for practical and not ideological reasons, a protracted conflict forced the insurgents to look for outside aid and arms where they could get them (p. 87).

## SCANDALOUS WESTERN AID
## TO DEMOCRATIC FORCES IN AFRICA

Paradoxically, the West, which is so vociferously championing the cause of democracy all over the world, might be a problem for the democracy movement in Africa. It is sympathetic but confused about what the situation requires and so dogmatic in its confusion that for all its good intentions, it is posing serious problems for the movement.

—Claude Ake, a Nigerian scholar.

The West acquiesced to the institution of tyranny in Africa in many ways. It tended to view Africa with different degrees of acuity. It would focus sharply on the abominable apartheid system in South Africa while its vision of the equally heinous tyranny in black Africa was blurred. Imagining that two Africas existed (South Africa and the rest of Africa), the West saw each with its own distinct problems and dichotomized its policy responses accordingly. In South Africa the West sought to promote political reform and to dismantle apartheid. In the rest of Africa the West sought to alleviate economic deprivation by partially cancelling foreign debts, providing economic aid, and introducing structural adjustment and other measures to promote economic reform.

This bifurcated Western approach to the crisis in Africa was based on the erroneous assumption that economic and political reforms were mutually exclusive. But the political reform needed in South Africa was the same reform needed in the rest of Africa. And the economic reform needed in the rest of Africa was precisely the same type needed in South Africa. The Western attempt to enforce a separation between economic and political reform not only was costly and self-defeating but also compounded the crisis for all of Africa.

The dual approach to Africa was due to the application of a double standard: one for black African leaders and the other for white rulers. This in turn originated from the prevailing Western mentality which held that blacks, enslaved in the past, must now be elevated to sainthood. This Western focus on the past oppression and enslavement of blacks effectively shielded corrupt black African leaders from condemnation in the West. White rulers in South Africa could be condemned, but not black African leaders guilty of the same political crimes.

The Western media, for example, avoided criticizing black leaders lest they be accused of being racist. In addition, the few blacks who offered such criticisms were regarded with deep suspicion.[5] But oversensitivity to racial issues produced a "silence" regarding the atrocities of black African tyrants, giving them free rein to perpetrate heinous atrocities against their people. Thus, if Marcias Nguema slaughtered 10,000 black Africans in Equatorial Guinea, the Western media organizations might not carry the story because it could be perceived as "too negative" or "offensive to blacks."

The apartheid system in South Africa provided another shield. Its repugnant system of racial segregation long held hostage and emasculated any public discussion of human rights violations and the institution of despotism in the rest of Africa, because however despicable the tyranny in black Africa, it could never be compared to the morally atrocious system of apartheid in South Africa. Criticisms of African leaders were viewed as an attempt to divert attention from the noble struggle of South African blacks. The few who dared to criticize were denounced as "racist apartheid supporters" if they were white or "traitors" if they were black. Consequently, the equally abominable de facto "apartheid" regimes in independent Africa escaped public scrutiny and condemnation in the West.

Western myths and misconceptions about Africa compounded these difficulties. Some Westerners, making vague references to "despotic African chiefs," steadfastly maintained that "democracy is alien to Africa." Consequently, corruption, acts of moral turpitude, arrogant despotism, and blatant barbarism on the part of some African leaders were "accepted" by Westerners as "part of African culture."

Another group of Westerners, pointing to Chile, Hong Kong, Singapore, and South Korea, contended that democracy was not essential to economic development. Development could successfully occur under authoritarian regimes. Meanwhile another group of Westerners proffered "compassion" and "understanding." But more often than not it was compassion for the tyrants, not the victims.

The result of all this was a severe intellectual paralysis, making it extremely difficult for Africa to come to grips with its problems. Westerners did not understand the complexity of African issues, were unwilling to discuss the truth about Africa because of racial sensitivity and, more maddening, were unwilling to listen to what Africans themselves had to say about their own condition and experience. Africans were not supposed to know what was good for them.

Although virtually all Western political leaders made lofty statements about the virtues of democracy, they did little to aid and establish it in Africa.[6] There have been more than 150 changes of government in Africa, but one would be hard pressed to name five countries that the West successfully democratized from 1970 to 1990. Indeed, the general belief that Western-style democracy could not exist in Africa held sway for a long time. Carola Kaps wrote:

> It was felt that multiparty systems would only lead to discord, strife and bloody quarrels among the different tribes; only the one-party system under a strong leader could pacify Africa's diverse people and hold them together. The few examples of pluralistic systems, like Senegal or neighboring Zambia, which functioned to some extent, were considered exceptions rather than the rule. Even the United States, the champion of democracy in other parts of the world, turned a blind eye to Africa; except for rather half-hearted attempts to press for observance of human rights, there were few efforts on the American side towards democratization of the African countries (Frankfurter Allegmeine, May 19, 1990; p. 2).

Accordingly, many African leaders projected themselves as "The Big Man" to win Western support. The clearest example of this was Mobutu Sese Seko. "It's me or chaos," he declared. The West bought his argument, as well as his anticommunist predilections, without paying much attention to his corrupt and antidemocratic government.

But then, when Africans and other people rose up against despotic officials, the West was quick to take the credit. For example, when Eastern Europe overthrew the yoke of communist dictatorships, it was widely reported that Eastern Europe had "adopted Western values." Specifically, at the 1989 Malta Summit between Mikhail Gorbachev and George Bush, the Soviet leader expressed indignation at the U.S. President's repeated references to the triumph of "Western democratic values." Before the summit, Mr. Bush had been using statements such as these: "And now the beautiful thing about it is, I think, as we look at Eastern Europe and other places in the world, we see that it's the American values that are prevailing" and "Our overall aim is to overcome the division of Europe and to forge a unity based on Western values" (*The Washington Times* (Jan 2, 1990; p. A6).

So what exactly are "Western values"? Did President Bush mean to say that only Westerners love liberty and that non-Westerners love tyranny? And when Africans rise up against tyranny, would that mean they have "adopted Western values"?

After being hounded by bloodthirsty Kenyan security forces, Gitobu Imanyara, editor of the *Nairobi Law Monthly*, supplied an articulate answer: "What makes people in the Soviet Union say 70 years of single-party rule is enough is the same human spirit that is moving these African countries to say that a quarter of a century of one-party rule in Africa is enough. What moved Nelson Mandela 27 years ago to offer his life for the achievement of the basic right to human dignity is the same spirit that moved that lone Chinese student at Tiananmen square to hold still armored tanks for time enough for the world to appreciate the universality of the yearning for freedom" (*Africa Report*, May-Jun 1990; p. 20).

President Bush subsequently corrected his statement by affirming that the love of liberty is "universal among all people." To many it may sound like an emotive gloss of a trivial, unguarded statement by an American president. But such statements were not helpful to the democratization of Africa.

Third and finally, the West provided a great deal of aid to Africa, much of which went to support tyrannical regimes. More than $300 billion in aid and various forms of credits and financial assistance have been pumped into Africa since the 1960s. In fact, according to Whitaker (1988), "Even in 1965, almost 20 percent of Western countries' development assistance went to Africa. In the 1980s, Africans, who are about 12 percent of the developing world's population, were receiving about 22 percent of the total, and the share per person was higher than anywhere else in the Third World—

amounting to about $20, versus about $7 for Latin America, and $5 for Asia" (p. 61). Between 1980 and 1988 sub-Saharan Africa received $83 billion of aid. Yet all that aid failed to spur economic growth and to arrest Africa's economic atrophy or promote democracy. Africa is littered with a multitude of "black elephants" (basilicas, grand conference halls, new capitals, and show airports) amid institutional decay, deteriorating infrastructure and environmental degradation. The standard of living in black Africa fell by 1.2 percent a year from 1960 to 1980. "Overall, Africans are almost as poor today as they were 30 years ago (at independence)," according to the World Bank (1989; p. 1). Nor did the aid buy much influence or leverage for the West since many of the aid programs were ill-conceived and economically unsound. Western backers tended to support almost any gaudy and extravagant project. Even Jean-Bedel Bokassa's coronation and Felix Houphouet-Boigny's basilica had Western financiers. Tanzania's less glamorous but ill-conceived *Ujaama* socialist experiment also received Western support. The *New York Times* reported that "at first, many Western aid donors, particularly in Scandinavia, gave enthusiastic backing to this socialist experiment, pouring an estimated $10 billion into Tanzania over 20 years. Yet, today as Mr. Nyerere leaves the stage, the country's largely agricultural economy is in ruins, with its 26 million people eking out their living on a per capita income of slightly more than $200 a year, one of the lowest in the world" (Oct 24, 1990; p. A8).

The 1990 *World Development Report* by the World Bank noted that Tanzania's economy contracted an average of 0.5 percent a year between 1965 and 1988. Average personal consumption declined dramatically by 43 percent between 1973 and 1988. *The Economist* observed that for all the aid poured into the country, Tanzania only had "pot-holed roads, decaying buildings, cracked pavements, demoralised clinics and universities, and a 1988 income per capita of $160 [lower than at independence in 1961]" to show for it (Jun 2, 1990; p. 48).

Western governments and development agencies failed to exercise prudence in granting aid and loans to Third World governments. Alan Woods, who was the administrator for the Agency for International Development, reported the scandalous failure of Western aid in a February 1989 report. Noting that the United States had provided some $400 billion in aid to the developing countries, he pointed out that no country receiving U.S. aid since 1968 has graduated from a less-developed to a developed status. Worse, he concluded, "only a handful of countries that started receiving U.S. assistance in the 1950s and 1960s has ever graduated from dependent status" (Woods, 1989; p. 112). A 1989 bipartisan congressional task force of the U.S. House of Representatives Foreign Affairs Committee confirmed this: "Current aid programs are so encrusted in red tape that they no longer either advance U.S. interests abroad or promote economic development" (*Wall Street Journal,* Mar 2, 1989; p. A16). In a more general indictment, Eberstadt (1988) wrote:

> Western aid today may be compromising economic progress in Africa and retarding its development of human capital. Overseas development assistance (ODA), after all, provides a very substantial fraction of the operating budgets of virtually all governments in sub-Saharan Africa. In 1983, ODA accounted for two-fifths of Liberia's central government budget, for three-quarters of Ghana's, and four-fifths of Uganda's. Western aid directly underwrites current policies and practices; indeed, it may actually make possible some of the more injurious policies, which would be impossible to finance without external help (p. 100).

A blistering affirmation came from a very unlikely source. Sir William Ryrie, executive vice-president of the International Finance Corporation, a World Bank subsidiary, declared that "the West's record of aid for Africa in the past decade [1980s] can only be characterised as one of failure" (*Financial Times,* Jun 7, 1990; p. 5).

Much of the aid to Africa was used to finance grandiose projects and to underwrite misguided, repressive policies. The rest was embezzled by elite gangsters. The West knew that billions of dollars were being transferred to Swiss banks by greedy African leaders. "Every franc we give impoverished Africa, comes back to France or is smuggled into Switzerland and even Japan" wrote the Paris daily, *Le Monde* in March 1990. Even famine relief assistance to Africa was not spared. Dr. Rony Brauman, head of *Medecins sans Frontiers* (Doctors without Borders), which operates in Ethiopia, lamented: "We have been duped . . . Western governments and humanitarian groups unwittingly fuelled—and are continuing to fuel—an operation that will be described in hindsight in a few years' time as one of the greatest slaughters of our time." But it would be very wrong and naive to pretend that it was only the West that supported tyrants in Africa.

The former Soviet Union, Eastern Europe, China, and Cuba offered no assistance whatsoever to democratic forces in Africa. After all, it was from these countries that the despicable one-party state system was imported. Nor did assistance come from other Third World countries, most of which were in solidarity with African dictators in the discredited Non-Aligned Movement—a movement which congregated in Havana to bash only the West. In recent times Arab countries have become more visible in their support of African despots. For example, Saddam Hussein of Iraq supported President Ould Yaya of Mauritania and Iran lent support to Omar Bashir of Sudan.

If foreign countries have not provided effective aid to democratic forces in Africa, how about blacks in diaspora?

## BLACKS IN DIASPORA

There is little black Americans could or should do directly to help foster or affect political change in Sub-Saharan Africa . . . I don't think it is our business to meddle in their affairs.

—Benjamin Hooks, former executive director of the NAACP, at Yamassoukrou
(April 1991).

Of blacks in diaspora, three groups may be distinguished: black Americans, Caribbean blacks, and African exiles. The role each group played in aiding and abetting tyranny in Africa will now be examined.

### *Black Americans*

In North America, black Americans constitute the only group of blacks in diaspora with sufficient clout, credibility and experience to help their black brothers and sisters in Africa in their struggle for freedom. The experience gained in the civil rights struggle in the 1960s could have been helpful to black Africans but, in practice, turned out to be more of a hindrance.

Black Americans tended to see the campaign against apartheid as an extension of their own civil rights struggle. This was understandable since the oppressors and exploiters in both cases were white, the oppressed and exploited, black. But many Africans saw apartheid as merely a special case of the oppression that was rampant across the continent. Further, the analysis of African problems in a rigid "civil rights" or black-white paradigm was not appropriate. In black Africa color was not the issue. Blacks ruled themselves. Although in the past their oppressors and exploiters were white colonialists, today they are black. Perhaps, the innocent oversight of this fundamental difference rendered many black Americans extremely hostile to the notion that some black African leaders head more ruthlessly oppressive regimes than the apartheid system in South Africa, notwithstanding the fact that apartheid is institutionalized.

It is true that in the 1950s black Americans provided vital support to Africans in the liberation struggle against colonialism.[7] In recent times, black Americans have been indefatigable in the campaign for one-man, one-vote for blacks in South Africa. But to the blacks in independent Africa fighting for the *same* political rights, black Americans have offered little or no support.

Unbelievably, black Americans actually helped black dictators to oppress black people in black Africa.

This was eloquently demonstrated at an African/African-American Conference in Yamassoukrou (in the Ivory Coast) in April 1991. The delegates were effusive in expressions of solidarity to combat the rising tide of racism in America. "We are a community of resistance united in a fight against racism, apartheid and forced indebtedness," intoned Capt. Blaise Compaore, the military despot from Burkina Faso. But no one in that congregation of civil rights leaders, which included Coretta Scott King and the Rev. Jesse Jackson, talked about the rising slaughter of blacks in West Africa and the senseless civil wars which had produced mounting refugees and grisly spectacles of emaciated bodies of famine victims. Not one single black American civil rights leader condemned Arab apartheid in Mauritania and Sudan and the present-day enslavement of blacks by Arab masters. Only two, Rep. William H. Gray III (D-Pa) and Vivien Lowery Derryck, president of the African-American Institute, distinguished themselves with muted references to civil rights. Said Gray: "We keenly are interested in human rights and democratic institutions. Human rights must be in the forefront of our relationship, and this principle must apply to all of Africa" (*Washington Post,* Apr 20, 1991; p. A18).[8]

Unfortunately, black Americans are not well informed about events in Africa, and myths and misconceptions about the continent still persist in the black, as well as the white, American community. But some black Americans refuse to be informed of the painful truth about Africa and, worse, disparage and attack those courageous enough to speak the truth. One victim was Jeffrey Goldstein, a history teacher in a Brooklyn High School.

> Hundreds of black and Hispanic students, incensed by a history teacher's remark that they deemed racist, walked out of classes in a Brooklyn high school yesterday morning, smashing display cabinets and forcing the school to close early, the police and school officials said . . . .
>
> The students were angry about a remark that Jeffrey Goldstein, a white teacher, made during a discussion of South Africa . . . Mr. Goldstein told his students that American blacks were concerned about racism in South Africa but did not express the same concern about the subjugation of blacks in West African nations (*The New York Times,* Oct 4, 1989; p. B3).

Which "brothers and sisters" in Africa do black Americans seek to protect? In Mali, "soldiers shot and killed five women in a crowd protesting military killings of demonstrators for democracy, then chased protesters into a building and set it ablaze . . . A human rights activist said at least 80 people

died and doctors said hundreds were injured" (*Washington Post*, Mar 24, 1991;
p. A26). While black Americans were being wined, dined and suckered in
the Ivory Coast, black Africans were being butchered in Cameroon, Congo,
Liberia, Togoland, and other countries. In particular, at about the same time
that black Americans were feasting on imported French delicacies and
expensive wines, 26 bodies of pro-democracy demonstrators were being
dredged from the Lome Lagoon (Togoland). One of the corpses was that of
a woman with a baby strapped to her back.

Asked about political turmoil and carnage in these black African countries,
Benjamin Hooks, director of the NAACP—the world's largest civil rights
organization—replied that "there is little black Americans could or should
do directly to help foster or affect political change in Sub-Saharan Africa...
I don't think it is our business to meddle in their affairs." Said one incredulous
Ivorian student: "I wish some of these (black) Americans would take to the
streets with us instead of supporting the old order" (*Washington Post*, Apr 18,
1991; p. A41). A more searing query came from a Liberian exile in the Ivory
Coast: "Why have you black Americans let us down?" (*Washington Post*, Apr
20, 1991; p. A18).

Life has been tough for Ivorians, as we saw in Chapter 8. President
Houphouet-Boigny blamed their hardships on "Western commodity speculators." But Ivorians pointed to the rampant corruption ($456 million is
illegally removed from the country every year) and the basilica at
Yamassoukrou—a magnificent "black elephant." The Rev. Leon H. Sullivan,
the black American civil rights leader known for his "Sullivan Principles" for
South Africa, hailed the basilica as the "world's greatest expression of religious faith and praised Houphouet-Boigny for his 30 years of impeccable
leadership" (*Washington Post*, Apr 18, 1991; p. A41).[9] To opposition critic
Professor Laurent Gbagbo, Houphouet-Boigny is "a reckless rogue, criminal
and a big thief." Funding for that useless monument to vanity (cost: $360
million) came from his own pocket, according to Houphouet-Boigny. Some
pocket.

While Africans were struggling to rid themselves of hideous dictators,
black American institutions were showering the dictators with honors and
degrees. The Central State University of Ohio awarded Flight Lt. Jerry
Rawlings an honorary doctorate in law. "It also made him the honorary
chairman of the World African Chamber of Commerce" (*West Africa*, May
21-27, 1990; p. 864).

Another honorary doctorate in law was awarded by the University of
Maryland (Eastern Shore) to President Paul Biya of Cameroon in April 1991.
The timing could not have been more callous. The University of Yaounde

in Biya's own country had been in a virtual state of siege in that very month, with clashes between pro-democracy students and security forces. "According to the National Coalition of Cameroon Students, 58 students were killed and over 200 arrests made, a claim backed by the Cameroon Human Rights Organization, which produced a list of students missing and presumed dead" (*West Africa*, May 20-26, 1991; p. 799).

Cameroonian students in the United States were irate: "'We will picket at the commencement . . . because of the corruption, the embezzlement . . . the jailing of people without reason,' said Ernest Ehabe, an organizer of the students . . . A high-ranking State Department official, who asked not to be identified, said the Biya government imposed harsh controls on Cameroon after the (1984) coup attempt, suspending most political parties and torturing and killing some political prisoners" (*Washington Post*, May 3, 1991; p. A10). Nevertheless, "university authorities rejected the students' appeal on the grounds that the award ceremony was already scheduled" (*West Africa*, May 20-26, 1991; p. 799).

Even more outrageous were plans by Coppin State College in Baltimore to present a degree to Maj. Gen. Justin Lekhanya of Lesotho. College authorities were thoroughly embarrassed when Lekhanya was deposed in a coup.

If black Americans are unwilling to help their true black brothers and sisters fight tyranny and Arab apartheid in the rest of Africa, then perhaps it would be best if they stayed out of Africa. The African people are becoming more and more irate at being let down not only by their heads of state but also by duplicitous "friends" and "brothers" in the West, who lack the courage to stand up to black African tyrants.

## Caribbean Blacks

There are also differences in perceptions and attitudes between Caribbean blacks and black Africans, although they are not as pronounced as that between black Americans and black Africans. Unlike black Americans, Caribbean blacks are more likely to be critical of black African leaders in private. But the gulf between Caribbean blacks and black Africans often revolves around ideology. Many Caribbean blacks still hold such African nationalist and socialist leaders as Kenneth Kaunda, Dr. Kwame Nkrumah, and Julius Nyerere in very high esteem and even worship them. It is difficult to persuade some Caribbean blacks that, while these leaders may have enjoyed high international stature, they were domestic failures.

### African exiles

Africans in the West constitute the last but most important group of blacks in diaspora. Among them are university professors, professionals, students, and economic and political refugees. Of these, two groups can be distinguished. The first constitute the "Lost Tribe"—those Africans abroad who do not care two hoots about Africa. In fact, they have written the continent off completely and are not interested in democracy there. The second are those who care and can do much to aid the second liberation of Africa for three reasons.

First, these Africans know and understand much better the real conditions at home than do most black Americans or Caribbean blacks. Being economic and/or political refugees, they have experienced first-hand the economic destitution, political oppression, and the general state of repression and hopelessness that prevail at home. Second, Africans abroad have liberties, such as freedom of expression, which their compatriots at home are denied. They can write newspaper articles, books, and monographs, exposing the misdeeds of African dictators and the institutionalized looting that is rampant across Africa, and call for political reform. In educating or creating an awareness of misrule in Africa, Africans abroad can be invaluable in mobilizing public opinion and support for the cause of freedom.

Third, Africans abroad have better resources than their brethren at home. They can provide funds and the materiel (word processors, copiers, fax machines, paper, printing materials, etc.) to support the democratic struggle in Africa. In countries where even typing paper is scarce, these items can be vital for pro-democracy movements. Consider this example: "A former Iranian diplomat, Assad Homayoun, is quietly organizing moderate Iranian exiles. His goal: to topple the mullahs with a fax revolution much as the Chinese dissidents attempted in 1989. Homayoun hopes to flood Iran with foreign broadcasts, underground newspaper and faxes" (*Newsweek*, Mar 30, 1992; p. 6). Even Africans at home with limited resources are replicating this strategy: "The opposition United Front for Multiparty Democracy in Malawi has sent dozens of faxed messages into the country from neighboring Zambia, urging peaceful demonstrations against Banda's rule" (*West Africa*, Mar 23-29, 1992; p. 518).[10]

There are at least 20,000 Ghanaians and over 500,000 Africans working in North America and Europe. If each contributes $100 a year, that is $2 million or over $50 million right there to fund the campaign for democracy in Ghana or Africa. How much is freedom worth to these Africans?

Shamefully, the actual level of support provided by Africans abroad to the struggle for democracy at home is, to say the least, despicably low in many instances. Some of these Africans drive around in BMWs and claim they are "socialists." But ask them to make a contribution to the cause of African freedom and the excuses are legion: "My son is sick," "I have to pay my mortgage," "My grandmother died" (she died in 1960). But come Saturday one sees them doing the watusi at the disco with four women dangling from their arms. Yet they are the same ones who insist that their government back home has its priorities all messed up. Instead of help, they offer plenty of hot air and useless rhetoric.

In November 1991 this author attended a fund-raising event in Washington, D.C. to solicit contributions to aid the democracy struggle in an African country. The 200 people who attended gave only a total of $420, which worked out to be a fraction over $2 a person. "Illiterates" back home understand the value of freedom and some have been quite willing to put their lives on the line, to stand up and challenge the hideous despots running amok in Africa. Yet the attendees, including several who were university professors and World Bank employees, could not put their money where their mouth was. One speaker pompously got up and, in pedantic language, quoted from the *American Sociological Review* to question whether multi-party democracy would solve Africa's problems. He demanded to know if polls had been taken to show that Africans unequivocally desired multi-party democracy. "The U.S. itself is not democratic," he declared. The rage seething in the audience could be felt. He was hooted down.

Most serious-minded Africans have come across such intellectual *gu-nu-gu* (a Sierra Leonian word for buzzards). Stiffly dressed in nine-piece suits with colors mismatched (flaming red tie over lime green shirt and purple pants), they come to meetings hours late, sweat cascading over fat cheeks and bloodshot eyes glazed. They won't just sit quietly and shut up but must wax eloquent on procedural detail, scuttling the program and agenda. They pedantically insist on decorum and the order of business, without realizing that punctuality is part of the order of business. They pontificate ad nauseam on constitutional intricacies and rule others out of order.

"Ask one of these African 'intellectuals' to discourse on Africa's problems and from their mouths will issue a whole stream of theories from Professor Higgins and Professor Biggins; they will quote Marx and Engels and Churchill and the columnist from the (London) *Times* who hardly knows where Africa is!" says Anver Versi, deputy editor of *New African* (Jun 1991).

These intellectual buzzards spend hours haranguing about "proper procedures" so that by the time they come to the real purpose of the meeting everybody has gotten fed up and left! Talks or seminars are even worse. Often the speaker is unprepared, with no notes. Some academics come prepared with typed papers. But then some insist on reading a 50-page text in full in the 20 minutes allocated for delivery. Open the floor for questions and each person who gets up insists upon making a speech and recounting a lengthy personal anecdote, most of which are irrelevant to the issue at hand.

There is so much Africans abroad can do to help the second liberation struggle in Africa. For example, they have the freedom to write. But how many of them write? How many African intellectuals in the West have written books? Produce a book and it will last centuries.

Few of us want to write because we are afraid of reprisals against our families at home. "I don't want to rock the boat. I will live here quietly until conditions at home improve so that I can go back and become president," many say to themselves. If all Africans act this way, how do we remove the tyrants back home? Few of the educated Africans abroad are willing to make the sacrifice and a modest contribution to help liberate Africa. They want somebody else to do it for them. But then they would hardly support someone who courageously takes the initiative. Instead, they attack him.

In offering criticism, we African elites all have Ph.D.s ("pull-him-down"). We won't write articles or books on Africa but let somebody else write them and we will bare our fangs, dripping with venom, to attack. If the author is a white Westerner, we will attack him for "racist biases and insensitivity." If an African, we will denounce him for being an "imperialist stooge" or "neocolonial lackey."

Self-criticism is extremely useful but we get a zero when it comes to organization. We need to be far more serious-minded, and must show a better sense of purpose, direction, and discipline. If the "illiterate" peasants could build empires, pyramids, temples (Great Zimbabwe), and produce kente cloths, those of us educated Africans abroad ought to be able to put together something of a formidable African organization to push for democracy in Africa. Must we always look up to Westerners to do it for us?

True, there are thousands of African organizations and associations. But each is too small to be effective. Worse, each is very parochial: the KYX Secondary School Association, the Kundu State Association, the Nigerian Students Association in Ohio, the Kenyan American Association, and so on. The irony is that we deplore tribalism, preach African unity and pan-Africanism. Yet we are only interested in events in our own little countries.

It is time to *adopt* another African country. Become an expert and write about an African country *other than your own*, not only to foster pan-Africanism but also for reasons of *safety*. A Malawian should befriend a Kenyan, adopt and write about Kenya. President Moi cannot take reprisals against a Malawian's family in Kenya because he does not have one there. A Liberian should write about Somalia. Both countries have been devastated by military barbarians. A Mozambican should adopt Angola: Both countries have been ruined by civil war and discredited Marxist-Leninism. A Tanzanian should adopt Zambia, and so on.

---

## NOTES

1. One such official in Senegal was Jean Collin, secretary-general of the Presidential Office. According to *West Africa* (Jun 4-10, 1990): "Perhaps the most hated public figure in opposition circles, Jean Collin has worked for the Senegalese administration since 1947, holding such ministerial seats as home office and finance. He was not noticed by the general public but when President Diouf said Collin taught him almost everything he knew about public affairs and nationalism, the Senegalese were naturally irritated" (p. 935).

2. Not everyone viewed U.S. policy toward Africa as one of benign neglect and containment of Soviet inroads. According to Nzongol-Ntalaja (1986, p. 19), U.S. policies were highly interventionist and domineering.

3. In 1991, $4 billion of Angola's $8.7 billion foreign debt was owed to the former Soviet Union. On July 1, 1991, President Eduardo dos Santos said: "military debts were not usually honored," implying that Angola would not pay it (*The New York Times*, Jul 8, 1991).

4. Angola and Mozambique benefited more from arms supplies.

5. Black Americans, naturally, played a significant role in creating this intellectual environment with their unwavering solidarity with African heads of state. Many black Americans tended to regard criticisms of black African leaders in particular as racially motivated. Insisting on solidarity with "their brothers and sisters" in Africa, too many black Americans blindly defended African tyrants without distinguishing between the tyrants and the victims of tyranny.

6. Nor elsewhere, according to Irving Kristol, publisher of the American magazine, *The National Interest*: "In the entire history of the US, we have successfully 'exported' our democratic institutions to only two nations— Japan and Germany, after war and an occupation. We have failed to establish a viable democracy in the Philippines, or in Panama, or anywhere in Central America. Why should anyone think we can do so in Eastern Europe or Southeast Asia (or Africa)?" (*The Wall Street Journal*, Jun 7, 1990).

7. Among those who deserve mention are Marcus Garvey, W.E.B. Du Bois, and George Padmore.

8. It is true that black Americans have criticized African dictators, but the criticism has been selective. Only the pro-West dictators such as Doe of Liberia, Mobutu of Zaire, and Moi of Kenya were excoriated while Marxist and socialist tyrants such as Kaunda, Mengistu, and Rawlings were shielded by black Americans. But as pointed out earlier, ideology is not relevant to African problems.

9. The "Sullivan Principles" were guidelines drawn for U.S. companies operating in South Africa to help provide equal opportunity for blacks in the workplace. Specifically, these companies were encouraged to institute job-training programs to help ease blacks into jobs reserved for whites under apartheid. Other programs included providing education, health, and other social services which the racist regime neglected to provide for blacks.

10. It should now become clear why uncensored communication is vital to the democratic struggle and why control of the media should be wrested out of the hands of African governments.

# Chapter 12

## Internal Props of
## Tyrannical Regimes in Africa

The most durable civilian governments in Africa so far have been disproportionately governments of one-party states; while the casualties of military intervention in Africa have been disproportionately multi-party states . . . The strongest case for the one-party state in Africa is to be found in those African societies which are ethnically dual: consisting primarily of two ethnic groups, one of which is well over half of the total population and the other is a permanent minority (Algeria, Burundi, Rwanda, Zimbabwe) . . . A dual society with a multi-party system in Africa seemed to be a prescription for a political caste system, with "Shona Brahmins" and "Ndebele Harijans" or their equivalent, for the foreseeable future.

—Ali Mazrui (*The Africans*, 1986; p. 197).

The absence of certain institutions, such as a free media, an independent judiciary, and freedom of expression, contributed immensely to the entrenchment of despotism in Africa. The role played by the military was obvious. Less conspicuous but still important were the roles played by African intellectuals and opponents of despotism.

## AFRICAN INTELLECTUALS

The saddest aspect of Africa's postcolonial descent into tyranny was the blatant support provided by some of Africa's best and brightest. Without the support of Africa's intellectuals and scholars, the institution of repression would scarcely have been possible. These intellectuals offered various arguments to justify the institution of one-party socialist/Marxist systems and military regimes in Africa.

Some of the arguments were partly ideological (aversion to Western capitalism and civilization). One strand in these arguments maintained that multipartyism was a "Western phenomenon" and that "democracy is alien to Africa." The other arguments were partly situational and partly mischievous. They echoed the dictators' call for "national unity" among Africa's numerous tribes. Single-party systems were necessary to suppress tribalism and channel all national energies into real development for the people. Dissent and opposition politics were divisive. But as we saw in Chapter 5, all these promises proved hollow and false.

In the 1960s the cause for which African intellectuals compromised their principles was independence from colonial rule. This overriding goal kept many African intellectuals from discussing participatory forms of government and from challenging dictatorships. Believing that the end justified the means, many intellectuals expected the masses to make sacrifices to fight colonialism. These sacrifices included political rights. Few intellectuals were willing to challenge the denial of these rights and risk being portrayed as colonial agents.

The rights, however, were not restored after independence. Shrewd African despots manufactured the specter of neocolonialism and other enemies, and demanded additional sacrifices from the people to fight these specters. The political systems they proposed ranged from African socialism to African unity. Africa's intellectuals were willing to accept any tyrant who would assert African pride by standing up to or humiliating colonialists and imperialists; for example, the intellectuals were ecstatic when Idi Amin made British residents of Uganda carry him on their shoulders. Thus, during the 1960s and 1970s African intellectuals abandoned critical inquiry and supported tyrants for various causes: promoting African unity, fighting apartheid and colonialism, and taking "drastic action" to deal with emerging economic crises.

The development promised by Africa's despots never occurred. In fact, the only real development that took place was in the wallets of the *wabenzi* ("Mercedes-Benz men"). While African economies were being mismanaged, the elites were raiding the national treasury. Famine and starvation appeared while Africa's foreign debt zoomed to a staggering $270 billion. "National unity" proved elusive. One-party rule, which was supposed to promote social equality, national unity, and harmony, failed to achieve any of those objectives. On the contrary, it was divisive and characterized by coercion and intolerance. For example, one-party rule exacerbated ethnic divisions since top party and government positions were often filled by members of the president's tribe. Attempts to enforce unity fanned separatist movements in

Angola (Cabinda), Ethiopia (Eritrea), Cameroon (Anglophones), Somalia (the north), Sudan (the south) and Tanzania (Zanzibar). As Wolfgand Dourado, a former Zanzibar attorney general, put it: "There was an enforced unifying process through the one-party system that is bringing about this disintegration. If they had gone to multipartyism before, Somalia would have been saved. Sudan could have been saved. They are now paying the price of one-party dictatorship. They tried to force disparate people into union without accommodating minority rights" (*The Washington Post*, Mar 25, 1992; p. A29).

Back in the 1960s, most of the intellectuals who ardently supported one-party states never contemplated the danger of disintegration after they collapsed. More unbelievable, the soldiers who stepped in "to clean up the mess" were hailed by intellectuals as "saviors." Some intellectual crackpots even argued that soldiers were "professional," "apolitical," "dedicated," "competent," and "efficient." As professionals, soldiers would put the national interest above all others and inject discipline into government administration. But as we saw in Chapter 7, the soldiers proved themselves to be no saviors and were themselves remarkably undisciplined.

So many of Africa's professors sold out by singing the praises of tyrannical regimes in exchange for an appointment or a Mercedes-Benz! And so many journalists flouted the imperatives of their own profession—objectivity and balance—to please autocratic regimes. Even the barbarous military regimes of Idi Amin of Uganda and Samuel Doe of Liberia could find professors to serve at their beck and call. Professional standards, ethics, integrity, and probity were sold off by Africa's "educated" to win favors. To cite just one example: "Dr. S.K.B. Asante, chairman of the Committee of Experts that drafted the proposals for Ghana's constitution, has admitted that the new proposal for a president and a prime minister was the *result of a direct PNDC order requiring the committee to arrive at such a conclusion*" (*West Africa*, Sep 23-29, 1991; p. 1576; emphasis added.)

Ismail Rashid, a Sierra Leonian exile in Waterloo, Canada, provided a few other examples:

> We should not forget the opportunism, cowardice and unprincipled role of a section of the so-called intelligentsia in leading us into our present quandary. Lawyers, doctors, professors and a whole host of other "educated" people willingly participated in the general repression and corruption that was characteristic of APC (All People's Congress) rule . . .
>
> In 1980 and 1985, this elite remained muted and in some cases condemned the widespread protests against the APC dictatorship and the deteriorating

economy by workers and students. In fact, it endorsed the punitive measures taken against these protestors. A classic representative of this class is the present Vice President, Dr. Abdullai Conteh, who came to power on the crest of student protest in 1977, and who criticized President Momoh's succession to power as the work of an insidious "cabal which will only destroy the nation." Needless to say, Dr. Conteh ended in that same cabal as a leading actor.

Finally, the nation cannot forget the opportunism and cowardice of the SLPP (Sierra Leone People's Party). After the death of so many people in the 1977 elections to ensure that the SLPP had a voice in parliament, its leading members, including its present chairman Salia Jusu-Sheriff, crossed over to the APC. For over 13 years, they also partook in the rape of the country (*New African*, May 1992, p.10).

It was this type of collaboration that allowed tyranny to become entrenched in Africa. Doe, Mobutu, Kaunda, and other dictators stayed in power by buying off or co-opting Africa's academics and opposition leaders. For a pittance, many would sacrifice principle to serve under an army sergeant whose level of education hardly matched half of theirs. Kwaku Annor, a Ghanaian, berated:

> "Liberia's tragedy should be an object lesson to Africa's academics, who, all too often embrace any coup leader no matter his intelligence or record. Had the Movement for Justice in Africa (MOJA) group on the campus of the University of Liberia not provided Doe with 'intellectual' legitimacy, he may not have destroyed Liberia. African universities should be the breeding ground for democratic interchange and compromise, not hotbeds for rabid radicalism" (*West Africa*, Oct 15-21, 1990; p. 2648).

One lesson for Africa's academics is that singing praises to a tyrannical regime offers them no protection against future missteps: "Six Malawian and two European Bishops were detained by Malawian authorities for circulating a pastoral letter which denounced 'unfairness and injustice . . . bribery and nepotism in political, economic and social life' and claimed that the suppression of dissent had created 'a climate of mistrust and fear.' President Banda expressed bewilderment at the letter, claiming 'the very same Bishops had praised me to the sky' " (*West Africa*, Mar 23-29, 1992; p. 518).

But are Africa's intellectuals capable of learning? According to Yoweri Museveni, Uganda's head of state, "Many so-called 'educated' Africans seemed to have sent their brains on holiday and hired out their hands to Western academics" (*Africa Forum*, Vol. 1, No. 2; p. 11). That may be so, but at least that was a little better than the brains of some African leaders—thoroughly eaten by insects, to use President Moi's own words.

## THE OPPOSITION IN AFRICA

The most unlikely support for tyranny in Africa often came from the very groups organized to oppose tyranny. One cannot heap all the blame for Africa's ruination on the dictators. Their primary impulses are well-known: to perpetuate themselves in power, to loot the country and to squelch criticism. And they succeed not so much because of their ingenuity or craftiness, but because of the inadequacies and weaknesses of the opposition. A force dominates either because a counterforce is non-existent or weak. In Africa, the forces of despotism dominated simply because of the nature and character of the opposition. Quite frankly, the type of opposition offered in Africa leaves much to be desired.

In many places in Africa the opposition has been hopelessly fragmented, disorganized, and prone to squabbling. In 1991, there were 120 opposition parties in Zaire alone, challenging Mobutu and 48 parties in Mali. When Mobutu announced his intention to allow multi-party democracy in April 1990, Zairean opposition groups met in Brussels to plot a strategy. But fancy what happened: "At least three Zairians were injured when violence erupted during an opposition press conference in Brussels. Representatives from the Union for Democracy and Social Progress (UDPS) were attacked by members of the audience while outlining their response to the reforms introduced recently by President Mobutu Sese Seko. The attack has been attributed to factionalism within the UDPS" (*West Africa*, May 28-Jun 3, 1990; p. 914).

In the fall of 1989, Liberian dissidents met in Washington, D.C. to devise ways of overthrowing Samuel Doe. Before the meeting was over, a heated argument erupted over who should be the next president. Word of this stupid bickering got out and by the time these dissidents showed up in Monrovia, Doe was waiting for them—with machine guns ready.

Most of the opposition leaders in Africa are themselves closet dictators, exhibiting the same tyrannical tendencies they so loudly denounce in the leaders they hope to replace: Many are obsessed with political power and are grossly intolerant of criticism. *Newsweek* reported that Charles Taylor had authoritarian tendencies: "Taylor may already be heading down the same authoritarian path traveled by Doe himself, who consistently ignored the pleas and criticisms of his own people" (Jul 16, 1990; p. 38). In the past, many such "liberators" transformed themselves—in less than a year—into another set of tyrants, far worse than the despots they replaced.

It is true that some opposition leaders have endured great personal suffering: detention, torture, exile, loss of employment, property, and so forth. It may sound callous, but that gives them no ownership rights over the presidency of the country. Winning independence for an African country or saving a country from a corrupt and despotic regime gives no one the license to impose himself on the country. It is the people of the country who must decide who should rule them.

Furthermore, some opposition group leaders lack imagination and are totally unsophisticated in their choice of tactics to oust an entrenched dictator. In fact, some of their methods are downright foolish; for example, blowing up power lines, bridges, rampaging through the city, looting and burning private cars. These are blind terroristic acts. They often claim innocent victims who have nothing to do with the hated regime. A sabotage of the electricity supply, for example, affects both supporters and opponents of the government, as well as innocent people. The strategies must be *surgical*, impinging only on the regime and with little collateral damage.

In many cases the tyrants being dealt with are brutal, calculating, and vicious, with tremendous resources and firepower at their disposal. Risks and methods must be weighed carefully before action is taken since one careless mistake could result in the deaths of scores of people. For example, the astute opposition leader does not issue a call for a general strike without carefully weighing all the risks involved. A failed general strike can also be extremely demoralizing. People will have little faith in the next strategy and will not make the effort necessary to make it work if they believe that that strategy too will fail. It becomes a kind of self-fulfilling prophecy. A strategy will fail if people do not make the effort required to help it succeed.

One of the most unimaginative methods was the issuance of a series of ultimatums by opposition groups to the military regime in Ghana: "Hand over by such-and-such a date, or else . . ." More than 15 such ultimatums have been issued between 1982 and 1992. Deadlines passed and nothing happened. Even pro-democracy forces dismissed them as a joke. If the opposition does not have the means to enforce a deadline, then it should not issue one. Otherwise, it will damage and weaken its own credibility. Besides, it is irresponsible to issue a deadline and not follow through with credible action because it puts the whole population at risk. The paranoid government will tighten security as the deadline approaches, arresting people on the flimsiest shred of evidence.

The second most useless method of ousting a military dictatorship is through "mass action" such as public demonstrations and rallies. Their use betrays the functional illiteracy of the opposition leaders. Just because these strategies worked in the 1950s against the colonialists does not mean they will also work against black neocolonialists. Mass demonstrations work to arouse public emotion and are effective if public assemblies are allowed and if the news media are free. But this is not the case in many African countries. The problem is a lack of imagination or inability to adapt strategies to suit changing circumstances. Today, thanks to advances in modern weaponry, the military can mow down a crowd of 10,000 people in an instant.

Though the military has an offensive superiority in weapons, it is *numerically* inferior. Soldiers constitute less than 0.1 percent of the population in *any* African country. The trick is to exploit their numerical inferiority by stretching them geographically. Dispersion, rather than concentration, should be the key.[1]

Three successful ways of removing military dictatorships have emerged in Africa. The first is through armed insurrection, as in Ethiopia, Liberia, Somalia, and Uganda. But this is not to be recommended since the cost is prohibitive: destruction of the country, the loss of thousands of lives and the creation of refugees. The second is through a palace coup, but then that does not get rid of the military regime (for example, Acheampong overthrown by Akuffo, Traore overthrown by Toure in Mali). The third is when the soldiers themselves hold elections and return to the barracks.

In the post-colonial era no military regime has been removed through mass demonstrations. These may work *indirectly* but are chancy, costly, and largely ineffective. They result in deaths when police and military barbarians rain bullets on the demonstrators: "Police opened fire on a student-led demonstration in the town of Zomba (Malawi) on March 16, 1992, killing several" (*West Africa*, Mar 23-29, 1992; p. 518). The deaths often elicit both strong domestic and international condemnation. This puts further pressure on the regime to reform. But the outcome is not predictable. Out of the chaos and confusion, another military adventurer may seize power and, as Africans would say, "he comes to do the same thing."

Time and time again those who set out to liberate their countries from tyranny end up fighting among themselves, sowing confusion and carnage. Even before Samuel Doe was overthrown and killed in September 1990, Charles Taylor and Prince Yormie Johnson were squabbling, each threatening to kill the other. Much the same thing has happened in Kenya:

> After battling the Kenyan government and forcing a change to a multi-party system, Kenya's democracy movement began to self-destruct, with two factions each claiming to be the legitimate voice of the opposition.
>
> The confusion became apparent when two separate groups of opposition leaders arrived at Chester House to announce formation of political parties. Both groups claimed the name Forum for the Restoration of Democracy (FORD).
>
> One group is led by Martin Shikuku (a Luhya) and the other by Oginga Odinga (a Luo) (*The Washington Post*, Dec 7, 1991; p. A21).

When Kenneth Matiba, a Kikuyu, declared his intention of seeking the presidency of the association, "everyone began discussing an imminent split between the Luo and the Kikuyu in the ranks of FORD" (*New African*, Apr 1992; p. 17). These leaders were the same who accused President Moi of "tribalism."

In neighboring Sudan, the Sudanese People's Liberation Army (SPLA) in the south has been battling the brutal Islamic fundamentalist regime in Khartoum. But the SPLA split into two factions in 1991—a Nuer faction led by Riak Machan and the other by the long-established leader, John Garang, and his Dinka supporters.

> The two sides first clashed in January 1992, near the town of Bor, and the aftermath saw one of the worst massacres in the long Sudanese tragedy.
>
> Mr. Garang's troops were routed and the victorious Nuer warriors swept into the town shooting and stabbing every person and animal in sight. Two hundred thousand Dinka refugees fled south, and a video shot by a worker with the Norwegian People's Aid group shows the horrors that ensued along the road to Mongalla.
>
> Between 2,000 and 5,000 civilians were murdered—tied up and then speared or garrotted—and in a particularly creative act of cruelty, thousands of cattle were blinded with pangas. (The Dinka revere their cows, and regard them almost as part of the family) (*Washington Times*, Apr 1, 1992; p. G4).

In Somalia, following the ouster of Siad Barre, internecine rivalry erupted between the United Somali Congress (USC) and the Somali National Movement (SNM). The USC controlled the south, including the capital, Mogadishu, while the SNM controlled the north. But factionalism emerged within the ranks of the USC. One faction was led by interim President Mahdi Mohamed and the other by Gen. Mohamed Farah Aidid, both members of the Hawiye clan. Mogadishu became a divided city. Gen. Aidid controlled most of the southern sector while Mahdi's stronghold was the Kaaraan district and other northern areas. There was more ammunition in Somalia than food and medicine (*Washington Times*, Jan 10, 1992; p. A7).

Like Liberia, Somalia's dictator (Siad Barre) had been ousted and in the process the country had been devastated—reduced to an ash heap of charred buildings and burned-out vehicles, with decomposing bodies littering the streets. Yet, "educated" barbarians waged a fierce battle to determine who should be president, totally unconcerned about the plight of their people. Said one frustrated official of UNICEF, Mr. Rupert Lewis, "These people are fighting over abandoned streets, shattered, looted buildings of no damn value. It's insane, it's mad and it probably won't stop" (*Washington Times*, Mar 2, 1992;

p. A9). Africa Watch affirmed that "the level of discipline among the troops [was] so low, the number of free guns so high and the need to loot for food so great that firefights [would] undoubtedly continue" (*Washington Times,* Mar 2, 1992; p. A9). Between November 1991 and March 1992 an estimated 41,000 had been killed. Most of the victims were civilians, half of them women and children.

When former Marxist dictator Mengistu Haile Mariam fled the country in May 1991, most Ethiopians thought the end of the long civil war would herald an era of peaceful development. But not for long:

A sharply escalating feud between Ethiopia's dominant political force and its main coalition partner has pushed this battle-fatigued country into the danger zone between war and peace.

Military skirmishes between the Ethiopian People's Revolutionary Democratic Front [which drove out Mengistu] and the Oromo Liberation Front, the main body that represents Ethiopia's largest ethnic group, have increased steadily. Hundreds and perhaps thousands have died in the fighting.

The hostilities between the Democratic Front and the Oromo Front have spread across much of the south and east and even into the western reaches of the country. A growing wave of armed banditry and inter-clan fighting have compounded the problem. Among the victims of the resurgent violence have been aid workers and peasants suffering from the ravages of 30 years of civil war (*The Washington Post,* Apr 4, 1992; p. A19).

Soon after independence in 1975, fighting broke out in Angola between UNITA and the MPLA, the two main anti-colonial forces, plunging the country into a 16-year civil war. Warfare also erupted between ZANU and ZAPU in Zimbabwe after independence in 1980. Feuding also broke out between Nkrumah and Danquah after Ghana's independence. And now between the ANC and Inkatha in South Africa. Said a Ghanaian, P. K. Boateng living in Umtata, Transkei (South Africa): "Not a day passes without someone being killed in the black townships. Whether the killing is done by rival black political organizations or by an unknown Third Force, we must remember that the root cause is intolerance . . . If democracy has any chance of survival in Africa, a cure must be found to intolerance. Else we are dead" (*New African,* May 1992; p. 7).

Violence breaks out not only among parties or organizations but within the organizations themselves. For Nigeria's transition to civilian rule, the military government has decreed the creation of two parties: the Social Democratic Party (SDP) and the National Republic Convention (NRC).

But warfare has broken out. One faction of the NRC has engaged another in physical battle at their Enugu-branch head office. Several persons were wounded and part of the edifice housing the NRC headquarters was damaged before the members of the invading rival group escaped in a car which they seized in the compound. Police later made some arrests.

Meanwhile three separate meetings of the SDP were broken up by violent protests. At one meeting in a plush hotel, a rival faction released noxious gas, which created such a stink that the meeting broke up in chaos. Then the local police issued a warning after two SDP officials narrowly escaped being shot on their way to work. Spoiling for a fight, they had been attacked by a rival faction, which opened fire but did not hit anyone. So they set fire to the two men's Toyota van instead . . .

In September, 1991, at least three NRC officials from Ogun state were killed in an inter-faction fight which started when they visited the national liaison office of the party (*New African*, Dec 1991; p. 20).

The level of intellectual and political maturity in many parties is deplorably low. For example, Prince Yormie Johnson claimed the presidency of Liberia because it was he who killed Samuel Doe. In Mozambique, Martin Bilal, president of the Liberal and Democratic Party of Mozambique (PALMO), "asserted that his own vice-president was an alcoholic" (*New African*, Nov 1991; p. 16). Such asinine infighting can only please the tyrant in power.

For a mere post, some opposition leaders have been eager to abandon the democratic struggle and join the despot. In this way, African tyrants, such as Mobutu Sese Seko and Robert Mugabe, coopted and neutralized the opposition. One example was Nguza Karl I Bond, a vocal critic of the corrupt Mobutu regime. In October 1981, he became the spokesperson for a coalition of three parties exiled in Belgium. But he later abandoned them to accept a post in Mobutu's cabinet. Another example was Joshua Nkomo. On December 22, 1987, he signed an agreement merging his ZAPU party with Robert Mugabe's ZANU and thereby paved the way for the establishment of a one-party state in Zimbabwe and a Mugabe dictatorship. Nkomo offered this fatuous defense:

"Let me say to you, what is continued here is a true feeling of both these political parties. The document may appear incomplete, but what is important is the spirit behind it" (*New African*, Feb 1988; p. 28).

The true "spirit" behind it was the reward: minister without portfolio in Mugabe's cabinet.

Opposition groups not only fight each other and claim innocent victims but also fight among themselves before, during, and after the ouster of a tyrant. There is one word which describes all this—idiocy. If we African "liberators" cannot get our acts together, then let the oppressors (the Bothas, the Rawlings, the Mois, the Bandas, and the Biyas) stay!

---

## NOTES

1. Had the nationalists adopted this strategy in their anti-colonial struggle, independence would probably have come to Africa sooner. The French, for example, had a small garrison stationed at Dakar, whence they quickly dispatched troops to suppress revolts across Francophone Africa. If there had been a *simultaneous* rebellion in *all* the colonies, the French would not have been able to deal with it.

# Chapter 13

## The Second Liberation of Africa

Democracy should not be a toy for the elite to play with. It should involve even the so-called "ignorant peasant." Because only when you involve the bulk of the people can you have a real check to central authority.

—Meles Zenawi, Interim president of Ethiopia (October 22, 1991).

By the beginning of the 1980s it was obvious that something had gone terribly awry in Africa. The continent was moving inexorably from one crisis to another. At a U.N. special session on Africa in May 1986, African leaders themselves admitted that consolidation of power was wrong and that misguided policies and economic mismanagement had played a significant role in precipitating Africa's economic crisis. They agreed to restructure their economies away from statism, and by 1990 more than half of the black African nations had signed a structural adjustment agreement with the World Bank and the IMF.

On the political front, the winds of change in Africa began to gather into a storm at the dawn of the 1990s. But, according to Nigerian scholar Claude Ake, it would be incorrect to characterize African demands for democratization as a by-product of the revolutionary changes in Eastern Europe:

The origins and aspirations of the democracy movements in Africa, as well as its form and content, have no connection with events in Eastern Europe. Far from mimicking these events, the democracy movement in Africa predates them. For nearly a century Africans have been struggling determinedly for democracy at much greater cost. But these struggles were not accorded international legitimacy. Not surprisingly. Because they were partly directed against the West which has been the bane of democracy in Africa by virtue of its role in slavery, colonialism, support of reactionary African regimes as Cold War allies and collusion in authoritarian development strategies. Thus, democratic struggles in

Africa were represented as ethnic conflicts, communal violence, anarchic tendencies, lack of consensus, extremist interest articulation, lawless political competition, systemic crisis and breakdowns.

What has changed is not what is happening in Africa but how the World perceives it. Africa's striving for democracy is now being recognized for what it is and what it has been all along. This change in perception was prompted by the changes in Eastern Europe. (*Africa Forum*, Vol.1, No.2, 1991; p. 13).

In his article, Claude Ake went on to provide a background to the democracy movement in Africa. He argued that most African regimes have been so alienated and so violently repressive that their citizens see "the state and its development agents as enemies to be evaded, cheated and defeated if possible, but never as partners." The leaders have been so engrossed in coping with the hostilities which their misrule and repression have unleashed that they are unable to take much interest in anything else, including the pursuit of development.

By 1990 it had become clear that the state was the *problem* and *not* the solution in Africa. A tribal chief in a rural farming community in Lesotho summed it up beautifully: "We have two problems: rats and the government" (*International Health and Development*, Mar-Apr 1989; p. 30). To solve Zaire's economic crisis, Amina Ramadou, a peasant housewife, suggested: "We send three sacks of angry bees to the governor and the president. And some ants which bite. Maybe they eat the government and solve our problems" (*The Wall Street Journal*, Sep 26, 1991; p. A14). The message is getting through. Citing "the credibility gap between the people and the leadership built up through years of mismanagement," Mr. Mohammed Boudiaf, the head of Algeria's High Executive Council (HEC), lamented: "A large segment of the population has, I am afraid, lost confidence in the capacity of the leadership to provide jobs, housing, health care and its ability to combat corruption" (*Financial Times*, Jun 17, 1992; p. 4).

Almost all African regimes have been characterized by an enormous concentration of both economic and political power in the hands of the state. Concentration of economic power creates several problems. It turns the state into a huge patronage machine and breeds cronyism. It fosters the erroneous belief that the state can solve all problems. The state cannot eradicate poverty, unemployment, and inflation; it can only lessen them. The economic controls and regulations instituted by the state breed corruption, as people offer bribes to circumvent them. Concentration of economic power in the hands of the state also encourages capital flight. Foreign exchange is controlled by the state and only top government officials have access. Finally, concentration of economic power transforms the state into a prize or plum, for which all sorts of individuals and groups compete. The winner subsequently uses the instruments of state power to advance the economic welfare of his group. In fact, virtually all of Africa's problems can be explained in terms of fierce competition among the elites for this power.

The state was captured by the white race in South Africa (apartheid); by Arabs in Mauritania and Sudan (Arab apartheid); by the Tutsi and Chewa minority tribes in Burundi and Malawi, respectively; by one political organization in Angola, Mozambique, Tanzania, and others (one-party state system); by socialists in Zambia (Swiss-bank socialism); by the military in Benin, Ghana, Togo, and others (stratocracy); by vampire elites in Cameroon, Kenya, Nigeria, and Zaire (kleptocracy).

Concentration of *political* power in the hands of the state also creates problems. It leads to abuse of power, denial of human rights, election fraud and drift toward one-person dictatorship. "Power corrupts and absolute power corrupts absolutely," as the cliché goes. Too much power in the hands of one individual leads to intolerance of dissent, brutal suppression of the opposition, and militarism. Enormous expenditures are made on the military to back up the political legitimacy of the government.

Those African politicians and elites who in the 1960s, heaped one power after another onto the head of state, never had the sense to arm themselves with mechanisms to take that power back should it be abused. There is one and only one solution to all this nonsense and that is to have a situation where nobody can capture and monopolize the powers of the state. That entails stripping the state of much of the power that it has been given. The less power vested in the state, the less its attraction. Politically, it means adopting a system with less power at the center, as in a confederation. Economically, it means *decentralization* (devolution of economic decisionmaking) liberalization toward a *market economy* so that private individuals can determine for themselves what to produce, how much, and where to sell it.

## THE FAILURE OF STRUCTURAL ADJUSTMENT
## AND REFORMS TO MAKE IT VIABLE

Intolerance, restrictions on the freedom and human rights of individuals and groups as well as overconcentration of power with attendant restrictions on popular participation in decisionmaking has constrained development on the continent.

—Economic Commission on Africa: The Khartoum Declaration on the Human Dimensions of Africa's Economic Recovery and Development, March 1988

> We affirm that nations cannot be built without the popular support and full participation of the people, nor can the economic crisis be resolved and the human and economic conditions improved without the full and effective contribution, creativity and popular enthusiasm of the vast majority of the people. After all, it is to the people that the very benefits of development should and must accrue. We are convinced that neither can Africa's perpetual economic crisis be overcome, nor can a bright future for Africa and its people see the light of day unless the structure, pattern and political context of the process of socio-economic development are appropriately altered.
>
> —African Charter for Popular Participation in Development Transformation, Arusha Declaration, February 1990.

The foreign aid donor community has been involved in Africa since the 1960s, and the focus was always on economic liberalization. But the earlier attempts at economic reform were generally unsuccessful because of stiff resistance from African leaders. However, following the emergence of the debt crisis and African leaders' own admissions of policy failures in 1986, a renewed effort at economic reform was made under the label "structural adjustment."

Typically, a structural adjustment agreement provides loans to a developing country to revamp its economy and reorient it toward greater reliance on markets and private-sector participation. Such programs entail selling unprofitable state enterprises, revamping the public sector to make it more efficient, reducing budget deficits, removing price controls, devaluing exchange rates, and generally dismantling the machinery of state intervention.

Where implemented, these reforms have achieved some spectacular results. In the latter part of the 1980s, Ghana, Guinea, Mali, Niger, Nigeria, Somalia, Tanzania, and Zaire eliminated price controls and allowed private traders greater market freedom. The peasants' initial response was a phenomenal increase in production. In 1987, for example, Tanzania reaped bumper harvests of corn, tea, coffee, and cotton. In fact, cotton production rose to 450,000 bales, double the output in 1986. But the shameful aspect of the economic reform process was that it was external institutions and agencies that told African leaders—who should know more about their own heritage—to sell off the state enterprises and to remove the price controls. These things did not exist in traditional Africa.

After years of economic decline, Ghana also registered a stellar 6.2 percent rate of Gross Domestic Product growth from 1986 to 1989 and by 1990 was considered by the World Bank as a role model for all of Africa. Unfortunately, the optimistic expectation for economic progress in Africa was premature. Both domestic and foreign investment in Africa sagged and the spectacular achievements became ephemeral. Overall, the experience with economic restructuring in black Africa was generally disappointing.

This has raised more doubts about the efficacy of structural adjustment in reversing the economic slide of black Africa. While it was overwhelmingly agreed that African economies needed restructuring, structural adjustment, as conceived and administered by the World Bank, was conceptually flawed for two reasons. First, it is illogical for a country that has truly discovered the magic of the free market to seek loans from governments. Western provision of credit, although well intentioned to encourage economic liberalization, instead reinforces the offensive notion of state hegemony in credit allocation. Furthermore, the supply of funds on a large scale to governments in Africa only strengthens the role of the state in the economy and undermines the trend toward a market economy and a vigorous private sector.

Second, in most cases in Africa structural adjustment amounts to reorganizing a bankrupt company and placing it, together with the massive infusion of new capital, in the hands of the same incompetent management that ruined it in the first place. A new management is imperative for a reorganized company. Even if these concerns were met, for structural adjustment to be successful in Africa several additional requirements would have to be satisfied. These include installing competent leadership, improving the development environment, improving the policy environment, achieving political reform, establishing fiscal austerity, and introducing freedom of expression, national debate, and consensus.

## Installing Competent Leadership

Competent leadership is vital for successful economic reform. African leaders cannot improve their countries' economic conditions without understanding how their economies run. Displaying such ignorance, many African leaders manage their economies by issuing decrees, orders, and threats. Others believe that making appeals, exhortations, and calls for sacrifice will produce efficient economies. These measures may work temporarily, but sooner or later civilians will ask why their sacrifices have not put food on their tables.

When an economic crisis emerges in Africa, the leadership usually fails to acknowledge that the problem may have internal as well as external causes. Rather, they insist that the causes are neocolonial and imperialist conspiracies. *The Economist* noted the consequences of the economic ignorance of Kenneth Kaunda and most of Africa's postcolonial leaders when it stated that "Mr. Kaunda has never known the first thing about economics. Nor did most of the whole generation of Africa's post-independence leaders. The consequences of their incompetence, together with the collapse of export prices and the aftermath of drought, put the arm-lock on their successors" (May 9, 1987, p. 13). Julius Nyerere, another African leader of Kaunda's generation, when asked to assess the economic situation in Africa and the options the continent had, replied: "The situation is a neocolonial one and African economies are not going to change until the neocolonial relationship is changed. It is not a question of debts. Debt is a symptom. It is the result. It is not the problem" (*West Africa*, Jun 6, 1988; p. 1034).

Nyerere's statement betrayed his lack of understanding of the origins of Africa's debt crisis. For 24 years, he adhered dogmatically to a socialist path that led Tanzania to economic ruin. Angola, Benin, the Congo, Mozambique, Tunisia, Zambia, and many other African countries suffered similar fates. Clearly the methodologies, rationalizations, and analyses of the first African postcolonial leaders have become obsolete. New ways of thinking and intellectual flexibility are urgently needed to tackle Africa's economic crisis.

To succeed in repairing Africa's economy the new leaders will require not only economic competence but the capacity to change course when things are obviously wrong, the readiness to accept suggestions and sound ideas, the willingness to examine alternative possibilities, and the disposition to face reality.

## Improving the Development Environment

Experts and African leaders assume that development takes place in a vacuum despite abundant evidence that the environment in black Africa has proven to be inimical to development. Africa's environment is characterized by infrastructural deterioration and political strife with its attendant violence. Noting that an environment conducive to production and efficiency has two parts—incentives and the physical infrastructure, the World Bank observed that most African countries have a neglected infrastructure that is chronic in some cases (World Bank, 1989; p. 5).

The World Bank also noted the negative effect of state violence and civil war on development in Africa: "Sometimes the military have deposed unpopular regimes. But often this has led to more, not less, state violence and lawlessness. Occasionally, it has led even to civil war . . . In southern Africa destabilizing policies have disrupted the development of South Africa's neighbors" (World Bank, 1989; p. 23).

Needless to say, private investment in black Africa has been dwindling. It dropped from a peak of $2.3 billion in 1982 to $500 million in 1986, and by 1987 some African countries were experiencing disinvestment. Foreign investors withdrew $50 million from Nigeria and $8 million from Ghana in 1987 (*World Development Report*, 1989; p. 206). Even Francophone Africa was not spared: "French direct investment in sub-Saharan Africa ran at $1 billion a year in 1981-83; by 1988, that had translated into a net outflow of more than $800 million" (*The Economist*, Jul 21, 1990; p. 82).

## Improving the Policy Environment

The policy environment in much of Africa is no better than the development environment. It is characterized by leaders' plundering state treasuries, haphazardly commissioning extravagant pet projects, establishing inappropriate priorities, and implementing dishonest economic reform. Fiscal accountability exists only in theory. As Claude Ake asserted, "Tyranny has eroded every vestige of accountability of rulers to the ruled, with the result that public policy is dissociated from social needs and from developmental relevance (*West Africa*, Mar 26-Apr 1, 1990; p. 491).

African governments, with the support of Western donors and institutions, restructure their bloated bureaucracies, not to scrap them but to save their regimes. As economic conditions improved, these governments would abandon restructuring and reinstate it only when a crisis reemerged. Such was the case in Sudan, Equatorial Guinea, Zaire, and Liberia. Even during restructuring, measures were often implemented perfunctorily, without the conviction, the commitment, or the dedication needed to carry them through. In many cases public confidence in the program was shattered by governmental dishonesty, insincerity, and incompetence. Governments preached one policy and practiced precisely the opposite. In Ghana, for example, the military government declared its willingness to allow private-sector participation in the economy after decades of socialist management and ruin. But its actions proved incongruous with its pronouncements. The government arbitrarily seized the commercial properties of burgeoning indigenous entrepreneurs without due process of law.[1]

Ghana also drew up an elaborate investment code to attract foreign investors with guarantees that their commercial properties would be safe. But it was an exercise in futility: "All categories of investment fell in 1988, including 100 percent Ghanaian owned, joint ventures and foreign equity projects. There was a fall in the number of new projects and in the number of capacity-increasing investments" (*West Africa*, Jan 7, 1990; p. 2165). Similar purported attempts to develop the private sector in Tanzania and Angola also suffered because the government was not sincere in its reform efforts.

These inconsistencies in policy reform doomed structural adjustments in many parts of black Africa and explain why the World Bank and the IMF had difficulty finding lasting success stories. In fact, the World Bank's own internal Report on Adjustment Lending II (*Policies for the Recovery of Growth - R90-51/IDA/R90-49, Mar 26, 1990*) concluded that "adjustment lending appeared to have been relatively less successful in the highly indebted countries and in sub-Saharan Africa" (p. 2).


## Establishing Fiscal Austerity

Structural adjustment often involves introducing measures to reduce government expenditures. The affected parties are primarily the elites—the military, civil servants, urban workers, and university students—who should recognize the need for the cutbacks and equally share the burden of adjustment. It would be grossly unfair, for example, to place the burden of adjustment on students and urban workers without imposing any cutbacks on the military. In addition, the program will fail if one group refuses to accept the austerity measures and shifts the burden to the rest of the population. Under these circumstances the other groups will attack the program and do all in their power to sabotage it. This is what happened in Africa.

In Ghana, for example, while students were asked to accept reduced allowances and civil servants were laid off, the military was spared and was actually expanded (*West Africa*, Jun 6, 1988; p. 1046). The military governments of Cameroon and Nigeria also grew while the rest of the population was asked to accept austerity measures. It was blatantly unjust to impose austerity on the people of Africa while the military rapaciously devoured scarce resources during an economic crisis. According to Whitaker, "The proportion of African funds going to equip and pay the military has been steadily rising, for example, over 40 percent in Ethiopia, and 25 and 20 percent respectively in drought-ravaged Mauritania and Mali" (Whitaker, 1988; p. 43).

Donor governments and multilateral lending institutions must take a hard look at how much African governments spend on the military. It makes little sense to support an economic recovery program that allocates more and more resources to the military. These expenditures need to be open to public scrutiny. Perhaps donor countries might consider refusing aid to any African country that spends more than 10 percent of its budget on the military. Mercifully, Japan has moved in this direction: "Japan, the world's largest foreign aid donor, will base future aid decisions partly on whether it thinks a potential recipient spends too much on its military" (*Washington Times*, Apr 11, 1991; p. A2).

The next group of African elites—the bureaucrats—has done much to thwart economic restructuring. Perhaps because the military has been unwilling to accept austerity measures, the bureaucrats saw no reason why they should bear the brunt of structural adjustment. Why should civil servants reduce the size of the public sector by privatizing state-owned enterprises and eliminating their own jobs? Rather, they embezzled and squandered government money.

Considerable evidence exists of sabotage and deliberate negligence in implementing reform in Africa. For example, the head of state of Ghana, Flight Lt. Jerry Rawlings, lamented that "expectations of substantial improvement in living conditions have not been fully realized because of the failure to put government programmes into action" (*West Africa*, Jul 11, 1988; p. 1276). In addition, President Lansana Conte of Guinea admitted that "generalized corruption, incessant embezzlement, laxity in implementing budget estimates and malfunctioning of our administrative system have created a situation that has finally paralysed all the recovery programs that have been launched" (*West Africa*, Oct 17-23, 1988; p. 1974).

The only way for structural adjustment to succeed in Africa is to have all the groups participate in the decisionmaking process and reach a consensus on the need for and the type of sacrifice to be made. Then all groups must equally share the burden. This is not possible in Africa because freedom of expression and national debates and consensus-building at the national level do not exist. Hence, structural adjustment is doomed. More perniciously, attempted adjustments have impeded democratic reform and have helped perpetuate dictatorships in black Africa.

Note that in all this discussion of reform, the peasant majority has not been mentioned. African peasants have little or no access to government subsidies and largesse. In addition, they have no voice, no representation in government, and no protection from the police. Since independence, many parties have spoken on behalf of these peasants but little has actually been done for them.

Because structural adjustment merely seeks to rationalize the public sector and to remove a balance of payment disequilibrium, it does not affect the institutional framework the elites have established to oppress the productive class—the peasants. For example, the IMF measures do not address the basic question of economic and political liberties for peasants to go about their activities. Although the government can remove price controls so that peasants can receive higher prices for their products, these measures are meaningless when harassment, brutality, and the denial of basic freedom destroy the incentive to produce. True reform requires dismantling the alien state control apparatus that the elites have erected for their own benefit. The elites, not the peasants, purchase commodities at lower, government-subsidized prices and have access to foreign exchange and Swiss bank accounts. But the peasants' sweat and toil earn the foreign exchange.

## Achieving Political Reform

The contention that we need to have a sound economic base before the restoration of political pluralism only betrays the undemocratic character of those who push it. Perhaps they imagine that politics can be separated from economics and that the people can be excluded from the choice of economic arrangements that will facilitate the establishment of the solid base.

—Movement for Freedom and Justice in Ghana, August 1, 1990

Until the beginning of the 1990s the donor community did not push for political reform in Africa for a variety of reasons. The obvious one was diplomatic: there was a risk of being charged with meddling in the internal affairs of sovereign African nations. The cold war provided another cover: the need to support ideological allies in Africa. Furthermore, many development experts disputed the connection between democracy and development. Pointing to Chile, South Korea, Taiwan, and the other "Asian Tigers," they argued that successful development can occur under authoritarian regimes. Unfortunately, these countries' experiences have been the exceptions, as more than 120 developing countries with authoritarian regimes have attempted economic reform and most have failed.[2]

Since political culture influences the successful outcome of structural adjustment, economic reform alone is insufficient. Events in Yugoslavia, the former Soviet Union, and elsewhere have demonstrated that, without better governance and a viable political structure in place, economic reform is an exercise in futility.

In Africa, no authoritarian regime has been able to generate lasting economic prosperity. Cameroon, Gabon, the Ivory Coast, Malawi, Morocco, Kenya, and Togoland at one time or another used to be called "African economic success stories." But by the early 1990s, "their economic prospects had faded under institutionalized looting and stiff official resistance to democratic reform" (*The Wall Street Journal*, Oct 18, 1991; p. A13). In Liberia and Somalia, the gains achieved by economic reform under authoritarian regimes were wiped out in revolutionary convulsions. Their ex-leaders' bull-headed refusal to yield to popular demands for democratic reform was to blame.

In the 1980s more and more Africans, including even a few African leaders, began emphasizing democracy in the development process. Claude Ake argued that "the democracy movement sees the economic regression as the other side of political regression. It recognizes that the cause of development is better served by a democratic approach which engages the energy and commitment of the people, who alone can make development sustainable" (*Africa Forum*, Vol.1, No. 2, 1991; p. 14).

Africans themselves increasingly came to the realization that Western aid to support economic reform was not helping them. In fact, in many cases it actually retarded the process of democratization in Africa. As *Africa Report* noted:

> The analysis of the IMF and the World Bank that the Sudanese economy has been mismanaged fundamentally misreads what the "state" really is in Sudan. State policies do not represent the general interest of the Sudanese people, but the interests of a few social groups: the military, wealthy merchants and land-owners, Islamic banks and high-level bureaucrats . . .
>
> With its almost exclusive emphasis on the east-central region of Sudan, World Bank lending has also reinforced the country's uneven pattern of resource distribution (Sep-Oct 1990; p. 61).

During the late Samuel Doe's brutal reign in Liberia (1980-1990), Patrick Sayon, former Vice-President of the University of Liberia, begged the U.S. government to stop sending aid to Doe's regime. He said that "this money enabled Doe to oppress, suppress and repress the people so that they are denied their fundamental rights" (*West Africa*, Apr 16-22, 1990; p. 613). The United States did not listen.

Maina wa Kinyatti, an exiled former MP, added his voice: "I see the aid which is given to Moi as a weapon to fight the people of Kenya. So the aid should be tied to the human rights situation in the country since Congress has the power to push Moi in this direction as well as to ensure that he respects our national constitution which gives our people freedom of speech and freedom of movement" (*Africa Report*, Jul-Aug 1989; p. 58).

Stephen Duah, a Ghanaian, was particularly irate: "If Western governments and the IMF would stop giving loans to dictators in the Third World, they would not be able to survive to terrorise their nations, let alone extend their acts into the international arena" (*New African*, Nov 1988; p. 47).

Emile Zinzou, the civilian president of Benin from May 1968 to December 1969, was also adamant about the need to end foreign aid to his country:

"Kerekou has fooled everyone particularly in the West. . .What would help us is for the international creditors to stop helping him. By continuing to give assistance, the U.S. and other Western powers are inevitably helping Kerekou to remain in power" (*New African*, Nov 1989; p. 18).

An indignant Baffour Ankomah, a Ghanaian columnist, wrote in *New African*, "It is no good for the West to insist on democracy before doing business with Eastern Europe, while supporting dictatorships in Africa. That is hypocrisy of the first order!" (Jun 1990; p. 26). General Olusegun Obasanjo, former head of state of Nigeria, added: "The Western nations themselves, which are applauding tentative democratic beginnings in some countries and demanding democracy for all countries in Africa, have themselves all too frequently used financial aid to shore up the power of the worst African despots for reasons of political and economic expediency" (cited in *Frankfurter Allgemeine*, May 19, 1990; p. 2).

Even Flight Lt. Jerry Rawlings, Ghana's head of state (who was described by U.S. Assistant Secretary of State for African Affairs Herman Cohen as "allergic to democracy") agreed that political reform should precede economic restructuring: "There can be no economic development in an undemocratic atmosphere" (*West Africa*, May 28-Jun 3, 1990; p. 913). Similarly, President Yoweri Museveni of Uganda, in a speech before the OAU in Addis Ababa, observed: "There is no way you can develop the economy without democracy" (*New York Times*, Jul 10, 1990; p. A3). On August 1, 1990, the Movement for Freedom and Justice in Ghana asserted, "To ask for the solution of economic problems before the restoration of multiparty democracy is in our view tantamount to putting the cart before the horse."

Finally, after the "revolution" in Eastern Europe, the donor community began to act and pay more attention to democratic reform. As *The Economist* put it: "Aid donors were embarrassed to be seen backing freedom in Eastern Europe, while hobnobbing with dictators in Africa . . . So the donors, already 'totally fed up' with Africa's performance, according to a senior aid official, changed their tune" (Feb 22, 1992; p. 20).

Accordingly, both the World Bank and the United Nations began stressing the importance of democratic institutions to secure political renewal and human development (World Bank, 1989; p. 6; *Human Development Report*, May 1990). At a conference on "The Prospects for Africa in the 1990s" held in the British House of Commons on June 9, 1990, British Secretary of State for Foreign and Commonwealth Affairs Douglas Hurd asserted the need for political pluralism to achieve economic success: "Economic success depends to a large degree on effective and honest government, political pluralism and observance of the rule of law, as well as freer, more open economies." He called on aid donors to direct their support to countries "tending toward pluralism, public accountability, respect for the rule of law, human rights, and market principles" (*The Times* [London], Jun 7, 1990). In addition, *New African* reported that John Major, as Britain's chancellor of the exchequer, warned the African nations in a speech delivered to the IMF that they would have to make "sweeping political and social changes," including cutting military spending and moving to democratic political systems, to qualify for international aid (Jul 1990; p. 31).

Indeed, Malawi saw its aid from Britain halved to $8.6 million in 1992 and in that same year the United States suspended aid to Sese Seko of Zaire. In November 1991 the World Bank and other donors withheld aid to Kenya for six months until it instituted steps toward democratic reform.

Unfortunately, selective and inconsistent application of "political conditionality" diminished its effectiveness. "While international aid donors have made demands for political reform in Kenya a condition for aid, assistance to [neighboring] Tanzania [a one-party socialist state] has actually increased since 1986, as donors sought to show support for the economic reform program" (*The Washington Post*, Mar 24, 1992; p. A14).

In Francophone Africa, pro-democracy demonstrators were irate:

[In March 1992], protesters in Niger burned the French flag in the streets of Niamey, denouncing France's 'desertion' of the reformist government of Amadou Cheffou, the prime minister, in the face of what happened to be an attempted coup. But at the same time, France was sending 150 paratroops to the assistance of Chad's Colonel Idriss Derby.

The events are part of a larger pattern of muddle. In Feb 1990, President Felix Houphouet-Boigny of Côte d'Ivoire asked France for help when he thought [pro-democracy] demonstrators were about to overthrow his government. France refused. In December 1991, Togo's reformist prime minister, Joseph Kokou Koffigoh, requested French assistance after troops loyal to the dictatorial president, General Gnassingbe Eyadema, stormed his residence. France refused again, half-heartedly dispatching some troops to neighboring Benin instead. But, in May 1991, 9 million rounds of ammunition arrived in Cameroon on a ship from France, destined for the authoritarian government of President Paul Biya. Inconsistency on the ground reflects indecision in Paris (*The Economist*, Mar 7, 1992; p. 46).

## POLITICAL REFORM

We should not practice dictatorship under the guise of independence, because independence does not mean dictatorship. Without democracy, there can be no development. Democracy is the sine qua non for the effective administration of a modern state.

—Yoweri Museveni, president of Uganda, July 1990

The claim that the multiparty system is an imposition on African countries by the Western powers is to say the least ridiculous, having regard to the fact that the history of Ghana even in the colonial era is the history of struggles for basic freedoms and multiparty democracy.

—Professor Adu Boahen, chairman of the Movement for Freedom and Justice,
August 1990

During the 1980s not one of Africa's military and one-party dictatorships was democratized to permit political pluralism and freedom of expression and association. While a few African countries attempted political renewal, the results were negligible. For example, in Equatorial Guinea's first national elections since independence, which were held to familiarize the population with the electoral procedure and to start the process of democratization, the only candidate was President Obiang Mbasogo, who had been in power since 1979. He asserted that political opponents were kept in exile because "[p]olitical pluralism would send convulsions through the population" (*West Africa*, Jul 24-30, 1989; p. 1230). As we have already seen, Kenya, Ghana, Nigeria, Algeria, Tunisia, and Tanzania also had essentially one-party elections.

If Pretoria had declared South Africa a one-party state and insisted that blacks vote by queuing behind portraits of candidates (as in Kenya), or had decreed that only two black political parties—of its own choice and manufacture (as in Nigeria)—would be allowed to exist in the postapartheid era, or had insinuated that blacks were not yet ready to choose their president in national elections (as in Ghana), or that blacks must be educated and must pass two examinations to demonstrate their knowledge of how South Africa is governed before holding public offices, the governments of Ghana, Kenya, Nigeria, Tanzania, and Zambia would have vehemently denounced these measures as racist arrogance and palpable effronteries to black Africans. But if a Kenyan or Ghanaian had challenged these purportedly democratic practices in his own country, he would have been rewarded with a jail term or a death sentence.

Black African leaders reacted to the release of Nelson Mandela with euphoria. But those African leaders cheering the most wildly were the tyrants who have ruined Africa, slaughtered its people, looted its wealth, and imprisoned thousands. Where is the freedom for which Africans fought?

The reaction of African leaders to the upheaval in Eastern Europe is of particular interest because after independence many African states adopted the former East European model of one-party states, life-presidents, state controls, state enterprises, and the denial of freedom of expression. The initial reaction of most African leaders to the events in Eastern Europe was an exercise in self-delusion: they pretended that nothing had happened. Indeed, the state-controlled press in Africa gave the events in Eastern Europe little coverage. Mobutu said, "Zaire has no need for *perestroika*. Its one-party state system is the most elaborate form of democracy" (*South*, Nov 1989; p. 7). Rawlings of Ghana said that he hoped "reforms in the East will be reciprocated by similar changes in the West." The state-owned *Ghanaian Times* in a two-part editorial condemned the changes in Romania and elsewhere as the "work of imperialism." Presidents dos Santos of Angola, Gaddafi of Libya, Kaunda of Zambia, Mengistu of Ethiopia, Moi of Kenya, Nyerere of Tanzania, and many other leaders obstinately refused to consider the possibility of multiple parties. Events in Eastern Europe or the West had no relevance whatsoever to Africa, according to them. In August 1991 President Moi proclaimed in a speech that Kenya was "at least 200 years behind the West and therefore Kenyans should not expect to see multi-party democracy or fully guaranteed rights such as the West enjoys until a similar period has elapsed" (*The Washington Post*, Sep 9, 1991; p. A20). "The Party System Aborts Democracy" said Gaddafi's Green Book.

Africans no longer accept these inane justifications for a one-party state. Even Zambia's minister of state agreed that the one-party system did not benefit the people: "The one-party state has been turned into an employment exchange for loyal party cadres, instead of remaining a dynamic political system for the welfare of the people" (*The African Letter*, Apr 16-30, 1990; p. 10).

Naturally, those in power and in prominent positions in the ruling party despise any talk of political pluralism or power-sharing. They prefer a continuation of the present one-party state system as they benefit immensely from it. The gulf between these leaders and their people could hardly be wider. Despite counsel from hordes of diplomats, foreigners, Africans, intellectuals, and chiefs, these leaders stubbornly cling to power—at their own peril. In the Ivory Coast, "Professor Laurent Gbagbo predicted 'death' for the President, members of his PDCI, some ministers and his family—saying 'what happened in Romania will automatically take place here.' He called on Ivorians to always come out to the streets and express their national feelings on Houphouet-Boigny's dictatorial policies" (*New African*, Jul 1990; p. 19). When popular demonstrations and strikes erupted in 1990 to demand multiple parties and the resignations of heads of state, African dictators met the protesters with tear gas, stun grenades, arrests, kidnappings (Benin, Ivory Coast, Senegal, and Zaire), bullets (Niger, where more than 11 were killed), and curfews (Gabon). Others promised new constitutions and renamed the ruling one-party state (Burkina Faso). Nevertheless the people of Africa, especially in Francophone Africa, are continuing to vent their rage at single-party governments—whether they are civilian, military, civilianized, socialist, or capitalist—for failed economic development, gross official corruption, neglect of agriculture, and rampant human rights violations. In Senegal, school students demonstrated against shortages of school furniture and laboratory equipment in 1990. Subsequently the opposition called for the removal of President Abdou Diouf and the holding of free elections. In Guinea, school teachers, once the vanguard of the radical revolutionary movement "Marxism in African Clothes," went on strike to demand more pay. In the Ivory Coast workers and students demonstrated against the government's demands for austerity while doing nothing to control the corrupt ruling elite. In Niger students protested austerity measures that reduced scholarships and other subsidies for university education. In Togoland protesters denounced the authoritarian, one-party government of President Gnassingbe Eyadema and demanded multiparty democracy.

In Ghana the Bar Association passed a 10-point resolution that challenged the Rawlings government's claim to going democratic and refuted the alleged popularity of the district assembly concept as an answer to Ghana's perennial search for genuine democracy. In addition, the Movement for Freedom and Justice, in an August 30, 1990, press release, asserted: "We are deeply convinced that only a political system that guarantees the fundamental human rights and political liberties of the people, that enables people of like-minded views freely to associate and form political parties to contest office, and in which the people elect their own leaders through free and fair elections can be considered truly democratic. That is what the multiparty system is all about."

Africans have made it clear that they will no longer tolerate one-party state systems, military dictatorships and life-presidents. Throughout 1990 and 1991, Africans, including peasants—in Cameroon, Mali, Niger, Togoland and other African countries, some were women with babies on their backs—braved bullets and demonstrated to demand democratic pluralism while academics argued furiously about whether democracy was essential to development. Not to be outdone, economists—my own profession—adamantly refused to acknowledge that all other things have *not* been constant since 1960 and therefore supplying more foreign aid to Africa would not accelerate development. Corruption, chaos, instability, tyranny, and senseless civil wars have produced an environment inimical to development. Angola, Ethiopia, Liberia, Mozambique, Somalia, and Sudan, to name only a few, are now in total economic ruins.

But it is also important to note that the democratization of Africa that began in the 1990s has all been elite-managed and controlled. The peasants have not been allowed to have much input. For far too long they have been the victims or guinea pigs in experiments with foreign systems conducted by the elites. It is time for the peasants to have a voice in the management of their own affairs, control over their own destinies, and the means to protect their own culture and heritage.

Recall the concentration of both economic and political power in the hands of the state, which in all African countries is controlled by the elites. Ultimately, true reform in Africa requires peasant empowerment— enfranchising the peasant majority to overthrow the tyranny of the elite minority that has monopolized not only power but also the channels of free expression. Without this empowerment the injustices against the peasants will continue, even under structural adjustment. For structural adjustment merely adjusts, it does not eliminate, the burdens of exploitation. Just as Africa overthrew the yoke of colonial oppression and exploitation, so too it will overthrow elite oppression and exploitation of the peasants.

That is when true reform and revolution will begin.

## INTELLECTUAL REFORM

Reforming a tyrannical state-controlled system requires measures in three distinct areas: economic, political, and intellectual. Intellectual reform has received scant attention, but it is the most critical and should supersede all. The events in Eastern Europe were caused by freedom of expression and thought. As people found that they could express their ideas and viewpoints freely, they began to demand change and a new system. The demands came from within. They were not dictated by American imperialists, the IMF, or the World Bank. With *glasnost,* Africans will make their own case for political reform, just as the Romanians and the Bulgarians did.

Ideally, the sequence of reform should run from the intellectual to the political before economic reform is undertaken. Only intellectual freedom can establish the free marketplace of ideas from which political and economic reform can be crafted. One Romanian, Dinu Buhaina, asserted: "We didn't start a revolution for more pork—we did it for freedom. We have waited 24 years under Ceausescu. If the economic revolution takes a little longer, well, I think we can wait" (*The Wall Street Journal*, Feb 12, 1990; p. A9). Indeed, unless political ideologies and systems are reformed to permit decentralized decision making processes, economic restructuring is not likely to be successful.

In Africa the greatest impediment to a broad reform program is intellectual repression; there is no freedom of expression in Africa. Criticism of government policies is not tolerated. The news media are controlled and owned by the state, one political party, or one individual. Newsprint into much of Africa is regulated by import licensing. A private newspaper or magazine that does not toe the government line is either denied an import license for newsprint or banned.

The print media are particularly important in the democratization process. They expose human rights abuses, corruption, repression, economic mismanagement, and a host of other evils associated with dictatorship. The print media also afford forums for publishing and exchanging ideas and solutions to problems. Obviously, Africa needs an information revolution to break the government monopoly over the media.

In Ghana the Committees for the Defense of the Revolution (CDRs), which had initially surveilled, brutalized, jailed, or killed dissidents, finally called on authorities to tolerate diverse opinions so that the people could take part in the decisionmaking process. According to *West Africa*, the "Secretary for CDRs, Mr. W. H. Yeboah . . . said democracy thrives on respect and recognition of the worth of each member of society" (May 28-Jun 3, 1990; p. 913).

All educated Africans, regardless of their ideological stripe, must demand the reinstitution of their native freedom of expression. In fact many Africans are demanding precisely this. At a press conference in Accra in July 1990, Secretary-General of the All African Students Union K. Kianikazowa called on African governments to " ' give a fair hearing to students' demands and respect academic freedom in general.' [Kianikazowa] urged that students should not be seen as antigovernment elements but rather be seen as a force than can contribute significantly to social progress" (*West Africa*, Jul 9-15, 1990; p. 2076). During that month the Catholic Bishops of Ghana endorsed eschewing "everything that operates as a constraint on the free exercise of speech" so that the people can "feel that their views are needed in the gigantic effort of nation building and that it is safe to be forthcoming with them" (*West Africa*, Jul 16-22, 1990; p. 2124). In South Africa, by contrast, after recent reform measures there is greater freedom:

> Today, the people of Soweto can call for toppling the government with little fear of persecution. They chant "Viva Mandela! Viva ANC!" and they are not arrested. The brave few who once defied authorities by wearing the black, green and gold colors of the ANC now have been joined by many. T-shirts with Mr. Mandela's picture on them are everywhere. Nearly everyone who spoke to this reporter in 1986 requested anonymity; this time, no one did.
>
> A new openness exists among South African blacks. Brian Sokutu, the Port Elizabeth correspondent for the *New Nation*, was among many black journalists jailed without trial, even without charges filed against them. His newspaper was shut down temporarily. He recalls having to conceal liberation literature, which he dared not keep at home. "I would have to go at night and fetch it," he says. "But after the unbanning, now people can just put their literature on top of their desk and read it anywhere," he says. "It's quite exciting" (*Wall Street Journal*, Apr 4, 1990; p. 1).

In how many black-ruled African countries can people demonstrate and speak freely without having soldiers fire bullets at them? And where in independent Africa is a journalist free to write and read literature of his choice? Indeed, the military government of Ghana abruptly cancelled the sixth Biennial Conference of the African Bar Association, scheduled to be held in Accra from September 17 to 22, 1989, because "the hosting of the conference was an elaborate plot by the leadership of the Ghana Bar Association to launch 'a destabilization campaign of economic sabotage, social turmoil and violence.' " (*West Africa*, Sep 25-Oct 1, 1989; p. 1617). The theme of the conference was to have been "Human Rights in Africa."

African leaders often allege the existence of destabilizing plots and assert the need for stability. They often fail to realize that they themselves create the very conditions for instability. Although conflicts arise in any sphere of development—economic, political, cultural, or religious—there are ways of resolving these conflicts.

Dialogue is the first and most fundamental step in conflict resolution. After a successful dialogue, the next step is negotiation. If negotiation breaks down, confrontation (strikes or demonstrations) is the next step. If that fails, open conflict, hostility, or even war results. Barbarians resort to the use of clubs or military force without first engaging in dialogue and negotiation. But as we noted in Chapter 10, there can be no dialogue or negotiation without a forum and freedom of expression. Nor is this possible when those with whom there is to be a dialogue are in jail.

If the channels or means of dialogue are blocked, the inevitable result will be confrontation and armed conflict. Indeed, there are demonstrations, strikes, and civil wars throughout Africa. Clearly, African leaders cannot complain about instability or destabilization when they persistently refuse to establish the process of dialogue and negotiation and to guarantee freedom of expression.

Recall that in the indigenous system any peasant with a grievance against even a chief could see a councilor and receive a fair hearing. When a conflict between two families erupted, the elders would meet for a dialogue and negotiate a settlement. Disputes between individuals could be taken to courts and adjudicated fairly—from the family court to the chief's court and ultimately to the king's court of final appeal.

But modern Africa has no such processes of arbitration and conflict resolution. Instead, "educated" leaders offer kangaroo courts, military tribunals, arbitrary arrests, summary executions, government monopoly of the media, and the denial of freedom of expression. Asha Mnzavas of Dar es Salaam, Tanzania, identified the problem: "We need more democracy for our mass media where people could voice their feelings more freely and question the ill-doings of party leaders, not the current newspapers that are always full of party propaganda" (*New African,* Jun 1990; p. 4).

Africans who criticize the government or complain about food shortages risk imprisonment. Recall that in 1990 the Rev. Lawford Ndege Imunde of Nairobi's Presbyterian Church of East Africa was arrested, held incommunicado for 10 days, charged with printing and being in possession of a seditious publication (his personal diary, which contained words offensive to President Moi) and jailed for six years (*New African,* Jun 1990; p. 21).

Everyone who wishes to see Africa's economic recovery should denounce this type of senseless barbarism. Flight Lt. Rawlings of Ghana observed that development cannot take place in an undemocratic atmosphere. Neither can it take place in an atmosphere of intimidation and a culture of silence. Africans cannot find solutions to their problems when people are arrested for entries in their diaries and conferences are stopped by the military.

The importance of intellectual freedom in the sequence of reform became apparent in Sierra Leone:

> The first open signal was fired by a lecturer and students of the Makeni Teachers College with leaflets circulated at Makeni town on the multiparty system. Security officials moved in and those involved were questioned by the Makeni

police. Thereafter, numerous articles and editorials on the multiparty system appeared in most of the independent weeklies.

The Freetown-based tabloid, *New Shaft*, went to the extent of publishing a form asking all those interested in multipartyism to fill it in and send it back to the paper for forwarding to the State House. The paper claims it received 25,000 responses from a wide range of people—teachers, labourers, lawyers, students and members of parliament (*West Africa*, Jun 4-10, 1990; p. 935).

Exactly one year later President Momoh accepted a draft multiparty constitution and announced a timetable for the reintroduction of a multiparty system (*West Africa*, Jun 3-9, 1991; p. 917). The importance of freedom of expression cannot be overemphasized.

To be fair, Cameroon made efforts to introduce openness and transparency in official affairs. Ministers were to be subject to tough questioning by the press. Information Minister Henri Bandolo was chosen to kick off the new era of ministerial press conferences. Over a period of three months three other government ministers appeared on television to answer questions from journalists. But each performance was an exercise in deception. *New African* reported that the questions were harvested a week or two before the program, the embarrassing questions were eliminated, and written responses were prepared by the ministers' staffs and read at the time the program was filmed. "The tame questions and evasive answers read from prepared notes have exposed the parody of the whole arrangement even to the most illiterate peasants" (Jul 1990; p. 22). This is a disgrace.

## Building on the Indigenous Systems

The solutions to Africa's numerous problems lie in Africa itself—in its own backyard, not in the corridors of the World Bank or the inner sanctum of the Cuban presidium. Africa's backyard is its own indigenous institutions and systems. And its salvation lies in returning to these roots and building upon its indigenous traditions of participatory democracy and free village markets. Africa had a system of government based upon consensus that by its very definition precluded despotism. No one was barred from the decisionmaking process. No African chief declared his village to be a one-party state. Nor were the African people ruled by soldiers. But none of the modern leadership built upon Africa's own indigenous institutions, except in Botswana where it paid off handsomely, according to *Newsweek*: "Botswana built a working democracy on an aboriginal tradition of local gatherings called *kgotlas* that resemble New England town meetings; it has a record $2.7 billion in foreign reserves" (Jul 23, 1990; p. 28).

As one African scholar, John Mensah Sarbah (1864-1910), stated: "For any reform to be permanent and enduring, it must be based on and rooted in the principle of the aboriginal institutions" (cited in Langley, 1979; p. 98). The challenge for African elites and nationalists after independence was to build upon the aboriginal institutions and lead the continent on the road to development under indigenous impetus. But the elites and nationalists failed miserably. They denigrated the indigenous institutions and in fact attempted to destroy them. In an article entitled "Give Us Back Our Own Democracy," His Majesty King Moshoeshoe of Lesotho wrote: "The continuing African struggle for independence from foreign domination is a liberation struggle for the right to determine a culturally derived political and economic ideology capable of delivering African economic and political development. Without such an ideology, which we failed to define at the time of our original independence [in the 1960s], there can be no progress towards recognisable development for the African majorities" (*Index on Censorship*, Apr 1992; p. 10).

More and more Africans are now calling for a return to Africa's own indigenous roots. Professor Ali Mazrui, State University of New York at Binghampton, wrote: "The continent has much in its indigenous past to form the foundation of its democratic future" (*Index on Censorship*, Apr 1992; p. 9). According to Kwame Fred-Mensah, a Ghanaian doctoral candidate at School of Advanced International Studies (SAIS), John Hopkins University in Washington, "There is a growing consensus among some African and Africanist writers, development experts, and the donor community that indigenous institutions, values, and practices are the motor of grassroots participatory development strategies. Consequently, there is a growing call for not only the utilization of indigenous institutions, but also for their rationalization and formalization" (*SAIS Newsletter*, May 1992). Baffour-Ankomah, a columnist for *New African*, also suggested: "We must take a hard look at the way our societies were run by our fathers long before Europeans arrived on the African continent, and see whether we can borrow ideas from them" (May 1992; p. 16).

Building upon the indigenous has many merits.[3] First, it is part and parcel of African culture. Second, a building with no foundations will collapse in a short time. Many development projects and schemes set up across Africa using massive amounts of foreign aid, crumbled with unbelievable speed because they were not rooted in the traditional culture. As we have seen, even the World Bank now admits that more than half of its completed agricultural projects in Africa have failed. Development experts now admit that the approach of infusing foreign funds into Africa instead of building on its foundations was a mistake. A "bottoms-up" approach is now deemed superior. But one cannot start from the bottom without knowing what is there in the first place. What is at the bottom are the peasants and their indigenous institutions. The third and most important reason why building on the indigenous has merit is that many African peasants still go about their activities according to centuries-old traditions. One cannot hope to elicit sacrifices and increased output from these peasants without understanding their institutions, practices, attitudes, and motivations. See Ayittey (1991) for an extensive discussion of the peasants' economic, political, social, and legal institutions.

Exactly how these indigenous institutions are to be improved to assure participatory democracy is for the African people in each country to determine. But freedom of expression is imperative. A Yoruba proverb states: "Only the organism knows what is best for itself." In the same vein, only the African people know what is best for themselves; not what a military despot waving a bazooka dictates.

## HOW AN AFRICAN NATION SHOULD BE GOVERNED

There have been heated debates about political pluralism: one-party versus multiparty or no party. But the emotional debate about "multiparty versus no party" is irrelevant to the political needs of Africa. One-party states have failed miserably in Eastern Europe, where they originated and in such African countries as Benin, Cameroon, the Central African Republic, Congo, Gabon, Kenya, Mali, Tanzania, Zaire, Zambia, and even Ghana during the Nkrumah regime. Therefore, the one-party state *cannot* be a viable option. Neither is the "no-party" option. It is a euphemism for military rule, since the military is the only apolitical, non-party institution.

Great care, however, needs to be exercised in prescribing political systems. Just because the one-party state system has failed in Eastern Europe and Africa does not mean we should jump wholeheartedly on the Western multiparty bandwagon. It is not the number of political parties (or the absence thereof) which determines whether a political system is democratic or not.

A de facto one-party state system can exist where a large number of small, religiously and tribally-based parties are too weak to challenge the dominant party's lock on power, as in Egypt, The Gambia and Senegal in 1990. The fact that the United States has only two parties does not mean Nigeria must have exactly two parties to assure democracy.

The right to political opposition or to form parties is only one facet of a democratic system. Among others that are also required:

- A constitution with checks and balances, *freely* negotiated and adopted, *not* under duress or barrel of a gun.
- A secular, non-ideological, non-racialist, and non-tribalistic state.
- Separation of powers between the executive, the legislative and the judiciary.
- The rule of law.
- A Bill of Rights.
- Press and academic freedom.
- Independent trade unions.
- A neutral, professional army.
- Right of habeas corpus.
- Popular, non-exclusive participation in political affairs, through elections and comments or criticisms of government policies.

Any political system which lacks these institutions will become tyrannical, regardless of the number of political parties it has. Africa should not copy either from the East or the West but should develop its own constitution or political system based upon its unique culture, history, and experience.

Before a constitution is drafted there has to be a consensus on the conception or nature of the state— is it going to be a federal, confederal, or unitary (centralized) state? Obviously it would be ludicrous to draft a constitution for the government of a unitary state when a federal state has been envisioned. As we saw in Chapter 3, most indigenous African governments were based on *confederations*. The Ashanti kingdom was a loose confederation. The Ga kingdom was a confederation of six republics. Great Zimbabwe was a confederation also; not a one-party Marxist-Leninist state. A confederation is a political association in which the constituent provinces or units retain a great deal of autonomy and power relative to the center. A federation is a similar organization but the center has slightly greater powers than the constituent parts. In a unitary state, of course, all powers reside at the center.

The confederate type is the one which is rooted in indigenous African political culture. It guarantees a greater amount of autonomy than under the other types. It was this autonomy that allowed the various tribes to cultivate and maintain their own distinct identities. Cultural diversity is the hallmark of indigenous Africa. This diversity would not have been possible in a unitary system. In fact, African natives would have rebelled against unitary states because the love of freedom has always been the ruling passion among them.

But the elites thought differently. After independence they envisioned a strong, unitary state with all powers concentrated at the center. They looked at Britain, France, and the United States and saw powerful states with one language and dreamed of transforming Africa's motley of ethnicity into something similar. That was the wrong way of looking at it as it meant going against the grain of African tradition.

Therefore, on the basis of Africa's indigenous political tradition, the *confederate type of government ought to be adopted for every African nation composed of more than one tribe.* It would have little, if any, effect on the average person on the street. All that it would require is *extensive decentralization,* a process which, commendably, has already been started by many African governments.

The next issue to tackle is the constitution. Indigenous Africa had its own constitution before the Europeans arrived in Africa. Of course, it was not written but that does not mean it didn't exist. The fact that Africa had no written literature did not mean that African natives did not educate their children, or have any conception of history. Here is an indigenous African constitution that I have derived from oral tradition and customs.

## THE INDIGENOUS AFRICAN CONSTITUTION

### A. THE NATURE OF GOVERNMENT

   I. The people, the source of all power, shall be governed by a chief or a king (not a soldier), chosen by the founding or ancestral lineage. This criterion must be combined with others such as intelligence, bravery, and pleasant disposition. The choice of the "ruler" is subject to the approval of the people since the legitimacy of the "ruler" rests upon the consent of the people to be ruled (implicit contract).

  II. The chief or king, who is not a ruler but a leader, shall perform the following duties:
   a. Provide a vital link between the living and their ancestors.
   b. Maintain order, balance, and harmony among the cosmological elements: the sky, the earth, and the world.
   c. Promote peace, justice, social harmony, and prosperity among the people.
   d. Respect the laws of the ancestors and abide by the will of the people. (Rule of law).

 III. Failure to perform these duties could result in "destoolment" or regicide. In addition, the "ruler" shall be deposed for the following failings:

      a.  Drunkenness
      b.  Cowardice in war
      c.  Failure to listen to advice
      d.  Physical disfigurement
      e.  Oppression of the people
      f.  Looting the tribal treasury

IV. There shall be no standing army. The people are the army. In the event of imminent external threat, members of the young age grade or the warrior class shall be called up to defend the community. The army shall be disbanded when the threat subsides.

V. The "ruler" shall govern with a Council. The chief or king must remain silent as the Council deliberates on an issue.

      a.  Important decisions must be debated until unanimity is reached. If not, the issue shall be placed before a Village Assembly of commoners and debated until a *consensus* is reached.

      b.  The "ruler," together with the Council, shall ensure that the will of the people, arrived at by *consensus*, is carried out. The "ruler" shall not unilaterally abrogate the expressed will of the community.

      c.  The "ruler" shall not entertain or enter into any contract with a foreigner or a stranger without the full approval of the Council.

      d.  All decisions initiated by the "ruler" must be approved by the Council.

VI. Councilor positions are hereditary. Councilors are chosen by their respective lineages and cannot be removed by the "ruler." The "ruler" may nominate highly regarded persons to the Council but only with its concurrence.

VII. The primary duties of the government are to defend the community against external aggression, maintain law and order, and ensure the survival of the tribe by promoting peace, justice, harmony, and economic prosperity. It is not the function of the tribal government to operate commercial enterprises to the total exclusion of the subjects. The chief may operate a farm or business if he so wishes. But he cannot prohibit others from engaging in the same economic activity.

## B. BILL OF NATIVE RIGHTS

I. The people shall enjoy the following rights which cannot be questioned or nullified by the "ruler":

a. The right to economic livelihood to support the family without interference by the chief or the king or the government. The occupation of the individual is his/her own determination to make. It is the individual's prerogative to determine whether to become a farmer, a hunter, a fisherman, or a market trader. And how much he/she sells produce for at the village market is for the individual to determine. It is not the duty of the chief or king to fix prices or debar any individual from entering any commercial transaction or contract if he/she so wishes.

b. The right to the use of land. Land belongs to the royal ancestors, not the chief or the king. The "ruler" only holds land in trust to ensure fair distribution and equal access by all. The chief or king cannot dispossess or deny a tribesman the use of the land without full Council review.

c. The right to defend the family against intruders, even against harassment by the chief.

d. The right to live anywhere a person so chooses and the right to leave the community unmolested.

e. The right to an open and fair trial in case of alleged wrongdoing and the right to appeal to a higher court.

f. The right to participate in government and the decision making process, regardless of a person's status, sex, age, ethnicity, or religion.

g. The right to comment on and criticize government policy, since the legitimacy of the "ruler" is based upon the consent of the people.

h. The right to express an opinion freely and the right to be heard are fundamental to African culture and participatory democracy.

i. The right to associate with any group—socially, economically, and politically—if a person so chooses. A person may belong to an age group, a social club, a secret society, a guild, or a political faction if he/she so wishes. It is not the business of the chief or king to ban these associations.

j. The right to practice any religion of his/her own choosing.

II. The rights specified above are enshrined in the following freedoms upon which the chief, the king, or the government must not infringe:

a. Freedom of choice (to live anywhere, to engage in any occupation, to trade goods at whatever prices).

   b.  Freedom of expression (required to debate, criticize policies, and
       participate in the decision making process).
   c.  Freedom of association in the social, economic, and political
       arena.
   d.  Freedom of worship and
   e.  Freedom of movement.
III.  These freedoms shall be enjoyed within the boundaries defined by
      the community as a whole, not by the chief or king.

African experts have only to build upon this indigenous constitution. Copying the American, Russian, Chinese, or French constitution will not work
because in *every* constitution, there is a cultural imprint. Africans are not
Americans or Chinese.

A good constitution for a modern African nation is one which guarantees
the freedom of its people, not one which specifies in detail the duties of
government. A good constitution limits the powers of the state from en-
croaching upon the liberties of the people. In other words, a good constitution views the state as necessarily tyrannical and must therefore protect the
people from the government. This is in the indigenous African tradition. As
we saw in Chapter 3, so fearful were many African tribes of the state that
they chose not to have centralized authority at all: they were stateless or
acephalous societies. To protect the people against the state, the constitution
must have a bill of rights.

After the constitution has been drafted and approved in a national
referendum, copies should be lodged with the United Nations, OAU or some
foreign aid donor with *specific* instructions to the effect that this constitution
cannot be recalled or abrogated by *anyone* without the expressed approval of
the people. If African elites are serious about putting a stop to military
adventurism in politics, they ought to take effective steps. Enshrining in the
constitution a clause to the effect that "coups are illegal" makes as much sense
as putting up a gold-plated sign with the inscription: "Burglary is illegal." The
sign itself will be stolen the next day! If the elites abhor having their
constitution kicked around like a football by soldiers, then they should make
it more difficult for them to do so, not by placing clauses in the constitution
but by placing the constitution in a place more difficult to get at.

Furthermore, future coup-makers in Africa need to be reminded of a
little-known law passed by the U.S. Congress in 1988. If a constitutionally
elected government in the Third World is overthrown in a military coup,
American aid will immediately be suspended. Sudan became the first African

casualty of this law when Brigadier Omar Bashir overthrew the civilian government of Sadiq el Mahdi on June 30, 1989.

Now, here is how a modern-day African government should be structured, using Africa's own indigenous political tradition. At the very least, it should have the following:

1. A head of state,
2. A cabinet chosen by the head of state,
3. A council, chosen by the people.

Council members should be representatives of every identifiable and autonomous group in the society— farmers, fishermen, soldiers, students, teachers, lawyers, and so forth. Indigenous African political systems did not lock anyone out of the decision making process. In this scheme, political parties may be considered as "groups" of individuals sharing common ideological beliefs and they too should send their representatives to the council. (To prevent having a large number of councilors, we might consider allowing representation to only those identifiable groups whose members exceed, say, 200,000 or one million.) The emphasis on multi-partyism in the manner of Western systems excludes non-political groups, which is *un-African*.

The councilors cannot be removed by the head of state. How the councilors are chosen is for the various groups to decide. Furthermore, what exactly the council is called—*ndaba, mbuza* or National Assembly—is immaterial. But council there should be; not a military junta or a politburo. We now know that the indigenous system of government was one of participatory democracy, under chieftaincy, based on *consensus*.

There is no reason why the head of state should necessarily be the head of a political party. In the indigenous system, even a slave could be king (for example, Jaja of Bonny of the Niger delta in the nineteenth century). The head of state should be elected from the councilors or the representatives. In this way the leader of *any* group, can become president. There are other important advantages as well.

First, it is far easier to count and recount the votes of the councilors than those of the electorate at large. This scheme eradicates election rigging and vote fraud. Second, it would save a tremendous amount of resources that could be better spent elsewhere. The fact that the United States elects its president by universal suffrage at considerable expense does not mean African countries must do exactly the same for their political systems to be called "democratic." It is the use of imagination and intelligence which is important, not the ability to copy. And if elections are abhorred, the presidency may be rotated among the leaders of the various groups. The

Gikuyu of Kenya and the Yoruba of Nigeria have this rotational system of choosing their chiefs.

This is a rather rough sketch of a political system for a modern African country. The details need not detain us here. Of course, better systems can be devised by the experts. But then again, freedom of expression is needed to air and debate them.

---

## NOTES

1. One celebrated case was that of Dr. Kwame Safo-Adu, who secured a loan from the African Development Bank and World Bank to establish a pharmaceutical factory at Kumasi that employed about 30 workers. Strangely perceived as a political threat, his home was attacked by two brigades of military personnel in February 1988. Both groups were disguised as armed robbers and apparently mistaking the others as real robbers, shooting erupted between them. When it was over, two of them lay dead. Subsequently on November 3, 1989, the pharmaceutical factory was cordoned off and closed by a battalion of 400 armed soldiers (*TransAfrica Forum*, Summer 1991; p. 49).

2. Moreover, the "Asian Tigers" benefited from circumstances like the cold war, U.S. aid, and advantageous trade arrangements for the U.S. market.

3. I have called this "indigenism" in Ayittey (1991). "Returning to Africa's own roots," and "determining a culturally derived political and economic ideology" also convey the same notion.

# Chapter 14

## Conclusion:
## Aluta Continua! *(The Struggle Continues!)*

Those who feel that the citizen should not continue to fight against monolithic-
ism, political illiberalism, tribalism, patrimonialism, bureaucratic inefficiency,
public graft and corruption are at the end of the day the true enemies of Kenya
(and indeed all of Africa). And they probably need to learn the lesson, often too
bitterly learnt elsewhere, that those who do not accept the **FORCE OF ARGU-
MENT** have often had to give in to the **ARGUMENT OF FORCE**.

—Wachira Nzina and Chris Mburu in *The Nairobi Law Monthly*, No. 31,
March 1991

This book has attempted to present the true story about Africa's postcolonial
experience. It is a grisly picture of one betrayal after another: economic
disintegration, political chaos, inane civil wars, and infrastructural and institutional decay. These were not what Africans hoped for when they asked for
their independence from colonial rule in the 1960s. It is difficult to convey
their outrage and sense of indignation at the leaders who have failed them.

By the beginning of the 1990s economic and political conditions in Africa
had become intolerable. African socialism has been a dismal failure, one-
party rule has been a disaster, and international blindness to the nearly
universal corruption of the continent's leaders has made matters immeasurably worse.

Various actors, foreign as well as domestic, participated, wittingly or not,
in the devastation of Africa. It is easy for African leaders to put the blame
somewhere else; for example, on Western aid donors or on an allegedly
hostile international economic environment. But as the World Bank observed
in its 1984 report, *Toward Sustained Development in Sub-Saharan Africa*, "genuine
donor mistakes and misfortunes alone cannot explain the excessive number
of 'white elephants' " (p. 24). Certainly, donor blunders and other external

factors have contributed to the crisis in Africa, but in my view the internal factors have played a far greater role than the external ones.

Of the internal factors, the main culprit has been the failure of leadership. In many cases African leaders themselves created "black elephants" and state enterprises that were dictated more by considerations of prestige than by concerns for economic efficiency. Mobutu Sese Seko of Zaire once declared, "I know my people. They like grandeur. They want us to have respect abroad in the eyes of other countries" (*The Wall Street Journal*, Oct 15, 1986). Accordingly, half of Zaire's foreign debt of $6 billion went to build two big dams and the Inga-Shaba powerline, as well as a $1 billion double-decked suspension bridge over the Congo River. The upper level is for a railroad that does not exist. In many other cases elite *bazongas* (raiders of the public treasury) blatantly squandered part of the foreign aid money. Does Africa need more foreign aid?

In truth, Africa needs less—not more—foreign aid. David Karanja of Kenya wrote: "Foreign aid has done more harm to Africa than we care to admit. It has led to a situation where Africa has failed to set its own pace and direction of development free of external interference. Today, Africa's development plans are drawn thousands of miles away in the corridors of the IMF and World Bank" (*New African*, Jun 1992; p. 20).

Moreover, there are a number of ways that aid resources Africa desperately needs can be found in Africa itself. Maritu Wagaw wrote: "Let Africa look inside Africa for the solution of its economic problems. Solutions to our predicament should come from within not from outside" (*New African*, Mar 1992; p. 19). Indeed.

First, in 1989 Africa was spending $12 billion annually to import arms and to maintain the military. Second, the elites illegally transferred from Africa at least $15 billion annually during the latter part of the 1980s.[1] Third, at least $5 billion annually could be saved if Africa could feed itself. Foreign exchange saved is foreign exchange earned. Fourth, another $5 billion could be saved from waste and inefficiencies in Africa's 3,200-odd state enterprises. This might entail selling off some of them or placing them under new management. Fifth, the civil wars raging in Africa exact a heavy toll in lost output, economic development, and destroyed property. If Angola's civil war alone cost the country $1 billion annually, $10 billion would not be an unreasonable estimate of the average annual cost of civil wars throughout the continent. Adding up these savings and the foreign exchange generated from internal sources would yield at least $47 billion annually, compared with the $12.4 billion in aid Africa received from all sources in 1990.

A bucket full of holes can only hold a certain amount of water for a certain amount of time. Pouring in more water makes little sense as it will all drain away. To the extent that there are internal leaks in Africa—corruption, senseless civil wars, wasteful military expenditures, capital flight, and government wastes—pouring in more foreign aid is futile. As a first order of priority, the leaks should be plugged to ensure that the little aid that comes in, stays. But African dictators, impervious to reason, continue to wage destructive wars.

In 1990 the OAU finally began to show signs of awakening from its slumber. Delegates to the OAU summit in July of that year, which Nelson Mandela addressed, observed that the summit demonstrated realism and a laudable determination to make progress in the resolution of Africa's intractable problems. Delegates realized that if Africa is to resist Western pressure for reforms and find its own solutions, it must first put its house in order. There was a genuine desire to end civil wars and disputes between neighbors, to increase regional cooperation, and to advance development.

The delegates signed a declaration, pledging to establish more democracy on the continent. According to the *Washington Times*, the incoming OAU chairman, President Yoweri Museveni of Uganda, averred, "Africa must find African solutions to its problems." Emphasizing that democracy could take many forms, he said that all states must have regular, free elections, a free press, and respect for human rights. In addition, the *Washington Times* reported that Nigerian President Ibrahim Babangida told the assembly that Africa's leaders had failed their people. "Ever since the majority of our countries became independent in the 1960s we have conducted our lives as if the world owes us a living," he said. According to one African political analyst, the delegates realized that "unless they change they won't be coming to any other summits because they will no longer be in power" (*Washington Times*, Jul 13, 1990; p. A11). But rhetoric is one thing and action another.

While the delegates were speaking, the Babangida administration was continuing its crackdown on journalists and anyone suspected to be involved in the abortive April 22, 1990, coup attempt. In Uganda it may be recalled that journalists who put tough questions to visiting President Kaunda were arrested in spite of the free press that President Museveni called for.

If Africa is in a mess, the fault does not lie in any innate inferiority of the African people but rather in the alien, defective political systems instituted across much of the continent. It is not the charisma or the rhetoric of African leaders which makes a political system democratic and accountable. The *institutional approach*, as we argued in the previous chapter, is far superior.

Kwame Nkrumah, Julius Nyerere, Kenneth Kaunda and other nationalists were all great heroes with charisma. But they all established regimes which lacked the institutions of a free press, an independent judiciary, freedom of political association, and the most basic standards of accountability. Political systems which lack these institutions have the tendency to produce despots. As we saw in the previous chapter, virtually all African regimes have been characterized by an enormous concentration of both economic and political power in the hands of the state and, therefore, one individual.

Africa has more than its share of civilian autocrats, military dictators, and rapacious elites. As we saw in Chapter 3, Africa's indigenous system of government produced few tyrants. The modern leadership is a far cry from the traditional. In fact, by Africa's indigenous standards the modern leadership in much of Africa has been a disgraceful failure. They refuse to learn and keep repeating not only their own mistakes but those of others as well.

In an address to the Rotary International in Accra, retired Lt. Gen. Emmanuel Erskine, former commander of the United Nations Forces in Lebanon, remarked: "The fact that some African leaders get themselves emotionally identified with their country which they consider their personal property and that they and their minority ethnic clientele should lead the country and that they should rule until death is the single major phenomenon creating serious political crisis on the continent. Not even bulldozers can dislodge some of these leaders from office" (West Africa, May 6-12, 1991; p. 722).

## WHY AFRICAN DICTATORS CLING TO POWER

Recall from Chapter 6 that between 1957 and 1990, there were more than 150 African heads of state and only six relinquished power voluntarily. There are three main reasons why African heads of state refuse to step down when their people get fed up with them. First, they somehow get this absurd notion that the country belongs to them and them alone. Witness their pictures on the currency and in every nook and cranny in the country. Every monument or building of some significance is named after them: Houphouet-Boigny this, Houphouet-Boigny that, Moi National Park, and on and on. In Malawi, "President Hastings Kamuzu Banda's face is everywhere, from the buttons on Youth League uniforms to the dresses of dancers. Highways, stadiums and schools are named for him. A national holiday honors him. It is forbidden to call him by his last name; only 'Ngwazi,' meaning lion or protector, or 'the life president' are allowed (*Washington Post*, May 5, 1992; p. A22).

Second, insecure African heads of state surround themselves with loyal supporters, often drawn from their own tribes: the late Doe from the Krahn tribe, Mobutu of Zaire from the Gbande, Biya of Cameroon from the Bamileke, Moi of Kenya from the Kalenjin and Babangida of Nigeria from the Muslims. In Togoland, about 70 percent of General Eyadema's army were drawn from his own Kabye tribe (*Africa Report*, Jan-Feb 1992; p.5).

Other supporters are simply bought: soldiers with fat paychecks and perks; urban workers with cheap rice and sardines ("essential commodities"); students with free tuition and hefty allowances; and intellectuals, opposition leaders and lawyers with big government posts and Mercedes-Benzes.[2]

Even when the head of state is contemplating stepping down, these supporters and lackeys fiercely resist any cutbacks in government largesse or any attempt to open up the political system. This was precisely the case in The Gambia when Sir Dawda Jawara—in power since the country's independence in 1965—announced in March 1992 his intention to step down. Freeloaders and patronage junkies urged him to stay on! In Sierra Leone, Mr. Musa Gendemeh, the deputy agriculture minister, was quite explicit. On the BBC "Focus on Africa" program (Apr 24, 1990), he declared that,

"He won't give up his present privileged position for the sake of a multiparty system nor would one expect a policeman or soldier to give up his one bag of rice at the end of every month for the same . . .

He warned that anyone talking about another party would be committing treason . . . that ministers and MPs suspected of having something to do with the multiparty movement are now under surveillance . . . and that whenever there has been trouble in the country, his people, the Mende, have suffered the most and he warned them to be careful" (*West Africa*, Jun 4-10, 1990; p. 934).

To protect their perks and benefits, these sycophants lie, deceive, and misinform the head of state. They continually praise him to the sky, even when his own tail is on fire! Kenneth Kaunda was informed that he would have "no problem" winning the October 1991 elections as he had 80 percent of the popular vote and "everything else had been taken care of." But when the actual voting took place, he was resoundingly humiliated, garnering a pitiful 25 percent of the vote. Ghanaians would recall that "party stooges" and "sycophants" also misled Nkrumah. African leaders should remember that "it is better to have wise people reprimand you than have stupid people sing you praises" (Ecclesiastes 7:5).

The third reason why African heads of state are reluctant to relinquish power is *fear*. Many of them have their hands so steeped in blood and their pockets so full of booty that they are afraid all their past gory misdeeds will be exposed. So they cling to power, regardless of the cost and consequences. But eventually they are dislodged, and only few subsequently are able to live peacefully in their own countries, much less to enjoy the loot.[3]

## Three Ways of Removing African Tyrants

In the ouster of Africa's dictators, three scenarios have emerged since 1990. By the "Doe scenario," those leaders who foolishly refused to accede to popular demands for democracy only did so at their own peril and at the destruction of their countries: Doe of Liberia, Traore of Mali, Barre of Somalia and Mengistu of Ethiopia. (Doe was killed in September 1990; Barre fled Mogadishu in a tank in January 1991; and Mengistu to Zimbabwe in February 1991.) African countries where this scenario is most likely to be repeated are Algeria, Cameroon, Djibouti, Equatorial Guinea, Libya, Malawi, Sudan, Tunisia, and Uganda.

In the "Kerekou scenario," those African leaders who wisely yielded to popular pressure managed to save not only their own lives but their countries as well: Kerekou of Benin, Kaunda of Zambia, Sassou-Nguesso of Central African Republic, and Pereira of Cape Verde Islands. Unfortunately, they are the exceptions.

The "Eyadema scenario," the third, is by far the most common. In this scenario, they yield initially after considerable domestic and international pressure but then attempt to manipulate the rules and the transition process to their advantage, believing that they could fool their people. In the end, they only fool themselves and are thrown out of office in disgrace. African countries likely to follow this route are: Angola, Burkina Faso, Burundi, Ghana, Ivory Coast, Kenya, Mozambique, Nigeria, Rwanda, Sierra Leone, Tanzania, Zaire, Zambia, and Zimbabwe. Recent events in Togo and Zaire also show that the outcome of the Eyadema scenario is highly unpredictable and its impact on economic development deleterious. Political uncertainty discourages business investment and trade.

Regardless of their obstinacy and chicanery, African dictators cannot escape five laws of modern African governance that have devastating consequences for themselves, their associates, their tribesmen, and their countries after they have been overthrown.

## IMMUTABLE LAWS OF AFRICAN GOVERNANCE

### Law 1: Leaders' Misdeeds Eventually Catch Up with Them

In their zeal to "clean house," new rulers, often military, resort to draconian measures, declare states of emergency and suspend civil liberties. They start a witch-hunt for corrupt politicians of the preceding regime and brutalize those who stand in their way. For example, three Ghanaian judges were abducted and murdered in June 1982 because they had freed corrupt politicians of past regimes. The witch-hunt soon spreads to "dissidents," alienating large segments of the population. Even supporters of the new regime are not safe. In the initial stages of the "Rawlings revolution" in Ghana, the country's university students regularly demonstrated their support in 1982, as was also the case in the initial period of the late Samuel Doe's tenure in Liberia. But when Ghanaian students complained in 1983 about cutbacks in allowances, the reaction of the military government was swift: closure of the universities.

But as the inscription on one of the "mammy trucks" plying Accra roads says: "No condition is permanent."[4] Eventually the supporters of dictatorial regimes turn against them. High-ranking government officials resign or defect and start talking. Long-held secrets about looting and other misdeeds begin to feed the rumor mill, undermining the legitimacy of the regime. One such defector was Mr. Kwaku Boakye Danquah, chairman of one of Ghana's notorious public tribunals, which handed down harsh sentences, including death by firing squad, for economic and political "crimes." Recently, Danquah told *West Africa* that "the tribunals 'are part of the system that underpins the PNDC (government). It is a political instrument, ensuring PNDC dominance.' He charges that there is political interference and intimidation of tribunals to secure the judgements that the government wants" (Mar 30-Apr 5, 1992; p. 545).

In Togoland, "Mba Kabassema, who was Minister of Trade and Transport in Eyadema's government in 1977, alleged that Eyadema pillaged the country's resources with the connivance of a Moroccan adviser, Maurice Assor . . . Another delegate [to the national conference] alleged that Eyadema's personal fortune was 800 billion CFA francs ($2.8 billion) most of which has been put into foreign banks" (*New African*, Oct 1991; p. 12).

## Law 2: Leaders will be Hoisted by Their own Petard

African tyrants spend an inordinate amount on an elaborate security cum military structure to protect themselves and suppress their people. As *Africa Report* noted:

> According to military sources in Kinshasa, the Zairian army currently numbers around 100,000 personnel. The largest sector is the regular army known as the Zairian Armed Forces (FAZ), which numbers 81,000, 60,000 of whom are under arms. Next in size is the 12,000 strong civil guard, headed by General Kpama Baramoto, brother-in-law of Mobutu. But it is the Special Presidential Division (DSP), numbering 6,500 under arms, which represents the strong arm of Mobutu's rule. Both the Civil Guard and the DSP are answerable to the president, while the FAZ is under the control of the ministry of defense. Senior officers are largely from Mobutu's Equateur region" (Jan-Feb 1992; p. 28).

But quite often, it is the very same security apparatus that overthrows them. The next tyrant doesn't learn. Being a product of that structure, with intricate knowledge of its inner workings, he repairs the weaknesses and strengthens the structure. Eventually he too is overthrown by the same security apparatus. The law is this: The more an African head of state spends on security, the more likely he will be overthrown by someone from his security forces.

Recall that each year, African governments spend about $12 billion on the importation of weapons and maintenance of the military—an amount which is nearly equal to what Africa receives in aid from all sources. The futility of such military expenditures was pointed out by Archbishop Desmond Tutu. Speaking at the Teachers Hall in Accra on November 25, 1990, he noted cogently: "Freedom is cheaper than repression. When you are a leader chosen by the people you don't need security. All the money spent on weapons doesn't buy one iota of security," he said (*Christian Messenger*, Jan 1991; p. 1). But obstinate tyrants refuse to take heed.

On March 18, 1991, angry Malians took to the streets to demand democratic freedom from the despotic rule of Moussa Traore. He unleashed his security forces on them, killing scores, including women and children. But pro-democracy forces were not deterred and kept up the pressure. Asked to resign on March 25, he retorted: "I will not resign, my government will not resign, because I was elected not by the opposition but by all the people of Mali!" But two days later when he tried to flee the country, he was grabbed by his own security agents and sent to jail. From there, he lamented: "My fate is now in God's hands." The same happened to Joseph Momoh of Sierra

Leone, Buhari of Nigeria, and many others. They should have used their common sense.

Moreover, the security system, quite apart from the threat that can come from within, often fails to provide adequate protection to African despots. The late Samuel Doe of Liberia, for example, spent so much to keep his soldiers happy. In addition, he had crack Presidential troops, secretly trained by the Israelis. But they could not protect him from the Charles Taylor's ragtag rebels of 1,000. Note that Charles Taylor was not even a soldier but an ex-civil servant. Similarly, Comrade Haile Mariam Mengistu spend an enormous amount to build Africa's largest army with 200,000 under arms. Neither they too could protect Mengistu from a band of determined Eritrean and Tigray rebels. The same can be said for Siad Barre of Somalia.

### Law 3: The Certainty of Reprisals

The third law is that the head of state doesn't go down alone. Because he often surrounds himself with and awards top government positions to cronies and members of his own tribe, vengeful retribution is often taken against them when he is overthrown. The victims may often be innocent individuals who had nothing to do with the ousted leader but are brutalized nonetheless because of their association with him or their membership in a tribe that enjoyed special privileges when he ruled. The Krahn tribe under the Doe regime in Liberia, and the Marehan clan under the Barre regime of Somalia are examples. In Liberia, as we saw in Chapter 7, savage reprisals were taken against the Krahn, most of whom fled into neighboring countries.

On the fall of Samuel Doe, *West Africa* wrote in an editorial: "Another serious indictment of his rule, has to be the way he was unable to see that the crass pursuit of the interests of his own ethnic group, the Krahn, would in the long run grievously damage the future of that group, as well as the whole of Liberia. There are other African countries where the concentration of guns in the hands of one group (as in Togo or the Congo) creates a grievous political imbalance, even if it can bring spurious short-term stability. Doe's efforts over the years to pack his army with Krahn, many of them brought from over the Ivorian border, introduced a level of tribal animosity not previously known, despite historical roots" (Sep 17-23, 1990; p. 2469).

In Togo, "at least 1,600 northern Togolese, especially those from the Kabye tribe where President Gnassingbe Eyadema comes from, were forced to seek refuge in the grounds of the ruling party school in the capital Lome after they had been molested and thrown out of their homes by southern Ewe" (*New African*, Jun 1991; p. 16).

In Somalia, former president Siad Barre not only favored his own Marehan clan but also played off one clan against another to stay in power. The Galgalo and Darod clans were armed by Barre. After Barre's ouster in January 1991, almost all the men of the Galgalo clan were killed in reprisals. In Mogadishu, the Darod clan were humiliated by the Hawiye clan, from which the triumphant United Somali Congress (USC) drew its support. " 'The Darods have been forced out of Mogadishu, stripped of everything, and now they're bent on revenge,' said one man . . . 'The showdown is still to come' " (*Africa Report*, May-Jun 1991; p. 59).

These two cases should serve as a lesson to those elites, some with Ph.D.s, who, for a Mercedes-Benz, would readily sell off conscience and integrity to serve in ministerial and ambassadorial capacities under brutal dictatorships. What happened to all those top government officials in the Doe and Barre regimes? Specifically, what happened to the following people who served under Doe: Senate President Tambakai Jangaba; Justice Minister Jenkins Scott, Information Minister J. Emmanuel Bowier, Deputy Minister of Foreign Affairs Elbert Dunn, Finance Minister Emmanuel Shaw, Deputy Minister of Agriculture Kekura Kpoto?

Over a third of them, including top banking officials, abandoned their posts in July 1990 during official missions abroad and were searching for political asylum. Mr. Shaw, the finance minister, sent a telex to notify Doe of his resignation, citing "family pressures." The remaining top government officials fled. Mr. Kpoto, the deputy minister of agriculture, was discovered in hiding in Bo (Sierra Leone). A few unlucky ones did not make it out of Liberia; they were killed.

The plight of the Krahn and the Marehan clan should also serve as a lesson to the Beti of Cameroon, the Baule of the Ivory Coast, the Ewe of Ghana, the Kalenjin of Kenya, the Muslims of northern Nigeria, the Gbande of Zaire, the Chewa of Malawi, and the Arabs of Mauritania and Sudan. Those African heads of state who exhort others to eschew "tribalism" ought to detribalize *themselves* and their regimes or risk reprisals against their tribesmen when they fall. If not, then members of these tribes themselves should remove their disgraceful kinsmen. The Krahn and the Marehan clan failed to do so.

But the retribution often extends beyond the country's borders to foreign governments and multilateral institutions which provided extensive credits to the hated, ousted regime. For example, in Ghana when Busia was overthrown in 1972, there were, for a brief period, cries of *"Yentua"* ("We won't pay our foreign debt") amid strong anti-Western feelings. These same feelings are bound to erupt when Mobutu, Moi, and Banda are overthrown.

Western governments and institutions ought to distinguish between the true people of Africa and the vampire elites who rule them.

## Law 4: Rulers' Receptivity to Political Change Determines the Country's Fate

The fourth inviolable law is that the greater their resistance to political change or reform, the greater the potential for the destruction of their countries, as seen in Angola, Ethiopia, Liberia, Mauritania, Mozambique, Somalia, South Africa, Sudan, and Uganda. Banda, Biya, Kaunda, Moi, Mugabe, Rawlings, and others may overconfidently believe they can resist change to the last minute. But in the end, they will only succeed in destroying their own countries.

This lesson or law should have been learned from Africa's own liberation struggle against colonialism. There were three main colonial powers in Africa in the 1950s: the French, the Portuguese, and the British. In general, the French offered the least resistance and the Portuguese the fiercest to African demands for freedom and self-determination. African countries where there was little resistance from the colonialists were spared destructive change and rabid ideological radicalism: This was the case in Francophone Africa, except Algeria. Where the colonialists stubbornly resisted independence, there was a degeneration of the liberation struggle into civil war and the adoption of rigid Marxism: This was the case in most of Lusophone Africa (ex-Portuguese colonies) such as Angola, Mozambique, Guinea-Bissau, and Algeria under the French.

Until recently this lesson was lost on the apartheid regime in South Africa which, for decades, doggedly resisted black aspirations for political freedom. But race or color is not the determining factor. Rather, it is the nature of the *resistance* to political change that is crucial. The greater this resistance, whether in South Africa or black Africa, the greater the potential for a violent revolution with cataclysmic consequences. Currently, dark clouds hang over the following African countries because of the stiff resistance to political change at the top level: Burundi, Cameroon, the Central African Republic, Congo, Ethiopia, Equatorial Guinea, Ghana, Mauritania, Sierra Leone, Sudan, Uganda, Zaire, Zimbabwe, and others. As Tom Paine, an African exile in Los Angeles, warned: "The Rawlingses, the arap Mois and the Robert Mugabes of today are behaving just like the Portuguese of old (*West Africa*, May 6-12, 1991; p. 692).

*Law 5: The Chaotic Aftermath of a Violent Overthrow*

A period of chaos, insurgency, and instability often tends to follow the violent overthrow of a government in Africa. Usually, various disparate groups and elements join forces to dislodge a hated regime. But when the regime is ousted or near its downfall, these groups often begin fighting among themselves, sowing seeds of confusion and carnage: Liberia (the conflict between Taylor and Johnson); Somalia (between the SNM and USC); South Africa (between Inkatha and the ANC); Angola (between UNITA and the MPLA); Mozambique (between RENAMO and FRELIMO); Zimbabwe (between ZAPU and ZANU), and so on. It should be pointed out, however, that this is not unique to Africa alone. The Mujihadeen rebels, after routing Soviet forces in Afghanistan, also began fighting among themselves. So too did the various ethnic groups after they joined forces to overthrow communist dictatorships in Yugoslavia, Romania, and even Poland.

Somalia provides another example of factional hostility in the aftermath of a violent overthrow. On May 19, 1991, northwest Somalia, under the control of the Somali National Movement (SNM), seceded. The new state, called the Somaliland Republic, was created out of the area that formed British Somaliland before it merged with the adjoining Italian-administered area to form Somalia in 1960. That area is under the control of the United Somali Congress (USC), but it too is likely to break up into two pieces: one controlled by the USC and the other, in the southern part of the country, under the thumb of Barre—the former president—and remnants of his army.

In November 1991, fighting broke out between clan leaders, Mohammed Ali Mahdi and Mohammed Farah Aidid, for the control of Mogadishu. This resulted in the deaths of 41,000 people between November 1991 and March 1992, and hundreds of thousands of refugees. And who was to blame for all that carnage? "Africa Watch and Physicians for Human Rights accused the U.S. of not doing enough to promote peace . . . The two aid groups contend the United States did not make a serious effort to head off the fighting and should have pressured United Nations officials to act sooner" (*The Washington Times*, Mar 27, 1992; p. A8).

This blame, however, was grossly misplaced on the United States. As the *Washington Times* noted: "Somalis blame their descent into anarchy on every organization that has tried to stop the civil war. They blame the United Nations, Red Cross, Arab League and Organization of African Unity. They blame everyone except [their leaders]" (Jun 6, 1992; p. A7).

By August 1992 the situation had deteriorated immeasurably into anarchy and chaos. Over 100,000 Somalis had perished, and more than a million were near death from starvation. Once again, emaciated bodies of famine victims were paraded before the world to appeal for humanitarian assistance while the idiots continued a pitched battle for control of Mogadishu, totally unconcerned about the immense suffering. Were they liberators? Even relief workers who went to assist were attacked: "Two U.N. military observers — a Czech and an Egyptian — were shot and wounded, even though their vehicle bore the U.N. flag" (*The Washington Post*, Aug 30, 1992; p. A33). The same wars and quests for political power produced carnage, famine, and massive human suffering in Angola, Ethiopia, Liberia, Mozambique, and Sudan.

Those intellectuals and government officials who loathe seeing the destruction of their countries ought to draw up a procedure—now!—by which a head of state can be removed peacefully.

Traditionally, Africans have solved their problems peacefully in village meetings, convened under "a big tree," debating issues until they reached a consensus. These village meetings were variously called *pitso* by the Xhosa, *ndaba* by the Zulu, *kgotla* by the Tswana, and *asetena kese* by the Asante. In the early 1990s this indigenous African tradition was revived by pro-democracy forces in the form of "national conferences" to chart a new political future (Benin, Cameroon, Congo, Mali, Niger, Togoland, Zaire).

Benin's nine-day "national conference" began on February 19, 1990, with 488 delegates, representing various political, religious, trade union, and other groups encompassing the broad spectrum of Beninois society. The conference, whose chairman was Father Isidore de Souza, held "sovereign power" and its decisions were binding on all, including the government. It stripped President Matthieu Kerekou of power, scheduled multiparty elections, and ended 17 years of autocratic Marxist rule.

Congo's national conference had more delegates (1,500) and lasted longer (three months). But when it was over in June 1991, the 12-year-old government of Gen. Denis Sassou-Nguesso had been dismantled. The Constitution was rewritten and the nation's first free elections were scheduled for June 1992. Before the conference, Congo was among Africa's most rigidly Marxist-Leninist states. "Without any question, it's a uniquely African process for resolving problems," said James Phillips, the U.S. ambassador to Congo. "This is how they do it in the villages" (*The New York Times*, Jun 25, 1991; p. A8). A Western business executive added, "The remarkable thing is that the revolution occurred without a single shot being fired . . . (and) if it can happen here, it can happen anywhere." Indeed, it could and should happen everywhere in Africa. The elites must demand a national conference whenever there is a crisis. It is a shame that it was Westerners who recognized this "uniquely African way" of solving problems and not African leaders.

## HOW CAN THE WEST HELP IN AFRICA?

It must be restated that it is *not* the responsibility of the West but that of Africans to clean up the mess in Africa. To be sure, the West has contributed to Africa's economic decline, not least by supporting brutal dictatorships. But so too did the East (the countries of Eastern Europe, the Soviet Union, China) and even the South (Cuba, India, Iran, Iraq). Once when I was asked on a Voice of America program what the United States should do to promote change in Africa, my response was curt: "Get out of Africa!"

To some that may sound contemptuous and arrogant. But there is a great deal of anger seething in Africans, not so much directed at the United States but at the hopelessness of the African situation. Realistically, there is little the United States can do without being accused of interfering in the internal affairs of sovereign African nations. As we saw in Chapter 11, United States involvement in Africa failed to achieve its own objectives—how much more can it expect to achieve in promoting Africans' welfare?

Theoretically the West can help Africans liberate themselves from tyranny. But in practice, Western help is more of a hindrance. Most Westerners do not understand the complexities and nuances of African problems. Americans, both black and white, are the worst, with a tendency to prescribe simplistic solutions. For example, whereas Westerners solve political problems by majority vote, Africans do so by *consensus*. Majority vote ignores minority positions while consensual decisionmaking takes minority views into account. Traditional African governments operated by consensus. In many African countries the application of the majority rules principle and the subsequent marginalization of the minority led to the outbreak of civil wars and demands for secession.

It would be helpful if Westerners would listen to what Africans themselves have to say about solving their own problems. But the arrogant "we-know-best" attitude of some Westerners stands in the way. Even when the West chooses to act, it is hobbled by colonial, racist, and imperialist baggage that renders its help suspect and ineffective. It is annoying when Westerners cannot denounce African dictators for reasons of "racial sensitivity" but then stand in the way of true African democrats who want to get at these hideous tyrants.

There are many Africans who believe that foreign aid does not help them and would like to have it terminated. But getting Western aid policies changed is even worse—a frustrating experience because of institutional resistance. Aid has become an "industry," with its own powerful lobbyists who seek a continuation of current programs at increased funding. Since Congressional requirements and regulations channel about 60 percent of all U.S. aid projects to American contractors, there is every incentive on the contractors' part to clamor for continued funding.

The West has most assuredly used diplomatic channels, economic leverage, and aid linkage to promote democracy in Africa. But during the 1980s, Western pontification, arm-twisting, and tutelage democratized not a single African country. Africans were deeply offended and angered when, during a brief visit to Zaire, U.S. Assistant Secretary for Africa Herman Cohen, said, "Mobutu is enthusiastic for democracy" (*The Washington Post*, Apr 1, 1992; p. A28).

It has now become apparent that the West values human dignity and the lives of people according to their continent or place of origin, the state of development of their country, the political ideology of their ruling regime, and their race. "All men are created equal [and] are endowed with liberty," we are told. But some are born a little more free and a little more equal than others. Blacks in America have one word for this—discrimination.

In Africa, Western application of a peculiar standard that defines freedom only in terms of color is bound to worsen the suffering of all black Africans, including those in South Africa. Until the West recognizes that oppression is oppression, irrespective of the tyrant's skin color, Western leaders have no business pontificating about freedom for black Africans. Thus, the West can be of little practical help to Africans if its own prejudices and misconceptions prevent it from condemning black tyranny.

In the struggle for democracy you lead, follow, or get out of the way. If it were up to this author, the West would stay out of the political arena in Africa and concentrate on promoting its own Western economic interests. It cannot do "business as usual" and then hand money over to African dictators, hoping that they will reform themselves. As we saw in the previous chapter, this is not only futile but, worse, it impedes the African struggle for freedom. More significantly, the demonstrations and strikes that forced political changes in Benin, Cape Verde, Sao Tome, and other African countries, were all internally generated, occurring with little or no help from the West. Irate Africans simply did not wait for Western help or for Western governments and intellectuals to make up their minds. The Africans initiated the action and took to the streets themselves.

But there are some Westerners who are sincerely desirous of helping Africans or at least facilitating change, since a prosperous Africa is in the West's best interest too. In that case, a few observations can be made.

It is heartening to note that in the West there have been talks of linking trade or aid to political pluralism. In March 1990 Carla Hills, the U.S. trade representative, declared: "We seek a normalization of relations with Eastern European countries to the extent that they are taking steps toward political pluralism, respect for human rights, a willingness to build a friendly relationship with the U.S. and a movement toward market-oriented economies" (Wall Street Journal, Mar 8, 1990; p. A16).

In May 1990 the U.S. Congress and the White House attempted to reshape the U.S. foreign aid program in light of global political changes and reordered priorities. President Bush sought new flexibility to boost aid to emerging democracies in Eastern Europe, Panama, and Nicaragua. Assistant Secretary of State for Africa Herman J. Cohen announced in May 1990 that, along with economic adjustment and the observance of human rights, democratization will soon be included as the third prerequisite for U.S. development aid. The policy of tying bilateral aid to political conditions was followed by a U.S. Congressional call to do the same for multilateral aid. As the largest stockholder in the World Bank and the IMF, the United States will therefore insist that these organizations as well tie economic assistance to political demands for democracy.

Smith Hempstone, Jr., the U.S. ambassador to Kenya, relayed this message to Africa in an address at the Rotary Club of Nairobi in June 1990. The U.S. Congress, the Ambassador said, would concentrate economic assistance on countries that "nourished democratic institutions, defended human rights and practised multiparty politics" (New African, Jul 1990; p. 17).

The U.S. Congress is now showing greater sensitivity to human rights issues. The Christian Science Monitor reported: "The 1991 foreign-aid appropriations bill now wending its way through Congress sets restrictions on money for Zaire, Somalia, and Sudan, among others whose actions have raised Congressional ire" (Jul 12, 1990; p. 7). But to improve its credibility and standing among Africans, the U.S. Congress must also come down hard on the leftist regimes in Angola, Burkina Faso, Ethiopia, the Central African Republic, Ghana, Mozambique, Zambia, Zimbabwe, and other nations. There are regimes on both the left and the right that have failed their people. Ideology is not particularly relevant to African human rights issues.

The Europeans' attitude toward Africa has also begun to change. In the 1990s it is most likely that Europeans will abandon Africa to focus on Eastern Europe. Indeed, at least three European Community (EC) countries are planning to cut back their Third World development cooperation budgets in favor of granting more aid to the emerging East European democracies, according to British analyst Nigel Twose, the London director of the Panos Institute, a nongovernmental development research and analysis group (*African Letter*, Dec 1-15, 1989; p. 4). The November 1989 World Bank report, *Sub-Saharan Africa: From Crisis to Sustainable Growth*, called for a 4 percent growth per year in Western aid to the region over the next decade, to reach $22 billion per year by the year 2000. But according to Twose, "The World Bank report was totally dismissed by the three EC countries. The calls for more aid are also going to be dismissed by other donor countries" (*African Letter*, Dec 1-15, 1989). In Italy, aid cuts in favor of Eastern Europe were already imminent. At the Francophone African summit at La Baule (June 20, 1990), French President François Mitterand was explicit: "France will link its contribution to efforts designed to lead to greater liberty and democracy" (*The Independent* [London], Jun 21, 1990).

While it may be desirable to link Western aid to political renewal or democracy, three problems loom. First, political conditionality can be added to current aid programs only at the exclusion of an existing criterion. A principle enunciated in the 1960s by Dutch economist Jan Tinbergen reminds us that one instrument—foreign aid—cannot be used to achieve multiple objectives—debt reduction, economic development, environmental protection, trade, human rights, foreign investment, and now democracy. The number of instruments must at least equal if not exceed the number of objectives. Otherwise, inconsistencies will emerge that will render some objectives unachievable, as has often been the case.

On April 1, 1992, U.S. Secretary of State James Baker III was interviewed by Tom Brokaw on *NBC Nightly News* regarding $5 billion in U.S. aid to Russia and the Commonwealth of Independent States (CIS). The secretary replied that there would be a few conditions attached to the aid. First, the countries should adopt credible economic reform programs; second, they should continue to support democracy; third, they should continue to support freedom; and fourth, they must permit free emigration.

The second problem with linking aid to democracy is that radical governments would denounce the linkage as unwarranted imperialist interference in their internal affairs, and others might fear that adopting political reform measures risks the criticism of capitulating to foreign dictates. For example, Ghana's secretary for finance and economic planning, Dr. Kwesi Botchwey, criticized the "emergent calls for Western aid to Africa to be tied to political reform as 'a slippery slope that can only lead to further erosion of the sovereignty and independence of African countries already severely constrained by the reality of economic dependence' . . . He said the democracy that all must strive for must be distinguished by whether it enables the people to control the use of state power and to appoint and remove office holders through free elections" (*West Africa,* Jun 11-17, 1990; p. 996).

Dr. Botchwey did not acknowledge that office holders in the PNDC administration, including himself, were irremovable since there were no free elections in Ghana. Ghana, incidentally, was one of the five Economic Community of West African States (ECOWAS) countries that sent troops to Liberia in July 1990 to enforce a cease-fire in Liberia's civil war, to install an interim government, and to hold free and fair elections.

Meanwhile, President Ali Hassan Mwinyi of Tanzania denounced the West's linkage of aid to adoption of a multiparty system as political and economic blackmail of the poor. According to *West Africa,* he asserted that it was not proper for external powers to force political standards on others. The correct approach was to allow the people of each country to discuss and eventually arrive at their own consensus on what form of government was suitable for them (Jun 18-24, 1990; p. 1049). But where in Africa do the people have the freedom of expression to allow them to do this?

The third problem is that linking Western aid to democratic reform has not been particularly effective in Africa, even in those countries allied to the West. The obstacle is the prevailing anticolonial and anti-imperialist mindset that is hostile to Western influence. Julius Nyerere, for example, characterized the World Bank and the IMF as "imperialist institutions and devices by which powerful nations maintain their power over poor nations" (*Time,* Jan 16, 1984; p. 39). Marxists charge that the real objective of the IMF-sponsored liberalization measures in Africa is not domestic economic recovery but rather the "penetration of imperialist capital."

In view of these roadblocks to externally directed reform, it would be best if Africans themselves make their own case for reform. Internally generated reform has a better chance of lasting success. More importantly, it is up to the African people to decide which political and economic systems are the most workable for them. Mitterand said as much to *Le Monde:* "It is for the Africans themselves to decide who rules them and how" (cited in the *Wall Street Journal,* Jun 21, 1990; p. A10).

But Africans cannot make this decision in a "culture of silence" or an atmosphere characterized by intolerance of alternative viewpoints and brutalities against dissidents. Nor can they shape their own destiny when decisions regarding foreign aid allocation are made behind closed doors. For example, at the Paris Consultative Group meetings, foreign aid donors meet only with representatives of tyrannical African regimes to determine the need and level of aid funding. Aid is not free but rather a "soft" loan. Loans given or taken by African governments should be authorized, or at least subject to review, by their people. In virtually all cases, Africans seldom know what kind of debt obligations their governments are entering into on their behalf behind closed doors. This must change, and the process must be opened up. U.S. Congressional committees hold hearings on budgetary allocations and other important matters before taking legislative action. Similar hearings should be held by the Paris Consultative Group to allow the opposition, or any other group that may so wish, to cast its opinion on the allocation of foreign aid to that African country. It is instructive to note that at an April 1992 Lusaka conference Malawian exiles formed an interim committee, which gave Chikufwa Chihana—a prominent labor leader—a mandate to return to Malawi to begin organizing an opposition party. More importantly,

> The interim committee also called for international donors to cut all but human-itarian aid for Malawi's 1 million Mozambican refugees and relief for the worst drought until specific demands are met. They also appealed to donors to make no new pledges when they meet with Malawian officials in Paris for a Consulta-tive Group meeting in May 1992.
>
> The interim committee demands also included a practical demonstration by the Malawi government of its commitment to free speech and association by allowing the national pro-democracy conference to go ahead.
>
> To this end, the delegates demanded that all political prisoners inside Malawi jails be released and all political exiles granted a general amnesty. Article 4 of the constitution should also be repealed so that other political parties could form (*Africa Report*, May-Jun 1992; p.23).

Indeed, on May 13, 1992, "the World Bank and Western donor nations suspended most aid to Malawi citing its poor human rights record, a history of repression under its nonagenarian" life-president" Hastings Banda . . . The decision came after protest by workers turned into a violent melee in Blantyre. Shops linked to Banda and the ruling party were looted and government troops fired point-blank at the protesters, killing at least 38 (*The Washington Post*, May 14, 1992; p. A16).

Note that it was Malawians, not "imperialist institutions," who *first* called for cuts in foreign aid and laid down conditionalities. They, as well as other African groups, should be given a hearing at the Paris Group meeting. Giving opposition leaders a hearing has many advantages. It would establish a channel of communication and possibly provide some leverage over the opposition. In the past, opposition leaders simply emerged victorious from a bush war to assume power with outmoded ideas and unworkable models.

Establishing early contacts with them would help "educate" them before they take power.

Note also that one of the demands by the Malawians was "a commitment to free speech." While donor emphasis on political conditionality is important, it ignores a far more paramount need—freedom of expression. Indeed, the free market system that Western governments and institutions hope to establish in Africa is unachievable without a free marketplace of ideas. The most effective aid the West or the world can ever give Africa is to help reinstitute its native freedom of expression. As noted in Chapter 3, this freedom, contrary to the belief of many African dictators, is not a Western invention and therefore a Western imposition on Africa. Freedom of expression is rooted in indigenous African political tradition. The chief could be criticized, and dissidents were not detained or killed. This freedom of expression cannot be overemphasized, because without it Africa will never find solutions to its problems.

Unfortunately, the West has been deficient in promoting freedom of expression in Africa. Except for the National Endowment for Democracy, a private, nonprofit corporation that receives an annual appropriation from the U.S. Congress but has no power to impose political or economic sanctions, there is little institutionalized machinery for promoting democracy. Institutions to promote intellectual freedom are virtually nonexistent. There are, of course, the British Broadcasting Company, Radio Free Europe, Radio Marti, and the Voice of America. For the most part, however, these mainly carry commentaries by Westerners on events in iron-curtain countries. In fact, Africans themselves should be able to make these commentaries in their own countries freely. Clearly, greater emphasis must be placed on promoting freedom of expression in Africa since freedom of expression is the most vital of all human rights.

This does not require creating an additional layer of bureaucracy in the West. Instead the West can refocus the priorities of existing institutions charged with monitoring human rights conditions with primary emphasis on restoring freedom of expression. For example, the U.S. Department of State may seek to promote greater freedom of the press, help create a more conducive intellectual climate, and help free the media from the clutches of state control. The United Nations may also wish to enforce Article 19 of its own Universal Declaration of Human Rights more strenuously with Boutros Boutros-Ghali, an Egyptian, as the new Secretary-General.

Since economic reform is currently under way in many African countries, it needs to be coupled with political and, more important, intellectual reform. Indeed, the World Bank itself made a statement to this effect: "Ultimately, better governance requires political renewal which means, among other things, encouraging public debate and nurturing a free press" (*Sub-Saharan Africa: From Crisis to Sustainable Growth,* Nov 1989; p. 6).

Western governments could accelerate the process of total reform by providing direct aid and credit for the establishment of newspapers, radio stations, and telecommunications by private individuals in Africa. Almost everywhere in Africa in 1991 the complaint was the same: lack of freedom of expression and of association—demonstrations were banned; the media was controlled by the state, access was denied to those with opposing views; and editors and journalists were languishing in jail. But frustrated Africans resorted to other means: faxing political messages, holding secret meetings, surreptitiously placing posters, circulating tracts and cassette tapes, and even writing political commentaries on currency notes.

For example, on May 25, 1991, Kwesi Pratt and Owusu Gyimah of the Movement for Freedom and Justice (MFJ) in Ghana were arrested for putting up "unauthorised posters." According to news reports the Movement said "the decision to mount the poster campaign to put its views across to Ghanaians had been prompted by the national media being closed to its views due to state control. Posters and leaflets have therefore become the only way in which the organization can put its views across to Ghanaians" (*West Africa,* Jun 3-9, 1991; p. 914). It should be obvious to pro-democracy forces why no future government in Ghana, or Africa in general, should exercise monopoly control over the national media.

Grants or loans may be given to private individuals for the purchase of simple technologies (computer networks, and copy and facsimile transmission machines) that enhance the free flow of information. Any African government that bans or shuts them down would jeopardize its Western aid.

The existence of independent newspapers is vital and can only be ensured by providing direct aid for the importation of newsprint or by removing newsprint from the list of import-controlled items. In South Africa the European Community provided funding to a trust, run by a group of churches, for the establishment of three strongly anti-apartheid weekly newspapers: *New Nation* in Johannesburg, *South* in Cape Town, and *New African.* EC funding is channeled through the Kasigo Trust in South Africa. The trust decides which organizations receive funds to avoid the appearance of editorial manipulation by particular EC countries (*South,* Jun 1990; p. 113). A similar trust should be set up for the rest of Africa. Consider: "Of the 10 new publications which appeared on news-stands around the country since August 1991 (when parliament voted in favor of a new Constitution abolishing the one-party state), only *The Weekly Post* is independent. The rest are offshoots of the government-owned *Times of Zambia* newspaper group" (*Index on Censorship*, Mar 1992; p. 41).

The West should take the following additional steps to encourage the introduction of freedom of expression in Africa:

1. Under structural adjustment agreements the World Bank has been persuading African governments to sell state enterprises. Since the media in much of Africa is owned by the state, obviously this state-owned operation must be the first strategic enterprise to be placed on the auction block. Otherwise, there should be no structural adjustment loan.

2. Political acceptability of the restructuring programs can be enhanced and intellectual discourse promoted by having African governments draw up their own programs or commission a group of local experts to do so. Almost all African central banks have statistical research units. There are universities in Africa too. Let Africans draw up their own programs and debate them to determine which program is best for them. The World Bank and the IMF can then accept, reject, or modify the program in light of their objectives.

3. Withhold aid to any African country where there is ongoing civil war. It makes little sense to supply funds to build bridges that insurgents subsequently destroy. Such aid should be placed in escrow to give combatants the incentive to resolve differences at the negotiating table.

4. The Brady Plan, which provides economic relief assistance on the condition that economic restructuring be adopted, or debt cancellation should be restricted to those African governments that announce a date for and carry out free and fair elections. This would give the incoming administration much greater flexibility to act.

Western church organizations should more vigorously defend religious freedom, freedom of worship, and freedom of expression. As the *Wall Street Journal* observed in a June 22, 1990, editorial, "The Arabs have a saying that 'the state eats the green and the dry.' They mean that an authoritarian government consumes everything in its path. It captures the labor unions, the guilds, the bar and the middle class. It allows no bourgeois opposition and renders exiled political leaders almost powerless by strangling their domestic support. There is only one refuge, the church" (p. A8). Recall the persecution of the Catholic Church in Equatorial Guinea under Marcias Nguema and also Ghana's Religious Bodies Registration Act of 1989. The churches in Africa must be protected from tyrannical governments.

Finally, black Americans can play a historic role in the democratization process by demanding the institution of freedom of expression, the principle of one man one vote, and the holding of free, multiparty elections in every African nation. Their true brothers and sisters are the victims of oppression, not the dictators upon whom they award honorary degrees.

Furthermore, they should shun diplomats from undemocratic African countries. Too often, black Americans invite these ambassadors of tyranny to play a prominent role in social functions (for example, keynote speaker) to the distress of oppressed Africans. These diplomats should be told, in no uncertain terms, that what their governments do to their own citizens is a disgrace to black people.

## HOW AFRICANS CAN HELP THEMSELVES

Given the political situation and the intellectual climate in the West, it has become apparent that Africans will have to fight their own battles and expect little help from foreigners. They must join with Fela Anikulapo Kuti, the Nigerian musician who declared: "I will fight any government that has no respect for law and order" (West Africa, Apr 24-30, 1989; p. 659). This author will also fight any barbarous government in Africa that has no respect for freedom of expression. In many places in Africa, students, workers, and even peasants are already battling failed dictatorships.

Naturally, the strategies to fight tyranny will vary from one African country to another. But broad generalities can be made. Violations of human rights must be vigorously exposed by Africans themselves. This requires the establishment of a *free* press or media, as we saw in Chapter 9. All Africans must demand of their governments strict adherence to the United Nation's 1948 Universal Declaration of Human Rights and the OAU's African Charter of Human and Peoples' Rights. Fortuitously, a group of African professionals from different walks of life met in Brazzaville, Republic of Congo, in 1989 to form the African Commission of Health and Human Rights Promoters (*Commission African des promoteurs de la santé et de droits de l'homme* [CAPSDH]). It is a non-governmental, non-political, non-sectarian and non-profit organization dedicated to the defense and promotion of the ideals enshrined in the UN and OAU charter on human rights but with emphasis on the health and rehabilitation of victims of human rights violations.

In May 1992 a branch of CAPSDH was opened in Accra, Ghana, and its director, Dr. Edmund N. Delle, told *West Africa* that "the idea to establish the Ghana branch was born some five years ago in Geneva but it was only last year that he and a group of concerned Ghanaians, who had recognized the ignominy, degradation and waste of lives of victims of human rights abuses, became concerned enough to want to take positive steps to redress the shameful and dehumanising situation" (Jun 15-21, 1992; p. 1008). The Ghana branch will cater to Anglophone Africa while the Brazzaville office is for the Francophone countries.[5]

Africans must not only expose the appalling human rights record of tyrannical regimes on the continent but also go after the *external* and *internal* props of such regimes. African dictators cannot survive without such external and internal support. The trick is to identify these props and sever them methodically. In the past, various groups—African and non-African—have sought to sever the external support by lobbying for a cut in U.S. or Western aid to a tyrannical African regime. Unfortunately, this strategy has not proven itself to be effective. For one thing, the aid was never suspended permanently. It was restored as soon as human rights conditions improved in some nebulously defined way. For another, the strategy had little effect on tyrannical regimes on the left that did not receive much Western aid. As we saw in Chapter 11, not only the West supports dictatorial regimes in Africa. The Eastern bloc, Third World nations, and even African governments have their puppets in Africa.

That Angola, Benin, Ethiopia, Mozambique, Guinea-Bissau, and the Central African Republic have been client states of the former Eastern bloc is well known. Also known is the support Cuba has provided to governments in Angola, Ethiopia, and Ghana. Iraq supplied arms to the Eritrean rebels, the Bashir regime in Sudan, and the government of Mauritania. Saudi Arabia provided funds to the Renamo (*Resistencia Nacional Mocambicana*) rebels in Mozambique. Renamo also enjoyed support from the Moi government of Kenya. Colonel Gaddafi of Libya provided military support to governments in Burkina Faso, Chad, Ghana, Sudan, and Uganda as well as to the Liberian rebels led by Charles Taylor. Taylor's forces were also backed by the Ivory Coast and Burkina Faso.

Regardless of the origin of these external supports, they have operated to the detriment of the African people, the very people so many profess to care about. There is only one way to end this hypocrisy and outrage—by adopting measures to stanch the flow of external and internal support of governments that oppress their people.

If the West can impose sanctions against Libya and South Africa, then Africans can call for sanctions against their own illegal regimes. Any foreign government or institution—Western, Eastern, Third World, or even African—that extends credit to a military or one-party state in Africa should do so at its own risk.

In the field of international law, a loan to an illegitimate government constitutes illegitimate debt to its people. After 1992, any foreign loan or credit to a military dictatorship or a one-party state in Africa, without authorization of their people, will not be paid back. If foreign governments and agencies wish to throw away their money in Africa, they are at liberty to do so. But they should not expect Africans to pay for that indiscretion (Author's testimony before the House Foreign Affairs Sub-Committee on Africa, U.S. House of Representatives, Nov 12, 1991 in *Congressional Records*).[6]

For example, President Mobutu, not the Zairian people, should be held personally liable for any foreign loan contracted. In Tanzania, Chama Cha Mapinduzi (CCM), the sole legal party, should be held liable for the country's foreign debt; in Angola, the MPLA; in Burkina Faso, the military; in Ethiopia, the military; in Mozambique, FRELIMO; in Kenya, KANU; in South Africa, the whites; in Zambia, UNIP; in Zimbabwe, ZANU-PF; and so on. The African people are fed up with huge foreign loans that have allegedly been contracted on their behalf but without their authorization or ultimate benefit. Ethiopia, Liberia, and Somalia now lie in ruins with their people starving. Yet they must shoulder huge foreign debt burdens. What benefits did they derive from those loans?[7] Indeed, many other Africans are already thinking along these lines, especially members of Zairian opposition groups: "Because Mobutu is openly accused of corruption and embezzlement by the U.S. Congress, by the UDSP and other opposition parties, these groups threaten that the moment they come to power they will obtain the repatriation of Mobutu's assets abroad. They think that Mobutu's private hoard could wipe out most of Zaire's $9 billion overseas debt" (*New African*, Jun 1990; p. 19).

The most treacherous support for tyrannical regimes in Africa, however, has come from within Africa itself—the military, the civil service, journalists profession and the intellectual community. In fact, the West could not impose a Mobutu on Africa if there were no internal supports. And where these internal supports have been lacking, many dictatorships have been overthrown despite Western or foreign supports. Therefore the internal supports—the military, the civil servants, intellectuals, urban workers, trade unions, and the mass media—must also be cut off.

As we saw in Chapter 7, the military itself has become the problem in many African countries. Obviously a general movement toward establishing professionalism in the military would reduce its involvement in politics. But this is unlikely because most military regimes seldom return to the barracks. Nevertheless, the people can reform the military by neutralizing its superiority in weapons and exploiting its numerical inferiority by staging a civil service strike. The military does not have the manpower to run the civil service. For example, in Benin the strike by civil servants and students that began in February 1989 ultimately drove Brig. Gen. Mathieu Kerekou from office by virtually paralyzing the operation of all government offices (*Africa Report*, Mar-Apr 1990; p. 8). In Ghana two successive civil service strikes created environments that enabled palace coups to topple the military governments of General I. K. Acheampong in 1978 and Lt. Gen. Frederick Akuffo in 1979. No civilian lives were lost. It turned out that the military government of General Akuffo itself set up a commission of enquiry into the civil service strike of November 1978. The report, which was published in April 1979 and freely sold to the Ghanaian public, detailed the planning and execution of the strike and concluded that the civil service was the key to the successful operation of the central government: "The fact should not be overlooked that the Civil Service is, in the final analysis, the machinery of Central Government. Without it, the policies and plans of Government will fail, and Government itself will collapse" (*Report of the Commission of Enquiry into the Civil Service Strike of November 1978*, Accra: Government Printer, paragraph 291, page 67).

Word of the success of civil service strikes is spreading. Consider: "Zairean civil servants have now been on strike for nearly two months and there appears to be little prospect of a settlement. The strike began on July 9, 1990 with the strikers seeking a 500 percent increase in salaries. The government has offered 100 percent but this has been rejected. The strike has severely disrupted work in a number of ministries, with the customs service particularly badly affected (*West Africa*, Sep 3-9, 1990; p. 2410).

Independent trade unions, the removal of price controls, and a free press should also help weaken some of the internal supports that enable tyrannical regimes to survive. Over the decades, African dictators have used price controls, ostensibly imposed to make food less expensive, to solidify political support among urban workers. The use of price controls partly explains President Kenneth Kaunda's dilemma when, in 1987 and 1990, he reluctantly attempted to remove subsidies on cornmeal, a local staple. His moves provoked urban riots; the peasants did not participate. He reinstated the subsidies to end the riots.

While urban workers can be bought politically with a few subsidies, African intellectuals, journalists, and even opposition leaders, who should know better, can be bought even more cheaply. Africa's tyrants get away with it because the elites do not exact any punishment for collaboration. For example, in March 1992, opposition groups in Burkina Faso finally managed to put together a coalition to confront the barbaric military dictatorship of Blaise Compaore in a national forum. But,

> Only a day to the forum, the already-divided coalition broke even further when one of its leading members, the Alliance for Democracy and Federation of Herman Yameogo, announced its withdrawal . . .
>
> Yameogo's compensation for his withdrawal came 10 days after the suspension of the forum, when he was appointed a minister of state in a surprise cabinet reshuffle. He joined the government together with three other opposition figures, thereby strengthening Compaore's [hand] . . . It had been rumored that Yameogo had struck a deal with the authorities for this post (*West Africa*, Mar 9-15, 1992; p. 41).

African elites should learn from the "illiterate" peasants. During the struggle against colonial rule those chiefs who collaborated with the oppressors were destooled, some even disposed of. Even today, in some parts of Africa, the peasants still go after collaborators of evil regimes. For example, in July 1991 Zairean opposition leader Tshikesedi was warned that if he accepted a prime ministerial post from Mobutu, his house would be burned down. Tshikesedi backed off. Later, he accepted the position with the full approval of the opposition but in October was "fired" by Mobutu. Bernardin Mungul-Diaka was appointed as the new prime minister. He was also warned not to accept the position. His house was burned down when he refused.

These peasant efforts should be replicated by placing the elites on notice: "After 1992, any African intellectual or civilian who serves under a military regime or a one-party state system in a capacity above that of Assistant Principal Secretary (for example, principal secretaries, ministers, ambassadors, governors of banks, vice-chancellors, etc.) will be disqualified from serving under any future democratic civilian government, from holding employment in any such government agency or institution and from any contractual dealings with such a government."[8] Collaborating with an alien regime is just as treacherous as collaborating with the colonialists. There should be no place in a future democratic Africa for intellectual collaborators of dictatorial regimes. The worst of the lot are Africa's chameleon diplomats, who strenuously defend repressive regimes at home and then, come a change of government, suddenly start to sing a different tune.

New, democratically-elected heads of state should clean up Africa's diplomatic missions abroad by assigning new functions and clearing out the "career diplomats," who have served one brutal regime after another. The new democrats should then extend the crusade to neighboring countries and the OAU itself. At an AFL-CIO function in Washington, D.C. on February 15, 1992, Zambia's freely elected president, Frederick Chiluba observed: "In Africa today, the era of dictators, of hypocrisy and lies is over . . . In this present crisis, government alone is not the solution to our problems. For too long, the government was the problem." Excellent message, but delivered at the *wrong* place. Chiluba should have taken this message to neighboring Angola, Malawi, Mozambique, Tanzania, Zaire, Zimbabwe, and on to the OAU. But as soon as democrats like Chiluba are elected into office, they forget that other Africans are waging the *same* struggle and therefore need help too.

All of Africa's newly-elected presidents, academics, intellectuals, and journalists must stand for diversity of opinion and the freedom of expression to air their views. *Intellectual pluralism* ought to be the objective. Furthermore, each profession should practice *group* as well as *inter-group solidarity*. It is true that journalists, writers, and academics have been persecuted in the past but nobody is going to defend them if each profession is not willing to defend itself. One useless body has been the Pan-African Writers Association (PAWA). Like the OAU, PAWA meets for an annual jamboree while numerous writers are jailed and killed in Africa. It has yet to pry one member of its own from prison.

> One reason why the press is relatively free in Nigeria is that if one editor is detained, all journalists demand his release. Henceforth, if one editor/journalist is seized, all must go to his aid and demand his release. If one lecturer is snatched, all must go to his aid. If one student is detained, all must go to his aid.
>
> If the educated do not understand what group solidarity is, they should beat up just one soldier and see what the military establishment will do (interview given by the author to *Christian Messenger,* Accra, Jan-Feb 1992; p. 3).

On June 15, 1992 the Nigerian Bar Association called a strike to demand that the Babangida regime produce four human rights activists, who had been detained without charge. "Authorities finally presented the activists (Campaign for Democracy Chairman Beko Ransome-Kuti, lawyers Gani Fawehinmi and Femi Falana, Baba Omojola, and student leader Olusegun Mayegun) before a magistrate's court in Gwagwadala, a village in central Nigeria" (*Washington Post,* Jun 16, 1992; p. A16). But when three Ghanaian judges were abducted and brutally murdered in 1983 by PNDC operatives, the Ghana Bar Association did nothing. Nor did the Ghana Journalist Association when George Naykene, editor of the *Christian Chronicle,* was detained in November 1991. He wrote that members of the Armed Forces

Revolutionary Council (AFRC), which ruled briefly in 1979, benefitted from an illegal loan the civilian government of the PNP took from an Italian businessman.

If a student body or any other association is under siege, all other professions and associations must go to its aid. Remember that "the stick used to beat your enemy is the same stick that will be used to beat you too," says a Fanti proverb. Translation: the powers used to clobber a student organization are the same ones that will be used to beat the bar association. The essence of this proverb was expressed by the Rev. Dartey, General Secretary of the Christian Council of Ghana, at a symposium on multi-party democracy in January 1992. He warned Christians that if they do not take steps to fight creeping dictatorship they may one day end up like Pastor Nimbohlor, who before he died recorded in a confession as follows: "First they came for the Jews, but because I was not a Jew I did not speak out. Then they came for the gypsies, but because I was not a gypsy I did not speak out. Then they came for the trade unionists, but because I was not a trade unionist, I did not speak out. And then they came for me. But by then, there was no one left to speak for me" (*West Africa*, Feb 7-23, 1992; p. 283; the original version is attributed to Martin Niemoeller).

In France, many spoke out for one African writer: "A Moroccan dissident expelled from France as a danger to state security returned to Paris after a court overturned a Government decision to deport him ... The June 20, 1991 expulsion of the writer, Abdelmoumen Diouri, raised a furor in France from rights groups and opposition politicians. Critics accused the Government of expelling Mr. Diouri because his forthcoming book accused Morocco, a French ally, of corruption" (*The New York Times*, Jul 17, 1991; p. A4).

The final internal support has often been the opposition itself. In past efforts to democratize Africa, the focus was on tyrannical regimes. But democratic values have to be instilled in the opposition, too. As we saw in Chapter 12, the opposition in many parts of Africa inspires little confidence. It is often fragmented and given to petty bickering. Facing a disorganized opposition, an African dictator does not require much skill to survive. The opposition in Africa needs to improve its preparation and organization.

Political events in Bangladesh, Czechoslovakia, Nicaragua, Poland, and other countries outside Africa have demonstrated eloquently that one person alone seldom succeeds in the battle to remove a tyrant. Nor does one political group or organization. A *coalition* of forces, groups, or organizations is imperative. This implies that coordination of pro-democracy activities is mandatory.

In Nicaragua a coalition of 13 opposition parties, including ideologically mortal enemies (communists and capitalists), succeeded in ousting the Marxist dictatorship of Daniel Ortega in March 1990. The opposition coalition did not field 13 presidential candidates. Sensibly, they put forward only Violeta Chamorro. Had they put forward six or even three candidates, Daniel Ortega would have won easily since the opposition vote would have been split.

Here is the mathematics of it. A tyrant in power always has some supporters. Let us assume this support to be, say, 30 percent of the vote. That means the overwhelming majority of the electorate is opposed to the government in power. Now suppose the opposition fields five presidential candidates. If they split the opposition vote equally, each would get only 14 percent of the vote, which is not enough to defeat the tyrant with 30 percent of the vote. This was what happened in Benin (only a second run-off election defeated Mathieu Kerekou) and in the Ivory Coast (although there was some election rigging).

There are two ways in which this can be prevented. One is to insert in the constitution a clause stipulating *run-off* elections if no one wins at least 50 percent of the plurality of votes. In the case of Benin, Mathieu Kerekou was eliminated in the second round of balloting. The other way to defeat a tyrant electorally is for the coalition of opposition parties to field only one candidate, as in the case of Nicaragua and Zambia.

If a coalition president (like Chiluba) is chosen, he should be restricted to only one term of office and if an interim president is chosen to oversee the transition process, he should be debarred from running in the coming presidential elections, as was the case of Liberia's interim president, Amos Sawyer, in 1991. He was to serve only one term.

Obviously a great deal of coordination and calculation are required on the part of the opposition in strategies adopted to remove a tyrant through the ballot box. But squabbling inevitably erupts. The main reason why opposition leaders bicker is that they lack focus. Personal ambitions and beliefs get in the way. Each leader's secret ambition is to be president and, since each sees the other as a rival, it is impossible for them to trust and work with each other. For public relations consumption they may put up a facade of cooperation and amity. But beneath the surface they are busy tearing each other apart. This arrant stupidity can only aid the tyrant in power.

Opposition leaders claim they are fighting for "democracy," yet they do not practice it in their own organizations. They denounce the tribalistic tendencies of the government in power. Yet the opposition groups are no better, drawing their memberships overwhelmingly from particular tribes;

for example, the ANC from the Xhosa, Inkatha from the Zulu, and UNITA from the Ovimbundu. How are these ethnically-based political associations different from South Africa's Nationalist Party, composed mostly of whites? Obviously each opposition group in Africa needs to broaden its support base to include other ethnic groups.

Every year each opposition party should hold a vote of confidence in its leader. Voting should be by secret ballot. Some leaders run their organizations like their own personal property and refuse to stand down even when they have lost all credibility. How are they different from the tyrants they seek to replace? Those who preach democracy ought to practice it "at home"—in their own organizations.

Every opposition leader must take an oath to the effect that he is prepared to step down should a majority of members so desire. Too many opposition leaders are driven by personal ambition and the obsession to become head of state. One does not have to be the head of state of an African country to be a "somebody." As a matter of fact, the presidency can be hazardous to one's health. How many of Africa's numerous heads of state are alive and still living in their countries as free men? In 1991 the number was less than seven, out of over 150 leaders that Africa has had since 1960. But it is the smell of loot that keeps attracting hyenas.

Once a year, membership rosters of all opposition groups should be reviewed. If there is a preponderance of one ethnic group in the organization, it is an indication that the leader has failed to broaden the base of the organization and he should be replaced.

It is probably true that opposition to a hated regime often comes from a motley coalition of groups with diverse interests and beliefs, which disintegrates into factionalism once the common enemy is vanquished. It is also true that when a people, long kept in a boiling cauldron of oppression, suddenly find the lid removed, they spend their remaining energy battling chimerical enemies. But such explanations offer little comfort to the victims and the wanton destruction.

Steps should be taken to avoid destructive internecine feuds and competition for political power. The first step is to *educate* the opposition leaders on the requisites of true democracy and political maturity. The second is to define the *focus* of the struggle, and the third is to get all parties to sign a *covenant* of rules which all must agree to play by.

## Education of Opposition Leaders

It is sad and painful to admit that the level of political sophistication and intellectual maturity of some of our opposition leaders is disgustingly low. All opposition groups and leaders must recognize that the political arena is a free marketplace and they are like merchants, peddling political ideas and solutions. If they demand the right to propagate their political philosophy, they cannot deny anyone else the right to do so. If their philosophy has any merit, the people will buy it. If not, they will reject it. It is not up to the opposition leaders to make this determination, but the people.

Furthermore, most opposition leaders define "democracy" only in terms of their right to form political parties, to hold rallies, and to criticize foolish government policies. But as we saw in the previous chapter, institutions such as the rule of law, freedom of expression, and an independent judiciary are far more important.

## Focus

The primary focus of all opposition groups in Africa should be on removing the tyrant in power and establishing a level political playing field. If the tyrant is crafting a dubious transition process, the focus should be on halting or changing that process. All other issues (such as who should be president, what type of ideology the country should follow, a political platform, whether the country should have a new currency or flag) are secondary.

## The Covenant

Quite clearly, the opposition in Africa needs to "get its act together." One effective way of doing this is to draw up a covenant, a set of rules by which all opposition groups agree to abide.[9] At a meeting of all opposition leaders, a covenant should be signed containing the following stipulations:

1.  Politics is a competitive game, and therefore the rules of competition must be established and respected by all. The term of the president will be limited to two terms (of four years each) in office.

2.  All must agree on the safeguards and the necessary structures to be adopted to ensure free and fair elections. Political maturity requires accepting electoral defeat graciously and congratulating the winner. Political violence and voter intimidation must be eschewed. Severe sanctions, such as disqualification or heavy

fines, must be imposed against any political party that is guilty of murder of political opponents.

3. Ultimately, it is the African people themselves who must determine what is best for them; not what one person imposes upon them. To do this, the African people need the means and the forum as well as the freedom to participate in the decisionmaking process.

4. Each opposition leader must agree to respect and honor the OAU's Charter of People's and Human Rights. This Charter is explicit on freedom of expression, freedom from arbitrary arrests, press freedoms, and so forth.

5. No one person or party shall monopolize the means or the forum by which the people can participate. All leaders will undertake to respect the right of every African to air his opinion freely, without harassment or intimidation, even if his view diverges from that of the head of state. Tolerance of diversity of opinion is a sign of intellectual maturity.

6. The media shall be taken out of the hands of the government. Religion and foreign ideology must be kept out of government. All leaders must pledge to build on or improve Africa's indigenous institutions and culture.

7. All must agree on sanctions to be applied against any leader or political party acting in violation of this covenant. Such sanctions must be determined by the leaders themselves.

After all is said and done, it becomes apparent that it is the educated elites—the leaders and the intellectuals—who have failed Africa. The Vai of Liberia have a proverb most appropriate for this situation. If after spending their meager savings to educate a child, he returns to the village an ignoramus, Vais elders may look upon him and ruefully remark: "The moon shines brightly but it is still dark in some places." Doesn't this describe postcolonial Africa and its elites?

Common sense has probably been the scarcest commodity among the elites in postcolonial Africa. Most of the "educated" leaders lacked it, intellectuals flouted it, and the opposition, in many cases, was woefully deficient in it. The peasants may be "illiterate and backward," but at least they can use their common sense. Obviously, a *common sense revolution* is what is urgently needed in African government.

It would be fitting to end this book with a poem written by Mahjoub Mohamed Sherif, known in Sudan as "The People's Poet." The poem is dedicated to African dictators: [10]

Hey . . . Buffoon
cling,
beware falling apart,
beware and be all alert
and lend your ears to every move
and look as well to your shadow
and when the leaves rustle
seclude yourself
keep still
it is so dangerous
you buffoon

Fire on everything, bullet everything
every word uttered
every breeze passing without
your permission
Mr Buffoon

Teach the sparrow
the village lanterns
the towns' windows
and all stalks to report to
You

Make the ants infiltrate
and join the securitat
ask the rain drops
to write its reports
You buffoon

(Translated from the Arabic by Africa Watch and reprinted by
*Index on Censorship*, Feb 1991; p. 22).

While battling current despots, Africans should be vigilant, think ahead, and formulate strategies against the next buffoon. Since the winds of democratic change began sweeping across Africa in 1990, all sorts of intellectual crackpots, corrupt former politicians, charlatans, and unsavory elements have suddenly jumped on to the "democracy bandwagon" to hijack the democratic revolution. In 1992, Kaunda, and Nyerere, for example, were all preaching multiparty democracy. Where were they back in 1985 when true democrats were laying their lives on the line to demand political pluralism? As this book has attempted to show, the African story is one of betrayal—by one buffoon after another.

---

## NOTES

1. These elites had too little faith to invest their ill-gotten wealth in their own economies. Yet they urged foreigners to invest in Africa.

2. Nigerian columnist, Pini Jason, observed that one of the driving motivations to office has been the power to dispense largesse, the power to appoint and dismiss, and the power to make and unmake. Therefore, the first official act of Nigerians in office has been to create offices and appointments to be handed out. The customary method has been to dissolve the boards of government corporations. Jason wrote: "And so the Lagos State governor was acting within both his right and tradition when he dissolved all the boards of government agencies in his state. Absolutely nothing wrong with that, except that His Excellency did not know that there were no boards in the first place. They were dissolved by his predecessor!" (New African, Apr 1992; p. 21).

3. If fear is the primary motivating factor, there is a *sensible* way out of this dilemma. The wise head of state would call a meeting of all opposition leaders in a spirit of "national reconciliation" and negotiate a way out. Items for negotiation might include an indemnity, safe passage out of the country in return for the repatriation of the country's wealth that was looted by his regime. An apology or compensation to the families of those executed might also be discussed. Another African head of state, a World Bank official, or some foreign ambassador should be invited as an observer. But the military regime in Ghana did not adopt this method. It convened a Consultative Assembly to draw up Ghana's constitution and after the Assembly had finished work on the constitution, the military regime clandestinely inserted an "indemnity" clause at the eleventh hour and presented the constitution to the people as "final." Ghanaians were outraged.

4. A "mammy truck" is a vehicle used to transport both people and goods. It is made by constructing a wooden cabin over a truck chassis. Seating is provided by a carefully arranged rows of planks that can be removed to provide space for goods.

5. In May 1992 the clinic took in 45 ex-detainees to start them on the slow, painful road to recovery. "On their arrival at Dr. Delle's clinic where the commission is based, the ex-detainees were taken through counselling, especially those who were victims of torture. Dr. Delle said a number of them had marks on their bodies that conformed to internationally categorised signs of torture . . . The ex-detainees included people from all walks of life—shoe makers, armed forces personnel, *mallams*, staff of

the Bureau of National Investigations. Most of them testified to the commission, in writing, that they were never tried so they never found out the actual reason for their detention . . . There were those who had spent 6 years in detention, others 9 nine years without trial, they told the commission" (*West Africa*, Jun 15-21, 1992; p. 1009). In 1991 the PNDC regime vehemently denied an accusation by the Movement for Freedom and Justice (MFJ) that there were scores of political detainees in Ghana.

6.  This testimony was reprinted in the following African publications: *Ghana Drum* (Gaithersburg, Md., Jan 1992; p. 6), *The African Mirror*, (Silver Spring, Md., Jan 1992; p. 8), and *African Economic Digest* (Nigeria, Dec 2, 1991; p. 21).

7.  In November 1990 the main opposition parties in Bangladesh warned donor countries and agencies that aid given during the rule of President Hussain Mohammad Ershad would not be paid back. "The military junta of President Ershad is plundering public money, and to make that up every year new taxes and levies are being imposed . . . People will not pay the loans back," said Sheik Hasina Wajed, the head of the Awami League. Donors should help a representative government and not "a government run with the power of the gun," she said, adding that proper accounts of aid funds are not available.

    Begum Khaleda Zia, head of the Bangladesh Nationalist Party, accused Mr. Ershad and his cronies of hoarding aid in foreign bank accounts and said, "people will not bear the pressure of paying back the debt" (*The Washington Times*, Nov 7, 1990; p. A2).

    Two weeks later, the military government of President Ershad collapsed when aid donors withheld funds.

8.  Author's statement, published in *Christian Messenger*, Accra, Jan-Feb 1992; p. 3).

9.  It is instructive to note that in 1991 the Nigerian Trade Union Congress adopted a covenant that mandates a general strike if a civilian government is overthrown in a coup. The civil service in *every* African nation should draw up and adopt such a covenant.

10. Mahjoub Sherif was repeatedly arrested and jailed in 1971, 1974, 1976, and 1979 by the Numeiry regime for writing "seditious" and "dangerous" poems. The poems were banned by the two government-controlled radio stations in Sudan. He was again arrested on September 20, 1989, by the Bashir regime and held without charge in a Port Sudan prison.

# APPENDIX

## STATE REPRESSION OF FREE EXPRESSION

The following representative cases have been culled from *Index on Censorship*. Dates of issue are in parentheses.

**ALGERIA:** On October 3, 1988, Abdennour Ali-Yahia, president of the (non-authorized) Algerian Human Rights League, was officially charged with damaging "the reputation of an established body" (i.e., the state). He was interrogated by a judge about two articles published in the French press. The first, published by *Le Monde* on September 30, 1988, was a review of a press conference he gave about the human rights situation in the country; and the second, published on September 19 by *Liberation*, was about a death threat he had received from anonymous phone callers. (1/89)

**BENIN:** Leon Yelone (30) and Moussa Mama Yori (37) were arrested on October 14 and 24, 1988, respectively, on suspicion of having links with left-wing opponents of the government. Neither has yet been charged. Both were previously detained without charge or trial from 1979 until the presidential amnesty in 1984. Yelone is currently held at Camp Guezo military camp in Cotonou, the capital, where political detainees have often been tortured. Yori's whereabouts are unknown. More than 200 people are believed to be in detention in connection with their nonviolent opposition to President Kerekou's government. A recent "restrictive" amnesty has been denounced by the Lagos-based Committee for the Defence of Human Rights, which wants a "general and total amnesty" and a lifting of the ban on meetings. (3/89)

**BURKINA FASO:** Over 30 trade unionists were arrested throughout the country in June 1987, following a complaint submitted by the Confederation Syndicate Burkinabe (CSB) to the International Labor Organization in April about restrictions on trade union activities. The arrests followed the detention of four leading members of CSB in May: Soumane Toure, Salif Kabore, Adama Toure, and Louis-Armand Ouali. (9/87)

Boukary Dabo, a medical student at the University of Ouagadougou who was among 16 students arrested in May 1990, is reported to have died in custody in early October 1990, probably as a result of torture. Eight of the others are believed to have been forcibly conscripted into the armed forces. (1/91)

**BURUNDI**: Leon Bantigira, a civil servant, Aloys Habonimana, a lecturer at Bujumbura University, Deo Hakizimana, a journalist, Terence Ndayakire, a financier, Leonce Ndikumana, a lecturer at the university, Augustin Nasnse, a history lecturer, and Salvator Sunzu, an engineer, were all arrested in September 1988 after signing an open letter to President Buyoya criticizing the government's policy toward members of the Hutu community and the killing in August of thousands of Hutu by government troops. The prisoners' whereabouts are unknown. (10/88)

**CAMEROON**: In the 1960s the country had 15 private newspapers; now only the *Cameroon Times* publishes. (The *Cameroon Tribune* is state-owned.) The National Documentary Centre, the country's secret police, can enter the editorial offices, arrest and detain journalists, and seize publications it judges "detrimental to public order."

In 1983 Charles Ndi-Chia, an editor, and his senior reporter, Andu Bello, were picked up by the secret police and kept under inhumane conditions for eight days. Their offense was to have published a newspaper without prior censorship. Another journalist, Nkemayang Paul, was detained for eight days, on orders of a district officer, when he refused to surrender certain documents at his disposal. (5/86)

Intellectuals in the country protested the arrest of academics and journalists following a debate on political literature held in March 1987. Among those in custody are Ambroise Kom, author and head of conferences at Yaounde University, Bassek Ba Khobio, author and literary critic at Radio-Cameroon, Martin Soua Ntyam, reader, Ebona Myetam, editor-in-chief, David Ndachi, cultural editor, and Jean-Marie Nzekoue, reporter, all working for the *Cameroon Tribune*. Dismissed were Jean Mboudou and Jean Luc Kuomo from the *Cameroon Tribune*. (1/88)

Professor Ambroise Kom made "irrelevant comments" about the head of state during the debate and criticized writers "who sang the praises of the government." (6/87)

Three members of the editorial board of the *Cameroon Tribune*, Zambou Zoleko (director general), Jean Mboudou (editorial director), and Jean Luc Kouamo (assistant editor-in-chief) were arrested in February 1987 for printing a decree that was not entirely authorized by President Biya. (4/87)

Albert Mukong, the politician and writer arrested on June 16, 1988, while returning from neighboring Nigeria, is now believed to have been charged with "secession" and distributing false news. His arrest followed an interview he gave to the BBC in which he criticized corruption among high-ranking government officers. He was previously imprisoned for six years in the 1970s. His book, *Prisoner without a Crime*, published in English in 1986, has been banned. The maximum penalty for "secession" is 15 years' imprisonment (or the death sentence if a state of emergency is declared). (3/89)

Yondo Black, a former president of the Cameroon Bar Association, Albert Mukong, a writer and former prisoner of conscience, Anicet Ekane, a company director suffering from a gastric ulcer, Rodolphe Bwanja, an accountant, Charles Njoh Njon, a journalist, and Henriette Ekew, a freelance translator, are among some 12 people detained since February 1990 on suspicion of attempting to set up a political party in this one-party state. None has so far been charged. (4/90)

Martina Agbor, a police officer, Abraham Abenyan Mboh, a public relations consultant, and Chrysanthus Agha were arrested on or around September 26, 1990, apparently in connection with their possession of documents connected with the Cameroon Democratic Party, an opposition group based outside the country. They were reportedly being held in the cells of the *Brigade Mixte Mobile* prison in Douala and may have been tortured. (1/91)

**CENTRAL AFRICAN REPUBLIC:** Seventeen people, including radio journalist Thomas Koazo, were arrested in Bangui, the capital, between October 13 and 17, 1990, after calling for a national conference to discuss multiparty democracy. The others were Adjerou Abdouraman, Nicaise Abourou, Oumarou Chaka, Robert Djoimer, Joseph Griss-Bembe, Ibrahim Houssein, Issa Ibrahim, Jean-Hilaire Kovomatchi, General Thimothee Malendoma, Godefroy Mokamanede, Jean-Firmin Mosseba, Dieudonne Namti, Tobie N'Garagba, Sakabede, Feikeram Sam and Arsene Yema. The public meeting they held on October 13 to discuss conference organization was dispersed by security forces. (1/91)

**CHAD:** Thomas Koazo, a Pana desk journalist, was sentenced to three years in prison for "misinforming the public" and "offending the head of state" on August 17, 1987. (10/87)

Saleh Gaba, a journalist arrested by the security forces on June 14, 1987, died in detention, possibly as long ago as June 1988. Gaba, who was in his early 30s, previously worked for *Agence France Presse* and Associated Press. He had been arrested twice before, in 1981 and 1984, in connection with his journalistic activities. During his last detention he was never formally charged or tried. (2/89)

At least 20 supporters of the transitional Government of National Unity, which ruled the country from 1979 to 1982, were arrested by the security services in June and July 1988 and held in secret detention. No formal charges had yet been brought against them by the end of the year. (2/89)

Moukhar Bachar Moukhtar, secretary of state at the Ministry of Agriculture, has been in detention at a military camp since July 1988 on suspicion of expressing opinions critical of President Hisseni Habre's policies. He has been denied medical attention and access to his lawyers. (5/89)

Six members of the Hadjerai ethnic group, including Gamane Moussa, a retired member of the French colonial army, Djibrine Daoud, and Kaffine Abouzarga, a trader, were arrested on or after January 24, 1989, and have since been held in secret detention. No reasons have been given for their arrests. (5/89)

EGYPT: Over 100 journalists staged a sit-down protest at the Journalists' Union headquarters to protest police harassment and restrictions imposed by Interior Minister Zaki Badr. They also demanded the abolition of restrictions on newspaper publishing included in the Press Law of 1980. (2/88)

Mustafa Mohammed Said El-Sharkawi, Mohammed Hussein, Ibrahim Sallam and Hassan Mohammed Isma'eel Mohammed have been held in continous detention without trial (under the 1978 Emergency Act) since September 28, 1990. Their only "crime" is that they were born to Muslim fathers but chose to embrace the Christian faith. They have all been ill-treated or tortured in prison. (2/91)

ETHIOPIA: Martha Kumsa, a writer for the Oromo-language newspaper, *Barissa*, was arrested in February 1980 and detained without charges in Alem Bekagne ("end of world") prison. She wrote about the rights of Ethiopia's Oromo minority.(5/86)

Ten long-term political detainees, including Gezahegne Kassahun, former deputy chairman of the All-Ethiopian Trades Union, and Kebede Demissie, a former Ministry of Agriculture official, have reportedly disappeared from detention. They had all been detained without trial since 1980. (6/87)

GABON: Georges Koupangoye and Louis de Dravo, general manager and editor, respectively, of the national daily *L'Union*, have been dismissed from their jobs by a presidential decree. This action was allegedly in response to the paper's column "Makaya," which was thought to be insulting to some government officials when it said, "Freedom stops where that of others begins." (1/88)

The November 1987 issue of *Taxi Ville*, an African magazine published in Paris, has been banned in Gabon for publishing an article, "Gabon, All Is Not Well." The article suggested that the country was in economic difficulties and that there was "friction" in its relations with France. (3/88)

GAMBIA: Sana Menneh, editor of the *Torch* independent newspaper, was arrested in Banjul on October 18, 1988, and detained overnight. He claims to have been interrogated about an article he wrote accusing Lamine Saho (minister of information and tourism), Mamadou Cadi Cham (minister of public works and communications), Saihou Sabally (minister of agriculture), and Jallow Sonko (minister of local administration) of using their public positions corruptly to enrich themselves. (1/89)

GHANA: The following were arrested on suspicion of seditious activities in relation to their membership in two opposition organizations, the New Democratic Movement (NDM) and the Kwame Nkrumah Revolutionary Guards (KNRG): Yaw Tony Akoto-Ampaw, general secretary of NDM, Kwesi Pratt, a journalist and secretary general of KNRG, Kwame Karikari, a lecturer at the University of Ghana School of Journalism and Mass Communications, and a former director general of the Ghana Broadcasting Corporation, Akwasi Adu-Amankwah, head of the political department of the Trade Union Congress, Yaw Graham, press and information secretary of NDM and a former government official, and John Ndebugre, a former agriculture minister and acting general secretary of the KNRG. (9/87)

Ben Ephson, a freelance journalist for *West Africa*, was arrested by officers from the Bureau of National Investigation on September 22, 1987, on charges of "gathering economic intelligence." (2/88). He was later released.

The December 1988 issue of the London-based monthly magazine, *New African*, was confiscated by the authorities for carrying an interview with Major (retired) Boakye Djan (a former colleague of head of state Flight Lt. Rawlings), who now lives in exile in Britain. The issue also carried an article by the magazine's assistant editor, Baffour Ankomah, critical of the 1988 district elections. (3/89)

GUINEA: Bakary Sakho, a former member of parliament, Nansadi Berete, an engineer, and N'Vanfing Kourouma, a businessman, have been detained in prison since August 1990 in connection with their distribution of an edition of the newspaper of the *Rassemblement du Peuple's Guineen* (Guinean People's Organization) which accused the government of corruption. They have been charged with endangering the internal security of the state. (1/91)

**IVORY COAST:** Honore Ade, Jean Agbre, Jean Amea, Andre Tata Dable, Bertin Ganin (deputy secretary general of a school teachers' union), Lucien Guei, Dominique Kamanan, Tiburce Koffi, Philipp Yapo, Bernard Zougon, and one other, were arrested between mid-September and mid-October 1987 in connection with a dispute concerning the school teachers' trade union, Le Syndicat National des Enseignants du Second Degre de Côte d'Ivoire. The authorities have announced that they are being conscripted into the army to do their national service and to receive a civic and moral education. Since the end of October, they have been held in a military camp in Seguela. (3/88)

Three members of the same family were arrested on February 19, 1990: Senin Don Mello Ahoua, leader of the Yamoussokro branch of the Syndicat Nationale de L'Enseignement Superieur teachers' union, student Senin Don Mello Eloge (17), and student Senin Don Mello Cyriac (21). No reasons were given, but it is thought that they may have been arrested in connection with distribution of the magazine, *L'Evenement*, produced by the opposition Ivorian Popular Front (not recognized in this one-party state). The first edition of *L'Evenement* was published in January. It called for a peaceful transition to democracy and modernization of the country's political institutions. Several people were detained for short periods in Gagnoa and Bouaffle for selling the paper, and on February 12 the interior minister banned its printing and distribution to "protect public order." (5/90)

**KENYA:** Since March 1986 more than 200 people have been arrested and held incommunicado illegally and without official acknowledgment. Many are reported to have been tortured. Abuya Abuya, an outspoken member of parliament, was picked up by security police and taken to an unknown destination on January 25, 1987. During a press conference on January 18, 1987, while on a visit to Kenya, U.S. Rep. Howard E. Wolpe, chairman of the House Foreign Affairs Committee, accused the Kenyan police of silencing Kenyans with whom he tried to discuss human rights abuses. He confessed himself "frankly stunned" when a meeting he was having with a church leader was interrupted by a policeman who warned the pastor that his meeting was "not in the interest of the state." (3/87)

"The first few months of 1987 have boded ill for Kenyans believing in liberty. There has been unprecedented repression against religious and nongovernment organizations, foreign diplomatic missions, politicians and civil servants . . . Said U.S. Congressman, Rep. Wolpe, 'human rights and democracy are fast deteriorating' " (*New African,* April 1987; p. 18).

In 1987 ten people, including Gibson Kamau Kuria, one of the country's leading lawyers, were detained under the Preservation of Public Security Act. This provides for detention for an indefinite period without charge or trial to maintain public security. (6/87)

Jaramogi Oginga Odinga, a key figure in the early years of independence, has criticized President Moi's government for its "gradual slide towards tyranny." He criticized the "erosion of democratic traditions," detention without trial, and the practice of holding people incommunicado and subjecting them to "brutal and inhuman indignities." (6/87)

Kiraitu Murungi, a prominent lawyer, has issued four separate summonses on Kenya's attorney general, Matthew Muli, alleging illegal detention and torture of two prominent lawyers (Wanyiri Kihoro and Mirugi Kariuku), a university lecturer (Mukaru Mg'ang'a), and a carpenter (Stephen Wanjema). All four had been beaten, starved, and deprived of sleep in an effort to make them sign confessions. According to reports by independent monitoring sources, over 70 illegally detained suspects have been tortured. (7/87)

Peter Karanka Njenga, a businessman who "disappeared" after being arrested on February 7, 1987, was identified at the morgue in Kenyatta National Hospital in Nairobi. He died as a result of torture. There were wounds on his neck and elsewhere. Charles Kariuku, a councilor and local official of KANU was arrested and held without charge. Peter Kinyajui, Danson Mahogo, and George Kilhara Mwangi, businessmen from the town of Nakuru, were arrested for suspected opposition to the government in February 1987. (5/87)

The minister of state for internal security has refused to grant the usual remission to the historian and university lecturer, Maina wa Kinyatti. He insists that the scholar serve the full six years of his jail sentence. (1/88) On Kinyatti's behalf, Wole Soyinka wrote an open letter to the Kenyan high commissioner that was published in the *Guardian* of July 23, 1987. Excerpt:

> The name MAINA WA KINYATTI must be familiar to you. Maina, a senior lecturer in history at Kenyatta University, was arrested on June 3, 1982. He is acknowledged as the leading scholar whose research and published writing has supported the interpretation of the freedom struggle in Kenya as a nationalist movement . . . What justifies keeping an African scholar under these conditions?

What needs of security make the state confine a brilliant mind among certified lunatics? But, finally, what stops the government of Kenya, and President arap Moi very specifically, from releasing Maina wa Kinyatti this moment? (He was released on October 17, 1988, and subsequently fled to the United States.)

In April 1988 Gitobu Imanyara, editor of the *Nairobi Law Monthly*, appeared in court on charges of "theft and misuse of a publishing licence" after publishing articles dealing with political detention and trials. (6/88)

John Muugai Wariru, a detainee for alleged links with the banned *Mwakenya*, died in prison on May 5, 1988. He had been severely tortured. (7/88)

David Owak, a real estate agent, was arrested at his offices on December 1, 1988, by plainclothes policemen. He has not been charged, but is probably being held on political grounds. Owak was an associate and former employee of Oginga Odinga, the former vice president whose well-known, left-wing views have caused embarrassment to Daniel arap Moi's government. (2/89)

**LIBERIA:** The independent *Suntimes* and *Cocorico* were banned for creating tension and instability by publishing articles deemed to be hostile to the government in February 1988. A *Suntimes* journalist was detained. In April *Footprints Today* was also banned after a number of independent newspapers announced that they would cease publication to protest recent attacks on press freedom. Isaac Bantu, Siaka Konneh, Arthur Massaquioi, Andrew Robinson, and Michael Saa, all *Footprints* journalists, were detained. (6/88)

Nathaniel Nimley Choloply, a student, has been in detention without charge or trial since being arrested in December 1987, shortly after returning from the United States. He is suspected of having associated with critics of the government while abroad. He is reported to be suffering ill-health due to poor prison conditions.

**LIBYA:** Amnesty International has called on Libyan leader Muammar Gaddafi to renounce his policy of "liquidating exiled political opponents." Thirty-seven such attacks have been attributed to government agents in the past seven years, leading to twenty-five deaths. On June 26, 1987, Yousef Khreybish of the National Front for the Salvation of Libya was gunned down in Rome. On May 20, 1987, former diplomat Izzedin Gadamsi escaped an assassination attempt in Vienna. The Libyan National Organization's Muhammad Fehelma was killed in Athens on January 7, 1987. (9/87)

"The first Gaddafi Human Rights Prize has been received by Zenani Mandela on behalf of her father, the gaoled ANC leader Nelson Mandela" (*West Africa*, Jun 26-Jul 2, 1989; p. 1072).

On February 19, 1990, the London-based Arab daily, *Al-Arab*, reported that the authorities had sent a note to all Arab publications imported into Libya warning them that they would be banned if they contained advertisements of American products. (5/90)

International PEN records the following writers and journalists in prison: Mostafa El Hashmi Ba'yu, Ahmed Muhammad El Fitouri, Omar Belgassem, Shelig El Kikli, Sa'ad El Saui Mahmoud, Idris Juma' El Mismari, Al Muhammad Hadidan al Rheibi, Muhammad Muhammad El Fgih Salih, Idris Muhammad Ibn Tayeb, and Khalifa Sifaw Khaboush. (5/90)

MALAWI: "The government has begun arresting senior state employees, including teachers and doctors, in a renewed crackdown on political opposition of Malawi's President for Life Kamuzu Banda. Three detainees were either killed or died in detention in March 1989. Most of detainees had earlier been fired or prematurely retired from state employment, apparently only because they were from northern Malawi, an area that has come in for criticism from Life President Banda. Among those arrested was Dr. George Mtafu, Malawi's only neurologist, detained in secret custody after he refused to apologize for challenging remarks by the President that state employees in northern Malawi were 'pursuing their own interest' " (*Amnesty International*, May-Jun 1989).

The Malawi government has banned the books of Nigerian writers Wole Sonyinka (1986 Nobel laureate) and Chinua Achebe because they fall foul of the "political, cultural, and religious tastes" of Malawi. Sonyinka in particular was singled out as "a bad man who had been chased out of his country." Books by Nkrumah of Ghana are also banned in Malawi. (8/88)

Malawian poet Jack Mapanje, former head of the English Department at the University of Malawi, continues to be held in detention. His crime? Writing poetic commentaries on the Malawian political scene. (3/88)

Jonathan Kuntambila, chief editor of the *Daily Times*, and Malawi News Agency editors Sandy Kuwale and Paul Akomenji, were in jail for more than a year for publishing a statement by President Hastings Banda's official hostess, Cecilia Tamanda (which she later denied) that "men cannot do without women." (3/86)

MALI: "Four engineering students, Adama Coulibaly, Souleymane Dembele, Ibrahima Tangara, and Boulkassoum Kire, are reported to have been tortured following their detention in mid-June 1989. Amnesty International believes they have been imprisoned for nonviolent expression of their political views and has adopted them as prisoners of conscience.

"No reason has been given for their arrest but it is thought it could be in connection with their activities in an unofficial organization, the Association of Malian School and University Students. They are reported to have distributed tracts complaining about material difficulties faced by students, including delays in grant payments" (*West Africa*, Aug 7-13, 1989; p. 1312).

**MAURITANIA: APARTHEID IN MAURITANIA** - "More than 500 noncommissioned officers of Negro stock have been expelled from the armed forces, the Forces de Liberation Africaine de Mauritania (Flam), a movement of black intellectuals said in a communique issued in Dakar. According to Flam, some 30 civilian prisoners arrested during prolonged agitation among the Black African community in Mauritania in 1986 have been transferred to the Oulata prison... The mass purge of black Mauritanians followed 'unspecified incidents' said to have occurred after the December executions of three black army officers for plotting a coup . . . Black Mauritanians, who constitute a third of the country's 2 million population, have made sporadic protests in the past few years against the predominant positions of power held by the majority Moors of Arab-Berber stock." (*West Africa*, Feb 8, 1988; p. 229).

Ibrahima Sarr, formerly a radio and television journalist at the *Office de radio-diffusion et de television de Mauritanie* in Nouakchot, who was arrested in September 1986 in connection with the distribution of a pamphlet showing discrimination against the black population, has been imprisoned "solely on account of the exercise of his right to freedom of expression." (2/88)

Well-known writer Tene Youssouf Gueye (60) died in detention in September 1988. He was among a group of 36 political prisoners tried in 1986 and 1987 and sentenced to long-term imprisonment in connection with the distribution in September 1986 of a document entitled *Le Manifeste du Negro-Mauritanien Opprime* ("The Manifesto of the Oppressed Black Mauritanian"), which criticized the predominantly Arab-Berber government for discriminating against the country's black population. (10/88)

Lieutenant Abdoul Ghoudouss Ba, Ibrahim Sarr, a radio journalist, Amadou Moctar Sow, an engineer, and Ly Mamadou Bocar, a former government minister, are believed to have died in detention. All were detained in connection with the distribution of a document in September that criticized the ruling

Arab-Berber government of discriminating against the country's black population. (1/89)

**MOROCCO:** On December 10, 1988, 37 political prisoners serving sentences of between 15 years and life in Kenitra Central Prison went on a 24-hour hunger strike in protest against their conditions of detention and the repression directed against political prisoners and their families. (2/89)

Mohamed Labrini and Abdelkader Himer, director and editor, respectively, of the daily opposition newspaper *al-Ittihad al-Ichtiraki,* were brought to trial in October 1990 on defamation charges as the result of an article which described the long delays common in examination and judgment cases in Casablanca's courts and tribunals, and raised the issue of corruption in the courts. (1/91)

**NIGERIA:** In January 1983 Ray Ekpu, a journalist of the National Concord, was arrested and charged with the murder of two persons who died in a fire that ravaged the NECOM House skyscraper. The police, displaying extraordinary imagination, accused him of what amounted to "murder by the pen." Ekpu had written a column highlighting a pattern of arson in Nigeria committed by corrupt officials seeking to destroy incriminating evidence. He warned that such was the scale of the arson that primary government buildings, such as NECOM House, would be set ablaze.

Unfortunately for the writer, his projection became a prophecy. The very day the article was published, NECOM House was set ablaze, thereby giving the police the sole evidence against the columnist. Mr. Ekpu languished in prison for 15 days before being acquitted. (4/86)

*Newswatch* was closed for six months in April 1987 for printing a leaked report from the Political Bureau. Concern is still felt about the murder of *Newswatch's* editor-in-chief, Dele Giwa. There are suspicions about government complicity. (10/87).

Four executives of the Nigerian Labor Congress—Alhaji Ali Chiroma, president, Lasisi A. Osunde, general secretary, Salisu Nuhu Mohammed, assistant general secretary, and S.O. Osidipe, national treasurer—were detained on December 14, 1987, for opposing the government's impending removal of the petroleum subsidy. They were held under State Security Decree No. 2 of 1984, which provides for up to six months' renewable detention without charge or trial. (3/88)

Pini Jason, a journalist, was detained in July 1988 for writing in *ThisWeek* magazine about the collapsing *naira,* intractable inflation, and the rise in armed robbery and hired killers (*New African,* Sep 1988; p. 17).

Chief Gani Fawehinmi, the radical lawyer who has been trying to prosecute two top security officers for allegedly murdering Dele Giwa (the editor of *Newswatch* magazine who was killed by a parcel bomb delivered to his house in October 1986), had his passport seized at the Murtala Muhammed International Airport in Lagos on September 27,1988, as he was about to travel to London. His passport had previously been impounded in September 1988, when he first wanted to make the trip. (1/89)

Etim Etim (26), the financial correspondent of the (Lagos) *Guardian*, was arrested by security officers on August 8, 1988, for disclosing details of a loan scheme by the Lagos State Water Authority involving a number of European banks before the federal government had made an official announcement. He is currently believed to be held under State Security Decree No. 2 of 1984. (1/89)

A new Media Council Decree signed by the military president, General Babangida, to replace a Press Council Decree of 1978, has been received with apprehension by journalists and media organizations, and who view it as inimical to the development of journalism. Particularly contentious are provisions for the registration of journalists and the definition of who qualifies to be registered. According to the constitution of the Nigerian Union of Journalists (NUJ), a journalist is "any person who is employed or has been employed as editorial staff" who earns 60 percent of his income from such employment. This includes reporters, feature writers, subeditors, editors, sports writers, photographers, artists, and information officers of government departments as well as public relations officers of companies and parastatal organizations.

But the newly promulgated decree insists that only journalism and mass communication graduates from approved institutions, with five years' experience in recognized news media, shall qualify for registration, and therefore be authorized by the Media Council to practice as journalists. Contravention could mean imprisonment of two years or a fine of 1,000 *naira*. "Where will an intending journalist get the five years' experience to qualify for registration since it is illegal to practise without being registered?" a columnist asked in a local newspaper. If applied strictly, the law will put an estimated 70 percent of those currently practicing as journalists out of employment. The decree empowers the government to appoint the majority of Media Council's membership, so it essentially gives government the power to recognize professional journalists—which, critics note, does not apply in other professions. Surprisingly, the decree has no provisions for freelance journalists, stringers, cartoonists, and photo-journalists. The *Vanguard* (Nigerian) summed up the mood: "The harsh fact of the matter is that in the true context of freedom, the Nigerian press is losing ground every day." (cited in *Index on Censorship*, May-Jun 1989; p. 5).

Chris Okole, editor-in-chief and publisher of *Newbreed* magazine, was arrested in Lagos on February 7, 1989, by members of the State Security Service for undisclosed reasons. His arrest followed the publication of an article, "A Harvest of Generals," believed to have offended the government. That was his second arrest in five months. Three other journalists on the magazine, Ishmael Raheem, the editor, Sola Oyeneyin, an assistant editor, and Toyin Egunjobi, a staff writer, were told to report to the police on February 9. The three had coauthored the offending article. (4/89)

**SOMALIA:** Safia Hashi Madar, a biochemistry lecturer who was arrested in July 1985 in connection with her alleged membership in a subversive organization, the Somali National Movement (SNM), is reported to be suffering from a kidney infection, severe depression, and chronic tooth pain. She is seriously underweight, has been tortured, and was raped repeatedly. (6/88) Abdi Ismail Yunis, formerly the head of Curriculum Development at the Ministry of Education, who has been in detention since 1982 for "belonging to an opposition organization," is now reported to be in ill-health and denied medical treatment. (10/88)

Diriye Sugal Roble, one of the five naval cadets forcibly returned from Egypt to Somalia on August 20, 1988, after they took part in a demonstration outside the Somali embassy in Cairo, is believed to have died in custody, possibly as a result of torture. (1/89) Abukar Hassan Yare, a former professor of law at the National University in Mogadishu, was arrested early in January after being discovered duplicating an Amnesty International report on the country. He was previously detained between 1981 and 1986, apparently for his socialist views and opposition to President Barre's government. (3/89)

Mahamoud Mohamed Mohamoud, an 18-year-old student in Mogadishu, died in the hospital on February 12, 1990, after being tortured. He had been arrested on February 9 or 10 by security officers and interrogated about his older brother, Abdirahim Mohamed Mohamoud, who fled the country in July 1989. On February 11, he was admitted in a coma to Mogadishu's Digfer Hospital. He never recovered. (4/90)

Fifty unarmed civilians, including Bulu Burti mayor Mohamed Sheikh Sharawe, former MP Mohamed Hassan Hawadleh, Haji Kabaweyne, a clan elder, and Sheikh Mohamed Balad, an Islamic judge, are reported to have been extrajudicially executed on November 12, 1990, in the town of Bulu Burti, 200 kilometres north of Mogadishu. (2/91)

**SOUTH AFRICA:** Zubeida Jaffer, a former reporter on the *Cape Times*, and her husband, Johnny Issel, are among the 335 still being held by the government under the state of emergency regulations. Another 294 are detained under the security law. Zubeida, three months pregnant, is being held incommunicado and has no access to her doctor. Her lawyer is also locked up. She was detained in 1980 for writing an article for the *Cape Times* on the families of victims shot by the police. Johnny Issel works for the United Democratic Front. (3/86)

The Detainees' Parents Support Committee reckons that 16,000 political and community leaders have been detained since the emergency began on June 12, 1986. They include almost the entire leadership of the 800 community organizations and labor unions affiliated with the UDF, the alliance of black nationalist groups. Allegations of torture persist despite denials by the authorities. However, then-Law and Order Minister Louis le Grange admitted that 464 detainees had been admitted to the hospital between July 12 and August 26. (1/87)

On March 9, 1989, a number of journalists were arrested in Cape Town while covering a series of protests against detentions. Journalists outside Parliament were ordered to leave the area and refrain from taking photographs; and demonstrators arrested in Greenmarket Square included the editor of *South*, Moegsien Williams, a Save the Press coordinator, Mansor Jaffer, and the staff of *Grassroots* newspaper. At St. George's Cathedral, police confiscated film belonging to photographer Eric Miller. (5/89)

*Grassroots* journalist Veliswa Mhlawuli was released after five months in detention on March 23, only to be charged with contravening the Internal Security Act. She was freed on bail of R 2,500. (5/89)

On March 25, 1989, seven journalists, including members of U.S. television crews, were questioned by police after filming a protest in solidarity with hunger-striking detainees in Durban. They had videotapes confiscated. (5/89)

"Under the state of emergency, imposed in 1985, the government has undermined the courts' legitimacy and made a mockery of judicial independence by taking the constitutional doctrine of parliamentary sovereignty, which elevates legislation beyond judicial review, to Banana Republic extremes. By passing a myriad of security laws that concentrate power in the executive branch and that can't be constitutionally challenged, the parliament has effectively excluded the courts from having any say over many government actions denying basic human rights. Cabinet ministers, without judicial scrutiny, have detained more than 30,000 people and held them without trial, restricted thousands of others, banned dozens of organizations and shut down a handful of newspapers. Law and Order Minister Adriaan Vlok justifies this by saying that if detainees were brought to court, they might be acquitted. 'In normal law,' he told reporters earlier in 1989, 'it's not always possible to find people guilty' " (*Wall Street Journal,* Jun 8, 1989; p. A11).

Police used tear gas and water cannons to break up a march by children in Cape Town on January 23, 1990. The march had been organized by the National Education Coordinating Committee. Several people were injured when they were crushed against razor-wire barricades strung across streets in the city center. (5/90)

Two people were shot dead and several wounded on January 24, 1990, after police used birdshot on crowds gathered outside Khutsong stadium near Carletonville. Some 5,000 people had gathered for the meeting, scheduled to precede a march to the Oberhozer police station to protest against police brutality and the death of 16-year-old Mbuyiselo Phiri, who died after being picked up for police questioning. (5/90)

SUDAN: On September 11, 1988, the Cabinet approved a new code of Islamic law denounced by Christian politicians as unacceptable. Among the punishment spelled out in the criminal code are: death by stoning for adultery, 100 lashes with a whip and five years in prison for homosexuality, and death for "the offence of apostasy," which is defined as "renunciation of the creed of Islam." (1/89)

Muhammad Madani Tawfiq, editor-in-chief of the biweekly *Al-Rayab* newspaper, was arrested at the beginning of March under the emergency laws. The Sudanese Journalists Association described the arrest as a violation of press freedom and democracy. (5/89)

TANZANIA: James Mapalala and Mwinyiguma Othuman Upindo have been held uncharged and without access to members of their family since October 22, 1986, for campaigning for the repeal of the law that authorizes only one political party in the country. They are detained under the Preventive Detention Act of 1962 (revised in 1985), which authorizes the president to detain for an indefinite period anyone considered a threat to "peace and good order." (3/87)

TOGOLAND: Yema Gu-Konu and Ati Randolph were arrested and held in detention for two years for possessing or distributing literature critical of the government. (5/87)

TUNISIA: On December 31, 1986, *al Mustaqbal*, the weekly newspaper of the Movement of Democratic Socialists (MDS)—the official opposition—was seized at the printing press. (3/87) Amnesty International has received reports that eight people—Ali al Bali, Abd Alah al-Aoubuidi, Ammar Amroussia, Kadri Amroussia, Yousef al-Zaidi, Hussein Zreiba, Abdel Ruzzak Athlili, and Ahbib al-Tabbasi, mostly students and teachers—were arrested in Gafsa between October and November 1986 and have been held incommunicado since then. (5/87)

On April 25, 1987, 12 trade union leaders and activists were arrested by police in Tunis. They included Tayeb Bakoush, Ali Ben Romdan, and Kamel Saad, all former members of the executive committee of the General Union of Tunisian Workers, as well as a number of former members of the administrative council of the central trade union. (6/87)

On May 23, 1987, Khamais Chamari, the secretary-general of the Tunisian League for Human Rights, was detained for three months on charges of disseminating false information, defaming the state, and offending the person of the prime minister. (7/87)

The Arab Organization of Human Rights has expressed "deep concern" over the progressive deterioration of human rights in Tunisia in recent months, including the arrests of hundreds of political opponents, the closure of opposition newspapers, the clampdown on Trade Union activities, and the torture of political detainees. (9/87)

Between September 1989 and January 1990, the authorities closed down seven Tunis bookshops for selling "undesirable publications." Al Huda publishers also had their offices closed down. (5/90)

On March 4, 1990, a tribunal in Tunis sentenced Najib Azzouz, director of the weekly Les Annonces, and his editor-in-chief, Abdelaziz Jridi, to two months in prison and fined them 500 dinars for defamation. In November 1989 the newspaper had published an article accusing the country's ambassador in Vienna of corruption when he was the country's interior minister. (5/90)

On October 6, 1990, Hamadi Jebali, director of the Islamic weekly Al-Fajr, was sentenced to a jail term of six months suspended and fined in connection with an article published in June 1990 which the authorities found provocative and an incitement to disobey the country's laws. (1/91)

UGANDA: President Museveni, addressing a news conference on February 25, 1987, threatened to put journalists under preventive detention if they write stories which, in the view of the government, discredit the National Resistance Army. (4/87)

Lance Seera Muwange, a human rights activist arrested in February 1987 following criticism of the actions of the ruling National Resistance Army during its operations against armed opponents in Northern Uganda, is still being detained without charge. (1/88)

John Kakooza, editor of *The Citizen*, was detained and questioned by the police on April 7, 1988, after publishing an article predicting that a peace agreement with the rebels would fail. (6/88)

**ZAIRE:** In its 1986 report, *Zaire: Reports of Torture and Killings Committed by the Armed Forces in the Shaba Region*, Amnesty International observed that over 100 people, mostly members or supporters of the Union pour la Democratie et le Progress Social (UDPS), were tortured and killed during mass arrests between October and December 1985.

Residents of Moba and surrounding villages described how people were seized from their homes and detained by Zairian troops. Prisoners were reported to have been taken to the headquarters of the armed forces and executed without any form of trial or hearing. Former prisoners described how they were whipped with barbed wire, subjected to electric shocks, and starved. Amnesty said one detainee, Kana Kange, who was arrested in October 1985 in Kinshasa, is known to have died in custody, and four other UDPS supporters are reported to have also died in custody (*West Africa*, March 24, 1986).

Koland Musena, a 28-year-old nurse, was arrested in Kinshasa on July 5, 1986, and imprisoned for distributing tracts calling for improved wages and better conditions of employment during a meeting of the Federation Nationale des Travailleurs de la Sante (National Federation of Health Workers). (1/87)

Amnesty International has received further information of nine people arrested and relegated (sent into internal exile). They are: Mpinga Shambuyi Makonda, Birkashira Birindwa, restricted to the village of Mwegerera, Epole Bolya Kodya Bassassi, restricted to the small town of Bolamba, Tshiongo Kanana, restricted to the village of Bera Mbala, Maliba Kibassa, held under house arrest in Lumumbashi, Maloba Ndiba Lumbu, held under house arrest, Ngiele Lasanga, restricted to the town of Sentery, Mpandanjila Ngalulu, restricted to the village of Tshihunde, and Mulumba Tshisekedi, restricted to the village of Mupompa. They belong to the banned Union pour la Democratie et le Progres Social (UDPS). (1/87)

Lokale-Topango, a law student, was arrested for "political reasons" in December 1986 and was believed to have been tortured in the Deuxieme Cite de l'OUA detention camp in Kinshasa. (7/87)

Two journalists with the Zairian Radio and Television Corporation, Makoko Musheni and Kafuka Rujamizi, were dismissed from their jobs on March 6, 1989, for presenting ill-timed information on a public broadcasting medium following student demonstrations in the country. (5/89)

The authorities closed Kinshasa University on February 16, 1989, because "students had disobeyed the party's line of action." Bakavu regional radio added: "Following the closure, no acts of violence or gatherings will be tolerated. Anybody who ignores this ban will be arrested and taken to court." (5/89)

**ZAMBIA:** Komani Kachinga, editor-in-chief of *The Times* newspaper,and Cyrus Sikazue, editor-in-chief of *The Mail*, were both removed from their posts in early December, 1990, apparently as a result of their growing outspokenness in favor of multiparty democracy. (2/91)

**ZIMBABWE:** Nathan Shamuyarira, the minister of information, has announced plans to move toward further control of the country's media. The Zimbabwe Mass Media Trust, set up by the government shortly after independence in 1980, has bought out the controlling interests and now owns the country's five main newspapers. The minister is also investigating how he could control the activities of the 70 film production and distribution units in the country. (1/87) The government of Prime Minister Robert Mugabe has prevented the *Chronicle*, an independent newspaper published in Bulawayo, from publishing an interview with Edgar Tekere, the controversial former secretary-general of the ruling ZANU (PF) party who was expelled from the party last September. In the interview Tekere was quoted as saying that he would form a political movement to fight parliamentary elections next year on a "clean administration" platform. The *Chronicle* has incurred the government's displeasure on several occasions over the past six months by printing stories of government corruption. Two prominent ministers have so far been forced to resign their seats following the paper's allegations. (5/89)

Students Christopher Giwa, Eric Nvundudu, Enoch Mhandhla, Servia Sibanda, and Kapofo were arrested on October 25 and 26, 1990 following demonstrations at the University of Zimbabwe. (2/91)

# BIBLIOGRAPHY

*Africa Review* 1988. Lincolnwood, IL: National Textbook Company.

Amoah, G.Y. (1988). *Groundwork of Government For West Africa*. Illorin (Nigeria): Gbenle Press, Ltd.

Andreski, Stanislav (1969). *The African Predicament: A Study in the Pathology of Modernization*. New York: Atherton Press.

Apter, David (1965). *The Politics of Modernization*. Chicago: University of Chicago Press.

_____(1972). *Ghana in Transition*. Princeton, NJ: Princeton University Press.

Arhin, Kwame (1985). *Traditional Rule in Ghana: Past and Present*. Accra, Ghana: Sedco Publishing.

Asante, Molefi (1989). *Afrocentricity*. Trenton, NJ: Africa World Press.

Austen, Ralph (1987). *African Economic History*. Portsmouth, NH: Heinemann.

Ayittey, George B.N. (1991). *Indigenous African Institutions*. Dobbs Ferry, NY: Transnational Publishers.

Bandow, Doug (1986). "The First World's Misbegotten Economic Legacy to the Third World." *Journal of Economic Growth*, Vol. 1, No. 4: 17.

Bankole, Timothy (1981). *From Cradle to Grave*. London: Garvin Press.

Baran, P.A. (January 1952). "The Political Economy of Backwardness." *Manchester School of Economics* (journal).

Barker, Jonathan S. (1971). "The Paradox of Development: Reflections on a Study of Local-Central Political Relations in Senegal." In *The State of the Nations; Constraints on Development in Independent Africa*, edited by M. F. Lofchie. Berkeley: University of California Press.

Barnes, Leonard (1971). *Africa in Eclipse*. New York: St. Martin's Press.

Bascom, William (1984). *The Yoruba Of Southwestern Nigeria*. Prospect Heights, IL: Waveland Press.

Bates, Robert H. (1981). *Markets and States in Tropical Africa*. Berkeley: University of California Press.

_____(1987). *Essays on the Political Economy of Rural Africa*. Berkeley: University of California Press.

Bauer, Ludwig (1934). *Leopold the Unloved*. London: European Books.

Bauer, Peter T. (1967). *West African Trade*. New York: Kelley.

_____(1972). *Dissent On Development*. Cambridge, MA: Harvard University Press.

_____(1984). *Reality and Rhetoric*. Cambridge,Mass: Harvard University Press.

Bell, Morag (1987). *Contemporary Africa*. New York: John Wiley & Sons.

Berg, E. J. (1964). "Socialism and Economic Development in Africa." *Quarterly Journal of Economics*: 549.

Berman, B. (1984). "Structure And Process In the Bureaucratic States Of Colonial Africa," *Development And Change*: Vol 15; pp. 161-202.

Biersteker, Thomas J. (1987). *Multinationals, the State, and Control of the Nigerian Economy*. Princeton, NJ: Princeton University Press.

Bing, Geoffrey (1968). *Reap the Whirlwind*. London: MacGibbon & Kee.

Birmingham, David (1981). *Central Africa to 1870*. London: Cambridge University Press.

Birmingham, Walter, Neustadt, I., and Omaboe, E. N. (1966). *A Study of Contemporary Ghana*, Vol. 1. Evanston: Northwestern University Press.

Boahen, A. A. (1986). *Topics in West African History*. New York: Longman.

Boahen, A. A., and Webster, J. B. (1970). *History of West Africa*. New York: Praeger.

Bohannan, Paul (1964). *Africa and Africans*. New York: The Natural History Press.

Bohannan, Paul, and Dalton, George, eds, (1962). *Markets In Africa*. Evanston: Northwestern University Press.

Bohannan, Paul, and Laura Bohannan (1968). *Tiv Economy*. London: Longmans.

Bourdillon, Michael (1976). *The Shona Peoples*. Gwelo (Zimbabwe): Mambo Press.

Bruckner, Pascal (1987). *The Tears of the White Man: Compassion as Contempt*. New York: The Free Press.

Bundy, Colin (1988). *The Rise and Fall of the South African Peasantry*. Cape Town: Lackshaws (Pty).

Busia, Kofi Abrefa (1951). *The Position of The Chief—In the Modern Political System of Ashanti*. London: Oxford University Press.

_____ (1967). *Africa in Search of Democracy.* New York: Praeger.

Caldwell, Don (1989). *South Africa: The New Revolution.* Saxonwold: The Free Market Foundation.

Calvocoressi, Peter (1985). *Independent Africa and the World.* New York: Longman.

Carlston, Kenneth S. (1968). *Social Theory and African Tribal Organization.* Urbana, IL: University of Illinois Press.

Chisiza, Dunduzi K. (1962). *Africa: What Lies Ahead.* New York: The African-American Institute.

Christensen, James Boyd (1958). "The Role of Proverbs in Fante Culture." *Africa.* Vol. 28, No. 3, pp. 232-43.

Cohen, Ronald (1970). "The Kingship in Bornu." In Crowder and Ikime (1970).

Colson, Elizabeth (1953). "Social Control And Vengeance In Plateau Tonga Society." *Africa,* Vol. 23, No. 3: 199-211.

Colson, Elizabeth, and Gluckman, M. (eds.) (1951). *Seven Tribes of British Central Africa.* London: Oxford University Press.

Coquery-Vidrovitch, C. (1977). "Research on an African Mode of Production." In Gutkind and Waterman (1977).

Coquery-Vidrovitch, C. (1985). *Africa: Endurance and Change South of the Sahara.* Berkeley: University of California Press.

Crowder, Michael and Ikime Obaro, eds. (1970). *West African Chiefs.* New York: Africana.

Curtin, Philip, Feierman, Steven, Thompson, Leonard, and Vansina, Jan (1988). *African History.* New York: Longman.

Daaku, Kwame Y. (1971). "Trade and Trading Patterns of the Akan in 17th and 18th Centuries." In Meillassoux (1971).

Davidson, Basil (1967). *African Kingdoms.* Chicago: Time/Life Books.

——— (1969). *The African Genius: An Introduction To African Cultural And Social History.* Boston: Atlantic Monthly Press.

——— (1970). *Discovering Africa's Past.* New York: Longman.

——— (1987). *The Lost Cities of Africa.* Boston: Little, Brown.

Decalo, Samuel (1976). *Coups and Army Rule in Africa: Studies in Military Style.* New Haven: Yale University Press.

deGraft-Johnson, J.C. (1986). *African Glory*. Baltimore: Black Classic Press.

deGraft-Johnson, K.E. (1964). "The Evolution of Elites in Ghana." In *The New Elites of Tropical Africa*, edited by P. C. Lloyd. London: Oxford University Press.

Diamond, Larry (1988). *Democracy in Developing Countries: Africa*. Boulder, CO: Lynne Rienner Publishers.

Dickson, David A. (1985). *US Foreign Policy Towards Sub-Saharan Africa*. Lanham, MD: University Press of America.

Dickson, Kwamina B. (1969). *A Historical Geography of Ghana*. Cambridge: Cambridge University Press.

Diop, Cheikh Anta (1987). *Pre-colonial Black Africa*. Westport, CT: Lawrence Hill.

Djoleto, Amu (1988). *Hurricane of Dust*. London: Longman.

Dostert, Pierre (1987). *Africa, 1986*. Washington, DC: Stryker-Post Publications.

Douglas, Mary (1962). "Lele Economy Compared with the Bushong: A Study in Economic Backwardness." In Bohannan and Dalton, eds. (1962).

Dumont, René (1966). *False Start in Africa*. London: Deutsch Limited.

Dupire, Marguerite (1962). "Trade and Markets in the Economy of the Nomadic Fulani of Niger (Bororo)." In Bohannan and Dalton, eds. (1962).

Eberstadt, Nicholas (1988). *Foreign Aid and American Purpose*. Washington, DC: American Enterprise Institute.

El-Affendi, Abdelwahab (1992). *Who Needs an Islamic State?* London: Grey Seal Books.

Ellis, George W. (1914). *Negro Culture in West Africa*. New York: Neale Publishing.

Evans-Pritchard, E. E. (1963). "The Zande State." *The Journal of the Royal Anthropological Institute*, Vol. 93, Part I, pp. 134-54.

Fallers, L. (1963). "Equality, Modernity and Democracy." In *New States: The Quest for Modernity in Asia and Africa*. New York: Free Press of Glencoe.

——— (1967). *Bantu Bureaucracy: A Century of Political Evolution Among the Basoga of Uganda*. Chicago: University of Chicago Press.

Falola, Toyin (1985). "Nigeria's indigenous economy." In R. Olaniyan, *Nigerian History and Culture*.

Feierman, Steven (1974). *The Shaamba Kingdom*. Madison: University of Wisconsin Press.

Ferkiss, Victor C. (1966). *Africa's Search for Identity*. New York: George Braziller.

Field, M. J. (1940). *Social Organization of the Ga People.* Accra: Government of the Gold Coast Printing Press.

Fieldhouse, D.K. (1986). *Black Africa 1945-80.* London: Allen & Unwin.

Fitch, Bob, and Oppenheimer, Mary (1966). *Ghana: End of an Illusion.* New York: Monthly Review Press.

Forde, Daryll, and Jones, G.I. (1950). *The Igbo and Ibibio-Speaking Peoples of South-Eastern Nigeria.* London: International African Institute.

Frank, A. G. (1969). *Capitalism and Under-Development in Latin America.* New York: Monthly Review Press.

Galli, Rosemary E., and Jones, Jocelyn (1987). *Guinea-Bissau: Politics, Economics and Society.* London: Frances Pinter.

Garlick, Peter (1971). *African Traders and Economic Development.* Oxford: Clarendon.

Gibbs, James L., Jr., ed. (1965). *Peoples of Africa.* New York: Holt, Rinehart & Winston.

Glazier, Jack (1985). *Land and the Uses of Tradition Among the Mbeere of Kenya.* Lanham, MD: University Press of America.

Gluckman, Max (1959). *Custom and Conflict in Africa.* Oxford: Basil Blackwell.

——— (1965). *Politics, Law and Ritual in Tribal Society.* Oxford: Basil Blackwell.

Gray, Robert F. (1962). "Economic Exchange in a Sonjo Village." In Bohannan and Dalton, eds. (1962).

Grayson, Leslie E. (1973). "The Role of Suppliers' Credit in the Industrialization of Ghana," *Economic Development & Cultural Change;* April: 543-551.

Gulliver, P. H. (1962). "The Evolution of Arusha Trade." In Bohannan and Dalton, eds. (1962).

Gutkind, Peter (1976). "Editor's Introduction." In *The Political Economy of Contemporary Africa.* Newbury Park, CA: Sage Publications, pp. 7-29.

Gutkind, Peter, and Waterman, Peter (1977). *African Social Studies: A Radical Reader.* New York: Monthly Review Press.

Gutteridge, W. F. (1975). *Military Regimes in Africa.* London: Methuen.

Guy, Jeff (1979). *The Destruction of the Zulu Kingdom.* London: Longman.

Hagen, E. E. (1962). *On the Theory of Social Change.* Homewood, IL: Dorsey Press.

Hamer, John H. (1970). "Sidamo Generational Class Cycles: A Political Gerontocracy." *Africa.* Vol. 40, No.1, pp. 50-70.

Harbison, F. H. (May 1962). "Human Resource Development, Planning in Modernising Economies." *International Labor Review*: 56-67.

Harris, Joseph E. (1987). *Africans And Their History*. New York: Penguin.

Hawkins, E. K. (1958). "The Growth of a Money Economy in Nigeria and Ghana". *Oxford Economic Papers* 10, No. 3:354.

Hayford, J. E. Casely (1897). *Gold Coast Native Institutions*. Excerpted in Langley (1979).

Heidenheimer, Arnold J., ed. (1970) *Political Corruption*. New York: Rinehart & Winston.

Herskovits, M. J., and Harwitz, M., eds. (1964). *Economic Transition In Africa*. Evanston: Northwestern University Press.

Hodder, B. W. (1962). "The Yoruba Rural Market." In Bohannan and Dalton, eds. (1962).

Hoffman, P. G. (1960). *One Hundred Countries, One and One Quarter Billion People*. Washington, DC: Brookings Institution.

Howell, T.A. (1972). *Ghana and Nkrumah*. New York: Facts on File.

Hull, Richard W. (1976). *African Cities and Towns Before The European Conquest*. New York: W. W. Norton.

Huntington, Ellesworth (1945). *Mainsprings of Civilization*. New York: Wiley.

Iliffe, John (1987). *The African Poor*. New York: Cambridge University Press.

Isichei, Elizabeth (1977). *History of West Africa Since 1800*. New York: Africana.

Italiaander, Rolf (1961). *The New Leaders of Africa*. Englewood Cliffs, NJ: Prentice-Hall.

Kelly, G. M. (1959). "The Ghanaian Intelligentsia." Unpublished Ph.D. dissertation, University of Chicago.

Kendall, Frances, and Gurley, John (1985). "Radical Analyses of Imperialism, The Third World, and the Transition to Socialism." *Journal of Economic Literature*, Vol. 23, No. 3: 1116.

Kendall, Frances, and Louw, Leon (1986). *After Apartheid: The Solution*. San Fransisco: Institute of Contemporary Studies.

Kenyatta, Jomo (1938). *Facing Mount Kenya*. London: Secker & Warburg.

Killick, Tony (1978). *Development Economics In Action: A Study of Economic Policies in Ghana*. London: Heinemann.

King, Coretta S., ed. (1987). *The Words Of Martin Luther King, Jr.* New York: Newmarket Press.

Klein, Martin A. (1968). *Islam and Imperialism: Sine-Saloum, 1847-1914.* Stanford, CA: Stanford University Press.

Kluckhorn, Richard (1962). "The Konso Economy of Southern Ethiopia." In Bohannan and Dalton, eds. (1962).

Kotecha, Ken C. with Adams, Robert W. (1981). *The Corruption of Power: African Politics.* Washington, DC: University Press of America.

Lamb, David (1984). *The Africans.* New York: Random House.

Lancaster, Carol, and Williamson, John, eds. (1986). *African Debt and Financing.* Washington, DC: Institute for International Economics.

Langley, J. Ayo, ed. (1979). *Ideologies of Liberation in Black Africa, 1856-1970.* London: Rex Collins.

Lappe, Frances and Collins, Joseph (1979). *Food First: Beyond the Myth Of Scarcity.* New York: Ballantine.

Lappe, Frances, and Kinley, David (1980). *Aid As Obstacle: Twenty Questions About Our Foreign Aid and the Hungry.* San Fransisco, CA: Institute For Food and Development Policy.

Lawson, Colin (1988) "Soviet Economic Aid to Africa", *Journal of African Affairs,* October: 324.

LeVine, R.A. (1962). "Wealth and Power in Gusiiland." In Bohannan and Dalton, eds. (1962).

———— (1966). *Dreams and Deeds; Achievement Motivation in Nigeria.* Chicago, IL: University of Chicago Press.

LeVine, Victor (1975). *Political Corruption; The Ghana Case.* Stanford: Hoover Institution Press.

Lewis, I.M. (1962). "Lineage Continuity and Modern Commerce in Northern Somaliland." In Bohannan and Dalton (1962).

Libby, Ronald T. (1987). *The Politics of Economic Power in Southern Africa.* Princeton, NJ: Princeton University Press.

Mandela, Winnie (1985). *Part Of My Soul Went With Him.* New York: W. W. Norton.

Manning, Patrick (1988). *Francophone Sub-Saharan Africa 1880-1985.* New York: Cambridge University Press.

Marris, Peter (October, 1968). "The Social Barriers to African Entrepreneurship." *Journal of Development Studies:* 125.

Martin, Phyllis M., and O'Meara Patrick, eds. (1986). *Africa.* Bloomington: Indiana University Press.

Marx, Karl (1915). *Capital: A Critique of Political Economy.* Chicago: Kerr.

Matthews, Ronald (1966). *The African Powder-Keg.* London: Bodley Head.

Maylam, Paul (1986). *A History of the African People of South Africa: From the Early Iron Age to the 1970s.* Cape Town: David Philip.

Mazrui, Ali (1986). *The Africans.* London: BBC Publications.

Mbiti, John S. (1970). *African Religions and Philosophies.* New York: Doubleday.

McCall, Daniel F. (1962). "The Koforidua Market." In Bohannan and Dalton, eds. (1962).

———, ed. (1969). *Western African History.* New York: Praeger Publishers.

Meillassoux, Claude (1962). "Social and Economic Factors Affecting Markets in Guro Land." In Bohannan and Dalton, eds. (1962).

———, ed. (1971). *The Development of Indigenous Trade and Markets in West Africa.* Oxford: Oxford University Press.

Melady, Thomas Patrick (1963). *Profiles of African Leaders.* New York: Macmillan.

Menkiti, Ifeanyi (1984). "Person and Community in African Traditional Thought." In Wright (1984).

Mensah Sarbah, John (1897). *Fanti Customary Laws.* Excerpted in Langley (1979).

Merton, R. (1957). *Social Theory and Social Structure.* Glencoe, IL: Free Press.

Messing, Simon D. (1962). "The Konso Economy of Southern Ethiopia." In Bohannan and Dalton, eds. (1962).

Millikan, R., and Rostow, W. W. (1956). *A Proposal, Key to an Effective Foreign Policy.* New York: Harper & Row.

Miracle, Marvin P. (1962). "African Markets and Trade in the Copperbelt." In Bohannan and Dalton, eds. (1962).

——— (1971). "Capitalism, Capital Markets, and Competition in West African Trade." In Meillassoux (1971).

Myrdal, G. (1971). *Asian Drama.* New York: Random House.

Nicol, Davidson, ed. (1969). *Black Nationalism in Africa, 1867.* London: Africana.

Nkrumah, Kwame (1957). *Ghana, An Autobiography.* London: Nelson.

———— (1963). *Africa Must Unite.* New York: International Publishers.

———— (1968). *Handbook on Revolutionary Warfare.* London: Panaf Publishers.

———— (1969). *Dark Days in Ghana.* London: Panaf Publishers.

———— (1973). *Revolutionary Path.* New York: International Publishers.

Northrup, David, (1978). *Trade Without Rulers: Pre-Colonial Economic Development in South-Eastern Nigeria.* Oxford: The Clarendon Press.

Nye, Joseph S. (June 1967). "Corruption and Political Development: A Cost-Benefit Analysis." *American Political Science Review.* 61, No. 2: 417-27.

Nyerere, Julius K. (1962). *Ujamaa: The Basis Of African Socialism.* Dar es Salaam: Government Printer.

———— (1966). *Freedom and Unity: A Selection From Writings and Speeches, 1965-67.* Dar es Salaam: Oxford University Press.

Nzongola-Ntalaja, ed. (1986). *The Crisis in Zaire: Myths and Realities.* Trenton, NJ: Africa World Press.

Obichere, Boniface I. (1974). "Change and Innovation in the Administration of the Kingdom of Dahomey." *Journal of African Studies,* Vol. 1, No. 3:325.

O'Connel, J. (1967). "The Inevitability of Instability." *Journal of Modern African Studies,* Vol. 2.

Ogot, B.A. (1967). *History of the Southern Luo.* Nairobi: East African Publishing House.

Oguah, Benjamin Ewuku (1984). "African and Western Philosophy: A Study." In Wright (1984).

Olaniyan, Richard, ed. (1985). *Nigerian History and Culture.* London: Longman.

Olivier, N.J.J. (1969). "The Governmental Institutions of the Bantu Peoples of Southern Africa." In *Recueils de la Societies Jean Bodin XII.* Bruxelles: Fondation Universitaire de Belgique.

Onwuanibe, Richard C. (1984). "The Human Person and Immortality in Igbo Metaphysics" In Wright (1984).

Ridley, Edgar J. (1982). "The Neurological Misadventure of Primordial Man," *The Journal of Black Male/Female Relationships,* Autumn.

Rimmer, D. (May 1966). "The Crisis in the Ghana Economy." *Modern African Studies:* 121-134.

Roberts, Brian (1974). *The Zulu Kings.* New York: Scribner.

Schapera, I. (1953). *The Tswana.* London: International African Institute.

───── (1955). *A Handbook of Tswana Law and Custom.* London: Oxford University Press.

───── (1957). "The Sources Of Law In Tswana Tribal Courts: Legislation And Precedent," *Journal of African Law,* Vol. 1, No. 3:150-162.

Sertima, Ivan (1977). *They Came Before Columbus: The African Presence in Ancient America.* New York: Random House.

─────, ed. (1987). *Blacks In Science: Ancient and Modern.* New Brunswick, NJ: Transaction Books.

Sithole, Ndabaningi (1979). "*African Nationalism.*" In Langley (1979).

Skinner, Elliott P. (1961). "Intergenerational Conflict Among The Mossi: Father And Son," *Journal of Conflict Resolution,* Vol. 5. No. 1: 55-60.

───── (1962). "Trade and Markets among the Mossi People." In Bohannan and Dalton, eds. (1962).

───── (1964). "West African Economic Systems." In Herskovits and Harwitz (1964).

───── (1973). *Peoples And Cultures Of Africa.* New York: Doubleday/Natural History Press.

Smith, Michael G. (1962). "Exchange and Marketing among the Hausa." In Bohannan and Dalton, eds. (1962).

Smith, Robert S. (1969). *Kingdoms of The Yoruba.* London: Methuen.

Snow, Philip (1988). *The Star Raft, China's Encounter with Africa.* London: Weidenfeld & Nicolson.

Stride, G. T., and Ifeka, Caroline (1971). *Peoples and Empires of West Africa.* Lagos: Thomas Nelson.

Tardits, Claudine, and Tardits, Claude (1962). "Traditional Market Economy in South Dahomey" In Bohannan and Dalton (1962).

Timothy, Bankole (1981). *Kwame Nkrumah: From Cradle To Grave.* London: Garvin.

United Nations (1990). *Human Development.* Report By United Nations Development Program, New York.

United Nations Development Program (UNDP) (1989). *African Economic and Financial Data.* New York: United Nations.

Vansina, Jan (1962). "Trade and Markets Among the Kuba." In Bohannan and Dalton, eds. (1962).

——— (1975). *Kingdoms of the Savannah*. Madison: University of Wisconsin Press.

——— (1978). *The Children of Woot: A History of the Kuba*. Madison: University of Wisconsin Press.

Vaughan, James H. (1986). "Population and Social Organization." In Martin and O'Meara (1986).

Whitaker, Jennifer S. (1988). *How Can Africa Survive?* New York: Harper & Row.

White, C.M.N. (1956). "The Role Of Hunting And Fishing In Luvale Society," *African Studies*, Vol. 15, No. 2: 75-86.

White, E. Frances (1987). *Sierra Leone's Settler Women Traders*. Ann Arbor: University of Michigan Press.

Wickins, Peter (1981). *An Economic History of Africa*. Oxford: Oxford University Press.

Wilks, Ivor (1975). *Asante in the Nineteenth Century: The Structure and Evolution of a Political Order*. Cambridge: Cambridge University Press.

Williams, Chancellor (1987). *The Destruction of Black Civilization*. Chicago: Third World Press.

Wilson, Peter J. (1967). "Tsimihety Kinship And Descent." *Africa*, Vol. 37, No. 2 pp. 133-153.

Woods, Alan (1989). *Development and the National Interest: US Economic Assistance into the 21st Century*. Report by the Administrator, Agency for International Development, Washington, DC.

World Bank (1984). *Toward Sustained Development in Sub-Saharan Africa*. Washington, DC.

World Bank (1989). *Sub-Saharan Africa: From Crisis to Self-Sustainable Growth*. Washington, DC.

World Bank, *World Development Report*, Annual. New York: Oxford University Press.

Wright, Peter (1988). *Spycatcher*. New York: Bantam Books.

Wright, Richard A., ed. (1984). *African Philosophy: An Introduction*. Lanham, MD: University Press of America.

Wrigley, Christopher (1960). "Speculations On The Economic Prehistory Of Africa." *Journal of African History*, Vol. 1, No. 2:189-203.

Yelpaala, Kojo (1983). "Circular Arguments and Self-Fulfilling Definitions: 'Statelessness' and the Dagaaba." *History in Africa*, 10:349-385.

Zinsmeister, Karl (1987). "East African Experiment: Kenyan Prosperity and Tanzanian Decline," *Journal of Economic Growth*, Vol 2, No. 2:28.

## PERIODICALS

*Africa Forum*, a private quarterly magazine published in New York by Olusegun Abasanjo (ex-head of state of Nigeria).

*Africa Report*, a monthly magazine published by the African American Institute in New York.

*African Guardian*, a private monthly magazine published in Lagos, Nigeria.

*The African Letter*, a private newspaper published by black Africans in Toronto, Canada.

*African Mirror*, a private monthly magazine published by black Africans in Silver Spring, MD.

*The Atlantic*, a private, monthly magazine published in Washington.

*Business Week*, private, published in the United States.

*Christian Messenger*, Presbyterian Church monthly; private, Accra, Ghana.

*The Continent*, a private newspaper published by black Africans in Washington, DC.

*Daily Graphic*, name changed to (*People's Graphic*), owned by the Government of Ghana; a daily newspaper, Accra, Ghana.

*Daily Nation*, a government-owned paper published in Nairobi, Kenya.

*Daily Sketch*, a private daily in Nigeria.

*The Economist*, a private weekly published in London.

*Financial Times*, a private weekly paper published in London.

*Ghana Drum*, a monthly newsletter published privately for the Ghanaian community in the Washington, DC, metropolitan area.

*The Independent*, a private daily published in London.

*Insight*, private monthly magazine published in Washington, DC; conservative.

*Ghanaian Times*, owned by the Government of Ghana; a daily newspaper, Accra, Ghana

*Index on Censorship*, a privately-owned monthly published in London and dedicated to the defense of freedom of expression; a must for writers and journalists.

*Izvestia*, a bulletin of news published by the Soviet government.

*National Concord*, private daily published in Lagos, Nigeria.

*New African*, a privately-owned monthly published in London.

*New Internationalist*, a private monthly magazine published in London.

*Newsweek*, a privately-owned weekly magazine, published in the United States.

*The New York Times*, a private daily published in New York; liberal.

*The Nigerian Tribune*, a private daily published in Lagos.

*Pravda*, an official Soviet newspaper.

*Punch*, a privately-owned weekly in Kumasi, Ghana.

*South*, a privately-published monthly from London; leftist.

*Time*, private weekly magazine; published in United States.

*The Wall Street Journal*, private daily published in New York; conservative.

*The Washington Post*, private daily published in Washington, DC; liberal.

*The Washington Times*, private daily published in Washington, DC; conservative.

*West Africa*, a privately-owned weekly, London.

*World Development Forum*, news bulletin by Hunger Project, non-profit, based in San Francisco.

## COLONIAL AFRICA, 1913

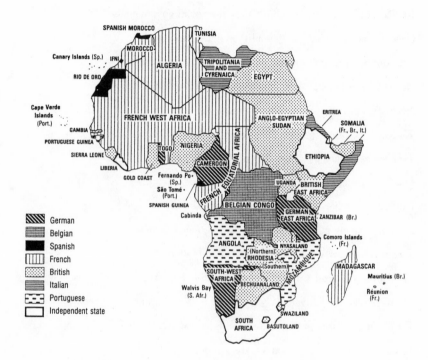

SPANISH MOROCCO
TUNISIA
Canary Islands (Sp.)
MOROCCO
IFNI
ALGERIA
RIO DE ORO
TRIPOLITANIA AND CYRENAICA
EGYPT
Cape Verde Islands (Port.)
FRENCH WEST AFRICA
GAMBIA
ANGLO-EGYPTIAN SUDAN
ERITREA
SOMALIA (Fr., Br., It.)
PORTUGUESE GUINEA
SIERRA LEONE
LIBERIA
GOLD COAST
TOGO
NIGERIA
Fernando Po (Sp.)
São Tomé (Port.)
SPANISH GUINEA
CAMEROON
FRENCH EQUATORIAL AFRICA
ETHIOPIA
UGANDA
BRITISH EAST AFRICA
Cabinda
BELGIAN CONGO
GERMAN EAST AFRICA
ZANZIBAR (Br.)
Comoro Islands (Fr.)
ANGOLA
NYASALAND
(Northern) RHODESIA
(Southern)
MADAGASCAR
Mauritius (Br.)
MOZAMBIQUE
Réunion (Fr.)
SOUTH-WEST AFRICA
Walvis Bay (S. Afr.)
BECHUANALAND
SWAZILAND
SOUTH AFRICA
BASUTOLAND

German
Belgian
Spanish
French
British
Italian
Portuguese
Independent state

Map reproduced by permission of the University of California Press, from C. Coquery-Vidrovitch, *Africa: Endurance and Change South of the Sahara* (1985). © The Regents of the University of California.

## THE POLITICAL MAP OF AFRICA, 1991

**Multiparty Democracies:** Benin, Botswana, Cape Verde Is., Eygpt, The Gambia, Mauritius, Namibia, Sao Tome & Principe, Senegal, Zambia.

Courtesy: The African American Institute

# INDEX